PRESENTED TO:

_____

FROM:

_____

DATE:

_____

Jesus Calling®

MORNING & EVENING
DEVOTIONAL

Jesus Always

Sarah Young

THOMAS NELSON
Since 1798

Jesus Calling *Jesus Always Morning & Evening Devotional*

Printed in China

18 19 20 21 22 DSC 5 4 3 2 1

PREFACE

Be still and know that I am God.

—Psalm 46:10

THIS NEW MORNING AND EVENING EDITION of *Jesus Calling*® and *Jesus Always* allows readers to begin each day focusing on the hope, peace, and joy that can be found only in Jesus and then, in turn, to go to bed each evening reflecting on His Word.

Let the morning bring me word of your unfailing love, for I have put my trust in you. Show me the way I should go, for to you I entrust my life. (Psalm 143:8)

Each morning devotion will open with a devotion from *Jesus Calling*®. What a gift it is to start the day knowing that God loves us and has a plan for us. Before the rush of the calendar and responsibilities takes over, while the world is still and the morning coffee is hot, take a moment to pause in the presence of Jesus. Starting your day in Scripture reading, prayer, and devotions provides you with strength and peace—both of which you are likely to need in the coming hours.

As the day winds to a close, thank the Lord for the joys and blessings of the day, acknowledging that He was with you each step of the way. As you read the evening devotions from *Jesus Always*, you can release your fears and cast your anxieties on Him, knowing that they are safe in His care and trusting that He is at work on your behalf. Rest peacefully, knowing that you are not in control but that the One who is in control is working to make all things to work together for good.

When you lie down, you will not be afraid; when you lie down, your sleep will be sweet. (Proverbs 3:24)

May you greet each day with His hope and peace in your heart, and may you sleep sweetly at night, sustained by the joy found in the promises of His Word.

Sarah Young

INTRODUCTION

DURING THE YEARS that I have been waiting in God's Presence—focusing on Him and His Word—I've found themes of His Peace becoming more prominent in my writing. I'm sure this tendency reflects, in part, my personal need. However, when people open up to me, I find that most of them also desire the balm of Jesus' Peace.

This practice of being still in God's Presence has increased my intimacy with Him more than any other spiritual discipline, so I want to share some of the writings I have gleaned from these quiet moments. In many parts of the world, Christians seem to be searching for a deeper experience of Jesus' Presence and Peace. The devotions that follow address that felt need.

The Bible is the only infallible, inerrant Word of God, and I endeavor to keep my writings consistent with that unchanging standard. I have written from the perspective of Jesus speaking, to help readers feel more personally connected with Him. So the first person singular ("I," "Me," "My," "Mine") always refers to Christ; "you" refers to you, the reader.

I have included Scripture references after each daily reading. As I waited in God's Presence, Bible verses or fragments of verses often came to mind. So I interwove these into the devotions. Words from the Scriptures (some paraphrased, some quoted) are indicated in italics. Certain Bible verses figure rather heavily in my writing. That is because God often uses these passages to strengthen and encourage me, raising my sights from my "light and momentary troubles" (2 Corinthians 4:17) to His eternal perspective.

Themes of thankfulness and trust recurred often during my listening times. These themes are quite prevalent in the Bible, and they are essential for a close relationship with the Lord.

The devotions in this book are meant to be read slowly, preferably in a quiet place—with your Bible open. Remember that Jesus is Immanuel, *God with us*. May you enjoy His Presence and His Peace in ever-increasing measure.

January

"For I know the plans I have for you," declares
the Lord, *"plans to prosper you and not to harm
you, plans to give you a hope and a future."*

JEREMIAH 29:11

COME TO ME with a teachable spirit, eager to be changed. A close walk with Me is a life of continual newness. Do not cling to old ways as you step into a new year. Instead, seek My Face with an open mind, knowing that your journey with Me involves being *transformed by the renewing of your mind.* As you focus your thoughts on Me, be aware that I am fully attentive to you. I see you with a steady eye because My attention span is infinite. I know and understand you completely; My thoughts embrace you in everlasting Love. *I also know the plans I have for you: plans to prosper you and not to harm you, plans to give you hope and a future.* Give yourself fully to this adventure of increasing attentiveness to My Presence.

PSALM 27:8 ESV; ROMANS 12:2; JEREMIAH 29:11

*D*O NOT DWELL ON THE PAST. *See, I am doing a new thing!* As you begin a fresh year, rejoice that I am continually working newness into your life. Don't let recent disappointments and failures define you or dampen your expectations. This is the time to make a fresh start! I am a God of unlimited creativity; expect Me to do surprising things in this year that stretches out before you.

Today is a precious gift. The present moment is where I meet with you, beloved. So seek My Face throughout *this day that I have made*. I have carefully prepared it for you—with tender attention to every detail. I want you to *rejoice and be glad in it*.

Search for signs of My loving Presence as you journey along *the path of Life*. Look for the little pleasures I have strewn alongside your pathway—sometimes in surprising places—and thank Me for each one. Your thankfulness will keep you close to Me and help you find Joy in your journey.

ISAIAH 43:18–19; PSALM 118:24 ESV;
PSALM 16:11 NKJV

R ELAX IN MY HEALING PRESENCE. As you spend time with Me, your thoughts tend to jump ahead to today's plans and problems. Bring your mind back to Me for refreshment and renewal. Let the Light of My Presence soak into you as you focus your thoughts on Me. Thus I equip you to face whatever the day brings. This sacrifice of time pleases Me and strengthens you. Do not skimp on our time together. Resist the clamor of tasks waiting to be done. *You have chosen what is better, and it will not be taken away from you.*

PSALM 89:15; PSALM 105:4; LUKE 10:39–42

I AM YOUR JOY! These four words can light up your life. Since I am always with you, *the Joy of My Presence* is continually accessible to you. You can open up to My Presence through your trust in Me, your love for Me. Try saying, "Jesus, You are my Joy." My Light will shine upon you and within you as you *rejoice in Me*, your Savior. Ponder all I have done for you and all that I am to you. This will lift you up above your circumstances.

When you became My follower, I empowered you to rise above the conditions in your life. I filled you with My Spirit, and this Holy Helper has limitless Power. I promised that *I will come back and take you to be with Me* in heaven—*that you may be where I am* forever. Whenever your world is looking dark, brighten your perspective by focusing on Me. Relax in My Presence, and hear Me saying, "Beloved, I am your Joy!"

PSALM 21:6; PHILIPPIANS 4:4 NKJV; JOHN 14:3

R EFRESH YOURSELF in the Peace of My Presence. This Peace can be your portion at all times and in all circumstances. Learn to *hide in the secret of My Presence*, even as you carry out your duties in the world. I am both with you and within you. I go before you to open up the way, and I also walk alongside you. There could never be another companion as devoted as I am.

Because I am your constant Companion, there should be a lightness to your step that is observable to others. Do not be weighed down with problems and unresolved issues, for I am your burden-bearer. In the world you have trials and distress, but don't let them get you down. *I have conquered the world and deprived it of power to harm you*. In Me you may have confident Peace.

PSALM 31:19–20 NASB; JOHN 16:33 AMP

*B*E STILL, AND KNOW *that I am God.* Most Christians are familiar with this command, but not so many take it seriously. Yet for those who *do*, blessings flow like *streams of living water.* As these believers sit in stillness—focusing on Me and My Word—their perception of Me expands and their troubles shrink in importance.

I want *you* to share in these blessings, beloved. Take time, take time with Me. While you rest in My Presence, I untangle your thoughts and help you view things more biblically. Remember: *My Word is a lamp to guide your feet and a light for your path.* Biblical thinking illuminates the path before you so you can find your way.

It's crucial to know not only that *I am God* but that *I made you and you are Mine.* You are a *sheep of My pasture.* Sheep have very limited understanding of what their shepherd is doing for them, but they follow him anyway. Similarly, as My "sheep," your job is to trust Me and follow wherever I lead.

PSALM 46:10 NKJV; JOHN 7:38;
PSALM 119:105 NLT; PSALM 100:3

I WANT YOU TO LEARN A NEW HABIT. Try saying, "I trust You, Jesus," in response to whatever happens to you. If there is time, think about who I am in all My Power and Glory; ponder also the depth and breadth of My Love for you.

This simple practice will help you see Me in every situation, acknowledging My sovereign control over the universe. When you view events from this perspective—through the Light of My universal Presence—fear loses its grip on you. Adverse circumstances become growth opportunities when you affirm your trust in Me no matter what. You receive blessings gratefully, realizing they flow directly from My hand of grace. Your continual assertion of trusting Me will strengthen our relationship and keep you close to Me.

PSALM 63:2; ISAIAH 40:10–11; PSALM 139:7–10

F IND JOY IN ME, for I am your Strength. It is vital to keep your Joy alive, especially when you're in the throes of adversity. Whenever you are struggling with difficulties, you need to guard your thoughts and spoken words carefully. If you focus too much on all the things that are wrong, you will become increasingly discouraged—and your strength will be sapped. As soon as you realize what is happening, stop this hurtful process immediately. Turn to Me, asking Me to help you with all your struggles.

Take time to praise Me: Speak or sing words of worship. Read scriptures that help you rejoice in Me.

Remember that your problems are temporary but *I* am eternal—and so is your relationship with Me. As you find Joy in Me, delighting in *My unfailing Love* for you, your strength will increase. This is *the Joy of the Lord,* which is yours for all time and throughout eternity!

NEHEMIAH 8:10; PSALM 66:1–3; PSALM 143:8

YOU CAN ACHIEVE THE VICTORIOUS LIFE through living in deep dependence on Me. People usually associate victory with success: not falling or stumbling, not making mistakes. But those who are successful in their own strength tend to go their own way, forgetting about Me. It is through problems and failure, weakness and neediness, that you learn to rely on Me.

True dependence is not simply asking Me to bless what you have decided to do. It is coming to Me with an open mind and heart, inviting Me to plant My desires within you. I may infuse within you a dream that seems far beyond your reach. You know that in yourself you cannot achieve such a goal. Thus begins your journey of profound reliance on Me. It is a faith-walk, taken one step at a time, leaning on Me as much as you need. This is not a path of continual success but of multiple failures. However, each failure is followed by a growth spurt, nourished by increased reliance on Me. Enjoy the blessedness of a victorious life through deepening your dependence on Me.

PSALM 34:17–18; 2 CORINTHIANS 5:7 NKJV

L ET *MY CONSOLATION*—My comfort—*bring Joy to your soul*. When anxiety is welling up within you, come to Me and *pour out your heart*. Then sit quietly in My Presence while I comfort you, helping you see things from My perspective. I remind you of your heavenly destination, for you are indeed on your way to Glory! I infuse My Joy and Peace into your heart, mind, and soul.

When you are joyful, this changes the way you view the world around you. Even though you see much darkness, you can also see the Light of My Presence continuing to shine. Moreover, the Joy in your soul gives you buoyancy, enabling you to rise above the countless problems in your life. Once you have gained this perspective, you will discover that you can comfort others in the midst of their troubles. They will find in you the consolation that you have found in Me. Thus your Joy becomes contagious, "infecting" those around you with Joy in *their* souls!

PSALM 94:19; PSALM 62:8; 2 CORINTHIANS 1:3–4

I AM ABLE *to do far beyond all that you ask or imagine.* Come to Me with positive expectations, knowing that there is no limit to what I can accomplish. Ask My Spirit to control your mind so that you can think great thoughts of Me. Do not be discouraged by the fact that many of your prayers are yet unanswered. Time is a trainer, teaching you to wait upon Me, to trust Me in the dark. The more extreme your circumstances, the more likely you are to see *My Power and Glory* at work in the situation. Instead of letting difficulties draw you into worrying, try to view them as setting the scene for My glorious intervention. Keep your eyes and your mind wide open to all that I am doing in your life.

EPHESIANS 3:20–21; ROMANS 8:6;
ISAIAH 40:30–31 NKJV; REVELATION 5:13

I T I S P O S S I B L E for My followers to be joyful and afraid at the same time. When an angel told the women who came to My tomb that I had risen from the dead, they were *"afraid yet filled with joy."* So do not let fear keep you from experiencing the Joy of My Presence. It is not a luxury reserved for times when your problems—and the crises in the world—seem under control. My loving Presence is yours to enjoy today, tomorrow, and forever!

Do not give in to joyless living by letting worries about the present or the future weigh you down. Instead, remember that *neither the present nor the future, nor any powers, nor anything else in all creation, will be able to separate you from My Love.*

Talk with Me about your fears, expressing your thoughts and feelings freely. Relax in My Presence and entrust all your concerns to Me. Then ask Me to bless you with My Joy, which *no one can take from you.*

MATTHEW 28:8; ROMANS 8:38–39;
JOHN 16:22 ESV

I T IS IMPOSSIBLE TO PRAISE OR THANK ME TOO MUCH. As it is written, *I inhabit the praises of My people.* Sometimes your adoration is a spontaneous overflow of Joy, in response to radiant beauty or rich blessings. At other times your praise is more disciplined and measured—an act of your will. I dwell equally in both types of praise. Thankfulness, also, is a royal road to draw near Me. A thankful heart has plenty of room for Me.

When you thank Me for the many pleasures I provide, you affirm that I am God, from whom all blessings flow. When adversity strikes and you thank Me anyway, your trust in My sovereignty is a showpiece in invisible realms. Fill up the spare moments of your life with praise and thanksgiving. This joyous discipline will help you live in the intimacy of My Presence.

PSALM 22:3 KJV; PSALM 146:1–2;
1 THESSALONIANS 5:18

T HE MORE OFTEN YOU TURN your thoughts to Me, the more you will enjoy My *perfect Peace*. This is a challenging goal, but it is also a glorious gift. I, *the Shepherd of your soul,* am always accessible to you.

You can train your mind to turn from other things and focus on Me. When you experience something beautiful, thank Me for it. When a loved one brings you joy, remember that I am the Source of this pleasure. Post reminders of My Presence in your home or car or office. It's also wise to memorize Scripture since it is ultimately about Me.

Turning your thoughts to Me demonstrates your trust in Me. Even undesired things such as pain and problems can be reminders to communicate with Me. Focusing on My Presence protects you from getting stuck on problems—going over and over them in your mind without making any progress.

Be creative in finding new ways to turn your thoughts toward Me. Thus you can enjoy the wondrous gift of My Peace.

ISAIAH 26:3 TLB; 1 PETER 2:25 NASB;
PHILIPPIANS 4:6–7

S OFTLY I ANNOUNCE MY PRESENCE. Shimmering hues of radiance tap gently at your consciousness, seeking entrance. Though I have all Power in heaven and on earth, I am infinitely tender with you. The weaker you are, the more gently I approach you. Let your weakness be a door to My Presence. Whenever you feel inadequate, remember that I am your *ever-present Help*.

Hope in Me, and you will be protected from despair and self-pity. Hope is like a golden cord connecting you to heaven. The more you cling to this cord, the more I bear the weight of your burdens; thus, you are lightened. Heaviness is not of My kingdom. Cling to hope, and My rays of Light will reach you through the darkness.

PSALM 46:1; ROMANS 12:12; ROMANS 15:13

IN ME YOU CAN DISCOVER JOY *inexpressible and full of Glory*! You will not find this kind of pleasure anywhere else; it is available only in your relationship with Me. So trust Me, beloved, and walk confidently along your life-path. As we journey together, you will encounter many obstacles—some of which are quite painful. Expect these difficulties each day, and don't let them throw you off course. Refuse to let adversity keep you from enjoying Me. In My Presence deep sorrow can coexist with even deeper Joy.

Your life with Me is an adventure, and there are always some dangers involved in adventurous journeys. Ask Me to give you courage so that you can face your troubles boldly. Keep your hope fully fastened on Me and on the heavenly reward that awaits you. Your Joy will expand astronomically—beyond anything you could possibly imagine—when you reach your eternal home. There you will see Me *face to Face*, and your Joy will know no bounds!

1 PETER 1:8 NKJV; 2 CORINTHIANS 6:10;
1 CORINTHIANS 13:12

I AM WITH YOU AND FOR YOU. When you decide on a course of action that is in line with My will, nothing in heaven or on earth can stop you. You may encounter many obstacles as you move toward your goal, but don't be discouraged—never give up! With My help, you can overcome any obstacle. Do not expect an easy path as you journey hand in hand with Me, but do remember that I, your *very-present Helper*, am omnipotent.

Much, much stress results from your wanting to make things happen before their times have come. One of the main ways I assert My sovereignty is in the timing of events. If you want to stay close to Me and do things My way, ask Me to show you the path forward moment by moment. Instead of dashing headlong toward your goal, let Me set the pace. Slow down, and enjoy the journey in My Presence.

ROMANS 8:31; PSALM 46:1–3 NKJV; LUKE 1:37

I AM YOUR TREASURE! Sometimes you feel frazzled—pulled this way and that by people and circumstances around you. Your yearning for meaning and deep connection drives you into more and more activity. Even when your body is still, your mind tends to race—anticipating future problems and searching for solutions. You need to remember that *all the treasures of wisdom and knowledge are hidden in Me.* Remind yourself of this glorious truth frequently, whispering: "Jesus, You are my Treasure. In You I am complete."

When you prize Me above all else, making Me your *First Love*, you are protected from feeling fragmented. Whenever you find your thoughts straying, you can train your mind to return to the One who completes you. This gives focus to your life and helps you stay close to Me. Living near Me, enjoying My Presence, involves seeking to *obey My commands.* I am telling you this *so that My Joy may be in you and that your Joy may be complete.*

COLOSSIANS 2:2–3; REVELATION 2:4 NKJV;
JOHN 15:10–11

EVERY TIME YOU AFFIRM YOUR TRUST IN ME, you put a coin into My treasury. Thus you build up equity in preparation for days of trouble. I keep safely in My heart all trust invested in Me, with interest compounded continuously. The more you trust Me, the more I empower you to do so.

Practice trusting Me during quiet days, when nothing much seems to be happening. Then when storms come, your trust balance will be sufficient to see you through. *Store up for yourself treasure in heaven* through placing your trust in Me. This practice will keep you in My Peace.

PSALM 33:20–21; PSALM 56:3–4;
MATTHEW 6:20–21

B EWARE OF OVERTHINKING THINGS— obsessing about unimportant matters. When your mind is idle, you tend to go into planning mode: attempting to figure things out and make various decisions before you really need to do so. This is an unproductive way of trying to grasp control, and it's a waste of your precious time. Often, you end up changing your mind or forgetting what you decided. There is a time for planning, but it's definitely not *all* the time—or even most of it.

Seek to live in the present moment, where My Presence awaits you continually. Refresh yourself in My nearness, letting My Love soak into your innermost being. Relax with Me, putting aside problems so you can be attentive to Me and receive more of My Love. *Your soul thirsts for Me*, but often you don't realize what you're really longing for: awareness of My Presence. Let Me *lead you beside quiet waters* and *restore your soul*. Just as lovers don't need to say much to communicate deeply, so it is in your relationship with Me—the Lover of your soul.

EPHESIANS 3:17–19; PSALM 63:1 NKJV;
PSALM 23:2–3

T RUST ME by relinquishing control into My hands. *Let go, and recognize that I am God.* This is My world: I made it and I control it. Yours is a responsive part in the litany of Love. I search among My children for receptivity to Me. Guard well this gift that I have planted in your heart. Nurture it with the Light of My Presence.

When you bring Me prayer requests, lay out your concerns before Me. Speak to Me candidly; pour out your heart. Then thank Me for the answers that I have set into motion long before you can discern results. When your requests come to mind again, continue to thank Me for the answers that are on the way. If you keep on stating your concerns to Me, you will live in a state of tension. When you thank Me for how I am answering your prayers, your mind-set becomes much more positive. Thankful prayers keep your focus on My Presence and My promises.

PSALM 46:10 AMP; COLOSSIANS 4:2; 2 PETER 1:3–4

*T*HERE IS A TIME FOR EVERYTHING, *and a season for every activity under heaven.* When you seek My Face and My will—searching for guidance—I may show you the next step on your journey without revealing the appointed time for you to take that step. Instead of going full speed ahead as soon as you know what is next, you must wait until I show you *when* I want you to go forward.

There is a season for everything. This means that even the most fulfilling times in life must eventually give way to something new. Whereas some of My followers "champ at the bit" to forge ahead into new territory, others hold back even when I am clearly directing them to go forward. Moving from a comfortable season of life into a new situation can feel scary—especially to those who dislike change. However, I want you to trust Me enough to cling to Me and follow wherever I lead, *whenever* I choose. *Your times are in My hands.*

ECCLESIASTES 3:1; ISAIAH 43:19;
2 CORINTHIANS 5:17 NKJV; PSALM 31:15

L ET ME PREPARE YOU for the day that stretches out before you. I know exactly what this day will contain, whereas you have only vague ideas about it. You would like to see a map, showing all the twists and turns of your journey. You'd feel more prepared if you could somehow visualize what is on the road ahead. However, there is a better way to be prepared for *whatever* you will encounter today: Spend quality time with Me.

I will not show you what is on the road ahead, but I will thoroughly equip you for the journey. My living Presence is your Companion each step of the way. Stay in continual communication with Me, whispering My Name whenever you need to redirect your thoughts. Thus, you can walk through this day with your focus on Me. My abiding Presence is the best road map available.

EXODUS 33:14; JOHN 15:4–7

*D*O NOT BE TERRIFIED OR DISCOURAGED, *for I am with you wherever you go.* It's easy for My followers to feel frightened and pessimistic when the mainstream voices in this world speak so heavily against them. Looking at this life through godless, biased lenses will indeed pull you down. Christian courage is the antidote to this poisonous input, and it is nourished by the knowledge that I am always with you.

It is crucial to remember that what you can see of reality is only a very small piece of the whole. When Elijah was deeply discouraged, he said he was the *only one* who had remained faithful. Yet there were thousands in Israel who had not bowed down to Baal. Elijah was blinded by his isolation and his discouragement. Similarly, Elisha's servant was terrified because he couldn't see what Elisha saw: *horses and chariots of fire all around* to protect them from enemy forces.

Beloved, not only am I with you, but I have unlimited resources to help you. So look beyond the way things appear, and *take courage!*

JOSHUA 1:9; 1 KINGS 19:14;
2 KINGS 6:17; MATTHEW 14:27

T RY TO VIEW EACH DAY as an adventure, carefully planned out by your Guide. Instead of staring into the day that is ahead of you, attempting to program it according to your will, be attentive to Me and to all I have prepared for you. Thank Me for this day of life, recognizing that it is a precious, unrepeatable gift. Trust that I am with you each moment, whether you sense My Presence or not. A thankful, trusting attitude helps you to see events in your life from My perspective.

A life lived close to Me will never be dull or predictable. Expect each day to contain surprises! Resist your tendency to search for the easiest route through the day. Be willing to follow wherever I lead. No matter how steep or treacherous the path before you, the safest place to be is by My side.

PSALM 118:24 NKJV; ISAIAH 41:10; 1 PETER 2:21

ALL THINGS ARE POSSIBLE WITH ME! Let these powerful words light up your mind and encourage your heart. Refuse to be intimidated by the way things look at the moment. I am training you to *live by faith, not by sight.*

The sense of sight is a spectacular gift from Me, to be used joyfully and gratefully. However, it's easy to be mesmerized by all the visual stimulation surrounding you—and forget about Me. Faith is a type of vision that connects you to Me. Instead of being so focused on the visible world, *dare* to trust in Me and My promises.

Live close to Me, your Savior and Friend, but remember: I am also infinite God. When I lived on your planet, *My miraculous signs revealed My Glory, and My disciples put their faith in Me.* I continue to do miracles in your world, according to My will and purposes. Seek to align your will with Mine and to see things from My perspective. Exert your faith to ask for big things, and *watch in hope for Me* to work.

MARK 10:27 ESV; 2 CORINTHIANS 5:7;
JOHN 2:11; MICAH 7:7

L ET ME BLESS YOU with My grace and Peace. Open your heart and mind to receive all that I have for you. Do not be ashamed of your emptiness. Instead, view it as the optimal condition for being filled with My Peace.

It is easy to touch up your outward appearance, to look as if you have it all together. Your attempts to look good can fool most people. But I see straight through you, into the depths of your being. There is no place for pretense in your relationship with Me. Rejoice in the relief of being fully understood. Talk with Me about your struggles and feelings of inadequacy. Little by little, I will transform your weaknesses into strengths. Remember that your relationship with Me is saturated in grace. Therefore, *nothing that you do or don't do can separate you from My Presence.*

1 SAMUEL 16:7; ROMANS 8:38–39

*Y*OU ARE FULLY KNOWN. I know absolutely everything about you, and I love you with perfect, *unfailing Love*. Many people are searching for greater self-understanding and self-acceptance. Underlying their search is a desire to find someone who truly understands them and accepts them as they are. I am the Someone who can fully satisfy this deep-seated longing. It is in your relationship with Me that you discover who you really are.

I encourage you to be real with Me—dropping all pretenses and opening yourself fully to Me. As you draw near, utter these inspired words: *"Search me, O God, and know my heart; test me and know my anxious thoughts."* In the Light of My holy gaze, you will see things you need to change. But don't despair; I will help you. Continue resting in My Presence, receiving My Love that flows freely into you through your openness to Me. Take time to let this powerful Love soak in deeply—filling up your empty spaces and overflowing into joyous worship. Rejoice greatly, for you are fully known and forever loved!

1 CORINTHIANS 13:12 HCSB;
PSALM 147:11; PSALM 139:23–24

January 15

M Y FACE IS SHINING UPON YOU, beaming out *Peace that transcends understanding.* You are surrounded by a sea of problems, but you are face to Face with Me, your Peace. As long as you focus on Me, you are safe. If you gaze too long at the myriad problems around you, you will sink under the weight of your burdens. When you start to sink, simply call out, "Help me, Jesus!" and I will lift you up.

The closer you live to Me, the safer you are. Circumstances around you are undulating, and there are treacherous-looking waves in the distance. *Fix your eyes on Me,* the One who never changes. By the time those waves reach you, they will have shrunk to proportions of My design. I am always beside you, helping you face *today's* waves. The future is a phantom, seeking to spook you. Laugh at the future! Stay close to Me.

PHILIPPIANS 4:7; MATTHEW 14:29–30;
HEBREWS 12:2

T HE CHRISTIAN LIFE is all about trusting Me: in good times *and* in hard times. I am Lord over all your circumstances, so I want to be involved in every aspect of your life. You can quickly connect with Me by affirming your confidence in Me here and now. When your world seems dark and you trust Me anyway, My Light shines brightly through you. Your display of transcendent faith weakens spiritual forces of evil. And My supernatural Light showing through you blesses and strengthens people around you.

Clinging to Me in the dark requires you to persistently exert your willpower. But while you're grasping onto Me, remember: My hand has an eternal grip on yours—I will never let go of you! Moreover, My Spirit helps you keep hanging on. When you feel on the verge of giving up, cry out for His assistance: "Help me, Holy Spirit!" This brief prayer enables you to tap into His limitless resources. Even when your circumstances look dark and threatening, My Light is still *shining on* in surpassing splendor!

1 JOHN 1:7; PSALM 62:8;
PSALM 139:10 NKJV; JOHN 1:5 AMP

January 16

C OME TO ME, and rest in My loving Presence. You know that this day will bring difficulties, and you are trying to think your way through those trials. As you anticipate what is ahead of you, you forget that *I am with you*—now and always. Rehearsing your troubles results in experiencing them many times, whereas you are meant to go through them only when they actually occur. Do not multiply your suffering in this way! Instead, come to Me, and relax in My Peace. I will strengthen you and prepare you for this day, transforming your fear into confident trust.

MATTHEW 11:28–30; JOSHUA 1:5, 9

W HEN THINGS ARE NOT GOING YOUR WAY, refuse to get flustered. Stop what you're doing and take some deep breaths. *Seek My Face*—spend a few moments enjoying My Presence. Tell Me about the matters that are frustrating you. I will help you see things from My perspective and sort out what is really important. Moreover, I will open up the way before you as you press on in trusting dependence, remaining in communication with Me.

Your desire to feel in control is often the culprit behind your frustration. You plan your day and expect others to behave in ways that expedite your plans. When that doesn't happen, you face a choice: to resent the situation or to trust Me. Remember that *I* am in control and *My ways are higher than yours—as the heavens are higher than the earth.* Instead of getting agitated about setbacks to your schedule, use them as reminders: I am your Savior-God, and you are My beloved follower. Relax in My sovereign control, *trusting in My unfailing Love.*

PSALM 27:8 NKJV; ISAIAH 55:9 NKJV;
PSALM 43:5; PSALM 13:5

COME TO ME WITH A THANKFUL HEART so that you can enjoy My Presence. This is the day that I have made. I want you to rejoice *today*, refusing to worry about tomorrow. Search for all that I have prepared for you, anticipating abundant blessings and accepting difficulties as they come. I can weave miracles into the most mundane day if you keep your focus on Me.

Come to Me with all your needs, knowing that *My glorious riches* are a more-than-adequate supply. Stay in continual communication with Me so that you can live above your circumstances even while you are in the midst of them. *Present your requests to Me with thanksgiving, and My Peace, which surpasses all comprehension, will guard your heart and mind.*

PSALM 118:24; PHILIPPIANS 4:19;
PHILIPPIANS 4:6–7 NASB

I BROUGHT YOU OUT *into a spacious place. I rescued you because I delighted in you.* You are in a spacious place of salvation—saved from being a *slave to sin.* Your salvation is the greatest, most lavish gift you could ever receive. Never stop thanking Me for this infinitely precious gift! In the morning when you awaken, rejoice that I have adopted you into My royal family. Before you go to sleep at night, praise Me for My glorious grace. Live in ways that help others see Me as the fountainhead of abundant, never-ending Life.

I delighted in you, not because of worthiness in you. Rather, I *chose* to delight in you and lavish My Love on you. Since your best efforts could never be sufficient to save you, I clothed you in My own perfect righteousness. Wear this *clothing of salvation* gratefully—with overflowing Joy. Remember that you are royalty in My kingdom, where Glory-Light shines eternally. *Live as a child of Light*, securely robed in radiant righteousness.

PSALM 18:19; JOHN 8:34;
ISAIAH 61:10 NLT; EPHESIANS 5:8

I AM LEADING YOU ALONG THE HIGH ROAD, but there are descents as well as ascents. In the distance you see snow-covered peaks glistening in brilliant sunlight. Your longing to reach those peaks is good, but you must not take shortcuts. Your assignment is to follow Me, allowing Me to direct your path. Let the heights beckon you onward, but stay close to Me.

Learn to trust Me when things go "wrong." Disruptions to your routine highlight your dependence on Me. Trusting acceptance of trials brings blessings that *far outweigh them all*. Walk hand in hand with Me through this day. I have lovingly planned every inch of the way. Trust does not falter when the path becomes rocky and steep. Breathe deep draughts of My Presence, and hold tightly to My hand. Together we can make it!

JOHN 21:19; 2 CORINTHIANS 4:17;
HABAKKUK 3:19

I AM ALWAYS DOING SOMETHING NEW in your life. So try to keep an open mind when you encounter things you have not seen before—or even imagined.

Do not recoil from the unfamiliar without even taking time to determine whether it might be from Me. Consider the trapeze artist: She must leave the safety of the swing she is on in order to move toward her goal. As she abandons the security of where she was, she will be briefly in flight—until she connects to the next trapeze.

At times *you* may feel as if you're "in flight" when you experience newness that feels uncomfortable. The temptation is to just criticize the changes and cling to the familiar. Instead of this knee-jerk response, come to Me in prayer. Tell Me your concerns, and ask Me to help you see the situation from My viewpoint. *I am always with you, and I hold you by your right hand. I guide you with My counsel*—helping you discern the best way to respond and go forward.

MATTHEW 9:17 ESV; PROVERBS 18:10 NKJV;
MATTHEW 11:28; PSALM 73:23–24

S EEK MY FACE, and you will find more than you ever dreamed possible. *Let Me displace worry at the center of your being.* I am like a supersaturated cloud, showering Peace into the pool of your mind. My Nature is to bless. Your nature is to receive with thanksgiving. This is a true fit, designed before the foundation of the world. Glorify Me by receiving My blessings gratefully.

I am the goal of all your searching. *When you seek Me, you find Me* and are satisfied. When lesser goals capture your attention, I fade into the background of your life. I am still there, watching and waiting, but you function as if you were alone. Actually, My Light shines on every situation you will ever face. Live radiantly by expanding your focus to include Me in all your moments. Let nothing dampen your search for Me.

PSALM 27:8 NKJV; PHILIPPIANS 4:7 MSG;
JEREMIAH 29:13

I CALL YOU BY NAME *and lead you. I know you*—I know every detail about you. You are never a number or statistic to Me; My involvement in your life is far more personal and intimate than you can comprehend. So *follow Me* with a glad heart.

After My resurrection, when Mary Magdalene mistook Me for the gardener, I spoke one word: *"Mary."* Hearing Me say her name, she recognized Me and *cried out in Aramaic, "Rabboni!" (which means Teacher).*

Beloved, I also speak *your* name in the depths of your spirit. When you read your Bible, try inserting your name into appropriate passages. Remember: *I called you out of darkness into My marvelous Light.* I chose to set My *everlasting Love* upon you. Take time to "hear" Me speaking to you personally in Scripture, reassuring you of My Love. The unshakable knowledge that I love you forever provides a firm foundation for your life. It strengthens you so that you can follow Me faithfully and joyfully—*proclaiming My praises* as you journey through your life.

JOHN 10:3, 27; JOHN 20:16; 1 PETER 2:9 NKJV;
JEREMIAH 31:3 NKJV

APPROACH THIS DAY WITH AWARENESS of who is Boss. As you make plans for the day, remember that it is I who orchestrates the events of your life. On days when things go smoothly, according to your plans, you may be unaware of My sovereign Presence. On days when your plans are thwarted, be on the lookout for Me! I may be doing something important in your life, something quite different from what you expected. It is essential at such times to stay in communication with Me, accepting My way as better than yours. Don't try to figure out what is happening. Simply trust Me and thank Me in advance for the good that will come out of it all. *I know the plans I have for you, and they are good.*

ISAIAH 55:9–11; JEREMIAH 29:11

REMEMBER THAT *THE FRUIT OF THE SPIRIT* includes Joy. Even in the midst of *severe suffering,* My Spirit can give you this wondrous gift. Feel free to ask Him to fill you with Joy—as often as you need. He resides in the deepest depths of your being, so His work within you is very effective. You cooperate with Him by saturating your mind with Scripture and asking Him to illuminate it to you.

One way the Holy Spirit increases your Joy is to help you think My thoughts. The more you see things from My perspective, the more accurately you view your life. You need not only to *know* biblical truth but to tell yourself the truth over and over each day.

The world continually assaults your mind with lies and deceptions, so you must be diligent to recognize falsehood, dispel it, and replace it with biblical teaching. The most glorious, life-changing truth is the gospel: I have died (to save all who *believe in Me*). I have risen. I will come again. *Rejoice in Me always*!

GALATIANS 5:22–23; 1 THESSALONIANS 1:6;
JOHN 3:16 ESV; PHILIPPIANS 4:4 NKJV

I WANT YOU TO BE ALL MINE. I am weaning you from other dependencies. Your security rests in Me alone—not in other people, not in circumstances. Depending only on Me may feel like walking on a tightrope, but there is a safety net underneath: *the everlasting arms.* So don't be afraid of falling. Instead, look ahead to Me. I am always before you, beckoning you on—one step at a time. *Neither height nor depth, nor anything else in all creation, can separate you from My loving Presence.*

DEUTERONOMY 33:27;
PROVERBS 16:9; ROMANS 8:38–39

To enjoy My Presence more fully, you need to think less and less about yourself. This is not an arbitrary demand; it's the secret to living *more abundantly*. Self-forgetfulness is a delightful way to live!

Try to become aware of how much time you spend thinking about yourself. Take a look at your mind's contents. Though your thoughts are not visible to other people unless you choose to share them, I see each and every one. When you realize your thinking is unworthy of Me, make every effort to change the subject. If you're struggling with a self-centered idea that recurs again and again, try connecting it to a favorite scripture or a brief prayer. This forms a bridge for your attention—away from yourself and toward Me. For example, praying "I love You, Lord" can quickly direct your focus to Me.

If you have to repeat this process many times, don't be discouraged. You are training your mind to *seek My Face*, and this endeavor is pleasing to Me. *Seek Me*, beloved, *and live* abundantly.

John 10:10 nkjv; Psalm 27:8 nkjv; Amos 5:4

S TRIVE TO TRUST ME in more and more areas of your life. Anything that tends to make you anxious is a growth opportunity. Instead of running away from these challenges, embrace them, eager to gain all the blessings I have hidden in the difficulties. If you believe that I am sovereign over every aspect of your life, it is possible to trust Me in all situations. Don't waste energy regretting the way things are or thinking about what might have been. Start at the present moment—accepting things exactly as they are—and search for My way in the midst of those circumstances.

Trust is like a staff you can lean on as you journey uphill with Me. If you are trusting in Me consistently, the staff will bear as much of your weight as needed. *Lean on, trust, and be confident in Me with all your heart and mind.*

PSALM 52:8; PROVERBS 3:5–6 AMP

I AM WORTHY of *all* your confidence, *all* your trust. There are people and things that deserve *some* of your confidence and trust, but only *I* deserve all of it. In a world that seems increasingly unsafe and unpredictable, I am the Rock that provides a firm foundation for your life. More than that, I am *your* Rock in whom you can *take refuge—*for I am *your God.*

You must not let your circumstances define your sense of security. Though it is natural for you to want to be in control of your life, I can empower you to live supernaturally, resting in My sovereign control. I am *a well-proved help in trouble,* and I am always present with you. I help you face unwelcome changes, and even catastrophic circumstances, without fear.

Instead of letting anxious thoughts roam freely in your mind, lasso them by voicing your hope in Me. Then bring those captive thoughts into My Presence, where I will disarm them. *Whoever trusts in Me is kept safe.*

PSALM 18:2; PSALM 46:1–2 AMP;
2 CORINTHIANS 10:5; PROVERBS 29:25

IT'S ALL RIGHT TO BE HUMAN. When your mind wanders while you are praying, don't be surprised or upset. Simply return your attention to Me. Share a secret smile with Me, knowing that I understand. Rejoice in My Love for you, which has no limits or conditions. Whisper My Name in loving contentment, assured that *I will never leave you or forsake you.* Intersperse these peaceful interludes abundantly throughout your day. This practice will enable you to attain *a quiet and gentle spirit*, which is pleasing to Me.

As you live in close contact with Me, the Light of My Presence filters through you to bless others. Your weakness and woundedness are the openings through which *the Light of the knowledge of My Glory* shines forth. *My strength and power show themselves most effective in your weakness.*

DEUTERONOMY 31:6; 1 PETER 3:4;
2 CORINTHIANS 4:6–7; 2 CORINTHIANS 12:9 AMP

I AM THE JOY THAT NO ONE CAN TAKE away from you. Savor the wonders of this gift, spending ample time in My Presence. Rejoice that this blessing is yours—I am yours—for all eternity!

Many things in this world can bring you pleasure for a while, but they are all passing away because of death and decay. In Me you have a matchless Treasure—Joy in the One who is *the same yesterday, today, and forever.* No one can take this pleasure away from you, for I am faithful and I never change.

Whenever you feel joyless, the problem is not in the Source (Me) but in the receiver. You may be so focused on other things—either pleasures or difficulties in your life—that you're neglecting your relationship with Me. The remedy is twofold: Remember that I am your *First Love*, and seek to put Me first in your life. Also, ask Me to increase your receptivity to My Presence. *Delight yourself in Me*, beloved, and receive Joy in full measure.

JOHN 16:22; HEBREWS 13:8 NKJV;
REVELATION 2:4 NKJV; PSALM 37:4

M Y PEACE is the treasure of treasures: *the pearl of great price.* It is an exquisitely costly gift, both for the Giver and the receiver. I purchased this Peace for you with My blood. You receive this gift by trusting Me in the midst of life's storms. If you have the world's peace—everything going your way—you don't seek My unfathomable Peace. Thank Me when things do not go your way, because spiritual blessings come wrapped in trials. Adverse circumstances are normal in a fallen world. Expect them each day. Rejoice in the face of hardship, *for I have overcome the world.*

MATTHEW 13:46 NKJV; JAMES 1:2–3;
JOHN 16:33 ESV

I AM *YOUR STRENGTH*! When you begin a day feeling weak and weary, it's all right. Your weakness can be a reminder of your need for Me. Remember that I am with you continually—ready to help you as you go along your way. Take My hand in joyful trust, letting Me guide you and *strengthen you*. I delight in helping you, My child.

Whenever you feel inadequate for the task ahead, stop and think about your resources. I, *your Strength*, am infinite: I never run out of anything. So when you work in collaboration with Me, don't set limits on what you expect to accomplish. I will give you what you need to keep moving forward, step by step. You may not reach the goal as quickly as you'd like, but you will get there in my perfect timing. Refuse to be discouraged by delays or detours. Instead, trust that I know what I'm doing—and just take the next step. Perseverance and trust in Me make a potent combination!

PSALM 59:16–17; PHILIPPIANS 4:13 NKJV;
ISAIAH 40:28–29

January 25

L ET MY LOVE ENFOLD YOU in the radiance of My Glory. Sit still in the Light of My Presence, and receive My Peace. These quiet moments with Me transcend time, accomplishing far more than you can imagine. Bring Me the sacrifice of your time, and watch to see how abundantly I bless you and your loved ones.

Through the intimacy of our relationship, you are *being transformed* from the inside out. As you keep your focus on Me, I form you into the one I desire you to be. Your part is to yield to My creative work in you, neither resisting it nor trying to speed it up. Enjoy the tempo of a God-breathed life by letting Me set the pace. Hold My hand in childlike trust, and the way before you will open up step by step.

HEBREWS 13:15; 2 CORINTHIANS 3:18;
PSALM 73:23–24

*T*HOUGH THE MOUNTAINS BE SHAKEN *and the hills be removed, yet My unfailing Love for you will not be shaken nor My covenant of Peace be removed.* Nothing on earth seems as enduring or immovable as soaring, majestic mountains. When you stand on their heights, breathing in that rarified air, you can almost smell eternity. Yet My Love and My Peace are even *more* enduring than the greatest mountain on earth!

Think deeply about *My unfailing Love.* One of the meanings of "unfailing" is *inexhaustible.* No matter how needy you are or how many times you fail Me, My supply of Love for you will never run low. Another meaning of "unfailing" is *constant.* I do not love you more on days when you perform well, nor do I love you less when you fail badly.

I Myself am your Peace. Live close to Me so you can enjoy this supernatural Peace. Come freely into My Presence, beloved, even when you're feeling bad about yourself. Remember who I am: *the Lord who has compassion on you.*

ISAIAH 54:10; ISAIAH 51:6;
EPHESIANS 2:14 NKJV

January 26

G IVE UP THE ILLUSION that you deserve a
problem-free life. Part of you is still hungering for the
resolution of all difficulties. This is a false hope! As I told My
disciples, *in the world you will have trouble.* Link your hope
not to problem solving in this life but to the promise of an
eternity of problem-free life in heaven. Instead of seeking perfection in this fallen world, pour your energy into seeking Me:
the Perfect One.

It is possible to enjoy Me and glorify Me in the midst of
adverse circumstances. In fact, My Light shines most brightly
through believers who trust Me in the dark. That kind of
trust is supernatural: a production of My indwelling Spirit.
When things seem all wrong, trust Me anyway. I am much
less interested in right circumstances than in right responses
to whatever comes your way.

JOHN 16:33; PSALM 112:4, 7

R ELAX, MY CHILD. I'm in control. Let these words wash over you repeatedly, like soothing waves on a beautiful beach, assuring you of My endless Love. You waste a lot of time and energy trying to figure out things before their time has come. Meanwhile, I am working to prepare the way before you. So be on the lookout for some wonderful surprises—circumstances that only *I* could have orchestrated.

Remember that you are My beloved. I am on your side, and I want what is best for you. Someone who is loved by a generous, powerful person can expect to receive an abundance of blessings. *You* are loved by the King of the universe, and I have good plans for you. As you look ahead into the unknown future, relax in the knowledge of who you are—*the one I love*. Cling to My hand, and go forward with confidence. While you and I walk together along *the path of Life*, your trust in Me will fill your heart with Joy and your mind with Peace.

JEREMIAH 29:11; DEUTERONOMY 33:12;
PSALM 16:11 NKJV

T RUST IS A GOLDEN PATHWAY TO HEAVEN. When you walk on this path, you live above your circumstances. My glorious Light shines more brightly on those who follow this path of Life. Dare to walk on the high road with Me, for it is the most direct route to heaven. The low road is circuitous: twisting and turning in agonizing knots. There the air hangs heavy—and dark, ominous clouds predominate. *Relying on your own understanding* will weigh you down. *Trust in Me absolutely, and I will make your path straight.*

JOHN 14:1–2; 2 TIMOTHY 4:18; PROVERBS 3:5–6

WALK WITH ME in close, trusting Love-bonds of joyful dependence. "Joyful dependence" may sound like an oxymoron, but it is the most fulfilling way to live. When you delight in relying on Me, you are living according to My perfect design for you.

The relationship I offer you is full of *glorious riches*: I am totally trustworthy, and I reach out to you with *unfailing Love*. I am closer than the very air you are breathing. I rejoice when you seek to live in trusting reliance on Me. This strengthens our relationship—building more and more bonds of affection between us.

A happily married man and woman are connected by much more than law and morality. Their warm memories of shared experiences create ties that draw them close and keep them committed to each other. Dear one, I want you to know that I am totally committed to *you*! I can fill your heart with loving memories as you *walk in the Light of My Presence*, joyfully depending on Me.

PHILIPPIANS 4:19; PSALM 52:8; PSALM 89:15–16

I AM WITH YOU ALWAYS. I spoke these words to My disciples after My resurrection. I continue to proclaim this promise to all who will listen. People respond to My continual Presence in various ways. Most Christians accept this teaching as truth but ignore it in their daily living. Some ill-taught or wounded believers fear (and may even resent) My awareness of all they do, say, and think. A few people center their lives around this glorious promise and find themselves blessed beyond all expectations.

When My Presence is the focal point of your consciousness, all the pieces of your life fall into place. As you gaze at Me through the eyes of your heart, you can see the world around you from My perspective. The fact that *I am with you* makes every moment of your life meaningful.

MATTHEW 28:20; PSALM 139:1–4

I MADE YOU A LITTLE LOWER than the heavenly beings and crowned you with glory and honor. You were made for greatness, beloved. Never doubt your personal significance, for *I created you in My own image*—in My likeness. I formed you with a magnificent brain that can communicate with Me, think rationally, create wonderful things, and much more. I gave you *dominion over the fish of the sea, the birds of the air, and every living thing that moves on the earth.* Of everything I created, only mankind is made in My likeness. This is a glorious privilege and responsibility; it makes every moment of your life meaningful.

One of your chief purposes in life is to glorify Me. I *crowned you with glory* so that you can *reflect My Glory*: lighting up this dark world and helping others come to know Me. I also want you to enjoy Me. I created you with unlimited capacity for pleasure in knowing Me. This Joy you find in Me here and now is a tiny foretaste of the eternal delights awaiting you in heaven.

PSALM 8:5; GENESIS 1:27–28 NKJV;
2 CORINTHIANS 3:18

K EEP YOUR FOCUS ON ME. I have gifted you with amazing freedom, including the ability to choose the focal point of your mind. Only the crown of My creation has such remarkable capability; this is a sign of being *made in My image.*

Let the goal of this day be to *bring every thought captive to Me.* Whenever your mind wanders, lasso those thoughts and bring them into My Presence. In My radiant Light, anxious thoughts shrink and shrivel away. Judgmental thoughts are unmasked as you bask in My unconditional Love. Confused ideas are untangled while you rest in the simplicity of My Peace. *I will guard you and keep you in constant Peace, as you focus your mind on Me.*

PSALM 8:5; GENESIS 1:26–27;
2 CORINTHIANS 10:5; ISAIAH 26:3 AMP

*Y*OU WILL SEEK *M*E AND FIND *M*E *when you seek Me with all your heart.* I don't expect perfection in this pursuit; it's not about that at all. It is the effort itself that pleases Me—when you keep on seeking Me even though it's so difficult. Actually, the intensity of this challenging search blesses you. As you strive to find Me in your moments, your focus is on Me. While you trudge toward Me through countless distractions, your awareness of Me increases. Even if you don't feel close to Me, you find yourself communicating with Me. So there is a sense in which your efforts to find Me are self-fulfilling: I am richly present in your striving. As a result, you feel more alive—more awake and real—when you are actively pursuing Me.

Your willingness to pour yourself into this glorious quest delights My heart. This joyful journey is all about *perseverance.* As long as you continue seeking Me, you are on the right path. Moreover, your success is certain: *I will be found by you!*

JEREMIAH 29:13–14; HEBREWS 12:1;
ROMANS 5:3 NKJV; 2 PETER 1:5–6

WORSHIP ME ONLY. Whatever occupies your mind the most becomes your god. Worries, if indulged, develop into idols. Anxiety gains a life of its own, parasitically infesting your mind. Break free from this bondage by affirming your trust in Me and refreshing yourself in My Presence. What goes on in your mind is invisible, undetectable to other people. But I read your thoughts continually, searching for evidence of trust in Me. I rejoice when your mind turns toward Me. Guard your thoughts diligently; good thought-choices will keep you close to Me.

PSALM 112:7; 1 CORINTHIANS 13:11;
PSALM 139:23-24 NASB

*I*AM MAKING EVERYTHING NEW*!* This is the opposite of what is always happening in your world of death and decay. Every day that you live means one less day remaining in your lifespan on this earth. Actually, this is very good news for My followers. At the end of each day, you can tell yourself: "I'm one step closer to heaven."

The world is in such a desperately fallen condition that there is only one remedy for it: making *everything* new. So do not be discouraged when your efforts to improve matters are unsuccessful. All things—including your efforts—are tainted by the Fall. Although I want you to endeavor to do your best, in dependence on Me, your world needs much more than a tune-up or an overhaul. It needs to be made completely new! And this is absolutely guaranteed to happen at the end of time, for *My words are trustworthy and true.*

You have good reason to rejoice, beloved, because I will make everything—including you—new and gloriously perfect!

REVELATION 21:5; PHILIPPIANS 1:21 NKJV;
ROMANS 8:22–23

I AM YOUR STRENGTH AND SHIELD. I plan out each day and have it ready for you long before you arise from bed. I also provide the strength you need each step of the way. Instead of assessing your energy level and wondering about what's on the road ahead, concentrate on staying in touch with Me. My Power flows freely into you through our open communication. Refuse to waste energy worrying, and you will have strength to spare.

Whenever you start to feel afraid, remember that I am your Shield. But unlike inanimate armor, I am always alert and active. My Presence watches over you continually, protecting you from both known and unknown dangers. Entrust yourself to My watch-care, which is the best security system available. *I am with you and will watch over you wherever you go.*

PSALM 28:7; MATTHEW 6:34;
PSALM 56:3–4; GENESIS 28:15

STRENGTH AND JOY are in My dwelling place. So the closer to Me you live, the stronger and more joyful you will be.

Invite Me to permeate your moments with My Presence. This helps you view people from a positive perspective. Whenever you're around someone who irritates you, don't focus on that person's flaws. Instead, gaze at *Me* through the eyes of your heart, and those irritants will wash over you without harming you—or hurting others. Judging other people is a sinful snare that draws you away from Me. How much better it is to *be joyful in Me, your Savior*!

The more you focus on Me, the more I can strengthen you. In fact, *I am your Strength.* You can train your mind to stay aware of Me even when other things are demanding your attention. I created you with an amazing brain that is able to be conscious of several things at once. Create a permanent place for Me in your mind, and My Light will shine on all your moments.

1 CHRONICLES 16:27; MATTHEW 7:1 NKJV;
HABAKKUK 3:18–19

February

Look to the LORD and his strength;
seek his face always.

PSALM 105:4

F OLLOW ME ONE STEP AT A TIME. That is all I require of you. In fact, that is the only way to move through this space/time world. You see huge mountains looming, and you start wondering how you're going to scale those heights. Meanwhile, because you're not looking where you're going, you stumble on the easy path where I am leading you now. As I help you get back on your feet, you tell Me how worried you are about the cliffs up ahead. But you don't know what will happen today, much less tomorrow. Our path may take an abrupt turn, leading you away from those mountains. There may be an easier way up the mountains than is visible from this distance. If I do lead you up the cliffs, I will equip you thoroughly for that strenuous climb. *I will even give My angels charge over you, to preserve you in all your ways.*

Keep your mind on the present journey, enjoying My Presence. *Walk by faith, not by sight*, trusting Me to open up the way before you.

PSALM 18:29; PSALM 91:11–12 AMP;
2 CORINTHIANS 5:7 NKJV

I AM *THE LIVING ONE who sees you.* I am more fully, gloriously alive than you can imagine. Someday you will see Me *face to Face* in all My Glory, and you will be awestruck! Now, though, *you see through a glass, darkly.* Your view of Me is obscured by your fallen condition. Nonetheless, I see *you* with perfect clarity. I know everything about you, including your most secret thoughts and feelings. I understand how broken and weak you are: *I remember that you are dust.* Yet I choose to love you with everlasting Love.

The gift of My Love was indescribably costly. I endured unspeakable suffering to save you from an eternity of agony. *I became sin for you so that in Me you might become the righteousness of God.* Ponder this wondrous truth: My righteousness is now yours! This gift of infinite value has been yours ever since you trusted Me as the God-Man who saved you from your sins. Rejoice that *the living One who sees you* perfectly is the Savior who loves you always!

GENESIS 16:13–14 AMP; 1 CORINTHIANS 13:12 KJV;
PSALM 103:14; 2 CORINTHIANS 5:21

I AM RENEWING YOUR MIND. When your thoughts flow freely, they tend to move toward problems. Your focus gets snagged on a given problem, circling round and round it in attempts to gain mastery. Your energy is drained away from other matters through this negative focus. Worst of all, you lose sight of Me.

A renewed mind is Presence-focused. Train your mind to seek Me in every moment, every situation. Sometimes you can find Me in your surroundings: a lilting birdsong, a loved one's smile, golden sunlight. At other times, you must draw inward to find Me. I am always present in your spirit. Seek My Face, speak to Me, and I will light up your mind.

ROMANS 12:2; HEBREWS 3:1; PSALM 105:4

I AM YOUR *EVER-PRESENT* *HELP*. Many people stumble out of bed in the morning and head straight for the coffee pot. Though they are not yet thinking clearly, they are awake enough to move toward something that will help unscramble their thoughts. I perform a similar function for you when your mind stumbles in My direction. Ask Me to clear out the confusion so you can communicate deeply with Me. You have this amazing capacity because I created you *in My own image*.

As you wait in My Presence, I not only unscramble your thoughts, I straighten your path through the day. I am sovereign over every aspect of your life, so opening up the way before you is no problem for Me. Some people assume they don't have time to begin their day with Me. They don't realize how much I can facilitate their activities—removing obstacles and giving insights that save time. When you spend precious moments with Me, I compensate you generously: I clarify your thinking and smooth out the circumstances of your life.

PSALM 46:1; GENESIS 1:27 NKJV;
JEREMIAH 32:17; PSALM 33:20

I AM WITH YOU AND FOR YOU. You face nothing alone—*nothing*! When you feel anxious, know that you are focusing on the visible world and leaving Me out of the picture. The remedy is simple: *Fix your eyes not on what is seen, but on what is unseen.* Verbalize your trust in Me, *the Living One who sees you always.* I will get you safely through this day and all your days. But you can find Me only in the present. Each day is a precious gift from My Father. How ridiculous to grasp for future gifts when today's is set before you! Receive today's gift gratefully, unwrapping it tenderly and delving into its depths. As you savor this gift, you find Me.

ROMANS 8:31; 2 CORINTHIANS 4:18;
GENESIS 16:13–14 AMP

*G*LORY IN MY HOLY NAME; *let the hearts of those who seek Me rejoice.* To "glory" in something is to give it praise and honor. Jesus is *the Name that is above every name*—it represents *Me* in all My sinless perfection. As My follower, you can whisper, speak, or sing My Name with confidence that I am listening. This draws you closer to Me and helps you find strength in My Presence. It also serves to drive away your spiritual enemies.

I'm delighted that you take time to seek Me, desiring to know Me better. Come freely into My loving Presence, letting your heart *rejoice in Me.* Remember that you are on *holy ground*, and breathe in the rarified air of My holiness. Release cares and concerns while you rest in the splendor of My Glory. Let My joyous Presence envelop you—permeating you through and through. As you delight in My nearness, time seems to slow down, enhancing your enjoyment of Me. Thank Me for these moments of sweet intimacy.

PSALM 105:3; PHILIPPIANS 2:9–11 NASB;
PHILIPPIANS 4:4–5 HCSB; EXODUS 3:5

B RING ME YOUR WEAKNESS, and receive My Peace. Accept yourself and your circumstances just as they are, remembering that I am sovereign over everything. Do not wear yourself out with analyzing and planning. Instead, let thankfulness and trust be your guides through this day; they will keep you close to Me. As you live in the radiance of My Presence, My Peace shines upon you. You will cease to notice how weak or strong you feel because you will be focusing on Me. The best way to get through this day is step by step with Me. Continue this intimate journey, trusting that the path you are following is headed for heaven.

PSALM 29:11; NUMBERS 6:24–26; PSALM 13:5

*I*T IS GOOD TO PROCLAIM MY LOVE *in the morn-ing and My faithfulness at night.* Proclaiming this Love is exceedingly good for you. When you declare the wonders of My loving Presence, you are strengthened and encouraged. This glorious blessing flows into you more fully as you speak these words out loud. Let this delightful declaration fill you with *Joy inexpressible and full of Glory*!

Ponder some of the qualities of My amazing Love: It is sacrificial, unfailing, priceless, boundless—*reaching to the heavens.* It shines so brightly that it can carry you through your darkest days. When you get to the end of each day, it is time to proclaim My faithfulness that *reaches to the skies.* Look back over the day, and notice how I helped you navigate your way through it. The more difficulties you encountered, the more help I made available to you. It is good to give voice to My great faithfulness, especially at night, so that you can *lie down and sleep in peace.*

PSALM 92:1–2; 1 PETER 1:8 NKJV;
PSALM 36:5–7; PSALM 4:8

S EEK MY FACE, and you will find not only My Presence but also My Peace. To receive My Peace, you must change your grasping, controlling stance to one of openness and trust. The only thing you can grasp without damaging your soul is My hand. Ask My Spirit within you to order your day and control your thoughts, for *the mind controlled by the Spirit is Life and Peace.*

You can have as much of Me and My Peace as you want, through thousands of correct choices each day. The most persistent choice you face is whether to trust Me or to worry. You will never run out of things to worry about, but you can choose to trust Me no matter what. I am *an ever-present help in trouble.* Trust Me, *though the earth give way and the mountains fall into the heart of the sea.*

ROMANS 8:6; NUMBERS 6:26 NKJV; PSALM 46:1–2

T HE JOY I GIVE YOU transcends your circumstances. This means that no matter what is happening in your life, it is possible to be joyful in Me. The prophet Habakkuk listed a series of dire circumstances that he was anticipating, then he proclaimed: *"Yet I will rejoice in the Lord, I will be joyful in God my Savior."* This is transcendent Joy!

I am training you to view your life from a heavenly perspective—through eyes of faith. When things don't go as you had hoped, talk with Me. *Seek My Face* and My guidance. I will help you discern whether you need to work to change the situation or simply accept it. Either way, you can teach yourself to say: "I can still rejoice in *You*, Jesus." This short statement of faith—expressing your confidence in Me—will change your perspective dramatically. As you practice doing this more and more, your Joy will increase. This training also prepares you to handle the difficulties awaiting you on your pathway toward heaven. *Rejoice in Me always.*

HABAKKUK 3:17–18; PSALM 105:4 NASB;
PHILIPPIANS 4:4

COME TO ME AND REST. I am all around you, to bless and restore. Breathe Me in with each breath. The way just ahead of you is very steep. Slow down and cling tightly to My hand. I am teaching you a difficult lesson, learned only by hardship.

Lift up empty hands of faith to receive My precious Presence. Light, Life, Joy, and Peace flow freely through this gift. When your focus turns away from Me, you grasp for other things. You drop the glowing gift of My Presence as you reach for lifeless ashes. Return to Me; regain My Presence.

MATTHEW 11:28–29; 1 TIMOTHY 2:8;
ZECHARIAH 1:3

R EJOICE THAT *I HAVE CLOTHED YOU* **with gar-**
ments of salvation. This *robe of righteousness* is yours
forever and ever! Because I am your Savior, My perfect righteousness can never be taken away from you. This means you
don't need to be afraid to face your sins—or to deal with them.
As you become aware of sin in your life, confess it and receive
My forgiveness in full measure.

It is essential also to forgive yourself. Self-hatred is not
pleasing to Me, and it is very unhealthy for you. I urge you to
take many looks at *Me* for every look at your sins or failures. I
am the perfect antidote to the poison of self-loathing.

Since you are already precious in My sight, you don't have
to prove your worth by trying to be good enough. I lived a
perfect life on your behalf because I knew that you could not.
Now I want you to live in the glorious freedom of being My
fully forgiven follower. Remember that *there is no condemnation for those who belong to Me.*

ISAIAH 61:10; MATTHEW 1:21 NKJV;
1 JOHN 1:9 NKJV; ROMANS 8:1–2

C OME TO ME FOR REST and refreshment. The journey has been too much for you, and you are bone-weary. Do not be ashamed of your exhaustion. Instead, see it as an opportunity for Me to take charge of your life.

Remember that *I can fit everything into a pattern for good*, including the things you wish were different. Start with where you are at this point in time and space, accepting that this is where I intend you to be. You will get through today one step, one moment at a time. Your main responsibility is to remain attentive to Me, letting Me guide you through the many choices along your pathway.

This sounds like an easy assignment, but it is not. Your desire to live in My Presence goes against the grain of the world, the flesh, and the devil. Much of your weariness results from your constant battle against these opponents. However, you are on the path of My choosing, so do not give up! *Hope in Me, for you will again praise Me for the help of My Presence.*

ROMANS 8:28 AMP; PSALM 42:5 NASB

*D*O NOT FEAR, *for I am with you. I will uphold you with My righteous right hand.* Let these words enfold you like a warm blanket, sheltering you from the coldness of fear and discouragement. When trouble seems to be stalking you, grip My hand tightly and stay in communication with Me. You can *trust and not be afraid, for I am your Strength and Song.* My powerful Presence is with you always. You face *nothing* alone! Moreover, I have promised to *strengthen you and help you.*

My strong hand supports you in both good times and bad. When things are going well in your life, you may not be attentive to My sustaining Presence. But when you are *walking through the valley of the shadow of death,* you become keenly aware of your neediness. During these difficult times, holding onto Me keeps you standing—and able to put one foot in front of the other. As you endure this adversity patiently—in trusting dependence on Me—I bless you with abundant Joy in My Presence.

ISAIAH 41:10; ISAIAH 12:2 NASB; PSALM 23:4 NKJV

I AM ABOVE ALL THINGS: your problems, your pain, and the swirling events in this ever-changing world. When you behold My Face, you rise above circumstances and rest with Me in *heavenly realms*. This is the way of Peace, living in the Light of My Presence. I guarantee that you will always have problems in this life, but they must not become your focus. When you feel yourself sinking in the sea of circumstances, say, "*Help me, Jesus!*" and I will draw you back to Me. If you have to say that thousands of times daily, don't be discouraged. I know your weakness, and I meet you in that very place.

EPHESIANS 2:6; MATTHEW 14:28–32; ISAIAH 42:3

My Love will never let you go! It has an eternal grip on you. You live in a world that is unpredictable and unsafe in many ways. As you look around, you see landscape littered with broken promises.

However, My Love is a promise that will never be broken. *Though the mountains be shaken and the hills be removed, yet My unfailing Love for you will not be shaken.* The prophet Isaiah is painting a picture of dire circumstances: quaking mountains and disappearing hills. No matter *what* is happening, My Love is unshakable. You can build your life on it!

Sometimes My children believe I care for them but still find it difficult to receive My Love in full measure. I want you to learn *to grasp how wide and long and high and deep is My Love for you.* Ask My Spirit to empower you *to know this Love that surpasses knowledge.* Break free from faulty self-images so you can view yourself as I see you—radiant in *My righteousness*, wrapped in luminous Love.

ISAIAH 54:10; EPHESIANS 3:16–19;
ISAIAH 61:10 NKJV

February 9

S EEK MY FACE more and more. You are really just beginning your journey of intimacy with Me. It is not an easy road, but it is a delightful and privileged way: a treasure hunt. I am the Treasure, and the Glory of My Presence glistens and shimmers along the way. Hardships are part of the journey too. I mete them out ever so carefully, in just the right dosage, with a tenderness you can hardly imagine. Do not recoil from afflictions, since they are among My most favored gifts. *Trust Me and don't be afraid, for I am your Strength and Song.*

PSALM 27:8 NKJV; 2 CORINTHIANS 4:7–8;
ISAIAH 12:2

R EJOICE THAT I UNDERSTAND YOU completely and love you with perfect, unending Love. Many people are afraid that anyone who comes to know them fully will look down on them or even reject them. So they strive to keep others at a safe distance, disclosing only the parts of themselves they think are acceptable. This way of interacting with others tends to feel safer, but it leads to loneliness.

Be thankful that there is One who sees straight through your defenses and pretenses. There is no hiding from Me! I know absolutely *everything* about you. So rest in the wonder of being *fully known*—yet delighted in! You don't have to work at trying to earn My Love. The truth is, nothing could ever *stop* Me from loving you. Because you are Mine—bought with My blood—you are accepted and treasured forever. You need to tell yourself this truth over and over, till it seeps into your inner being and changes the way you view yourself. Self-acceptance is the path to self-forgetfulness, which is the royal road to Joy!

PSALM 107:1, 43 ESV; 1 CORINTHIANS 13:12;
PSALM 149:4–5; EPHESIANS 1:5–6 NKJV

T RUST ME ENOUGH to spend ample time with Me, pushing back the demands of the day. Refuse to feel guilty about something that is so pleasing to Me, the King of the universe. Because I am omnipotent, I am able to bend time and events in your favor. You will find that you can accomplish *more* in less time after you have given yourself to Me in rich communion. Also, as you align yourself with My perspective, you can sort out what is important and what is not.

Don't fall into the trap of being constantly on the go. Many, many things people do in My Name have no value in My kingdom. To avoid doing meaningless works, stay in continual communication with Me. *I will instruct you and teach you in the way you should go; I will counsel you with My eye upon you.*

LUKE 10:41–42; HEBREWS 1:1–2;
PSALM 32:8 NASB

*C*OME TO *ME, and I will ease, relieve, and refresh your soul.* Approach Me confidently, dear one, knowing that I have perfect understanding of you and everything that concerns you. Tell Me your troubles candidly; let the Light of My Face shine on them and illuminate your thinking. Then rest with Me, slowly inhaling the beauty of My Presence. You can feel safe and secure in *My everlasting arms.* As you spend precious time with Me, let Me ease and relieve your soul.

Your soul is the most important part of you because it is eternal. The New Testament Greek word for "soul" is sometimes translated "life." When you are *heavy-laden and overburdened*, you may feel as if the life is draining out of you. But I offer wonderfully nourishing care for this vital part of you. *I restore your soul*—helping you to rest and see things from My perspective. As I am refreshing you, relax and feel My Life flowing into you. *Your soul finds rest in Me alone.*

MATTHEW 11:28 AMP; DEUTERONOMY 33:27 ESV;
PSALM 23:2–3; PSALM 62:1

M Y PEACE is like a shaft of golden Light shining on you continuously. During days of bright sunshine, it may blend in with your surroundings. On darker days, My Peace stands out in sharp contrast to your circumstances. See times of darkness as opportunities for My Light to shine in transcendent splendor. I am training you to practice Peace that overpowers darkness. Collaborate with Me in this training. *Do not grow weary and lose heart.*

2 THESSALONIANS 3:16;
JOHN 1:4–5 AMP; HEBREWS 12:3

*B*E JOYFUL ALWAYS; *pray continually.* The way to rejoice at all times is to find moment-by-moment pleasure in your relationship with Me—the Lover of your soul. This relationship is so full of comfort and encouragement that it's possible to *be joyful in hope* even when you're in the midst of adversity.

Give thanks in all circumstances. There is immense Power in praying, "Thank You, Jesus." These three words are appropriate for all times and in every situation because of My great sacrifice for you. I encourage you to praise Me for every good thing as soon as you become aware of it. This practice adds sparkle to your blessings—heightening your Joy.

When you are feeling sad or discouraged, it is still a good time to thank Me. This demonstrates your trust in Me and brightens your perspective. To enhance your gratefulness, ponder specific things about *Me* that delight you—My continual Presence, My lavish grace, *My unfailing Love.* Thanking Me in all circumstances strengthens your relationship with Me and helps you live more joyfully!

1 THESSALONIANS 5:16–18; ROMANS 12:12;
EPHESIANS 1:7–8; PSALM 143:8

February 12

I AM EVER SO NEAR YOU, hovering over your shoulder, reading every thought. People think that thoughts are fleeting and worthless, but yours are precious to Me. I smile when you think lovingly of Me. My Spirit, who lives within you, helps you to think My thoughts. As your thinking goes, so goes your entire being.

Let Me be your positive Focus. When you look to Me, knowing Me as *God with you*, you experience Joy. This is according to My ancient design, when I first crafted man. Modern man seeks his positive focus elsewhere: in sports, sensations, acquiring new possessions. Advertising capitalizes on the longing of people for a positive focus in their lives. I planted that longing in human souls, knowing that only I could fully satisfy it. *Delight yourself in Me; let Me become the Desire of your heart.*

PSALM 139:1–2; MATTHEW 1:23; PSALM 37:4

I OFFER YOU *INEXPRESSIBLE and glorious Joy*— straight from heaven itself! This *triumphant, heavenly Joy* can be found only in Me. It is easy to slide, ever so gradually, from delighting in Me to living for the next spiritual "high." Sometimes I bless you with a taste of heaven's splendor, but the primary purpose of these experiences is to whet your appetite for the next life. Do not underestimate the brokenness of the world you inhabit. Your enjoyment of My Presence will always intermingle with the sorrows of living in this fallen world—until *I take you into Glory*.

Someday you will see Me face to Face, but for now *you love Me without having seen Me. You believe in Me even though you do not see Me.* This love for Me is not irrational or whimsical. It's a response to My boundless passion for you, dramatically displayed on the cross and verified by My resurrection. You worship a risen, living Savior! *Blessed are those who have not seen Me and yet have believed.*

1 PETER 1:8 AMP; PSALM 73:23–24;
1 JOHN 4:19 NKJV; JOHN 20:29 NKJV

P EACE BE WITH YOU! Ever since the resurrection, this has been My watchword to those who yearn for Me. As you sit quietly, let My Peace settle over you and enfold you in My loving Presence. To provide this radiant Peace for you, I died a criminal's death. Receive *My Peace* abundantly and thankfully. It is a rare treasure, dazzling in delicate beauty, yet strong enough to withstand all onslaughts. Wear My Peace with regal dignity. It will keep your heart and mind close to Mine.

JOHN 20:19, 21; JOHN 14:27; PHILIPPIANS 4:7

I N MY PRESENCE there is *fullness of Joy*. As you peer into My Presence—remembering who I Am in all My Power and Glory—ponder also My eternal commitment to you. *Nothing in all creation will ever be able to separate you from Me!* Your relationship with Me has been rock-solid secure ever since you confessed your sinfulness and received My forgiveness. You are My beloved in whom I delight; *this* is your permanent identity.

You can find Joy even in this broken world, because *I have set eternity in your heart*. Spend time refreshing yourself in My Presence, where you can relax and learn to *delight yourself in Me* above all else. As the Love-bonds between us grow stronger, so does your desire to help others enjoy this amazing Life you have found in Me. When your love for Me overflows into other people's lives, there is abundant Joy both in heaven and on earth! As you go along this *path of Life*, I will lead you—and I'll bless you with *pleasures forevermore*.

PSALM 16:11 NKJV; ROMANS 8:39;
ECCLESIASTES 3:11; PSALM 37:4

G IVE YOURSELF FULLY to the adventure of today. Walk boldly along the path of Life, relying on your ever-present Companion. You have every reason to be confident because My Presence accompanies you all the days of your life—and onward into eternity.

Do not give in to fear or worry, those robbers of abundant living. Trust Me enough to face problems as they come, rather than trying to anticipate them. *Fix your eyes on Me, the Author and Perfecter of your faith*, and many difficulties on the road ahead will vanish before you reach them. Whenever you start to feel afraid, remember that *I am holding you by your right hand*. Nothing can separate you from My Presence!

PSALM 48:14; HEBREWS 12:2; ISAIAH 41:13

*L*ET *MY UNFAILING LOVE* *be your comfort.* One definition of "comfort" is a person or thing that makes you feel less upset or frightened during a time of trouble. Because you live in such a broken world, trouble is never far away. There are many sources of comfort in the world, yet only one of them is unfailing: My Love! Other sources will help you *some* of the time, but My tender Presence is with you *all* of the time.

My perfect, inexhaustible Love is not just a *thing* that makes you feel less upset; it's also a *Person. Nothing in all creation can separate you from Me.* And *I* am inseparable from My Love.

As My cherished follower, you can turn to Me for comfort at all times. Since you have this boundless Source of blessing—*Me*—I want you to be a blessing in the lives of other people. You *can comfort those in any trouble with the comfort you have received from Me.*

PSALM 119:76; JOHN 16:33 NKJV;
ROMANS 8:38–39; 2 CORINTHIANS 1:3–4

C OME TO ME with all your weaknesses: physical, emotional, and spiritual. Rest in the comfort of My Presence, remembering that *nothing is impossible with Me.*

Pry your mind away from your problems so you can focus your attention on Me. Recall that I am *able to do immeasurably more than all you ask or imagine.* Instead of trying to direct Me to do this and that, seek to attune yourself to what I am *already* doing.

When anxiety attempts to wedge its way into your thoughts, remind yourself that *I am your Shepherd.* The bottom line is that I am taking care of you; therefore, you needn't be afraid of anything. Rather than trying to maintain control over your life, abandon yourself to My will. Though this may feel frightening—even dangerous—the safest place to be is in My will.

LUKE 1:37; EPHESIANS 3:20–21; PSALM 23:1–4

I AM YOUR SHEPHERD—*to guide and shield you.* A good shepherd cares about his sheep and understands them very well. My care for you is wonderfully complete: I love you with perfect, *unfailing Love.* I know *everything* about you—your weaknesses and limitations, your struggles and sins, your strengths and abilities. So I am able to shepherd you exceptionally well.

I have designed you to walk through this perilous world in trusting dependence on Me. I lovingly go before you and open up the way, carefully preparing the path you will follow. I remove many dangers and obstacles from the road ahead, and I help you handle the difficulties that remain.

Even when you walk through the darkest valley, you need not be afraid, for I am close beside you. Enjoy My nearness, beloved, and communicate with Me. I will guide you carefully through this day and all your days. *For I am your God for ever and ever; I will be your Guide even to the end.*

PSALM 23:1 AMP; EXODUS 15:13;
PSALM 23:4 NLT; PSALM 48:14

T HANK ME for the conditions that are requiring you to *be still*. Do not spoil these quiet hours by wishing them away, waiting impatiently to be active again. Some of the greatest works in My kingdom have been done from sick-beds and prison cells. Instead of resenting the limitations of a weakened body, search for My way in the midst of these very circumstances. Limitations can be liberating when your strongest desire is living close to Me.

Quietness and trust enhance your awareness of My Presence with you. Do not despise these simple ways of serving Me. Although you feel cut off from the activity of the world, your quiet trust makes a powerful statement in spiritual realms. *My Strength and Power show themselves most effective in weakness.*

ZECHARIAH 2:13; ISAIAH 30:15;
2 CORINTHIANS 12:9 AMP

B EFORE YOU BEGIN A TASK—large or small—take time to pray about it. By doing so, you acknowledge your need for Me and your trust that I will help you. This enables you to go about your work in dependence on Me. There are many benefits to this practice. I can guide your mind as you think things out and make decisions. Just knowing I am involved in what you're doing gives you confidence, reducing stress. It's wise to thank Me often for My help and to keep asking Me to *guide you along the best pathway.*

Though the Bible instructs you to *pray continually,* at times you ignore this teaching. When you're feeling rushed, you find it hard to slow down enough to seek My perspective on the work at hand. However, diving in and forging ahead on your own is actually counterproductive. When you request My involvement *before* you begin, I can point you in the right direction—saving precious time and energy. I delight in helping you with everything, even simple tasks, because you are *My beloved.*

COLOSSIANS 3:23 NASB; PSALM 32:8 NLT;
1 THESSALONIANS 5:17; SONG OF SOLOMON 6:3 NKJV

I AM THE RISEN ONE who shines upon you always. You worship a living Deity, not some idolatrous, man-made image. Your relationship with Me is meant to be vibrant and challenging, as I invade more and more areas of your life. Do not fear change, for I am making you a *new creation, with old things passing away and new things continually on the horizon.* When you cling to old ways and sameness, you resist My work within you. I want you to embrace all that I am doing in your life, finding your security in Me alone.

It is easy to make an idol of routine, finding security within the boundaries you build around your life. Although each day contains twenty-four hours, every single one presents a unique set of circumstances. Don't try to force-fit today into yesterday's mold. Instead, ask Me to open your eyes so you can find all I have prepared for you in this precious day of Life.

MATTHEW 28:5–7; 2 CORINTHIANS 5:17

Y OU CAN FIND JOY in the most unexpected places. However, this requires effort: searching for the good and refusing to let your natural responses blind you to what is there. I will help you respond in a *supernatural* way, giving you eyes that see beyond the obvious and discover treasure hidden in your troubles. Simply ask Me.

Living joyously is a choice. Since you inhabit such a sinful, broken world, you must choose gladness many times daily. This is especially true during difficult times. When something happens that breaks the pattern of comfort and happiness in your life, you are being put to the test. Such trials can both prove and strengthen your faith, which is *much more precious than gold*. I am training you to *consider it pure Joy whenever you face trials of many kinds*.

I made the agonizing choice to *endure the cross for the Joy set before Me*—the eternal pleasure of *bringing My followers to Glory*. Choose Joy, beloved, by *fixing your eyes on Me* and looking for treasures in your trials.

1 PETER 1:6–7 NKJV; JAMES 1:2;
HEBREWS 12:2; HEBREWS 2:10 NKJV

February 18

I AM WITH YOU. These four words are like a safety net, protecting you from falling into despair. Because you are human, you will always have ups and downs in your life experience. But the promise of My Presence limits how far down you can go. Sometimes you may feel as if you are in a free fall, when people or things you had counted on let you down. Yet as soon as you remember that *I am with you*, your perspective changes radically. Instead of bemoaning your circumstances, you can look to Me for help. You recall that not only am I with you; *I am holding you by your right hand. I guide you with My counsel, and afterward I will take you into Glory.* This is exactly the perspective you need: the reassurance of My Presence and the glorious hope of heaven.

ZEPHANIAH 3:17; PSALM 73:23–26

I N M Y P R E S E N C E you can find *fullness of Joy, perfect Peace*, and *unfailing Love*. Walk with Me along *the path of Life*—enjoying My company each step of the way. Because I am always by your side, the Joy of My Presence is yours for the taking!

I will keep you in perfect Peace as you *fix your thoughts on Me*. Stay in communication with Me through your spoken words, thoughts, and songs. Spend ample time absorbing My Word—letting it speak into your heart, where it changes the way you think and live. As you ponder who I really am, My Light shines warmly into your mind, helping you live in My Peace.

Beloved, I want you to flourish in My Presence—*like an olive tree flourishing in the house of God*. As the sunlight of My Presence nourishes you, you are able to produce abundant fruit in My kingdom. And the more you *trust in My unfailing Love*, the more you will realize how utterly secure you are.

PSALM 16:11 NKJV; ISAIAH 26:3 NLT; PSALM 52:8

Y OU ARE FEELING WEIGHED DOWN by a plethora of problems, both big and small. They seem to require more and more of your attention, but you must not give in to those demands. When the difficulties in your life feel as if they're closing in on you, break free by spending quality time with Me. You need to remember who I am in all My Power and Glory. Then humbly bring Me your prayers and petitions. Your problems will pale when you view them in the Light of My Presence. You can learn to *be joyful in Me, your Savior*, even in the midst of adverse circumstances. Rely on Me, *your Strength; I make your feet like the feet of a deer, enabling you to go on the heights.*

EXODUS 3:14; PSALM 63:2; HABAKKUK 3:17–19

*S*ET ME BEFORE YOU CONTINUALLY; keep your eyes on Me. *I am at your right hand*, close by your side. This is the most reliable source of Joy: knowing that I am always near. Seek to strengthen your awareness of My Presence so you can enjoy Me in your moments and feel more secure.

Communicating with Me—in silent prayers, in whispers, in spoken words, in shouts of praise—is the best way to stay attentive to Me. I want you to be real with Me in your prayers. Instead of worrying or obsessing about things, turn those thoughts toward Me. Talk with Me about whatever is on your mind. I will show you *My* way to handle the person or situation that concerns you.

Study and meditate on Scripture. Let it saturate your heart and mind, changing your way of thinking. Permeate your prayers with biblical concepts and content. As you stay in close communication with Me, the Joy of My Presence is yours!

PSALM 16:8 NASB; PSALM 71:23;
PHILIPPIANS 4:6 NLT; PSALM 90:14

L EARN TO LIVE from your true Center in Me. I reside in the deepest depths of your being, in eternal union with your spirit. It is at this deep level that My Peace reigns continually. You will not find lasting peace in the world around you, in circumstances, or in human relationships. The external world is always in flux—under the curse of death and decay. But there is a gold mine of Peace deep within you, waiting to be tapped. Take time to delve into the riches of My residing Presence. I want you to live increasingly from your real Center, where My Love has an eternal grip on you. *I am Christ in you, the hope of Glory.*

1 THESSALONIANS 5:23;
COLOSSIANS 3:15; COLOSSIANS 1:27

D ON'T THINK OF PRAYER AS A CHORE. Instead, view it as communicating with the One you adore. *Delight yourself in Me*; this will draw you irresistibly into communion with Me. Remember all that I am to you, all I have done for you. I love you with perfect, everlasting Love, and *I take great delight in you*. Let My tenderness embrace you, convincing you that you are indeed My beloved. Rejoice in the One who will never let you go!

Often the easiest way to start talking with Me is to thank Me for being your Savior, Redeemer, and Friend. You can also give thanks for things that are happening in your life, your family, your church, and beyond. These grateful prayers connect you with Me and ease the way into other prayers.

You can talk freely with Me since I know everything about you and your circumstances. I never reject you because the penalty for your sins has been paid in full—with My blood. Trust Me enough to *pour out your heart to Me, for I am your Refuge.*

PSALM 37:4; ZEPHANIAH 3:17;
PSALM 118:28–29 NKJV; PSALM 62:8

T RUST AND THANKFULNESS WILL get you safely through this day. Trust protects you from worrying and obsessing. Thankfulness keeps you from criticizing and complaining: those "sister sins" that so easily entangle you.

Keeping your eyes on Me is the same thing as trusting Me. It is a free choice that you must make thousands of times daily. The more you choose to trust Me, the easier it becomes. Thought patterns of trust become etched into your brain. Relegate troubles to the periphery of your mind so that I can be central in your thoughts. Thus you focus on Me, entrusting your concerns into My care.

PSALM 31:14 NKJV, COLOSSIANS 2:6–7;
PSALM 141:8; 1 PETER 5:7

*P*UT ON THE ARMOR OF LIGHT. To wear this bright, protective covering, you have to *put aside deeds of darkness.* You live in a world where darkness is prevalent all around you. You need My Light-armor to help you see things clearly—protecting you from being led astray by the worldliness that surrounds you.

I want you to *walk in the Light* with Me. Make every effort to live close to Me, aware of My loving Presence. Just as you put clothes on your body, you can also *clothe yourself with Me.* Such nearness to Me will help you make good decisions. Sometimes, though, you will make bad choices that lead you into sin. Do not despair when this happens. Because I am your Savior, I have made provision for *all* your sin. Moreover, the blood I shed on the cross *cleanses you* and keeps you walking in the Light.

If you confess your sins, I forgive you and cleanse you from all unrighteousness. I am *faithful and just*, and I delight in your nearness to Me.

ROMANS 13:12; 1 JOHN 1:7 NKJV;
ROMANS 13:14; 1 JOHN 1:9 NKJV

Y OU NEED ME EVERY MOMENT. Your awareness of your constant need for Me is your greatest strength. Your neediness, properly handled, is a link to My Presence. However, there are pitfalls that you must be on guard against: self-pity, self-preoccupation, giving up. Your inadequacy presents you with a continual choice—deep dependence on Me or despair. The emptiness you feel within will be filled either with problems or with My Presence. Make Me central in your consciousness by *praying continually*: simple, short prayers flowing out of the present moment. Use My Name liberally, to remind you of My Presence. *Keep on asking and you will receive, so that your gladness may be full and complete.*

PSALM 86:7; 1 THESSALONIANS 5:17;
JOHN 16:24 AMP

ONE OF MY NAMES is *Wonderful Counselor.* I understand you far, far better than you understand yourself. So come to *Me* with your problems and insecurities, seeking My counsel. In the Light of My loving Presence you can see yourself as you really are: radiantly lovely in My brilliant righteousness. Though My righteousness is perfect, you will continue to struggle with imperfections—yours and others'—as long as you live in this world. Still, your standing with Me is secure. *Nothing in all creation can separate you from My Love!*

A good counselor helps you recognize truth and live according to it. *Actually, I was born and came into the world to testify to the truth.* So be open and honest when you bring Me your concerns. Also, fill your mind and heart with My Word, which contains absolute truth.

A *wonderful* counselor is not only extremely good at helping people but also able to inspire delight or pleasure. *Delight yourself in Me,* beloved, *and I will give you the desires of your heart.*

ISAIAH 9:6 NASB; ROMANS 8:38–39;
JOHN 18:37 NLT; PSALM 37:4

B E ON GUARD against the pit of self-pity. When you are weary or unwell, this demonic trap is the greatest danger you face. Don't even go near the edge of the pit. Its edges crumble easily, and before you know it, you are on the way down. It is ever so much harder to get out of the pit than to keep a safe distance from it. That is why I tell you to be on guard.

There are several ways to protect yourself from self-pity. When you are occupied with praising and thanking Me, it is impossible to feel sorry for yourself. Also, the closer you live to Me, the more distance there is between you and the pit. Live in the Light of My Presence by *fixing your eyes on Me*. Then you will be able *to run with endurance the race that is set before you*, without stumbling or falling.

PSALM 89:15; HEBREWS 12:1–2 NASB

I AM THE WORD OF LIFE—*eternal Life.* I have always existed: I am *that which was from the beginning.* Moreover, I am divine. As the apostle John wrote, *"The Word was God."* This divine Word brings Life to all who believe in Me.

From the beginning of creation, words have been associated with life. Originally, the earth was formless, empty, and dark. Then I said, *"Let there be light," and there was light.* I spoke everything into existence, including all the plants and animals. Finally, I spoke mankind into being.

The Life I offer you is *eternal.* It begins when you trust Me as your only Savior—but it never ends. You can enjoy immense freedom through knowing *there is no condemnation* for you. I have forever *set you free from the law of sin and death!* The best response to this glorious gift is grateful Joy—delighting in the One who loves you perfectly *and* eternally. Remember that I am always near you, closer than the air you breathe.

1 JOHN 1:1–2; JOHN 1:1 NKJV;
GENESIS 1:1–3; ROMANS 8:1–2

B E S T I L L I N T H E L I G H T of My Presence while I communicate Love to you. There is no force in the universe as powerful as My Love. You are constantly aware of limitations: your own and others'. But there is no limit to My Love; it fills all of space, time, and eternity.

Now you see through a glass, darkly, but someday you will see Me face to Face. Then you will be able to experience fully *how wide and long and high and deep is My Love for you.* If you were to experience that now, you would be overwhelmed to the point of feeling crushed. But you have an eternity ahead of you, absolutely guaranteed, during which you can enjoy My Presence in unrestricted ecstasy. For now, the knowledge of My loving Presence is sufficient to carry you through each day.

1 CORINTHIANS 13:12 KJV; EPHESIANS 3:16–19

*M*ORNING BY MORNING *I* AWAKEN YOU *and open your understanding to My will.* I'm always mindful of you, beloved. I never sleep, so I'm able to watch over you while you're sleeping. *When you wake up* in the morning, *I am still with you.* As you become aware of My loving Presence, I help you become more alert—smoothing out the tangles in your mind and enabling you to see Me more clearly. I invite you to spend time enjoying My Presence and nourishing your soul with My Word. When you respond to My Love-call by *drawing nearer to Me,* I am delighted.

This time dedicated to Me blesses and strengthens you immensely. I open your understanding to My Word—enabling you to comprehend Scripture and apply it to your life. As you make plans for your day, I help you discern My will. This collaboration with Me empowers you to handle *whatever* comes your way as you go through the day. I am training you to *trust Me at all times*—in all circumstances.

ISAIAH 50:4 TLB; PSALM 139:17–18 NLT;
JAMES 4:8 NKJV; PSALM 62:8

REST IN MY PRESENCE, allowing Me to take charge of this day. Do not bolt into the day like a race-horse suddenly released. Instead, walk purposefully with Me, letting Me direct your course one step at a time. Thank Me for each blessing along the way; this brings Joy to both you and Me. A grateful heart protects you from negative thinking. Thankfulness enables you to see the abundance I shower upon you daily. Your prayers and petitions are winged into heaven's throne room when they are permeated with thanksgiving. *In everything give thanks, for this is My will for you.*

MATTHEW 11:28 NKJV; COLOSSIANS 4:2;
1 THESSALONIANS 5:18 NASB

T HE LIGHT OF MY GLORY is shining on you, beloved. Look up to Me with worship in your heart. Let the radiance of My Love fall upon you and soak into the depths of your being. Savor these moments alone with Me. I am using them to make you more like Me. The more you keep your gaze on Me—in quiet times *and* busy times—the better you can *reflect My Glory* to other people.

Staying conscious of Me when you're busy can be quite a challenge. But I have created you with an amazing mind that can function on more than one "track." Practicing My Presence involves dedicating one track to your relationship with Me. This practice has many benefits: When you are aware that I am present with you, you're less likely to do or say something that's displeasing to Me. When you're struggling with difficult circumstances or painful feelings, awareness of My Presence offers courage and comfort. I can use *everything* in your life for good—*transforming you into My likeness with ever-increasing Glory.*

HEBREWS 12:2; 2 CORINTHIANS 3:18;
ROMANS 8:28 NLT

I AM LEADING YOU, STEP BY STEP, through your life. Hold My hand in trusting dependence, letting Me guide you through this day. Your future looks uncertain and feels flimsy—even precarious. That is how it should be. *Secret things belong to the Lord*, and future things are secret things. When you try to figure out the future, you are grasping at things that are Mine. This, like all forms of worry, is an act of rebellion: doubting My promises to care for you.

Whenever you find yourself worrying about the future, repent and return to Me. I will show you the next step forward, and the one after that, and the one after that. Relax and enjoy the journey in My Presence, trusting Me to open up the way before you as you go.

DEUTERONOMY 29:29; LUKE 12:25–26;
PSALM 32:8

MAN LOOKS AT THE OUTWARD APPEARANCE but I look at the heart. The ability to see is a great gift. I grant glimpses of My Glory via visual beauty in nature. Great paintings, sculptures, and cinematography can also help awaken your soul. Rejoice in these glorious gifts, but do not become enslaved to appearances. I am primarily interested in the condition of your heart, and I work to create beauty in it.

It is vital to set aside time for nourishing your heart. *Above all else, guard your heart, for it is the wellspring of life.* A wellspring is a source of abundant supply. Since you belong to Me, My own Life flows through you! However, to keep this Life flowing abundantly, you must protect your heart from evil influences and nourish it with Bible study and prayer.

Aligning your priorities with My teaching can be very freeing. When you don't like the way things look in your world, close your eyes and gaze at who I am. Remember that I am *Immanuel—God with you.*

1 SAMUEL 16:7; PROVERBS 4:23;
MATTHEW 1:23

KEEP YOUR EYES ON ME! Waves of adversity are washing over you, and you feel tempted to give up. As your circumstances consume more and more of your attention, you are losing sight of Me. Yet *I am with you always, holding you by your right hand.* I am fully aware of your situation, *and I will not allow you to be tempted beyond what you are able to bear.*

Your gravest danger is worrying about tomorrow. If you try to carry tomorrow's burdens today, you will stagger under the load and eventually fall flat. You must discipline yourself to live within the boundaries of today. It is in the present moment that I walk close to you, helping you carry your burdens. Keep your focus on My Presence in the present.

PSALM 73:23; 1 CORINTHIANS 10:13;
HEBREWS 3:13

I CAME INTO THE WORLD AS A LIGHT *so that no one who believes in Me should stay in darkness.* I did not just *bring* light into the world; I Myself am *the Light that keeps on shining in the darkness.* Since I am infinite and all-powerful, nothing can extinguish this illumination!

When you believed in Me, you became a *child of Light*, and the brightness entered into your inner being. This helps you see things from My perspective—both things in the world and things in your heart. This illumination of the contents of your heart can be very uncomfortable. However, when it leads to repentance and walking in My ways, it is the road to freedom.

Rejoice in your brightened perspective. *The god of this age has blinded the minds of unbelievers so that they cannot see the Light of the gospel of My Glory.* But because you are My cherished one, you have *the Light of the knowledge of My Glory* shining in your heart. Rejoice greatly!

JOHN 12:46; JOHN 1:5 AMP;
1 THESSALONIANS 5:5 ESV;
2 CORINTHIANS 4:4, 6

S TOP JUDGING AND EVALUATING YOURSELF, for this is not your role. Above all, stop comparing yourself with other people. This produces feelings of pride or inferiority, sometimes a mixture of both. I lead each of My children along a path that is uniquely tailor-made for him or her. Comparing is not only wrong; it is also meaningless.

Don't look for affirmation in the wrong places: your own evaluations or those of other people. The only source of real affirmation is My unconditional Love. Many believers perceive Me as an unpleasable Judge, angrily searching out their faults and failures. Nothing could be farther from the truth! I died for your sins so that I might *clothe you in My garments of salvation*. This is how I see you: *radiant in My robe of righteousness*. When I discipline you, it is never in anger or disgust; it is to prepare you for face-to-Face fellowship with Me throughout all eternity. Immerse yourself in My loving Presence. Be receptive to My affirmation, which flows continually from the throne of grace.

LUKE 6:37; ISAIAH 61:10 NASB; PROVERBS 3:11–12

Y OU ARE NO STRANGER TO ME, dear one. *Before I formed you in the womb I knew you.* My knowledge of you has continued without interruption: through your entrance into this world and onward throughout your life. I delight in transforming you more and more into the one I created you to be, much as a skilled potter delights in the work he is creating.

One implication of My uninterrupted Presence with you is that you are never alone. I am training you to be increasingly aware of Me, but I understand that you are human and your attention span is limited. Sometimes when you are suffering, you may feel as if you're alone or abandoned. However, I suffered alone on the cross so that you would *never* have to be alone in your struggles. *You are always with Me; I hold you by your right hand.*

The last enemy you will face is death, but My crucifixion and resurrection have decimated that foe! So trust Me to guide you through your life, and *afterward take you into Glory.*

JEREMIAH 1:5; PSALM 139:16; PSALM 73:23—24

Y OU ARE ON THE RIGHT PATH. Listen more to Me and less to your doubts. I am leading you along the way I designed just for you. Therefore, it is a lonely way, humanly speaking. But I go before you as well as alongside you, so you are never alone. Do not expect anyone to understand fully My ways with you, any more than you can comprehend My dealings with others. I am revealing to you the path of Life, day by day and moment by moment. As I said to My disciple Peter, so I repeat to you: *Follow Me.*

PSALM 119:105; JOHN 21:22

I CALLED YOU OUT OF DARKNESS *into My marvelous Light.* I brought you not only *out of darkness* but *into* My royal family. I clothed you with My personal *robe of righteousness*, making you fit for My kingdom. You are one of *My own special people*: You belong to Me, and I delight in you.

I have chosen to use imperfect ones like you to *proclaim My praises.* I know you cannot do this as well as you would like. Actually, without My help it is impossible for you to do. This gap between My call on your life and your ability to respond is part of My plan. It heightens your awareness of your utter insufficiency. Because you are Mine, I allow you to connect your inability to My boundless sufficiency. Instead of focusing on your inadequacy, work on staying close to Me. In everything you do, consciously rely on My help, living in the joyous wonder of self-forgetfulness. As you look to Me for all you need, your face will reflect the Light of My surpassing Glory.

1 PETER 2:9 NKJV; ISAIAH 61:10;
JOHN 15:5 NKJV; 2 CORINTHIANS 3:18

March

"*When he has brought out all his own, he goes on ahead of them, and his sheep follow him because they know his voice.*"

JOHN 10:4

W HEN SOMETHING IN YOUR LIFE OR THOUGHTS makes you anxious, come to Me and talk about it. Bring Me your *prayer and petition, with thanksgiving*, saying, "Thank You, Jesus, for this opportunity to trust You more." Though the lessons of trust that I send to you come wrapped in difficulties, the benefits far outweigh the cost.

Well-developed trust will bring you many blessings, not the least of which is My Peace. I have promised to *keep you in perfect Peace* to the extent that you trust in Me. The world has it backwards, teaching that peace is the result of having enough money, possessions, insurance, and security systems. *My* Peace, however, is such an all-encompassing gift that it is independent of all circumstances. Though you lose everything else, if you gain My Peace you are rich indeed.

PHILIPPIANS 4:6; ISAIAH 26:3;
2 THESSALONIANS 3:16 NKJV

I GIVE YOU JOY in your journey through the world. This sparkling gift is not a luxury; it's a necessity! There are bumps in the road ahead, as well as sharp curves, ascents, and descents. Without Joy in your heart, you will *become weary and discouraged.*

Joy is not dependent on the circumstances in your life. It can transcend them all! This is why impoverished people are often more joyful than those who have material wealth. Sick—and even dying—people can also be joyful when they're trusting in Me as Savior, Lord, and Friend.

Seek to spread Joy in the world around you. Let My Light reflect from your demeanor—through your smiles, your laughter, your words. The Holy Spirit will equip you to do this as you give Him space in your life. Ask Him to fill you with contagious delight. Concentrate on staying close to Me, and I will lead you along *the path of Life. In My Presence there is fullness of Joy.*

HEBREWS 12:3 NKJV; HABAKKUK 3:17–18;
PSALM 16:11 ESV

I AM THE RESURRECTION AND THE LIFE; all lasting Life emanates from Me. People search for life in many wrong ways: chasing after fleeting pleasures, accumulating possessions and wealth, trying to deny the inevitable effects of aging. Meanwhile, I freely offer abundant Life to everyone who turns toward Me. As you *come to Me and take My yoke upon you*, I fill you with My very Life. This is how I choose to live in the world and accomplish My purposes. This is also how I bless you with *Joy unspeakable and full of Glory*. The Joy is Mine, and the Glory is Mine; but I bestow them on you as you live in My Presence, inviting Me to live fully in you.

JOHN 11:25; MATTHEW 11:28–29;
1 PETER 1:8–9 KJV

*M*Y PATHS ARE BEYOND TRACING OUT! Come to Me with humility in your heart, bowing before My infinite intelligence. Relinquish your demand to understand; accept the fact that many things are simply beyond your comprehension. Because I am infinite and you are finite, the limitations of your mind make it impossible for you to understand much of what happens in your life—and in the world. So it's vital to make room for *mystery* in your worldview.

You are privileged to know many things that were formerly mysteries—things that had *been kept hidden for ages and generations*. The New Testament is full of revelations that came through My incarnation, life, death, and resurrection. You are immeasurably blessed to have this priceless knowledge!

Nonetheless, the ways I work in your world are often mysterious to you—beyond tracing out. This presents you with a choice: to resent My ways or to bow before Me in wonder and worship. Marvel at *the depth of the riches of My wisdom and knowledge*!

ROMANS 11:33; PROVERBS 3:5 NLT;
COLOSSIANS 1:26

I LOVE YOU FOR WHO YOU ARE, not for what you do. Many voices vie for control of your mind, especially when you sit in silence. You must learn to discern what is My voice and what is not. Ask My Spirit to give you this discernment. Many of My children run around in circles, trying to obey the various voices directing their lives. This results in fragmented, frustrating patterns of living. Do not fall into this trap. Walk closely with Me each moment, listening for My directives and enjoying My Companionship. Refuse to let other voices tie you up in knots. *My sheep know My voice and follow Me wherever I lead.*

EPHESIANS 4:1–6; JOHN 10:4

*M*Y LOVE CHASES AFTER YOU *every day of your life.* So look for signs of My tender Presence as you go through this day. I disclose Myself to you in a vast variety of ways—words of Scripture just when you need them, helpful words spoken through other people, "coincidences" orchestrated by My Spirit, nature's beauty, and so on. My Love for you is not passive; it actively chases after you and leaps into your life. Invite Me to open the eyes of your heart so you can "see" Me blessing you in myriad ways—both small and great.

I want you not only to receive My bountiful blessings but to take careful note of them. Treasure them and *ponder them in your heart.* Thank Me for these ways I show up in your life; write some of them down so you can enjoy them again and again. These signs of My Presence strengthen you and prepare you for difficulties on the road ahead. Remember that *nothing in all creation can separate you from My Love.*

PSALM 23:6 MSG; PSALM 119:11 NKJV;
LUKE 2:19; ROMANS 8:39

R EFUSE TO WORRY! In this world there will always be something enticing you to worry. That is the nature of a fallen, fractured planet: Things are not as they should be. So the temptation to be anxious is constantly with you, trying to worm its way into your mind. The best defense is *continual communication with Me, richly seasoned with thanksgiving.* Awareness of My Presence fills your mind with Light and Peace, leaving no room for fear. This awareness lifts you up above your circumstances, enabling you to see problems from My perspective. Live close to Me! Together we can keep the wolves of worry at bay.

LUKE 12:25–26; 1 THESSALONIANS 5:16–18;
PSALM 36:9

*B*LESSED ARE ALL THOSE WHO WAIT FOR ME! Waiting patiently does not come easily to you, but it is nonetheless very good for you. You long to plan ahead, make definitive decisions, and make things *happen*. There is a time for that, but this is not the time. Now is a time for sitting in My Presence, trusting Me with your whole being. This discipline will bring a wealth of blessings your way.

Some of the good things I offer you reside in the future. While you obediently wait on me, you are building up equity for those not-yet blessings. Because they are veiled in the mystery of the future, you cannot see them clearly. Other blessings are for the present. The very process of waiting for Me is beneficial. It keeps your soul on tiptoe, as you look up to Me in hope. You acknowledge that I am in control, and you rest in My goodness. Though you may not understand why you have to wait so long, I bless you as you choose to *trust Me with all your heart.*

ISAIAH 30:18; PSALM 143:8 NKJV;
PROVERBS 3:5 ESV

MAKE FRIENDS WITH THE PROBLEMS IN YOUR LIFE. Though many things feel random and wrong, remember that I am sovereign over everything. *I can fit everything into a pattern for good*, but only to the extent that you trust Me. Every problem can teach you something, transforming you little by little into the masterpiece I created you to be. The very same problem can become a stumbling block over which you fall if you react with distrust and defiance. The choice is up to you, and you will have to choose many times each day whether to trust Me or defy Me.

The best way to befriend your problems is to thank Me for them. This simple act opens your mind to the possibility of bene-fits flowing from your difficulties. You can even give persistent problems nicknames, helping you to approach them with familiarity rather than with dread. The next step is to introduce them to Me, enabling Me to embrace them in My loving Presence. I will not necessarily remove your problems, but My wisdom is sufficient to bring good out of every one of them.

ROMANS 8:28 AMP; 1 CORINTHIANS 1:23–24

I AM TAKING CARE OF YOU. Sometimes you feel alone and vulnerable—exposed to the "elements" of a fallen world. When you are feeling this way, stop and remind yourself, "Jesus is taking care of me." This reminder can comfort you and help you relax. It draws you back from obsessing about the future, trying to figure out and orchestrate what will happen.

When circumstances are confusing and you don't know which way to proceed, remember that you are in My watchcare. I know everything about you and your situation. I also know the future. A child in a good family with adequate resources doesn't need to know how his parents will provide for him tomorrow, next week, next year. *You* are in the best Family imaginable, and My resources are absolutely unlimited! So bring Me all your needs and concerns. Entrust them to Me and live confidently—as a child of the *King of kings*! Relax and rejoice, for I am taking good care of you.

1 PETER 5:7; ISAIAH 58:11;
REVELATION 19:16 NKJV

ONTINUE ON THIS PATH WITH ME, enjoying My Presence even in adversity. I am always before you, as well as alongside you. See Me beckoning to you: "Come! Follow Me." The One who goes ahead of you, opening up the way, is the same One who stays close and never lets go of your hand. I am not subject to limitations of time or space. I am everywhere at every time, ceaselessly working on your behalf. That is why your best efforts are trusting Me and living close to Me.

ISAIAH 41:10 NASB; HEBREWS 7:25; PSALM 37:3–4

D O N O T D R E A D *walking through the valley of the shadow of death.* My radiant Presence shines brightly in that *deep, sunless valley*—strengthening, encouraging, and comforting you. Since *I never sleep*, I am able to watch over you constantly. Moreover, no valley is so deep, no pit so dark, that I cannot see all the way to the bottom of it.

Even if you wander from Me at times and fall into a *slimy pit*, you can count on Me to rescue you. When you cry out to Me, I *lift you out of the mud and mire* and *set your feet on a rock*—giving you *a firm place to stand.* Find comfort in My commitment to help you, even when you slip up.

Whenever you start to feel afraid, remember that *I am with you.* I've promised *I will never leave you; I Myself go before you.* While you are walking through the valley of adversity, keep these words of comfort flowing through your mind: *I will fear no evil, for You are with me.*

PSALM 23:4 AMP; PSALM 121:2–3 NCV;
PSALM 40:1–2; DEUTERONOMY 31:8

L ET ME HELP YOU through this day. The challenges you face are far too great for you to handle alone. You are keenly aware of your helplessness in the scheme of events you face. This awareness opens up a choice: to doggedly go it alone or to walk with Me in humble steps of dependence. Actually, this choice is continually before you, but difficulties highlight the decision-making process. *So consider it all joy whenever you are enveloped in various trials.* These are gifts from Me, reminding you to rely on Me alone.

PSALM 46:1; PSALM 63:7–8; JAMES 1:2–3 AMP

*B*LESSED ARE THOSE WHO REJOICE *in My Name all day long and exult in My righteousness.* This Name represents *Me* in all of My glorious attributes. Used properly, it draws you closer to My loving Presence. Many people abuse My Name by using it as a swear word. Hearing this verbal abuse is exceedingly offensive to Me. However, My followers can lovingly utter the word "Jesus" *all day long*—to rejoice in Me and ask for help. *I am God your Savior, and I will help you for the Glory of My Name.*

I invite you to exult in My righteousness. To "exult" is to be delighted, elated, joyful, jubilant—especially because of triumph or success. Just before I died on the cross, I said, *"It is finished!"* I was announcing the accomplishment of the greatest triumph imaginable: victory over sin and death for everyone who believes in Me. Through this crowning achievement, My righteousness has been credited to you forever, beloved. *I have covered you with the robe of righteousness.* Wear My glorious *garments of salvation* with delight, elation, and joyful jubilation!

PSALM 89:16; PSALM 79:9;
JOHN 19:30 NKJV; ISAIAH 61:10 ESV

S AVE YOUR BEST STRIVING FOR SEEKING MY FACE. I am constantly communicating with you. To find Me and hear My voice, you must seek Me above all else. Anything that you desire more than Me becomes an idol. When you are determined to get your own way, you blot Me out of your consciousness. Instead of single-mindedly pursuing some goal, talk with Me about it. Let the Light of My Presence shine on this pursuit so that you can see it from My perspective. If the goal fits into My plans for you, I will help you reach it. If it is contrary to My will for you, I will gradually change the desire of your heart. *Seek Me first* and foremost; then the rest of your life will fall into place, piece by piece.

1 CHRONICLES 16:11;
PROVERBS 19:21 NKJV; MATTHEW 6:33

I ENABLE YOU TO STAND *on the heights.* This term "the heights" can refer to a number of things. Taken literally, it means that something is physically very high up. This is appropriate language for describing mountaintops or the uppermost floors of skyscrapers. Taken figuratively, the term can refer to euphoric pleasure *or* to something quite different: weighty experiences of responsibility. If you aspire to reach the heights—especially the high places of achievement and recognition—be prepared to shoulder the responsibilities that accompany success. But don't forget to enjoy the satisfaction of accomplishing good things with Me, through Me, and for Me.

Because you are Mine, you can *stand firm, with the belt of truth buckled around your waist* and *the breastplate of righteousness in place.* All of My teaching is absolutely true, for *I am the Truth.* This provides a firm foundation for you—solid rock on which to stand. My perfect righteousness has been credited to your account forever. No matter how much trouble you encounter, *this righteousness* can keep you standing!

2 SAMUEL 22:34; EPHESIANS 6:14;
JOHN 14:6 NKJV; ROMANS 3:22

R<small>EST IN</small> M<small>Y RADIANT</small> P<small>RESENCE</small>. The world around you seems to spin faster and faster, till everything is a blur. Yet there is a cushion of calm at the center of your life, where you live in union with Me. Return to this soothing Center as often as you can, for this is where you are energized: filled with My Love, Joy, and Peace.

The world is a needy place; do not go there for sustenance. Instead, come to Me. Learn to depend on Me alone, and your weakness will become saturated with My Power. When you find your completeness in Me, you can help other people without using them to meet your own needs. Live in the Light of My Presence, and your light will shine brightly into the lives of others.

G<small>ALATIANS</small> 5:22; 2 C<small>ORINTHIANS</small> 12:9;
1 J<small>OHN</small> 4:12

M Y WAYS ARE MYSTERIOUS and unpredictable, but they are good. When you look at world events—with so much rampant evil—it's easy to feel fearful and discouraged. You cannot comprehend why I allow such cruelty and suffering. The difficulty lies in the fact that I am infinite and you are not. Many things are simply beyond your comprehension. But do not despair. When you reach the limits of your understanding, trusting Me will carry you onward. Affirm your *trust in Me* through silent and spoken prayers. Stay in communication with Me!

Don't get trapped in a posture of demanding to know "Why?" That is the wrong question to ask Me. The right questions are: "How do You want me to view this situation?" and "What do You want me to do right now?" You cannot change the past, so start with the present moment and seek to find My way forward. Trust Me one day, one moment, at a time. *Do not fear, for I am with you. I will strengthen you and help you.*

PROVERBS 3:5 ESV; ECCLESIASTES 8:17 NLT;
PSALM 37:12–13; ISAIAH 41:10

Y OU ARE MINE FOR ALL TIME—and beyond time, into eternity. No power can deny you your inheritance in heaven. I want you to realize how utterly secure you are! Even if you falter as you journey through life, I will never let go of your hand.

Knowing that your future is absolutely assured can free you to live abundantly today. I have prepared this day for you with the most tender concern and attention to detail. Instead of approaching the day as a blank page that you need to fill up, try living it in a responsive mode, being on the lookout for all that I am doing. This sounds easy, but it requires a deep level of trust, based on the knowledge that *My way is perfect*.

1 PETER 1:3–4; PSALM 37:23–24; PSALM 18:30

*F*ROM THE FULLNESS OF *MY* GRACE, *you have received one blessing after another.* Stop for a moment, beloved, and ponder the astonishing gift of salvation—*by grace through faith* in Me. Because it's entirely a gift—*not as a result of works*—this salvation is secure. Your part is just to receive what I accomplished for you on the cross, believing with the faith that was given you. This undeserved Love and favor is yours forever. My grace has infinite value!

Multiple blessings flow out of grace because of its extraordinary fullness. Guilt feelings melt away in the warm Light of My forgiveness. Your identity as a *child of God* gives your life meaning and purpose. Relationships with other people improve as you relate to them with love and forgiveness.

The best response to My bountiful grace is a heart overflowing with gratitude. Take time each day to think about and thank Me for blessings in your life. This protects your heart from weeds of ingratitude that spring up so easily. *Be thankful*!

JOHN 1:16; EPHESIANS 2:8–9 ESV;
JOHN 1:12; COLOSSIANS 3:15 NASB

WALK BY FAITH, NOT BY SIGHT. As you take steps of faith, depending on Me, I will show you how much I can do for you. If you live your life too safely, you will never know the thrill of seeing Me work through you. When I gave you My Spirit, I empowered you to live beyond your natural ability and strength. That's why it is so wrong to measure your energy level against the challenges ahead of you. The issue is not your strength but Mine, which is limitless. By walking close to Me, you can accomplish My purposes in My strength.

2 CORINTHIANS 5:7 NKJV;
GALATIANS 5:25; PSALM 59:16—17

S EEK TO LIVE IN THE PRESENT—with *Me*! Your life is a gift from Me, consisting of millions upon millions of moments. These countless, tiny gifts can easily slip away unnoticed and unused. The best remedy to such wastefulness is to fill your moments with My Presence. You can begin your day connecting with Me by praying: "Thank You, Jesus, for this precious day of life. Help me stay aware of Your Presence with me."

Thankfulness keeps you linked to Me and anchored in the present. Worry, on the other hand, pulls you into the future, where you wander in barren places of uncertainty. However, you can always return to Me by whispering, "Lord, help me."

To live consistently in the present, seek to become more grateful. Look around you, searching for the many gifts I shower upon you. As you thank Me for these blessings, go into detail—express yourself enthusiastically! This will increase your gratitude and enhance your ability to grasp how blessed you really are.

PSALM 118:24; COLOSSIANS 2:6–7;
PSALM 13:5; 2 CORINTHIANS 9:15 NKJV

WAITING, TRUSTING, AND HOPING are intricately connected, like golden strands interwoven to form a strong chain. Trusting is the central strand because it is the response from My children that I desire the most. Waiting and hoping embellish the central strand and strengthen the chain that connects you to Me. Waiting for Me to work, with your eyes on Me, is evidence that you really do trust Me. If you mouth the words "I trust You" while anxiously trying to make things go your way, your words ring hollow. Hoping is future-directed, connecting you to your inheritance in heaven. However, the benefits of hope fall fully on you in the present.

Because you are Mine, you don't just pass time in your waiting. You can wait expectantly, in hopeful trust. Keep your "antennae" out to pick up even the faintest glimmer of My Presence.

JOHN 14:1; PSALM 27:14; HEBREWS 6:18–20

T HE JOY YOU HAVE IN ME is independent of your circumstances. *In My Presence is fullness of Joy,* and you are never separated from Me. *Search for Me* as you go along your pathway today. I delight in disclosing Myself to you. Sometimes I communicate with you in grand, unmistakable ways—"coincidences" that are clearly the work of My hands. At other times I display My unseen Presence in subtle ways. These are often so personal to you that others wouldn't even notice them. Yet these subtle signs can be a source of deep, intimate Joy.

The more attentive you are, the more you can find Me in the details of your day. So try to stay alert—be on the lookout for Me!

Fill your mind and heart with Scripture, where I reveal Myself most clearly. Let My promises permeate your thinking and keep you close to Me. *Listen to My voice. I know you, and you follow Me. I give you eternal Life; no one can snatch you out of My hand.* Rejoice!

PSALM 16:11 NKJV; JEREMIAH 29:13 NKJV;
JOHN 10:27–28

L EARN TO LIVE above your circumstances. This requires focused time with Me, the *One who overcame the world*. Trouble and distress are woven into the very fabric of this perishing world. Only My Life in you can empower you to face this endless flow of problems with *good cheer*.

As you sit quietly in My Presence, I shine Peace into your troubled mind and heart. Little by little, you are freed from earthly shackles and lifted up above your circumstances. You gain My perspective on your life, enabling you to distinguish between what is important and what is not. Rest in My Presence, *receiving Joy that no one can take away from you*.

JOHN 16:33 NKJV; PSALM 42:5 NASB; JOHN 16:22

*D*O NOT DWELL ON THE PAST, beloved. You can learn from the past, but don't let it become your focus. You cannot undo things that have already occurred, no matter how much you may yearn to do so. Instead of wishing for the impossible, come to Me and *pour out your heart.* Remember that I am *your Refuge; trust in Me at all times.*

Reinforce your confidence in Me by saying frequently: "I trust You, Jesus." Uttering those four words can brighten your day immediately. Dark clouds of worry are blown away by simple, childlike trust.

I am doing a new thing! Be on the lookout for all that I am accomplishing in your life. Ask Me to open the eyes of your mind and heart so you can see the many opportunities I've placed along your path. Don't fall into such a routine that you see only the same old things—and miss the newness. Remember that I can make a way where there appears to be no way. *With Me all things are possible!*

ISAIAH 43:18–19; PSALM 62:8; MATTHEW 19:26

D O NOT HESITATE TO RECEIVE JOY FROM ME, for I bestow it on you abundantly. The more you rest in My Presence, the more freely My blessings flow into you. In the Light of My Love, you are gradually *transformed from glory to glory*. It is through spending time with Me that you realize *how wide and long and high and deep is My Love for you.*

Sometimes the relationship I offer you seems too good to be true. I pour My very Life into you, and all you have to do is receive Me. In a world characterized by working and taking, the admonition to rest and receive seems too easy. There is a close connection between receiving and believing: As you trust Me more and more, you are able to receive Me and My blessings abundantly. *Be still, and know that I am God.*

2 CORINTHIANS 3:18 NASB;
EPHESIANS 3:17–19; PSALM 46:10

I REJOICE OVER YOU WITH SINGING. **Open** wide your heart, mind, and spirit to receive My richest blessings. Because you are My blood-bought child, My Love for you flows continuously from *the throne of grace*. Look up and receive all that I have for you. Listen and hear Me singing songs of Joy because of My *great delight in you*. You can approach Me boldly—with confidence—trusting that you are indeed *the one I love*.

The world teaches you that love is conditional: based on performance, appearance, and status. Even though you don't believe this lie, the constant onslaught of this message in the media can penetrate your thinking. That's why it is so important to spend time focusing on Me—soaking in My Presence, absorbing My Word.

Setting aside time to be alone with Me is countercultural, so this practice requires discipline and determination. However, it is well worth the effort. Living close to Me brightens your life immeasurably. *With Me is the fountain of Life; in My Light you see Light.*

ZEPHANIAH 3:17; HEBREWS 4:16;
DEUTERONOMY 33:12; PSALM 36:9

L ISTEN TO THE LOVE SONG that I am continually singing to you. *I take great delight in you. I rejoice over you with singing.* The voices of the world are a cacophony of chaos, pulling you this way and that. Don't listen to those voices; challenge them with My Word. Learn to take minibreaks from the world, finding a place to be still in My Presence and listen to My voice.

There is immense hidden treasure to be found through listening to Me. Though I pour out blessings upon you always, some of My richest blessings have to be actively sought. I love to reveal Myself to you, and your seeking heart opens you up to receive more of My disclosure. *Ask and it will be given to you; seek and you will find; knock and the door will be opened to you.*

ZEPHANIAH 3:17; MATTHEW 17:5; MATTHEW 7:7

I UPHOLD ALL THOSE WHO FALL *and lift up all who are bowed down.* Sometimes you and I are the only ones who know you have fallen. It's tempting at such times to gloss over what you have done (or failed to do). You may not be overwhelmed by feelings of shame, but you feel restless and unsettled—mildly guilty. Even at times like this, I continue to love you perfectly. Sometimes I display My Love for you in unexpected ways—humbling and delighting you simultaneously. This deepens your awareness of your sin, intensifying your desire to confess and draw near Me. As you settle into your rightful position, My redeemed one, your restlessness yields to calmness. This is how I lift you up when you've stumbled.

Remember that I can make *all things*—including your failures—*work together for good* because *you love Me and are called according to My purpose.* Realizing how much I cherish you even when you're not living well deepens your relationship with Me. It also helps you relax and rejoice in *My steadfast Love.*

PSALM 145:14; ROMANS 8:28 NASB;
LAMENTATIONS 3:22–23 RSV

I T IS GOOD THAT YOU RECOGNIZE YOUR WEAKNESS. That keeps you looking to Me, your Strength. Abundant life is not necessarily health and wealth; it is living in continual dependence on Me. Instead of trying to fit this day into a preconceived mold, relax and be on the lookout for what I am doing. This mind-set will free you to enjoy Me and to find what I have planned for you to do. This is far better than trying to make things go according to your own plan.

Don't take yourself so seriously. Lighten up and laugh with Me. You have Me on your side, so what are you worried about? I can equip you to do absolutely anything, as long as it is My will. The more difficult your day, the more I yearn to help you. Anxiety wraps you up in yourself, trapping you in your own thoughts. When you look to Me and whisper My Name, you break free and receive My help. Focus on Me, and you will find Peace in My Presence.

PHILIPPIANS 4:13 AMP; PROVERBS 17:22

I AM THE ANTIDOTE TO LONELINESS. *For I am the Lord, your God, who takes hold of your right hand and says to you, "Do not fear; I will help you."* Close your right hand, as if you are grasping onto *My* hand. This symbolic gesture helps you feel connected to Me—to My living Presence. Whenever you start to feel lonely or afraid, you need to reconnect with Me.

Tell Me about your feelings and the struggles you face. I already know about them, but it does you good to bring them to Me. Spend time basking in the Light of My Presence, realizing how safe and secure you are in Me. *I am with you* every nanosecond of your life. You are never alone!

Seek My Face and My perspective on your life. Sometimes it's beneficial to write out your concerns. This clarifies your thinking and provides a record of your prayers. It also helps you release your problems to Me. *I am watching over you* continually.

ISAIAH 41:13; MATTHEW 28:20 NKJV;
PSALM 27:8 NKJV; GENESIS 28:15

COME TO ME FOR UNDERSTANDING since I know you far better than you know yourself. I comprehend you in all your complexity; *no detail of your life is hidden from Me.* I view you through eyes of grace, so don't be afraid of My intimate awareness. Allow the Light of My healing Presence to shine into the deepest recesses of your being—cleansing, healing, refreshing, and renewing you. Trust Me enough to accept the full forgiveness that I offer you continually. This great gift, which cost Me My Life, is yours for all eternity. Forgiveness is at the very core of My abiding Presence. *I will never leave you or forsake you.*

When no one else seems to understand you, simply draw closer to Me. Rejoice in the One who understands you completely and loves you perfectly. As I fill you with My Love, you become a reservoir of love, overflowing into the lives of other people.

PSALM 139:1–4; 2 CORINTHIANS 1:21–22; JOSHUA 1:5

*N*OTHING IN ALL CREATION *can separate you from My Love.* Pause and ponder what an astonishing promise this is! You live in a world where separations abound: wives from husbands, children from parents, friends from friends, childhood dreams from adult realities. But there is one terrible separation you will never have to face: isolation from My loving Presence.

I want you to cling to Me with tenacious confidence. This gives you strength to cope with the uncertainties of living in such a broken, unstable world. Anxious thoughts can assault your mind and fill you with fear if you forget that My Love will never fail you. When you find yourself feeling afraid, grasp My hand in childlike trust. Rest in the protection of My Presence, and remember that *perfect Love drives out fear.*

The greatest wealth on earth is minuscule compared with the riches of My boundless Love. Yet this is My free gift to all who follow Me. *How priceless is My unfailing Love!*

ROMANS 8:38–39; ISAIAH 30:15 NKJV;
1 JOHN 4:18; PSALM 36:7

T RUST ME ONE DAY AT A TIME. This keeps you close to Me, responsive to My will. Trust is not a natural response, especially for those who have been deeply wounded. My Spirit within you is your resident Tutor, helping you in this supernatural endeavor. Yield to His gentle touch; be sensitive to His prompting.

Exert your will to trust Me in all circumstances. Don't let your need to understand distract you from My Presence. I will equip you to get through this day victoriously as you live in deep dependence on Me. *Tomorrow is busy worrying about itself; don't get tangled up in its worry-webs.* Trust Me one day at a time.

PSALM 84:12; 1 CORINTHIANS 6:19;
JEREMIAH 17:7 NKJV; MATTHEW 6:34

S TRIVE TO LIVE MORE FULLY in the present, refusing to *worry about tomorrow*. Striving involves devoting serious effort and energy to something; it usually includes struggle. You must exert continual effort if you want to live present-tense in My Presence. I urge you to make *Me* the major pursuit of your everyday life.

It's essential to resist the temptation to worry. You live in a fallen world, full of sin and struggles—you will never run short of things that can provoke anxiety. However, remember that *each day has enough trouble of its own*. I carefully calibrate the amount of difficulty you will encounter on a given day. I know exactly how much you can handle with My help. And I'm always near—ready to strengthen, encourage, and comfort you.

Pursuing a close walk with Me is the best way to live in the present. Keep bringing your thoughts back to Me whenever they wander. Return to Me joyfully, beloved. *I will take great delight in you* and *rejoice over you with singing.*

MATTHEW 6:34; ISAIAH 41:10 NKJV;
ZEPHANIAH 3:17

I SPEAK TO YOU FROM THE DEPTHS OF YOUR BEING. Hear Me saying soothing words of Peace, assuring you of My Love. Do not listen to voices of accusation, for they are not from Me. I speak to you in love-tones, lifting you up. My Spirit convicts cleanly, without crushing words of shame. Let the Spirit take charge of your mind, combing out tangles of deception. Be transformed by the truth that I live within you.

The Light of My Presence is shining upon you, in benedictions of Peace. Let My Light shine in you; don't dim it with worries or fears. Holiness is letting Me live through you. Since I dwell in you, you are fully equipped to be holy. Pause before responding to people or situations, giving My Spirit space to act through you. Hasty words and actions leave no room for Me; this is atheistic living. I want to inhabit all your moments—gracing your thoughts, words, and behavior.

ROMANS 8:1–2; COLOSSIANS 1:27;
1 CORINTHIANS 6:19

*Y*OU ARE READY FOR ANYTHING *and equal to anything* through your living relationship with Me. Rest in My Presence while *I infuse inner strength into you.* Because you are a child of the King of kings, you are capable of so much more than you realize. To benefit fully from your privileged position, however, you need to spend ample time with Me. As you relax in My Presence—delighting in Me and opening your heart to Me—I fill you with inner strength. This time spent together is not only pleasurable, it is empowering.

When there is much to do, it's tempting to rush through your time with Me and dive into the activities of the day. But just as eating a healthy breakfast helps you function at your best, so does feeding your soul a healthy diet of *Me.* Bask in My Word, asking My Spirit to make it come alive to you. Savor these words of Life! Your living relationship with Me helps you approach each new day with confidence—ready for anything that comes your way.

PHILIPPIANS 4:13 AMP; PSALM 37:4; PSALM 5:3

THANK ME FOR THE GLORIOUS GIFT OF MY SPIRIT. This is like priming the pump of a well. As you bring Me the sacrifice of thanksgiving, regardless of your feelings, My Spirit is able to work more freely within you. This produces more thankfulness and more freedom, until you are overflowing with gratitude.

I shower blessings on you daily, but sometimes you don't perceive them. When your mind is stuck on a negative focus, you see neither Me nor My gifts. In faith, thank Me for whatever is preoccupying your mind. This will clear the blockage so that you can find Me.

PSALM 50:14; 2 CORINTHIANS 5:5;
2 CORINTHIANS 3:17; PSALM 95:2 NKJV

S TOP YOUR INCESSANT WORRY-PLANNING! Draw your mind back from the future to the present moment, where My Presence lovingly awaits you. *Seek My Face* with a smile in your heart, knowing that I take delight in you. Talk with Me about all that concerns you and the tasks that are weighing on you. Call out to Me for help as you set priorities according to My will. Then keep returning your focus to Me and to the work at hand. Inviting Me into your activities increases your Joy and helps you to be more effective.

When you need to take a break, remember that I am your resting place. My *everlasting arms* are always available to support you and hold you close. When you relax in My company—waiting with Me for a time—this demonstrates genuine trust in Me. As you prepare to return to your tasks, make the effort to include *Me* in your plans. This protects you from worrying; it also helps you stay close to Me, enjoying My Presence.

LUKE 12:25–26; PSALM 27:8 NKJV;
PSALM 62:5–6; DEUTERONOMY 33:27

T RUST ME AND DON'T BE AFRAID, *for I am your Strength and Song.* Think what it means to have Me as your Strength. I spoke the universe into existence; My Power is absolutely unlimited! Human weakness, consecrated to Me, is like a magnet, drawing My Power into your neediness. However, fear can block the flow of My Strength into you. Instead of trying to fight your fears, concentrate on trusting Me. When you relate to Me in confident trust, there is no limit to how much I can strengthen you.

Remember that I am also your Song. I want you to share My Joy, living in conscious awareness of My Presence. Rejoice as we journey together toward heaven; join Me in singing My Song.

ISAIAH 12:2–3; PSALM 56:3 NKJV; PSALM 21:6

I AM TRAINING YOU not only to endure your difficulties but to transform them into Glory. This is a supernatural feat, and it requires the help of My supernatural Spirit. When problems are weighing heavily on you, your natural tendency is to speed up your pace of living, frantically searching for answers. But what you need at such times is to *slow down* and seek My Face. Invite the Spirit to help you as you discuss your difficulties with Me. Then *lay your requests before Me and wait in expectation.*

Even though you wait expectantly, I may not answer your prayers quickly. I am always doing something important in your life—far beyond simply solving your problems. Your struggles are part of a much larger battle, and the way you handle them can contribute to outcomes with eternal significance. When you respond to your troubles by trusting Me and *praying with thanksgiving*, you glorify Me. Moreover, your practice of praying persistently will eventually make a vast difference in *you*—My loved one *crowned with Glory.*

PSALM 5:3; PHILIPPIANS 4:6 NKJV; PSALM 8:5

REJOICE AND BE THANKFUL! As you walk with Me through this day, practice trusting and thanking Me all along the way. Trust is the channel through which My Peace flows into you. Thankfulness lifts you up above your circumstances.

I do My greatest works through people with grateful, trusting hearts. Rather than planning and evaluating, practice trusting and thanking Me continually. This is a paradigm shift that will revolutionize your life.

PHILIPPIANS 4:4; PSALM 95:1–2;
PSALM 9:10; 2 CORINTHIANS 2:14 NKJV

R EJOICE, BELOVED, because My sacrifice on the cross absorbed all your guilt: past, present, and future. *There is no condemnation for those who are in Me.* Your guilt-free status as My follower is good reason to be joyful each day of your life. Ever since the Fall in the Garden of Eden, mankind's worst problem has been sin. My sacrificial death provided the solution to this terrible problem. The gospel really *is* the best news imaginable: I took your sin—*I became sin for you*—and I gave you My perfect righteousness. This is an amazing, eternal transaction!

I want you to learn to enjoy more fully your guilt-free standing in My kingdom. *Through Me, the law of the Spirit of life set you free!* This is *not* an invitation to dive into a sinful lifestyle. Instead, I'm inviting you to live jubilantly, reveling in the glorious privilege of belonging to Me forever! This is your true identity, and it makes every moment of your life meaningful. Rejoice in knowing who you really are—a beloved *child of God.*

ROMANS 8:1–2; GENESIS 3:6–7;
2 CORINTHIANS 5:21 NKJV; JOHN 1:11–12 ESV

I AM A GOD of both intricate detail and overflowing abundance. When you entrust the details of your life to Me, you are surprised by how thoroughly I answer your petitions. I take pleasure in hearing your prayers, so feel free to bring Me all your requests. The more you pray, the more answers you can receive. Best of all, your faith is strengthened as you see how precisely I respond to your specific prayers.

Because I am infinite in all My ways, you need not fear that I will run out of resources. *Abundance* is at the very heart of who I AM. Come to Me in joyful expectation of receiving all you need—and sometimes much more! I delight in showering blessings on My beloved children. Come to Me with open hands and heart, ready to receive all I have for you.

PSALM 36:7–9; PSALM 132:15; JOHN 6:12–13

I AM THE RISEN ONE—your *living God*. Celebrate the Joy of serving a Savior who is exuberantly alive! Rejoice also in My promise to be with you continually—throughout time and eternity. These truths can sustain you through the greatest trials or disappointments you will ever encounter. So walk boldly along the path of Life with Me, trusting confidently in the One who never lets go of your hand.

Consider what I offer you: Myself, forgiveness of *all* your sins, forever-pleasures in heaven. This is all so extravagant and lavish that you cannot comprehend it fully. That is why worshiping Me is so important: It's a powerful way of connecting with Me that transcends your understanding. It also proclaims My Presence. There are numerous ways of worshiping Me: singing hymns and praise songs, studying and memorizing My Word, praying individually and with others, glorying in the wonders of My creation. Serving and loving others with My Love can also be worship. *Whatever you do, do it all for the Glory of God—My Glory!*

MATTHEW 28:5–6; PSALM 42:2;
COLOSSIANS 2:2–3 TLB; 1 CORINTHIANS 10:31

T HIS IS A TIME in your life when you must learn to let go: of loved ones, of possessions, of control. In order to let go of something that is precious to you, you need to rest in My Presence, where you are complete. Take time to bask in the Light of My Love. As you relax more and more, your grasping hand gradually opens up, releasing your prized possession into My care.

You can feel secure, even in the midst of cataclysmic changes, through awareness of My continual Presence. The One who never leaves you is the same One who never changes: *I am the same yesterday, today, and forever.* As you release more and more things into My care, remember that I never let go of your hand. Herein lies your security, which no one and no circumstance can take from you.

PSALM 89:15; HEBREWS 13:8; ISAIAH 41:13

N O MATTER HOW INADEQUATE you may feel, you can always look to Me for help. You don't need to go to a special place or assume a certain posture to *seek My Face*. Nor do you need to use elegant language or work to win My favor. I always look favorably on you because I see you clothed in My righteousness. I am alive in you, and I understand your thoughts perfectly. So a simple glance at Me—made in faith—is enough to connect you to My help.

You tend to waste energy trying to determine whether your resources are adequate for the day. You keep checking your "power gauge" instead of looking to Me for My provision. How much better to simply acknowledge your insufficiency when you awaken! This frees you to rely on My boundless sufficiency. If you stay in touch with Me, I will place enough Power at your disposal to meet your needs as they arise. Keep turning toward Me, your *ever-present Help*, and your strength will be equal to the demands of your day.

PSALM 105:4; ISAIAH 61:10 NKJV;
PSALM 46:1; DEUTERONOMY 33:25

L ET THANKFULNESS TEMPER ALL YOUR THOUGHTS. A thankful mind-set keeps you in touch with Me. I hate it when My children grumble, casually despising My sovereignty. Thankfulness is a safeguard against this deadly sin. Furthermore, a grateful attitude becomes a grid through which you perceive life. Gratitude enables you to see the Light of My Presence shining on all your circumstances. Cultivate a thankful heart, for this glorifies Me and fills you with Joy.

1 CORINTHIANS 10:10;
HEBREWS 12:28–29; COLOSSIANS 3:16

I AM THE RESURRECTION *and the Life. He who believes in Me will live, even though he dies.* I spoke this truth to Martha when her brother Lazarus had died, and she believed Me. Shortly thereafter, I commanded Lazarus to come out of his tomb, and he did. Even though he eventually died again—as all people do—he knew he would rise again to Life, as all believers will.

Shortly before My crucifixion, I taught My disciples: *"I am the Way, the Truth, and the Life."* I am everything you could possibly need—for this life and the next. I am the Treasure that encompasses all treasures. This truth can simplify your life immensely! I am the answer to all your struggles, the Joy that pervades all time and circumstances. I can make hard times bearable and good times utterly delightful. So *come to Me* just as you are, beloved; share more and more of your life with Me. Rejoice as you journey with Me—the Way who guides you always and the Resurrection who gives you eternal Life.

JOHN 11:25, 43–44; JOHN 14:6 NKJV;
COLOSSIANS 2:2–3; MATTHEW 11:28

March 26

WAITING ON ME means directing your attention to Me in hopeful anticipation of what I will do. It entails trusting Me with every fiber of your being instead of trying to figure things out yourself. Waiting on Me is the way I designed you to live: all day, every day. I created you to stay conscious of Me as you go about your daily duties.

I have promised many blessings to those who wait on Me: *renewed strength*, living above one's circumstances, resurgence of hope, awareness of My continual Presence. Waiting on Me enables you to glorify Me by living in deep dependence on Me, ready to do My will. It also helps you to enjoy Me; *in My Presence is fullness of Joy.*

LAMENTATIONS 3:24–26;
ISAIAH 40:31; PSALM 16:11 NKJV

A SK ME TO INCREASE YOUR THANKFULNESS. This will brighten your day and open your heart to Me. Seek to "see" Me in the midst of your circumstances. Look for signs of My unseen Presence as you walk along *the path of Life*. Gratefulness opens not only your heart but also your eyes. When you know Me intimately, you can find Me in myriad tiny details as well as in the big picture of your life. Take time to notice all My blessings—small and large—and to thank Me for them. This practice will help you enjoy My many gifts.

Ask Me also to train you in trusting Me more consistently. Well-developed trust enables you to go across treacherous terrain without stumbling. The more challenging your journey, the more frequently you need to voice your confidence in Me. You can pray, "Lord, *I trust in Your unfailing Love*." This short prayer reminds you that I am with you, I am taking care of you, and I love you forever. Rejoice, beloved, for I am truly worthy of your thankfulness and trust.

COLOSSIANS 2:6–7 NASB;
PSALM 16:11 NKJV; PSALM 52:8

B E S T I L L I N M Y P R E S E N C E even though countless tasks clamor for your attention. Nothing is as important as spending time with Me. While you wait in My Presence, I do My best work within you, *transforming you by the renewing of your mind*. If you skimp on this time with Me, you may plunge headlong into the wrong activities, missing the richness of what I have planned for you.

Do not seek Me primarily for what I can give you. Remember that I, the Giver, am infinitely greater than any gift I might impart to you. Though I delight in blessing My children, I am deeply grieved when My blessings become idols in their hearts. Anything can be an idol if it distracts you from Me as your *First Love*. When I am the ultimate Desire of your heart, you are safe from the danger of idolatry. As you wait in My Presence, enjoy the greatest gift of all: *Christ in you, the hope of Glory*!

ROMANS 12:2; REVELATION 2:4;
COLOSSIANS 1:27

*T*HROUGH MY RESURRECTION *from the dead, you have new birth into a living hope.* My work in you is all about "newness." Because you belong to Me, you're *a new creation; the old has gone, the new has come!* Your adoption into My royal family occurred instantaneously, at the moment you first trusted Me as Savior. At that instant, your spiritual status changed from death to life—eternal Life. You have *an inheritance that can never perish, spoil, or fade—kept in heaven for you.*

You are indeed a new creation, with the Holy Spirit living in you. But your becoming a Christian was only the *beginning* of the work I'm doing in you. You need *to be made new in the attitude of your mind and to put on the new self*—becoming increasingly godly, righteous, and holy. This is a lifelong endeavor, and it is preparing you for heaven's Glory. So receive this assignment with courage and gratitude. Be alert, and look for all the wonderful things I am doing in your life.

1 PETER 1:3–4; 2 CORINTHIANS 5:17;
EPHESIANS 4:22–24; ROMANS 6:4 NKJV

I AM A GOD WHO GIVES and gives and gives. When I died for you on the cross, I held back nothing; I poured out My Life *like a drink offering*. Because giving is inherent in My nature, I search for people who are able to receive in full measure. To increase your intimacy with Me, the two traits you need the most are receptivity and attentiveness. Receptivity is opening up your innermost being to be filled with My abundant riches. Attentiveness is directing your gaze to Me, searching for Me in all your moments. It is possible to *stay your mind on Me*, as the prophet Isaiah wrote. Through such attentiveness you receive a glorious gift: My perfect Peace.

PHILIPPIANS 2:17; MARK 10:15; ISAIAH 26:3 NKJV

A S YOU COME TO KNOW ME more intimately, you grow increasingly aware of your sins. This presents you with a choice: to focus on your flaws and failures or to rejoice in My glorious gift of salvation. When you keep your focus on my sacrifice for your sins, you live in the joyful awareness that you are wonderfully loved. There is *no greater Love than Mine*, and it is yours forever! The best response to such a fathomless gift is to *love Me with all your heart.*

Tragically, many people think they have little—or even nothing—for Me to forgive. They've been deceived by the prevailing lie that there is no absolute truth. They believe good and evil are relative terms, so they see no need for a Savior. These deluded ones do not seek My forgiveness, and their sins remain unpardoned. The evil one's deceptions have darkened their minds. But *I am the Light of the world*, and My Light can shine through you into their lives. Because you are My follower, *you never walk in darkness—you have the Light of Life*!

PSALM 13:5–6; JOHN 15:13 NKJV;
MATTHEW 22:37–39; JOHN 8:12

S TOP TRYING TO WORK THINGS OUT before their times have come. Accept the limitations of living one day at a time. When something comes to your attention, ask Me whether or not it is part of today's agenda. If it isn't, release it into My care and go on about today's duties. When you follow this practice, there will be a beautiful simplicity about your life: *a time for everything, and everything in its time.*

A life lived close to Me is not complicated or cluttered. When your focus is on My Presence, many things that once troubled you lose their power over you. Though the world around you is messy and confusing, remember that *I have overcome the world. I have told you these things, so that in Me you may have Peace.*

ECCLESIASTES 3:1; ECCLESIASTES 8:6–7;
JOHN 16:33

IF YOU WALK IN THE LIGHT—living close to Me— *My blood continually cleanses you from all sin.* When you become aware of sins, I want you to confess them and seek My help in making needed changes. Nonetheless, your status with Me is not based on confessing your sins quickly enough or thoroughly enough. The only thing that keeps you right with Me is *My* perfect righteousness, which I gave you freely and permanently when you joined My eternal family. Since you are Mine—gloriously attired *in a robe of righteousness*—I invite you to come confidently into My bright Presence.

Walking in the Light of My Presence blesses you in many ways. Good things are better and bad things are more bearable when you share them with Me. As you delight in My Love-Light, you can love other believers more fully and *have fellowship* with them. You are less likely to stumble or fall, because sins are glaringly obvious in My holy Light. *Rejoice in My Name all day long*, enjoying My Presence and *exulting in My righteousness*.

1 JOHN 1:7 NKJV; ISAIAH 61:10; PSALM 89:15–16

I AM TAKING CARE OF YOU. Trust Me at all times. Trust Me in all circumstances. *Trust Me with all your heart.* When you are weary and everything seems to be going wrong, you can still utter these four words: "I trust You, Jesus." By doing so, you release matters into My control, and you fall back into the security of *My everlasting arms.*

Before you arise from your bed in the morning, I have already arranged the events of your day. Every day provides many opportunities for you to learn My ways and grow closer to Me. Signs of My Presence brighten even the dullest day when you have eyes that really see. Search for Me as for hidden treasure. *I will be found by you.*

PROVERBS 3:5; DEUTERONOMY 33:27;
JEREMIAH 29:13–14

I AM THE *LIGHT FROM ON HIGH that dawns upon you, to give light to those who sit in darkness.* Sometimes your circumstances are so difficult and confusing that you feel as if you're surrounded by darkness. Your mind offers up various solutions to your problems, but you've already tried them—without success. So you fret and wonder what to do next, feeling helpless and frustrated. At times like this, you need to look up and see My Light shining down upon you. Gaze at Me in childlike trust, resting in My Presence. Let go of problem-solving efforts for a while. *Cease striving, and know that I am God.*

As you relax in My Presence, remember that I am the *Prince of Peace.* The more of Me you absorb, the more peaceful you will be. Breathe Me in with each breath. After resting with Me for a while, tell Me about your troubles—trusting Me to help you with them. Stay close to Me, My child, and I will *guide your feet into the way of Peace.*

LUKE 1:78–79 AMP; PSALM 46:10 NASB;
ISAIAH 9:6

TASTE AND SEE THAT I AM GOOD. The more intimately you experience Me, the more convinced you become of My goodness. I am *the Living One who sees you* and longs to participate in your life. I am training you to find Me in each moment and to be a channel of My loving Presence. Sometimes My blessings come to you in mysterious ways: through pain and trouble. At such times you can know My goodness only through your trust in Me. Understanding will fail you, but trust will keep you close to Me.

Thank Me for the gift of My Peace, a gift of such immense proportions that you cannot fathom its depth or breadth. When I appeared to My disciples after the resurrection, it was Peace that I communicated first of all. I knew this was their deepest need: to calm their fears and clear their minds. I also speak Peace to you, for I know your anxious thoughts. Listen to Me! Tune out other voices so that you can hear Me more clearly. I designed you to dwell in Peace all day, every day. Draw near to Me; receive My Peace.

PSALM 34:8; GENESIS 16:13–14 AMP;
JOHN 20:19; COLOSSIANS 3:15

*R*EJOICE THAT YOUR NAME IS WRITTEN *in heaven*—in the book of Life. Because you are Mine, you have Joy that is independent of circumstances. You have received eternal Life that will *never* be taken away from you. *Those who are justified* (through faith in Me as their risen Savior) *are also glorified.* There is a very real sense in which you are already *seated with Me in the heavenly realms.*

Joy is the birthright of all who belong to Me. It can coexist with the most difficult, heartrending circumstances. So come to Me each morning with open hands and an open heart, saying, "Jesus, I receive your Joy." Then wait with Me while the Light of My Presence shines upon you—soaking into the depths of your inner being. Thus I strengthen you, preparing you for the day that stretches out before you.

As you journey through this day, return to Me for fresh Joy as often as you need. I am a God of unlimited abundance, so I always have more than enough for you.

LUKE 10:20; ROMANS 8:30; EPHESIANS 2:6

April

In all your ways acknowledge him, and
he will make your paths straight.

PROVERBS 3:6

I AM CALLING YOU to a life of constant communion with Me. Basic training includes learning to live above your circumstances, even while interacting on that cluttered plane of life. You yearn for a simplified lifestyle so that your communication with Me can be uninterrupted. But I challenge you to relinquish the fantasy of an uncluttered world. Accept each day just as it comes, and find Me in the midst of it all.

Talk with Me about every aspect of your day, including your feelings. Remember that your ultimate goal is not to control or fix everything around you; it is to keep communing with Me. A successful day is one in which you have stayed in touch with Me, even if many things remain undone at the end of the day. Do not let your to-do list (written or mental) become an idol directing your life. Instead, ask My Spirit to guide you moment by moment. He will keep you close to Me.

1 THESSALONIANS 5:17; PROVERBS 3:6;
GALATIANS 5:25

I DELIGHT IN BRIGHTENING your perspective. That's why I ventured into your world, knowing full well the terrible price I would pay. I came *to open eyes that are blind, to free captives from prison, and to release from the dungeon those who sit in darkness.* When you find yourself imprisoned by ingratitude, ask Me to open your eyes and release you from that dark place.

You live in an age of entitlement, so you need to counteract the messages proclaiming that you deserve more. One way is to jot down some things you're thankful for each day. This changes your focus from things you wish you had to blessings you already have.

Saturating your mind with Scripture can help you see from My infinitely wise perspective. My Word is *sharper than any double-edged sword*; I use it to perform spiritual surgery on *the thoughts and attitudes of your heart.* As Scripture lights up your point of view, I set you free from the dungeon of ingratitude, releasing you to enjoy the pleasures of a thankful heart.

ISAIAH 42:7; PSALM 119:105; HEBREWS 4:12

April 2

I HAVE PROMISED *to meet all your needs according to My glorious riches.* Your deepest, most constant need is for My Peace. I have planted Peace in the garden of your heart, where I live, but there are weeds growing there too: pride, worry, selfishness, unbelief. I am the Gardener, and I am working to rid your heart of those weeds. I do My work in various ways. When you sit quietly with Me, I shine the Light of My Presence directly into your heart. In this heavenly Light, Peace grows abundantly and weeds shrivel up. I also send trials into your life. When you trust Me in the midst of trouble, Peace flourishes and weeds die away. Thank Me for troublesome situations; the Peace they can produce *far outweighs* the trials you endure.

PHILIPPIANS 4:19; 2 THESSALONIANS 3:16 NKJV;
2 CORINTHIANS 4:17

BELIEVING IN ME has many beneficial effects—
including *Joy that is inexpressible and filled with Glory*!
If something is inexpressible, it is too great and wondrous
to be described. But it *can* be experienced. So come into My
Presence expectantly; open wide your heart to Me. The Joy
you can have in Me is triumphant and filled with heaven's
Glory. I triumphed over sin and death once for all time! This
opens up the way to heaven for all who believe in Me.

No matter how many difficulties you face, the *outcome of
your faith—the salvation of your soul—*is secure. This is true
for all who really trust Me as Savior-God. As you rejoice in
your glorious heavenly future, *let your light shine before other
people.* My Spirit, the Spirit of truth, will help you speak truth
into others' lives. Align yourself with Me, for *I came into the
world to testify to the truth.* Join Me in this quest so that *people
living in darkness* can find Me and walk in My *great Light.*

1 PETER 1:8–9 ESV; MATTHEW 5:16 NKJV;
JOHN 18:37; ISAIAH 9:2

I N ME YOU HAVE EVERYTHING. In Me you are complete. Your capacity to experience Me is increasing through My removal of debris and clutter from your heart. As your yearning for Me increases, other desires are gradually lessening. Since I am infinite and abundantly accessible to you, desiring Me above all else is the best way to live.

It is impossible for you to have a need that I cannot meet. After all, I created you and everything that is. The world is still at My beck and call, though it often appears otherwise. Do not be fooled by appearances. *Things that are visible are brief and fleeting, while things that are invisible are everlasting.*

EPHESIANS 3:20; 2 CORINTHIANS 4:18 AMP

L OOK UP TO ME, BELOVED, for *My Face is shining upon you.* Be awed by the Glory of My holiness, and let the Light of My Love soak into your inner being. Remember that *I dwell in your heart through faith.* I am simultaneously Master of the universe—which I created and I control—and the Savior who lives inside you. My majestic greatness and My gentle humility combine to give you everything you need. You are rich beyond your wildest imagination!

Because you live in a terribly broken world, it can be hard to remember that you are royalty: adopted into the family of the *King of kings.* Your journey through this world may take you along paths of pain and problems, deserts of deprivation and distress. Do not be surprised by these fiery trials; rather, take them in stride, trusting in the One who never leaves your side. In due time I will take you into the realm of My Glory-Light where *there will be no more night.*

NUMBERS 6:24–25; EPHESIANS 3:16–17;
REVELATION 19:16 NKJV; REVELATION 21:25

I MEET YOU in the stillness of your soul. It is there that I seek to commune with you. A person who is open to My Presence is exceedingly precious to Me. My eyes *search to and fro throughout the earth*, looking for one whose heart is seeking Me. I see you trying to find Me; our mutual search results in joyful fulfillment.

Stillness of soul is increasingly rare in this world addicted to noise and speed. I am pleased with your desire to create a quiet space where you and I can meet. Don't be discouraged by the difficulty of achieving this goal. I monitor all your efforts and am blessed by each of your attempts to seek My Face.

ZECHARIAH 2:13; 2 CHRONICLES 16:9 NKJV;
PSALM 23:2–3 NKJV

*Y*OUR TIMES ARE IN *MY* HANDS. My holy hands are absolutely capable of caring for you and meeting your needs. I want you to relax in My sovereign watchcare, trusting Me to do what is best. Because I am totally trustworthy, it's safe to commit both the "whats" and the "whens" of your life into My care.

As long as you remain on this side of heaven, you will have to submit to the reality of time. Consider the following examples: A bride whose wedding date has been set may yearn to fast-forward to that magical day. But her longing does not change the passage of time; she must wait. Someone who is suffering may yearn for relief—and want it instantly—but he also must wait. I, however, live above the tyranny of time; I am its Master. If you're struggling with having to wait for something, turn to Me in trusting acceptance. Don't fight against what you cannot change. Instead, rejoice in the knowledge that the Master of time understands your struggles and loves you *with an everlasting Love.*

PSALM 31:14–15; PSALM 62:8 NKJV;
JEREMIAH 31:3 NKJV

L ET ME FILL YOU with my Love, Joy, and Peace. These are Glory-gifts, flowing from my living Presence. Though you are an *earthen vessel*, I designed you to be filled with heavenly contents. Your weakness is not a deterrent to being filled with My Spirit; on the contrary, it provides an opportunity for My Power to shine forth more brightly.

As you go through this day, trust Me to provide the strength you need moment by moment. Don't waste energy wondering whether you are adequate for today's journey. My Spirit within you is more than sufficient to handle whatever this day may bring. That is the basis for your confidence! *In quietness* (spending time alone with Me) *and confident trust* (relying on My sufficiency) *is your strength.*

2 CORINTHIANS 4:7 NASB;
EPHESIANS 3:16; ISAIAH 30:15

I WANT YOU TO *DRAW WATER from the wells of salvation with Joy!* Knowing that I have saved you forever from your sins can be a wellspring of Joy in your daily life. Because you know Me as your Savior, you have inside you *a spring of water welling up to eternal life.* Ponder the enormity of this amazing gift, and rejoice! Try to begin and end each day thanking Me for all I have provided.

My gift of salvation is designed to bless not only you but the people around you. As you trust in Me, *streams of living water will flow from within you.* Ask My Spirit, who dwells inside of you, to bless others through you—flowing into their lives. One way to make this request is to pray: "Holy Spirit, think through me; live through me; love through me." While His streams of living water are passing through you into the hearts of other people, I fill both them *and* you with Joy!

ISAIAH 12:3; JOHN 4:13–14; JOHN 7:38

Bring Me the sacrifice of thanksgiving. Take nothing for granted, not even the rising of the sun. Before Satan tempted Eve in the Garden of Eden, thankfulness was as natural as breathing. Satan's temptation involved pointing Eve to the one thing that was forbidden her. The Garden was filled with luscious, desirable fruits, but Eve focused on the one fruit she couldn't have rather than being thankful for the many good things freely available. This negative focus darkened her mind, and she succumbed to temptation.

When you focus on what you don't have or on situations that displease you, your mind also becomes darkened. You take for granted life, salvation, sunshine, flowers, and countless other gifts from Me. You look for what is wrong and refuse to enjoy life until that is "fixed."

When you approach Me with thanksgiving, the Light of My Presence pours into you, transforming you through and through. *Walk in the Light* with Me by practicing the discipline of thanksgiving.

PSALM 116:17 NKJV; GENESIS 3:2–4; 1 JOHN 1:7

E VEN THOUGH YOUR JOURNEY often feels haphazard, *your steps are directed by Me.* When the path that lies before you is veiled in uncertainty, the best thing you can do is cling to Me. Picture a young child walking along busy city streets with a trustworthy adult. The child may feel overwhelmed by all the sensory stimulation—fearful of getting separated and losing her way. However, if she keeps holding onto the adult's hand, she will come safely to her destination. Similarly, as you clasp My hand for help and guidance, you are ultimately safe.

Though you may not know the way you should go, you *do* know the One who is *the Way.* Because I am sovereign over your life, I *direct your steps and make them sure* even when they seem random to you. Talk with Me about your uncertainty, your fear of making wrong decisions. The most important choice you make moment by moment is to stay in communication with Me. *This* is how you cling to Me. This is how you trust My guiding Presence to keep you safe.

PROVERBS 20:24; JOHN 14:6 NKJV;
PROVERBS 16:9 AMP; 2 CORINTHIANS 5:7 NKJV

I AM THE POTTER; *you are My clay.* I designed you before the foundation of the world. I arrange the events of each day to form you into this preconceived pattern. My everlasting Love is at work in every event of your life. On some days your will and Mine flow smoothly together. You tend to feel in control of your life when our wills are in harmony. On other days you feel as if you are swimming upstream, against the current of My purposes. When that happens, stop and seek My Face. The opposition you feel may be from Me, or it may be from the evil one.

Talk with Me about what you are experiencing. Let My Spirit guide you through treacherous waters. As you move through the turbulent stream with Me, let circumstances mold you into the one I desire you to be. Say *yes* to your Potter as you go through this day.

ISAIAH 64:8; PSALM 27:8; 1 JOHN 5:5–6 NKJV

I GIVE ETERNAL LIFE TO YOU, *and you will never perish; no one will snatch you out of My hand.* This is astonishingly good news for all who know Me as Savior. Your promised inheritance is far more glorious than anything you can imagine! The gift of eternal Life provides a Light that shines on, even in your darkest days. So let this brightness beckon you onward, protecting you from discouragement. Refuse to let hard circumstances or the wickedness of this world drag you down. Instead, look ahead to the Glory that awaits you. See it sparkling in the distance, just beyond the horizon.

You may have to go through some deep waters on your journey, but remember: *I will be with you when you pass through the waters. They will not sweep over you.* Keep holding onto My hand in trusting dependence—confident that I love you and *nothing will be able to separate you from Me.* Rather than dreading the challenging times ahead of you, seek to enjoy the adventure of journeying with Me through your life.

JOHN 10:27–28 NASB; 1 PETER 1:3–4;
ISAIAH 43:2; ROMANS 8:38–39

I AM WITH YOU AND FOR YOU, your constant Companion and Provider. The question is whether you are with Me and for Me. Though I never leave you, you can essentially "leave" Me by ignoring Me: thinking or acting as if I am not with you. When you feel distance in our relationship, you know where the problem lies. My Love for you is constant; *I am the same yesterday, today, and forever.* It is you who change like shifting sand, letting circumstances toss you this way and that.

When you feel far from Me, whisper My Name. This simple act, done in childlike faith, opens your heart to My Presence. Speak to Me in love-tones; prepare to receive My Love, which flows eternally from the cross. I am delighted when you open yourself to My loving Presence.

GENESIS 28:15; ROMANS 8:31;
HEBREWS 13:8; COLOSSIANS 3:17 NKJV

*A*LWAYS BE PREPARED *to give an answer to everyone who asks you the reason for the hope you have.* It is easier to obey this command when you're well rested and your life is flowing smoothly. It's quite another matter when you're feeling exhausted and frazzled. Yet *this* may be the time when your hopeful answer will make the greatest impact. So make it your goal to be prepared *always.* You also need to be ready to answer *everyone* who asks you the reason for your hopefulness. It is tempting to judge some people as poor candidates for learning about Me and what I mean to you. But only *I* know their hearts and the plans I have for them.

Essential preparation for giving a good answer is living in awareness of My Presence—trusting Me fully as your Hope. This will steady you as you deal with the frequent ups and downs of your life. Whenever you're struggling, encourage yourself by pondering truths of the gospel and by gazing at Me, your glorious Hope.

1 PETER 3:15; ROMANS 5:5 NASB; PSALM 27:4

Y OU ARE MINE FOR ALL TIME; *nothing can separate you from My Love.* Since I have invested My very Life in you, be well assured that I will also take care of you. When your mind goes into neutral and your thoughts flow freely, you tend to feel anxious and alone. Your focus becomes problem solving. To get your mind back into gear, just turn toward Me, bringing yourself and your problems into My Presence.

Many problems vanish instantly in the Light of My Love because you realize you are never alone. Other problems may remain, but they become secondary to knowing Me and rejoicing in the relationship I so freely offer you. Each moment you can choose to practice My Presence or to practice the presence of problems.

ROMANS 8:38–39; EXODUS 33:14;
JOHN 12:46 NKJV

B E WILLING TO FOLLOW MY LEAD, beloved. Open yourself more fully to Me and My way for you. Don't get so focused on what you want that you miss the things I've prepared for you. Relax with Me while *I transform you by the renewal of your mind*—working My newness into your innermost being. Trust Me enough to let go of your expectations and demands. *Be still, and know that I am God.*

Sometimes you obstruct the very things you desire by trying too hard to make things go according to your will and timing. I know the desires of your heart, and I also know the best way to reach those goals. Instead of striving to be in control so you can get what you want, *seek My Face.* Talk with Me openly, and rest for a while in My Presence. When you are feeling more refreshed, invite Me to show you the way forward. *I will guide you along the best pathway for your life. I will advise you and watch over you.*

ROMANS 12:2; PSALM 46:10 NKJV;
1 CHRONICLES 16:11 NASB; PSALM 32:8 NLT

TRUST ME IN EVERY DETAIL of your life. Nothing is random in My kingdom. *Everything that happens fits into a pattern for good, to those who love Me.* Instead of trying to analyze the intricacies of the pattern, focus your energy on trusting Me and thanking Me at all times. Nothing is wasted when you walk close to Me. Even your mistakes and sins can be recycled into something good through My transforming grace.

While you were still living in darkness, I began to shine the Light of My Presence into your sin-stained life. Finally, I *lifted you up out of the mire into My marvelous Light.* Having sacrificed My very Life for you, I can be trusted in every facet of your life.

JEREMIAH 17:7; ROMANS 8:28 AMP;
PSALM 40:2 AMP; 1 PETER 2:9 NKJV

*G*REAT IS *MY LOVE, reaching to the heavens; My faithfulness reaches to the skies.* You can feel wonderfully secure in Love that has no boundaries or limits. My faithfulness also has no bounds.

Respond to these wondrous gifts with worship. The more you praise Me, the more you can *reflect My Glory* to other people. This is the work of the Holy Spirit, who is *transforming you into My likeness with ever-increasing Glory.* As you draw near Me through worship, I change you profoundly, equipping you to make Me known to others.

My Love not only reaches to the heavens but descends upon you from heavenly realms. Keep looking up to Me, beloved. See Me smiling on you in radiant approval. My limitless Love falls continually upon you, like heavenly snowflakes that melt into your upturned face. No matter how distressing your circumstances, this Love is sufficient to sustain you. Someday you will even ascend to heaven on it. I eagerly anticipate the time when *I will take you into Glory*—to be with Me forever!

PSALM 57:9–10; 2 CORINTHIANS 3:18;
NUMBERS 6:25–26 AMP; PSALM 73:23–24

T HIS IS THE DAY THAT I HAVE MADE. *Rejoice and be glad in it.* Begin the day with open hands of faith, ready to receive all that I am pouring into this brief portion of your life. Be careful not to complain about anything, even the weather, since I am the Author of your circumstances. The best way to handle unwanted situations is to thank Me for them. This act of faith frees you from resentment and frees Me to work My ways into the situation, so that good emerges from it.

To find Joy in this day, you must live within its boundaries. I knew what I was doing when I divided time into twenty-four-hour segments. I understand human frailty, and I know that you can bear the weight of only one day at a time. Do not worry about tomorrow or get stuck in the past. There is abundant Life in My Presence today.

PSALM 118:24; PHILIPPIANS 3:13–14;
HEBREWS 3:13

S EEK TO THINK MY THOUGHTS more and more. Enlist My Spirit's help in this endeavor, *for the mind controlled by the Spirit is Life and Peace.*

When the worries of this world are pressing in on you, take time to think things out in My Presence. Rest in Me, beloved. Let My *everlasting arms* enfold you in Peace. Take a break from your concerns, and *fix your thoughts on Me.* Intersperse quietness with reading Scripture and speaking or singing praises to Me. You can also use Bible verses in your prayers to Me. When your thoughts and prayers are permeated with Scripture, you're able to have more confidence in them.

I want you to *be transformed by the renewal of your mind.* The world exerts massive amounts of pressure on you through ever-present electronic communications. Instead of letting the world and its gadgets shape you, invite Me to transform the way you think. As I renew your mind, your ideals and attitudes will reflect *Me* more and more.

ROMANS 8:6; DEUTERONOMY 33:27 NKJV;
HEBREWS 3:1; ROMANS 12:2 ESV

T RUSTING ME is a moment-by-moment choice. My people have not always understood this truth. After I performed miracles in the wilderness, My chosen children trusted Me intensely—but only temporarily. Soon the grumbling began again, testing My patience to the utmost.

Isn't it often the same way with you? You trust Me when things go well, when you see Me working on your behalf. This type of trust flows readily within you, requiring no exertion of your will. When things go wrong, your trust-flow slows down and solidifies. You are forced to choose between trusting Me intentionally or rebelling, resenting My ways with you. This choice constitutes a fork in the road. Stay on the path of Life with Me, enjoying My Presence. Choose to trust Me in all circumstances.

EXODUS 15:22–25; PSALM 31:14

YOUR RELATIONSHIP WITH ME TRANSCENDS all your circumstances. This is why you can praise Me and enjoy My Presence in the midst of the darkest difficulties. To find Me in such times, you have to really exert your faith; but I am always near.

As a Christian, you live on two planes simultaneously: the natural world, where adverse situations abound; and the supernatural world, where I reign supreme. Your trust-muscles empower you to experience My Presence even in your hardest times. In fact, trials can both strengthen your faith and help you discern how much you actually trust Me.

I want you to work on strengthening your trust-muscles. One way is to fill your mind and heart with Scripture. Another is to *seek My Face continually.* Instead of getting stuck in intro-spection, turn your thoughts toward Me. Make it a practice to affirm your faith in Me frequently, whether you're feeling confident or inadequate. Remember that your adequacy rests in your relationship with Me. I make you *ready for anything and equal to anything* by *infusing inner strength into you*!

JAMES 1:2–3; PSALM 105:4 NASB;
PHILIPPIANS 4:13 AMP

WHEN I GIVE YOU no special guidance, stay where you are. Concentrate on doing your everyday tasks in awareness of My Presence with you. The Joy of My Presence will shine on you, as you do everything for Me. Thus you invite Me into every aspect of your life. Through collaborating with Me in all things, you allow My Life to merge with yours. This is the secret of not only joyful living but of victorious living. I designed you to depend on Me moment by moment, recognizing that *apart from Me you can do nothing.*

Be thankful for quiet days, when nothing special seems to be happening. Instead of being bored by the lack of action, use times of routine to seek My Face. Although this is an invisible transaction, it speaks volumes in spiritual realms. Moreover, you are richly blessed when you walk trustingly with Me through the routines of your day.

COLOSSIANS 3:23; JOHN 15:5; PSALM 105:4

S EEK TO INCLUDE ME in more of your moments by living in joyful dependence on Me. *I am with you, watching over you* continually. Nothing you do is beyond My sight. No task or opportunity is too small to ask for My help. Actually, your very existence—including each breath you breathe—depends on My sustaining Power.

When a difficult task lies before you, you usually remember to pray about it, both before you begin and throughout the challenging endeavor. You punctuate your work with brief prayers such as: "Help me, Lord" and "Thank You, Jesus." These communications increase both your reliance on Me and your gratitude for My continual Presence. When you're involved in less challenging activities, however, you often forget about Me and plunge ahead on your own. You may experience some degree of success, but you miss a far greater blessing that was available had you sought My help. Or you may fail miserably, whereas depending on Me would have brought success. So rely on Me in *all* you do; I have blessings waiting for you.

GENESIS 28:15; HEBREWS 1:3; PROVERBS 3:6 NASB

H EAVEN IS both present and future. As you walk along your life-path holding My hand, you are already in touch with the essence of heaven: nearness to Me. You can also find many hints of heaven along your pathway because the earth is radiantly alive with My Presence. Shimmering sunshine awakens your heart, gently reminding you of My brilliant Light. Birds and flowers, trees and skies evoke praises to My holy Name. Keep your eyes and ears fully open as you journey with Me.

At the end of your life-path is an entrance to heaven. Only I know when you will reach that destination, but I am preparing you for it each step of the way. The absolute certainty of your heavenly home gives you Peace and Joy to help you along your journey. You know that you will reach your home in My perfect timing: not one moment too soon or too late. Let the hope of heaven encourage you as you walk along the path of Life with Me.

1 CORINTHIANS 15:20–23; HEBREWS 6:19

Y OU ARE NOT YOUR OWN, *for you were bought with a price.* And that price was exorbitant—My very Life! I went through excruciating pain and humiliation as I sacrificed Myself for your sins. This was a gift of infinite value—an act of indescribable Love. However, only those who recognize their sinfulness, their need for a Savior, can receive this astonishing gift of Love. Hear My invitation calling out: *"Come to Me, all you who are weary and burdened, and I will give you rest."* Sin is a terrible, crushing burden, but I have paid the price *in full* to remove it from you forever.

When you awaken each morning, say to yourself: "I am not my own. I belong to Jesus." Then keep in mind Whose you are as you make your way through the day, especially as you make plans and decisions. Knowing that you belong to Me helps you keep your feet on *the path of Peace*. This knowledge meets deep-seated needs. You can find spiritual and emotional security by remembering that you are *Mine*—My beloved.

1 CORINTHIANS 6:19–20 ESV;
MATTHEW 11:28; LUKE 1:76–79

T RUST ME, *and don't be afraid.* Many things feel out of control. Your routines are not running smoothly. You tend to feel more secure when your life is predictable. Let Me lead you to *the rock that is higher than you* and your circumstances. *Take refuge in the shelter of My wings*, where you are absolutely secure.

When you are shaken out of your comfortable routines, grip My hand tightly and look for growth opportunities. Instead of bemoaning the loss of your comfort, accept the challenge of something new. *I lead you on from glory to glory*, making you fit for My kingdom. Say *yes* to the ways I work in your life. Trust Me, and don't be afraid.

ISAIAH 12:2; PSALM 61:2–4;
2 CORINTHIANS 3:18 NKJV

YOU CAN TRUST THE ONE who died for you. In this world of spin and scams, people often find it hard to believe anyone. They talk about requiring others to "earn" their trust by proving themselves. *I* am the quintessential Person who has earned the right to be trusted. For your sake, I left the glorious perfection of heaven and began life in your world as a helpless, stable-born infant. I resisted all temptations for thirty-three years so that My sacrifice for sinners would be sufficient. I lived a perfect life and freely gave My body to be tortured and executed—to pay the full penalty for sin. As a result of My death and resurrection, *whoever believes in Me has eternal Life*!

I want you to rely confidently on Me—not only as your Savior but also as the God-Friend who is taking care of you. I have already proved how trustworthy I am. Now I invite you to relax in My loving Presence and confide in Me. Tell Me your hopes and fears. *Cast all your anxiety on Me because I care for you.*

2 CORINTHIANS 8:9 NKJV; JOHN 3:36;
1 PETER 5:7

I AM CALLING YOU to a life of thankfulness. I want all your moments to be punctuated with thanksgiving. The basis for your gratitude is My sovereignty. I am the Creator and Controller of the universe. Heaven and earth are filled with My glorious Presence.

When you criticize or complain, you are acting as if you think you could run the world better than I do. From your limited human perspective, it may look as if I'm mismanaging things. But you don't know what I know or see what I see. If I pulled back the curtain to allow you to view heavenly realms, you would understand much more. However, I have designed you to *live by faith*, not by sight. I lovingly shield you from knowing the future or seeing into the spirit world. Acknowledge My sovereignty by *giving thanks in all circumstances.*

ISAIAH 6:3; 2 CORINTHIANS 5:7;
1 THESSALONIANS 5:18

*T*HIS IS THE DAY THAT *I* HAVE MADE. I invite you to rejoice in this day as you share it with Me. The more of Me you have in your life, the more joyful you will be.

Invite Me into your moments by talking with Me about everything that concerns you, whatever is on your mind. Your conversations with Me will radically change the way you think. If you've been preoccupied with something trivial, bringing Me into your thoughts helps you recognize how silly they are. If you're stuck in the past—yearning to change what has happened—My Presence lovingly draws you back into the present. Whatever you're facing, I can help you handle it better.

Seek to find Joy in this day I have made for you. I've hidden small pleasures along your pathway. Search for them, and thank Me for each one you find. Many of the little things that delight your heart are unique to you. I know you so intimately that I can provide just what you need to make you glad. *Rejoice*, beloved!

PSALM 118:24 NKJV; 1 THESSALONIANS 5:16–18;
PSALM 139:1–3 NASB

April 17

I AM TRAINING YOU IN STEADINESS. Too many things interrupt your awareness of Me. I know that you live in a world of sight and sound, but you must not be a slave to those stimuli. Awareness of Me can continue in all circumstances, no matter what happens. This is the steadiness I desire for you.

Don't let unexpected events throw you off course. Rather, respond calmly and confidently, remembering that I am with you. As soon as something grabs your attention, talk with Me about it. Thus I share your joys and your problems; I help you cope with whatever is before you. This is how I live in you and work through you. This is the way of Peace.

PSALM 112:7; 1 THESSALONIANS 5:17 AMP;
ISAIAH 41:10 NKJV

L ook to Me as your joyful Focus. You were *made* for Joy, and I am the boundless, overflowing Source of delight in your life.

I never run out of anything because I am infinite. If you draw too much from other pleasures, they will eventually let you down. The nature of addiction is that you need more and more of a substance to get the same effect as before. This is a self-destructive trap. However, the more you make *Me* your Focus, the less dependent you are on other things. You can still enjoy the good gifts I provide, but you don't need to grasp onto them, trying to milk every possible bit of pleasure from them.

Learn to fix your gaze on Me even as the world parades before you. Whisper My Name in remembrance that I am near, and tell Me about what troubles you. Thank Me for the things you enjoy—loved ones, shelter, food, sunlight, starlight, and *especially* My glorious Presence. *Seek My Face* and My will; *look to Me and My strength*.

HEBREWS 12:2 ESV; JOHN 15:11;
1 TIMOTHY 1:17 NKJV; PSALM 105:4

P EACE IS MY CONTINUAL GIFT TO YOU. It flows abundantly from My throne of grace. Just as the Israelites could not store up manna for the future but had to gather it daily, so it is with My Peace. The day-by-day collecting of manna kept My people aware of their dependence on Me. Similarly, I give you sufficient Peace for the present when you come to me *by prayer and petition with thanksgiving.* If I gave you permanent Peace, independent of My Presence, you might fall into the trap of self-sufficiency. May that never be!

I have designed you to need Me moment by moment. As your awareness of your neediness increases, so does your realization of My abundant sufficiency. *I can meet every one of your needs* without draining My resources at all. *Approach My throne of grace with bold confidence,* receiving My Peace with a thankful heart.

EXODUS 16:15–16; PHILIPPIANS 4:6–7, 19;
HEBREWS 4:16

THANK ME FOR THE GLORIOUS GIFT of forgiveness. I am your Savior-God, and I alone can give you this blessing. I went to exorbitant expense to procure this gift for you. You receive forgiveness and become My child by receiving *Me* and *believing in My Name*. This Name, Jesus, means *the Lord saves*. To receive this gift of salvation, you need to trust Me as your only Hope—the One who delivers you from all your sins.

There is no condemnation for those who are in Me. I want you to enjoy the wonder of walking through your life as My follower—totally forgiven! The best response to this wondrous gift is to live in gratitude, seeking to please Me above all else. You don't need to do good things to secure My Love, because it's already yours. Just let your desire to please Me flow readily out of your grateful heart. Thanking Me frequently will help you stay close to Me, ready to follow wherever I lead. Rejoice, beloved, for *through Me the law of the Spirit of Life has set you free!*

JOHN 1:12; ACTS 4:12 NASB; ROMANS 8:1–2

I LOVE YOU regardless of how well you are performing. Sometimes you feel uneasy, wondering if you are doing enough to be worthy of My Love. No matter how exemplary your behavior, the answer to that question will always be no. Your performance and My Love are totally different issues, which you need to sort out. *I love you with an everlasting Love* that flows out from eternity without limits or conditions. *I have clothed you in My robe of righteousness*, and this is an eternal transaction: Nothing and no one can reverse it. Therefore, your accomplishment as a Christian has no bearing on My Love for you. Even your ability to assess how well you are doing on a given day is flawed. Your limited human perspective and the condition of your body, with its mercurial variations, distort your evaluations.

Bring your performance anxiety to Me, and receive in its place *My unfailing Love*. Try to stay conscious of My loving Presence with you in all that you do, and I will direct your steps.

JEREMIAH 31:3; ISAIAH 61:10;
PSALM 31:16; PSALM 107:8

*Y*OU LOVE ME *because I first loved you.* I had My eye on you long before you were interested in Me. I noticed everything about you and followed you everywhere. I orchestrated circumstances and events in your life to help you see your need of Me. I provided people and teaching that told you the truth about Me in ways you could understand. My Spirit worked within you to make you spiritually alive—enabling you to *receive Me and believe in My Name.* All of this flowed out of My deep, powerful affection for you. *I have loved you with an everlasting Love!*

The more you realize the immensity of My ardor for you, the more fully you can love *Me.* This enables you to grow, little by little, into the person I designed you to be. As you spend time in My tender Presence, it becomes easier for you to delight in Me and to show kindness to other people. When you are with others, ask Me to help you love them—with *My* Love.

1 JOHN 4:19 NKJV; JOHN 1:12; JEREMIAH 31:3

D O NOT BE AFRAID, for I am with you. Hear Me saying, *"Peace, be still,"* to your restless heart. No matter what happens, *I will never leave you or forsake you.* Let this assurance soak into your mind and heart until you overflow with Joy. *Though the earth give way and the mountains fall into the heart of the sea,* you need not fear!

The media relentlessly proclaim bad news: for breakfast, lunch, and dinner. A steady diet of their fare will sicken you. Instead of focusing on fickle, ever-changing news broadcasts, tune in to the living Word—the One who is always the same. Let Scripture saturate your mind and heart, and you will walk steadily along the path of Life. Even though you don't know what will happen tomorrow, you can be absolutely sure of your ultimate destination. *I hold you by your right hand, and afterward I will take you into Glory.*

MARK 4:39 NKJV; DEUTERONOMY 31:6;
PSALM 46:2; PSALM 73:23–24

THIS DAY OF LIFE IS A PRECIOUS GIFT from Me. Treat it as the treasure it is by prayerfully prioritizing. As you look into the day that stretches out before you, *seek My Face* to help you discern what is most important. Set priorities according to My will, and use them to guide you as you go along your pathway. This practice will help you make good choices about the use of your time and energy. When you reach the end of the day, you can feel at peace about the things you have done—and also the things you have *not* done.

I encourage you to invite Me into everything you do. The briefest prayer, "Help me, Lord," is sufficient to involve Me in your activities. I delight in your acknowledgment that you need Me continually. And I want *you* to delight in your neediness, for it is a strong link to My radiant Presence. Although living in a dependent mode is countercultural, it is a blessed way to live—rejoicing in the Glory of My Presence.

PSALM 118:24 NKJV; 1 CHRONICLES 16:10–11;
JOHN 15:5; JUDE V. 24

L ET ME CONTROL YOUR MIND. The mind is the most restless, unruly part of mankind. Long after you have learned the discipline of holding your tongue, your thoughts defy your will and set themselves up against Me. Man is the pinnacle of My creation, and the human mind is wondrously complex. I risked all by granting you freedom to think for yourself. This is godlike privilege, forever setting you apart from animals and robots. *I made you in My image*, precariously close to deity.

Though My blood has fully redeemed you, your mind is the last bastion of rebellion. Open yourself to My radiant Presence, letting My Light permeate your thinking. *When My Spirit is controlling your mind, you are filled with Life and Peace.*

PSALM 8:5 NKJV; GENESIS 1:26–27; ROMANS 8:6

*T*HE PROSPECT OF THE RIGHTEOUS IS JOY. This means that your prospects are excellent, beloved. I lived a perfectly righteous life for you and died in your place, enduring the full punishment for your sins. This made it possible to clothe you in My own *robe of righteousness*. I invite you to wear the *garments of salvation* with overflowing gratitude and Joy.

A thankful, joyful attitude will help you live well, according to My will. Beginning your day in this positive frame of mind sets your feet on the right path. Thankfulness increases your Joy, which in turn augments your gratitude. There is delightful synergy between these two attitudes. When your ability to be joyful seems to be flagging, energize it with a hearty dose of thanksgiving! Reading psalms can help you with this, and so can singing hymns or praise songs. Making a list—mentally or on paper—of blessings in your life is another effective way to give thanks. I want you to remember the *great things I have done for you*; this will *fill you with Joy.*

PROVERBS 10:28; ISAIAH 61:10;
PSALM 13:6; PSALM 126:3

L ISTEN TO ME CONTINUALLY. I have much to communicate to you, so many people and situations in need of prayer. I am training you to set your mind on Me more and more, tuning out distractions through the help of My Spirit.

Walk with Me in holy trust, responding to My initiatives rather than trying to make things fit your plans. I died to set you free, and that includes freedom from compulsive planning. When your mind spins with a multitude of thoughts, you cannot hear My voice. A mind preoccupied with planning pays homage to the idol of control. Turn from this idolatry back to Me. Listen to Me and live abundantly!

PSALM 62:8 NKJV; JOHN 8:36;
PROVERBS 19:21; JOHN 10:27

*D*O NOT WORRY ABOUT TOMORROW! This is a most gracious command. I understand human frailty; I know that *you are dust.* This command is not meant to burden you or condemn you. It is meant to set you free from worldly cares.

Just before I gave this directive to My followers, I spoke about how to enjoy such freedom. Remember that *your heavenly Father knows what you need.* As you *seek first His kingdom and His righteousness,* your perspective changes. Worldly pursuits become secondary to matters of unseen, eternal reality—the advancement of My kingdom. So put more time and energy into developing your relationship with Me, seeking not only My Presence but also My will. Be ready to follow wherever I lead. I will guide you along adventurous paths that can fill your life with meaning.

I created you to enjoy My Presence in the present—entrusting your future into My care and keeping. As you *delight yourself in Me, I give you the desires of your heart.*

MATTHEW 6:32–34; PSALM 103:14 NKJV;
PSALM 37:4

K EEP YOUR EYES ON ME, not only for direction but also for empowerment. I never lead you to do something without equipping you for the task. That is why it's so important to seek My will in everything you do. There are many burned-out Christians who think more is always better, who deem it unspiritual to say no.

In order to know My will, you must spend time with Me—enjoying My Presence. This is not an onerous task but a delightful privilege. I will show you *the path of Life; in My Presence is fullness of Joy; at My right hand there are pleasures forevermore.*

PSALM 141:8; ISAIAH 48:17; PSALM 16:11 NKJV

I AM THE ONE AND ONLY *who came from the Father, full of grace and truth.* I came from Him and I returned to Him because I am God—the second Person of the Trinity.

I entered your world to provide a way for you to have a living, eternal relationship with your Father-God. People who do not know Me have often stated that there are many ways to God. But this claim is absolutely untrue: *I am the Way, the Truth, and the Life. No one comes to the Father except through Me.*

I come to *you*, beloved, *full of grace.* Because you have trusted Me to save you from your sins through My sacrificial death on the cross, you have nothing to fear. You don't need to dread failure or performing below expectations. Since I am your Savior—and you cannot save yourself—your security rests in My grace. Rejoice that I am both faithful and sufficient. In spite of all the trouble in this world, *in Me you may have Peace. I have overcome the world*!

JOHN 1:14; JOHN 14:6 NKJV; JOHN 16:33

REST IN THE STILLNESS of My Presence while I prepare you for this day. Let the radiance of My Glory shine upon you as you wait on Me in confident trust. *Be still, and know that I am God.* There is both a passive and an active side to trusting Me. As you rest in My Presence, focusing on Me, I quietly build bonds of trust between us. When you respond to the circumstances of your life with affirmations of trust, you actively participate in this process.

I am always with you, so you have no reason to be afraid. Your fear often manifests itself in excessive planning. Your mind is so accustomed to this pattern of thinking that you are only now becoming aware of how pervasive it is and how much it hinders your intimacy with Me. Repent of this tendency and resist it whenever you realize you are wandering down this well-worn path. Return to My Presence, which always awaits you in the present moment. I accept you back with *no condemnation.*

PSALM 46:10; ROMANS 8:1–2

I AM A *SHIELD for all who take refuge in Me.* On some days you feel your need of My shielding Presence more than on other days. At times you're not even aware that you need protection, but I am continually close by—watching over you. I delight in being your Protector, so you can always find shelter in Me.

One of the best ways to make Me *your Refuge* is to spend focused time with Me and *pour out your heart to Me.* Tell Me about the things that have wounded you: the unfair things done to you or said about you. Trust that I care about you and want to heal your hurts. Also, I know the truth about everything; My view of you is untainted by innuendos and half-truths.

Knowing that I understand you completely is vital to your healing. It is also crucial for forgiving those who have wounded you. Forgiveness is usually a process, so keep at it till you are free. Rejoice in Me, beloved, for I came to *make you free.*

PSALM 18:30; PSALM 62:8; JOHN 8:32 NKJV

M AKE ME YOUR FOCAL POINT as you move through this day. Just as a spinning ballerina must keep returning her eyes to a given point to maintain her balance, so you must keep returning your focus to Me. Circumstances are in flux, and the world seems to be whirling around you. The only way to keep your balance is to *fix your eyes on Me*, the One who never changes. If you gaze too long at your circumstances, you will become dizzy and confused. Look to Me, refreshing yourself in My Presence, and your steps will be steady and sure.

HEBREWS 12:2; PSALM 102:27; 1 JOHN 3:19–20

I AM THE TRUTH—unchanging, transcendent Truth! Many, many people believe that truth is relative—to the situation, the person, the day. But only absolute truth can provide a firm foundation for your life. Everything else is shifting sand.

Because I am inerrant Truth, *all the treasures of wisdom and knowledge* are hidden in Me. You can find everything you need in your relationship with Me. I provide the foundation on which to build your life, and I Myself *am* Life. So the closer you live to Me, the more alive you will feel!

Many people struggle with issues of identity, wondering who they really are and what they're supposed to be doing with their lives. But the more fully you know Me—*the Truth*—the better you can understand yourself and the meaning of your life. So make every effort to know Me as I truly am. Also, *be prepared* to tell others about the Savior-God who has redeemed you and *set you free.*

JOHN 14:6 NKJV; COLOSSIANS 2:2–3;
1 PETER 3:15; JOHN 8:32

WELCOME PROBLEMS as perspective-lifters. My children tend to sleepwalk through their days until they bump into an obstacle that stymies them.

If you encounter a problem with no immediate solution, your response to that situation will take you either up or down. You can lash out at the difficulty, resenting it and feeling sorry for yourself. This will take you down into a pit of self-pity. Alternatively, the problem can be a ladder, enabling you to climb up and see your life from My perspective. Viewed from above, the obstacle that frustrated you is only *a light and momentary trouble*. Once your perspective has been heightened, you can look away from the problem altogether. Turn toward Me, and see *the Light of My Presence* shining upon you.

2 CORINTHIANS 4:16–18; PSALM 89:15

*T*HERE WILL BE NO NIGHT in heaven, *for the Glory of God gives it Light.* You will not need nighttime for sleeping, because your glorified body will always be full of energy. Tiredness is one of the main things people have to contend with in this world, especially as they grow old or sickly. But there will be no fatigue in heaven and therefore no need for sleep.

The Glory-Light of heaven is perfect and brilliant, without a speck of darkness in it. There will be no sin there—nothing to hide. You will see everything through glorified eyes, as you've never seen before. Colors will be more vivid; faces will be more vibrant. You will be able to look fully into *My* Face. Your experience will be far better than that of Moses, who had to hide in the cleft of a rock while My Glory passed by. He was allowed to see only My back, but you will have no such limitations. In heaven *you will see Me face to Face*—in all My Glory!

REVELATION 21:23, 25; 1 JOHN 1:5;
EXODUS 33:22–23; 1 CORINTHIANS 13:12 NKJV

C OME TO ME with empty hands and an open heart, ready to receive abundant blessings. I know the depth and breadth of your neediness. Your life-path has been difficult, draining you of strength. Come to Me for nurture. Let Me fill you up with My Presence: I in you, and you in Me.

My Power flows most freely into weak ones aware of their need for Me. Faltering steps of dependence are not lack of faith; they are links to My Presence.

JOHN 17:20–23; ISAIAH 40:29–31

Y OU ARE TROUBLED BY FEAR OF FAILURE, but My Love for you will never fail. Let Me describe what I see as I gaze at you, beloved. You look regal, for I have clothed you in My righteousness and *crowned you with glory and honor.* You *are radiant*, especially when you are looking at Me. You are beautiful as you *reflect My Glory* back to Me. In fact, you delight Me so much that *I rejoice over you with shouts of Joy*! This is how you appear through My grace-filled vision.

Because I am infinite, I can see you as you are now and as you will be in heaven—simultaneously. Viewing you in the present, I work with you on things you need to change. Seeing you from the heavenly perspective, I love you as if you were already perfect.

I want you to learn to look at yourself—and others— through the lens of My unfailing Love. As you persevere in this, you will gradually find it easier to love yourself *and* others.

HEBREWS 2:7; PSALM 34:5 ESV;
2 CORINTHIANS 3:18; ZEPHANIAH 3:17 NASB

A s you look into the day that stretches out before you, you see many choice-points along the way. The myriad possibilities these choices present can confuse you. Draw your mind back to the threshold of this day, where I stand beside you, lovingly preparing you for what is ahead.

You must make your choices one at a time since each is contingent upon the decision that precedes it. Instead of trying to create a mental map of your path through this day, focus on My loving Presence with you. I will equip you as you go so that you can handle whatever comes your way. Trust Me to supply what you need when you need it.

LAMENTATIONS 3:22–26;
PROVERBS 16:9; PSALM 34:8 NKJV

*T*RUST IN ME AT ALL TIMES. *Pour out your heart to Me, for I am your refuge.* The more you rely on Me, the more effectively I can help you. Trusting Me is appropriate for all circumstances: joyful and sorrowful, peaceful and stressful. In fact, things that cause you stress can serve as reminders to *seek My Face.* I want you to remember that I am with you, taking care of you, even when life hurts. Talk with Me about your troubles and leave them with Me. Then rest in My Presence while I go to work on your behalf.

Tell yourself the truth about Me. Use words of Scripture to describe Me: "You are *my refuge and my fortress, my God, in whom I trust.*" I am indeed a refuge—a safe place to find shelter in the storms of life. Speaking or singing such truths is an effective way to draw near Me. Your mind usually has several thoughts or thought-fragments passing through it at once. Instead of just thinking about Me, speak out loud; this gives focus to your thoughts—and to your trust in Me.

PSALM 62:8; 1 CHRONICLES 16:11 NKJV;
1 PETER 5:7; PSALM 91:2

L ET ME TEACH YOU THANKFULNESS. Begin by acknowledging that everything—all your possessions and all that you are—belongs to Me. The dawning of each new day is a gift from Me, not to be taken for granted. The earth is vibrantly alive with My blessings, giving vivid testimony to My Presence. If you slow down your pace of life, you can find Me anywhere.

Some of My most precious children have been laid aside in sickbeds or shut away in prisons. Others have voluntarily learned the discipline of spending time alone with Me. The secret of being thankful is learning to see everything from My perspective. My world is your classroom. *My Word is a lamp to your feet and a light for your path.*

HEBREWS 12:28–29; PSALM 19:1 NKJV;
PSALM 119:105

I AM WORTHY of all your confidence, all your trust. So I refuse to let world events spook you. Instead, pour your energy into trusting Me and looking for evidence of My Presence in the world. Whisper My Name to reconnect your heart and mind to Me quickly. *I am near to all who call upon Me.* Let Me wrap you up in My abiding Presence and comfort you with My Peace.

Remember that I am both loving and faithful. *My Love reaches to the heavens, My faithfulness to the skies*! This means you can never come to the end of My Love. It is limitless and everlasting. Moreover, you can stand on the Rock of My faithfulness, no matter what circumstances you may be facing.

People routinely put their confidence in their abilities, education, wealth, or appearance. But I urge you to place your confidence fully in Me—the Savior whose sacrificial death and miraculous resurrection opened the way for you into *eternal Glory*!

PSALM 145:18 NKJV; PSALM 36:5;
2 CORINTHIANS 4:17

WHEN SOME BASIC NEED IS LACKING—time, energy, money—consider yourself blessed. Your very lack is an opportunity to latch onto Me in unashamed dependence. When you begin a day with inadequate resources, you must concentrate your efforts on the present moment. This is where you are meant to live—in the present. It is the place where I always await you. Awareness of your inadequacy is a rich blessing, training you to rely wholeheartedly on Me.

The truth is that self-sufficiency is a myth perpetuated by pride and temporary success. Health and wealth can disappear instantly, as can life itself. Rejoice in your insufficiency, knowing that *My Power is made perfect in weakness.*

JAMES 1:2–3; 2 CORINTHIANS 12:9 NASB

*L*ET ME SATISFY YOU *in the morning with My unfailing Love, that you may sing for Joy and be glad all your days.* People seek satisfaction in a vast variety of hurtful ways, many of which are addicting. Even good things can fail to satisfy you if you elevate them above Me. So come to Me each morning with your emptiness and longings. Sit quietly in My Presence, communing with Me. Invite Me to fill you up to the full with My limitless Love. Ponder *how wide and long and high and deep* is this vast ocean of blessing.

Finding your satisfaction in Me above all else provides a firm foundation for your life. Building on this solid foundation enables you to be joyful and glad as you go through your days. You will still encounter hardships because you live in such a broken world. However, I will lovingly guide you along your way as you cling to Me in trust. Then your life will be meaningful and satisfying while you're traveling toward your ultimate goal: the gates of Glory!

PSALM 90:14; EPHESIANS 3:17–19;
PSALM 73:24 NKJV

May

Ascribe to the Lord the glory due his name;
worship the Lord in the splendor of his holiness.

PSALM 29:2

Y OU ARE ON THE PATH of My choosing. There is no randomness about your life. Here and Now comprise the coordinates of your daily life. Most people let their moments slip through their fingers, half-lived. They avoid the present by worrying about the future or longing for a better time and place. They forget that they are creatures who are subject to the limitations of time and space. They forget their Creator, who walks with them only in the present.

Every moment is alive with My glorious Presence, to those whose hearts are intimately connected with Mine. As you give yourself more and more to a life of constant communion with Me, you will find that you simply have no time for worry. Thus, you are freed to let My Spirit direct your steps, enabling you to walk along *the path of Peace.*

LUKE 12:25–26; JUDE vv. 24–25; LUKE 1:79

T HE PRESENT MOMENT is the point at which time intersects eternity. It is also the place where you can encounter *Me*—your eternal Savior. So keep your thoughts focused on the present as much as you can, enjoying My Presence here and now.

Invite Me into whatever you are engaged in. Ask Me to help you *do your work heartily*. Working collaboratively with Me lightens your load and enables you to be more effective. Share with Me not only your work but also your leisure—thanking Me for both. When something upsets you, don't let fearful or obsessive thoughts take over your mind. Instead, talk with Me about whatever is troubling you. Then *cast all your anxiety on Me*, knowing that *I care for you.*

If you ask, I will open your eyes and awaken your heart so you can see more fully all that the present contains. I delight in meeting with you in your wide-awake heart! *I came into the world so that you may have life in abundance—till it overflows.*

COLOSSIANS 3:23 NASB; 1 PETER 5:7;
JOHN 10:10 AMP

L IVING IN DEPENDENCE ON ME is the way to enjoy abundant life. You are learning to appreciate tough times because they amplify your awareness of My Presence. Tasks that you used to dread are becoming rich opportunities to enjoy My closeness. When you feel tired, you remember that I am your Strength; you take pleasure in leaning on Me. I am pleased by your tendency to turn to Me more and more frequently, especially when you are alone.

When you are with other people, you often lose sight of My Presence. Your fear of displeasing people puts you in bondage to them, and they become your primary focus. When you realize this has happened, whisper My Name; this tiny act of trust brings Me to the forefront of your consciousness, where I belong. As you bask in the blessing of My nearness, My life can flow through you to others. This is abundant life!

PSALM 18:1–2; PROVERBS 29:25;
JOHN 10:10 NKJV

T RUSTING ME is the alternative to falling into despair
or escaping into unreality. When you're in the midst of
adversity, it can be hard to think clearly. Yet this is when it's
vitally important to make wise decisions. Sometimes it's as
if choices are swirling around you, waiting for you to grab
onto the right one. However, there is *one* choice that is always
appropriate and always effective: the decision to *trust Me with
all your heart and mind.*

If you're on the verge of sliding into the depths of despair,
stop and declare your trust in Me. Whisper it, speak it, shout
it! Spend some time thinking about all the reasons you have
for *being confident in Me.* Remember and rejoice in My endless, *unfailing Love* for you.

If you've been numbing your pain through denial of
reality, expressing your trust can bring you into contact
with *ultimate* Reality—Me! Confide in Me, beloved, for I
am infinitely knowing. I understand everything about your
circumstances, and *I will help you.*

PROVERBS 3:5 AMP; PSALM 52:8;
ISAIAH 41:13

Y OU CANNOT SERVE TWO MASTERS. If I am truly your Master, you will desire to please Me above all others. If pleasing people is your goal, you will be enslaved to them. People can be harsh taskmasters when you give them this power over you.

If I am the Master of your life, I will also be your *First Love*. Your serving Me is rooted and grounded in My vast, unconditional Love for you. The lower you bow down before Me, the higher I lift you up into intimate relationship with Me. *The Joy of living in My Presence* outshines all other pleasures. I want you to reflect My joyous Light by living in increasing intimacy with Me.

MATTHEW 6:24; REVELATION 2:4;
EPHESIANS 3:16–17; PSALM 16:11

I T IS ONLY AS *I WORK* that anything really works well. When what you are doing is pleasing to Me, I come alongside you—helping in your endeavor. Sometimes you're aware of My empowering Presence, and at other times you are not. But the more you turn to Me for guidance and help, the more blessings I shower on you. Some of the blessings are work-oriented; others are matters of the heart. Awareness of My Presence increases your sense of security and fills you with Joy.

I am training you to look for Me wherever you are, in all situations. There will be times when you have to look *through* your circumstances to find signs of My radiant Presence. Imagine gazing through a dirty window into a gorgeous, sun-drenched garden. If you focus on the dirt that's on the glass, you'll miss the exquisite beauty of the garden. Just as you can train your eyes to see the splendor beyond the window, you can learn to look through your circumstances and "see" *My Face shining upon you*. Seek to find Me everywhere.

COLOSSIANS 1:29; ACTS 2:28;
NUMBERS 6:24–25 NKJV

M EET ME IN MORNING STILLNESS, while the earth is fresh with the dew of My Presence. *Worship Me in the beauty of holiness.* Sing love songs to My holy Name. As you give yourself to Me, My Spirit swells within you till you are flooded with divine Presence.

The world's way of pursuing riches is grasping and hoarding. You attain *My* riches by letting go and giving. The more you give yourself to Me and My ways, the more I fill you with *inexpressible, heavenly Joy.*

PSALM 29:2 NKJV; PSALM 9:10; 1 PETER 1:8

I KNOW ABOUT EVERY ONE of your troubles. *I have collected all your tears and preserved them in My bottle.* So don't be afraid of tears—or of the hardships that cause them. Your problems are not random or meaningless. I'm calling you to trust not only in Me but also in My sovereignty. I know what I am doing!

Because My perspective is infinite—unlimited by time or space—My ways of working in the world are often beyond your comprehension. If it were possible for you to see things from My God-perspective, you would understand the perfection of My will—and revel in My Glory. But now you see *only a poor reflection*, so you must learn to live with mystery.

I have collected your tears in My bottle because you are exceedingly precious to Me. And someday *I will wipe every tear from your eyes. There will be no more death or mourning or crying or pain.* Rejoice in this glorious, heavenly future awaiting you!

PSALM 56:8 TLB; 1 CORINTHIANS 13:12;
REVELATION 21:4

COME TO ME for all that you need. Come into My Presence with thanksgiving, for thankfulness opens the door to My treasures. When you are thankful, you affirm the central truth that I am Good. *I am Light, in whom there is no darkness at all.* The assurance that I am entirely Good meets your basic need for security. Your life is not subject to the whims of a sin-stained deity.

Relax in the knowledge that the One who controls your life is totally trustworthy. Come to Me with confident expectation. There is nothing you need that I cannot provide.

PSALM 95:2; 1 JOHN 1:5;
PSALM 19:7; HEBREWS 4:16 ESV

I WANT YOU TO LINGER IN GRATITUDE. This is a most delightful place—where the Joy of My Presence shines warmly upon you.

You often pray fervently for something until you receive the answer you desire. When I grant your request, you respond joyfully and thankfully. But your tendency is to move on rather quickly to the next matter. I want you to remain for a while in an attitude of grateful Joy. Instead of experiencing only a short-lived burst of gratitude, let this pleasure flow freely into the future by training yourself to recall what I have done. One way is to tell others about it. This blesses both them and you, and it pleases Me. Another way is to write down the prayer-answer someplace where you will see it again and again.

Keep bringing your gratitude to Me. This thankfulness will bless you doubly—with happy memories of answered prayer and with the delight of sharing Joy with Me.

PSALM 95:2 NKJV; 1 CORINTHIANS 15:57;
1 CHRONICLES 16:12 NKJV

DO NOT SEARCH FOR SECURITY in the world you inhabit. You tend to make mental checklists of things you need to do in order to gain control of your life. If only you could check everything off your list, you could relax and be at peace. But the more you work to accomplish that goal, the more things crop up on your list. The harder you try, the more frustrated you become.

There is a better way to find security in this life. Instead of scrutinizing your checklist, focus your attention on My Presence with you. This continual contact with Me will keep you in My Peace. Moreover, I will help you sort out what is important and what is not, what needs to be done now and what does not. *Fix your eyes not on what is seen* (your circumstances), *but on what is unseen* (My Presence).

HEBREWS 3:1; ISAIAH 26:3 NKJV;
2 CORINTHIANS 4:18

*T*HIS IS WHAT I SAY—*I who made you, who formed you in the womb, and who will help you: Do not be afraid.* I have always been involved in your life, even before you were born. Because you are Mine, purchased with My own blood, you can count on My promise to help you as you journey through this world. This is how you gain victory over fear: through trusting in My *ever-present help.*

The problem arises when you gaze too long into the future, trying to visualize and take control of those not-yet events. A future-focus can easily deteriorate into a problem-focus. Weeds of worry and fear spring up quickly in this sort of "soil." When you realize this has happened, turn away from your worries and back to the One who is lovingly present with you. Rejoice that I will *still* be with you when you arrive at each coming stage of your journey. Lean hard on My Presence, trusting Me to help you today—and *all the days of your life.*

ISAIAH 44:2; PSALM 46:1;
PSALM 23:6 AMP

I F YOU LEARN TO TRUST ME—really trust Me—with your whole being, then nothing can separate you from My Peace. Everything you endure can be put to good use by allowing it to train you in trusting Me. This is how you foil the works of evil, growing in grace through the very adversity that was meant to harm you. Joseph was a prime example of this divine reversal, declaring to his brothers: "*You meant evil against me, but God meant it for good.*"

Do not fear what this day, or any day, may bring your way. Concentrate on trusting Me and on doing what needs to be done. Relax in My sovereignty, remembering that I go before you, as well as with you, into each day. *Fear no evil*, for I can bring good out of every situation you will ever encounter.

ISAIAH 26:4; GENESIS 50:20 NASB; PSALM 23:4

Y ou are a child of God. Someday you will *see Me as I am*—you will be face to Face with Me in Glory. Until then, I am training you *to be made new in the attitude of your mind, to put on the new self.* Although your new self is being conformed to My image, this process doesn't erase the essence of who you are. Instead, the more you become *like Me*, the more you develop into the unique person I designed you to be.

You have been a member of My royal family since you first trusted Me as Savior. Thus you're a *fellow heir with Me—sharing My inheritance.* However, *you must share My suffering if you are to share My Glory.* When you encounter hard times, search for Me in the midst of your struggles. Ask Me to help you suffer well, in a manner worthy of the King's household. Everything you endure can help you become more like Me. Remember the ultimate goal: *You will see My Face in righteousness—and be satisfied*!

1 John 3:2 nkjv; Ephesians 4:22–24;
Romans 8:17 amp; Psalm 17:15 nkjv

May 8
MORNING

JESUS CALLING

D O NOT LONG FOR THE ABSENCE of problems in your life. That is an unrealistic goal since *in this world you will have trouble.* You have an eternity of problem-free living reserved for you in heaven. Rejoice in that inheritance, which no one can take away from you, but do not seek your heaven on earth.

Begin each day anticipating problems, asking Me to equip you for whatever difficulties you will encounter. The best equipping is My living Presence, *My hand that never lets go of yours.* Discuss everything with Me. Take a lighthearted view of trouble, seeing it as a challenge that you and I together can handle. Remember that I am on your side, and *I have overcome the world.*

JOHN 16:33; ISAIAH 41:13; PHILIPPIANS 4:13

I REDEEM YOU FROM HELL—*crowning you with Love and mercy; I wrap you in goodness and renew your youth.*

I give you these magnificent gifts because *I take pleasure in you.* Let My delight in you soak into the depths of your being—satisfying your soul. Although I see your sins and flaws, my perfect Love never wavers. I look on you first and foremost as My redeemed one, wearing *a paradise crown and wrapped in beauty eternal.*

I want your identity as My beloved to be front and center in your mind. However, your thoughts often get stuck on trivial matters, especially when your mind is in neutral. This is why I urge you to *be alert and always keep on praying.* Invite Me to enter into your circumstances—including your thoughts, feelings, and decisions. Communicating with Me will help you focus less on trivial matters and more on glorious realities. While you wait in My Presence, I will *renew your strength.* Regardless of how old you are, *you're always young in My Presence!*

PSALM 103:4–5 MSG; PSALM 149:4 NKJV;
EPHESIANS 6:18; ISAIAH 40:31

D ON'T BE SO HARD ON YOURSELF. I can bring good even out of your mistakes. Your finite mind tends to look backward, longing to undo decisions you have come to regret. This is a waste of time and energy, leading only to frustration. Instead of floundering in the past, release your mistakes to Me. Look to Me in trust, anticipating that My infinite creativity can weave both good choices and bad into a lovely design.

Because you are human, you will continue to make mistakes. Thinking that you should live an error-free life is symptomatic of pride. Your failures can be a source of blessing, humbling you and giving you empathy for other people in their weaknesses. Best of all, failure highlights your dependence on Me. I am able to bring beauty out of the morass of your mistakes. Trust Me, and watch to see what I will do.

ROMANS 8:28; PROVERBS 11:2; MICAH 7:7

I MEET YOU in the place of your deepest need. So come to Me just as you are, leaving pretense and performance behind. You are totally transparent to Me: I know everything about you. Yet because you are My own—redeemed by My blood—I have unlimited, unfailing Love for you.

Ask My Spirit to help you be honest and open with Me. Don't be ashamed of your neediness; instead, use it to connect with Me in humble dependence. Invite Me to have My way in your life. Remember that *I am the Potter, and you are the clay.* The weakness you bring Me is malleable in My hands, and I use it to mold you according to My will.

Your deepest need is to *lean on, trust in, and be confident in Me.* Accepting your lack of strength helps you lean on Me in unashamed dependence. I am training you to trust Me *with all your heart and mind*—a lifelong endeavor. And the best way to *not be afraid* is to have confidence in Me, *your Strength.*

1 PETER 1:18–19; ISAIAH 64:8;
PROVERBS 3:5 AMP; ISAIAH 12:2 NASB

D O NOT RESIST OR RUN from the difficulties in your life. These problems are not random mistakes; they are hand-tailored blessings designed for your benefit and growth. Embrace all the circumstances that I allow in your life, trusting Me to bring good out of them. View problems as opportunities to rely more fully on Me.

When you start to feel stressed, let those feelings alert you to your need for Me. Thus, your needs become doorways to deep dependence on Me and increasing intimacy between us. Although self-sufficiency is acclaimed in the world, reliance on Me produces abundant living in My kingdom. Thank Me for the difficulties in your life since they provide protection from the idolatry of self-reliance.

JOHN 15:5; 2 CORINTHIANS 1:8–9;
EPHESIANS 5:20

Y OUR CHOICES MATTER, BELOVED. They are a vital part of My transforming work in you. You make most of your choices alone—in the solitude of your heart and mind. But remember: I am *Christ in you*! I know every thought before you think it, every decision before you make it. Your realization that I'm aware of everything going on within you can protect you from careless, selfish living. Let your desire to *please Me*, the One who knows you so intimately, change the way you think and live.

You may have assumed that your choices are mostly insignificant, but this is not true. A good decision you make today, however small, may set you on a path to accomplish something very important. A bad decision, seemingly minor, can lead to serious failure or loss in the future. Though your choices do indeed matter, remember that *there is no condemnation for those who belong to Me*. I am able to see all your flaws and failures, yet simultaneously love you with glorious, *unfailing Love*.

COLOSSIANS 1:27; 1 THESSALONIANS 4:1 NLT;
ROMANS 8:1–2 ESV; PSALM 13:5

THANK ME FOR YOUR PROBLEMS. As soon as your mind gets snagged on a difficulty, bring it to Me with thanksgiving. Then ask Me to show you My way to handle the situation. The very act of thanking Me releases your mind from its negative focus. As you turn your attention to Me, the problem fades in significance and loses its power to trip you up. Together we can deal with the situation, either facing it head-on or putting it aside for later consideration.

Most of the situations that entangle your mind are not today's concerns; you have borrowed them from tomorrow. In this case, I lift the problem out of today and deposit it in the future, where it is veiled from your eyes. In its place I give you My Peace, which flows freely from My Presence.

PHILIPPIANS 4:6; PSALM 25:4–5; JOHN 14:27

I AM YOUR BROTHER and your Friend. I'm *the Firstborn among many brothers*; you are *being conformed to My likeness*. This is an astonishing privilege and blessing! Some children are blessed to have a strong, loving older brother who helps and protects them. *You* have an all-powerful Big Brother who is constantly looking out for your interests. Even the most committed family member or friend cannot be with you always, but I never leave your side. I am the *Friend who sticks closer than a brother.*

My continual Presence with you should never be taken for granted. Remember that your faithful Friend is also *King of kings*. If you could glimpse Me in all My Glory, you would understand why *John fell at My feet as though dead* when he saw Me. *I am the First and the Last—the Living One who was dead and is alive forever and ever!* I want you to relate to Me with reverence because I am your Savior-God. Remind yourself that the glorious gift of salvation is yours forever—and honor Me with gratitude.

ROMANS 8:29; PROVERBS 18:24 ESV;
REVELATION 17:14 NKJV; REVELATION 1:17–18

L EARN TO RELATE to others through My Love rather than yours. Your human love is ever so limited, full of flaws and manipulation. My loving Presence, which always enfolds you, is available to bless others as well as you. Instead of trying harder to help people through your own paltry supplies, become aware of My unlimited supply, which is accessible to you continually. Let My Love envelop your outreach to other people.

Many of My precious children have fallen prey to burnout. A better description of their condition might be "drainout." Countless interactions with needy people have drained them, without their conscious awareness. You are among these weary ones, who are like wounded soldiers needing R & R. Take time to rest in the Love-Light of My Presence. I will gradually restore to you the energy that you have lost over the years. *Come to Me, all you who are weary and burdened, and you will find rest for your souls.*

PSALM 36:5; EXODUS 33:14; MATTHEW 11:28–29

*P*RAISE ME FOR THE HELP *of My Presence.* At all times and in all circumstances, it's appropriate to pray: "Thank You, Jesus, for being *with me* here and now." You may not sense My Presence with you, but I have promised—and that is enough!

An important part of your assignment as a Christian is to trust that *I am with you always.* In faith, talk to Me about your thoughts and feelings, your struggles and pleasures. Believe that I care for you deeply and I hear all your prayers. Seek My help with confident anticipation. Be on the lookout for all the ways I am at work: in you and through you. Rejoice that you and I together can *do immeasurably more than all you ask or imagine. My Power is at work within you*—especially as it connects with your weakness offered up to Me for My purposes.

Remember that *nothing is impossible with Me,* and refuse to be intimidated by daunting circumstances. Praise Me for the help of My Presence!

PSALM 42:5 NASB; MATTHEW 28:20 NLT;
EPHESIANS 3:20; LUKE 1:37 ESV

May 13

T HANK ME IN THE MIDST of the crucible. When things seem all wrong, look for growth opportunities. Especially look for areas where you need to let go, leaving your cares in My able hands. Do you trust Me to orchestrate your life events as I choose, or are you still trying to make things go according to your will? If you keep trying to carry out your intentions while I am leading you in another direction, you deify your desires.

Be on the lookout for what I am doing in your life. Worship Me by living close to Me, *thanking Me in all circumstances.*

1 PETER 5:6–7; PSALM 62:8; 1 THESSALONIANS 5:18

*S*TOP JUDGING *by mere appearances, and make a right judgment.* I made this statement at the temple in Jerusalem, teaching that judging can be either good or bad. I was speaking to people who had assessed Me on the basis of appearances: focusing on the letter of the Law rather than the spirit of the Law. What they were doing was wrong, but that doesn't mean *all* judgments are wrong. I forbid superficial, self-righteous, and hypocritical evaluations. But I do want My followers to make *righteous* assessments about moral and theological issues—based on biblical truth.

In this age of "tolerance," there is immense pressure on people to refrain from making statements that differentiate right from wrong. The fear of being labeled "intolerant" has silenced many people who know how to make right judgments. I want you to have the courage to *speak the truth in love* as I lead you to do so. The best preparation is to search the Scriptures and your heart. Then ask My Spirit to speak through you even as He loves others through you.

JOHN 7:24; MATTHEW 7:1 AMP; EPHESIANS 4:15

I AM A MIGHTY GOD. *Nothing is too difficult for Me.* I have chosen to use weak ones like you to accomplish My purposes. Your weakness is designed to open you up to My Power. Therefore, do not fear your limitations or measure the day's demands against your strength. What I require of you is to stay connected to Me, living in trusting dependence on My limitless resources. When you face unexpected demands, there is no need to panic. Remember that *I am with you.* Talk with Me, and listen while I talk you through each challenging situation.

I am not a careless God. When I allow difficulties to come into your life, I equip you fully to handle them. Relax in My Presence, trusting in My Strength.

LUKE 1:37; DEUTERONOMY 31:8;
2 CORINTHIANS 12:9

I AM ABLE to keep you from stumbling. I know how weak you are, how easily you would lose your footing if I were not holding onto you. You are *growing in grace,* but complete freedom from sin will not be possible as long as you live in this fallen world. So you need My help continually.

I am able to *present you faultless*—blameless, perfect, unblemished—*before the Presence of My Glory* because *I have clothed you with garments of salvation and arrayed you in a robe of righteousness.* I want you to wear these royal raiments with confidence. You are absolutely secure because it is *My* righteousness that saves you, not yours.

Exceeding Joy is for you and for Me. I delight in you now, but this Joy will be immeasurably magnified when you join Me in Glory. The jubilation you will experience in heaven is indescribable—far beyond any pleasure you could know in this world. Nothing can rob you of this glorious *inheritance that can never perish, spoil, or fade*!

JUDE vv. 24–25 NKJV; 2 PETER 3:18;
ISAIAH 61:10; 1 PETER 1:3–4

S PENDING TIME alone with Me is essential for your well-being. It is not a luxury or an option; it is a necessity. Therefore, do not feel guilty about taking time to be with Me. Remember that Satan is *the accuser of believers.* He delights in heaping guilt feelings upon you, especially when you are enjoying My Presence. When you feel Satan's arrows of accusation, you are probably on the right track. Use your *shield of faith* to protect yourself from him. Talk with Me about what you are experiencing, and ask Me to show you the way forward. *Resist the devil, and he will flee from you. Come near to Me, and I will come near to you.*

REVELATION 12:10; EPHESIANS 6:16;
JAMES 4:7–8

As you seek Me, I encourage you to *rejoice and be glad in Me.* Take time to praise Me in psalms and song. Think about who I am: I dwell in *splendor, majesty, and beauty.* Then remember how I left the Glory of heaven and came into the world—so I could bring you into My kingdom of everlasting Life and Light. All of this helps you to *be joyful in Me, your Savior.* This Joy ushers you further into My holy Presence, helping you draw nearer to Me. And this nearness gives you even more reason to rejoice!

Being joyful blesses not only you but other people. Your family and friends will benefit from your gladness, which can rub off on them. You can also influence many beyond your inner circle. When My followers are joyful, unbelievers are more likely to be drawn to Me. Joy shines in stark contrast to your ever-darkening world, and some people will ask you about it. *Always be prepared to give an answer to everyone who asks you the reason for your hope.*

PSALM 70:4; PSALM 96:6 ESV;
HABAKKUK 3:18; 1 PETER 3:15

I AM YOUR LORD! Seek Me as Friend and Lover of your soul, but remember that I am also King of kings—sovereign over all. You can make some plans as you gaze into the day that stretches out before you. But you need to hold those plans tentatively, anticipating that I may have other ideas. The most important thing to determine is what to do right now. Instead of scanning the horizon of your life, looking for things that need to be done, concentrate on the task before you and the One who never leaves your side. Let everything else fade into the background. This will unclutter your mind, allowing Me to occupy more and more of your consciousness.

Trust Me to show you what to do when you have finished what you are doing now. I will guide you step by step as you bend your will to Mine. Thus you stay close to Me on the *path of Peace*.

REVELATION 17:14; PROVERBS 19:21; LUKE 1:79

WHEN YOU BEGIN A DAY—or a task—feeling inadequate, remember this: *My grace is sufficient for you.* The present tense of the verb "is" highlights the continual availability of My wondrous grace. So don't waste energy regretting how weak you feel. Instead, embrace your insufficiency—rejoicing that it helps you realize how much you need Me. Come to Me for help, and delight in My infinite sufficiency! *My Power is made perfect in weakness.*

As you go about a task in joyful dependence on Me, you will be surprised by how much you can accomplish. Moreover, the quality of your work will be greatly enhanced by your collaboration with Me. Ponder the astonishing privilege of living and working alongside Me, the *King of kings and Lord of lords.* Seek to align yourself with My will, making yourself a *living sacrifice.* This is a form of worship, and it pleases Me. It also makes your life meaningful and joyful. This is a tiny foretaste of the immense, indescribably glorious Joy that awaits you in heaven!

2 CORINTHIANS 12:9; REVELATION 19:16 NKJV;
ROMANS 12:1; JUDE v. 24 NKJV

A s you sit quietly in My Presence, remember that I am a God of abundance. I will never run out of resources; My capacity to bless you is unlimited. You live in a world of supply and demand, where necessary things are often scarce. Even if you personally have enough, you see poverty in the world around you. It is impossible for you to comprehend the lavishness of My provisions: the fullness of My *glorious riches*.

Through spending time in My Presence, you gain glimpses of My overflowing vastness. These glimpses are tiny foretastes of what you will experience eternally in heaven. Even now you have access to as much of Me as you have faith to receive. Rejoice in My abundance—*living by faith, not by sight*.

PHILIPPIANS 4:19; PHILIPPIANS 3:20–21;
2 CORINTHIANS 5:7

*C*AST YOUR CARES ON *ME, and I will sustain you.* Carrying your own burdens is wearing you out. Your shoulders were not designed for carrying heavy loads, so I want you to learn to cast your burdens on *Me.* The first step is to recognize that something is weighing you down. Next, examine the difficulty to determine whether it is yours or someone else's. If it isn't yours, simply let go of it and leave it behind. If it *is* your problem, talk with Me about it. I will help you see from My perspective, and I'll show you the way forward.

Be prepared to take action as needed, but don't let problems weigh you down by becoming your focus. Make a concerted effort to cast your cares on Me, for I have very strong shoulders! Then simply do the next thing—in joyful dependence on Me.

Be encouraged by My promise to sustain you—to hold you up and provide what you need. *I will supply all your needs according to My riches in Glory.*

PSALM 55:22; ISAIAH 9:6 NKJV;
PHILIPPIANS 4:19 NASB

COME TO ME with your plans held in abeyance. *Worship Me in spirit and in truth,* allowing My Glory to permeate your entire being. Trust Me enough to let Me guide you through this day, accomplishing My purposes in My timing. Subordinate your myriad plans to My Master Plan. I am sovereign over every aspect of your life!

The challenge continually before you is to trust Me and search for My way through each day. Do not blindly follow your habitual route, or you will miss what I have prepared for you. *As the heavens are higher than the earth, so are My ways higher than your ways and My thoughts than your thoughts.*

JOHN 4:24; ISAIAH 50:4; ISAIAH 55:8–9 NKJV

T O INCREASE YOUR AWARENESS of My Presence, you need to learn the art of self-forgetfulness. You were not designed to stay focused on yourself. However, Adam and Eve's disobedience in the Garden of Eden made selfishness the natural bent of mankind. This inclination is a deadly trap, but I have equipped you to live *supernaturally*. Since the moment you asked Me to be your Savior, you have had My Spirit living in you. Ask this Holy Helper to free you from self-centeredness. You may pray as often as you like: "Help me, Holy Spirit."

One thing that traps you in self-absorption is being overly concerned about how you look—in the mirror or in the eyes of others. Instead of making yourself the object of your thoughts, gaze at *Me* and be attentive to the people around you. Ask My Spirit to help you look beyond yourself with eyes that really see. You are safe in My *everlasting arms* and complete in My loving Presence. So turn your attention to trusting and loving Me.

GENESIS 3:6–7; ROMANS 8:9;
JOHN 15:26 NKJV; DEUTERONOMY 33:27

I WANT YOU TO KNOW how safe and secure you are in My Presence. That is a fact, totally independent of your feelings. You are on your way to heaven; nothing can prevent you from reaching that destination. There you will see Me face to Face, and your Joy will be off the charts by any earthly standards. Even now, you are never separated from Me, though you must see Me through eyes of faith. I will walk with you till the end of time and onward into eternity.

Although My Presence is a guaranteed promise, that does not necessarily change your feelings. When you forget I am with you, you may experience loneliness or fear. It is through awareness of My Presence that Peace displaces negative feelings. Practice the discipline of walking consciously with Me through each day.

JOHN 10:28–29; 1 CORINTHIANS 13:12;
PSALM 29:11

Look for Me in the hard places of your life. It's easy to find Me in answered prayer, in beauty and heartfelt Joy. But I am also tenderly present in difficulties. In fact, your problems are fertile soil for growing in grace and encountering My loving Presence in greater depth and breadth. So search for Me in dark times—both past and present. If you're plagued by painful memories and hurtful past experiences, look for *Me* in them. I know all about them, and I am ready to meet you there. Invite Me into those broken places, and cooperate with Me in putting the fragments back together in *new* ways.

If you are walking through tough times in the present, remember to cling to My hand. Against the dark backdrop of adversity, the Light of My Presence shines in transcendent radiance. This Light blesses you abundantly—providing both comfort and guidance. I will show you the way forward step by step. As you walk close to Me, I will draw you into deeper, richer intimacy with Me.

PSALM 139:11–12 NASB;
JOHN 1:5 AMP; PSALM 73:23–24

W HEN YOUR SINS WEIGH HEAVILY upon you, come to Me. Confess your wrongdoing, which I know all about before you say a word. Stay in the Light of My Presence, receiving forgiveness, cleansing, and healing. Remember that *I have clothed you in My righteousness,* so nothing can separate you from Me. Whenever you stumble or fall, I am there to help you up.

Man's tendency is to hide from his sin, seeking refuge in the darkness. There he indulges in self-pity, denial, self-righteousness, blaming, and hatred. But *I am the Light of the world,* and My illumination decimates the darkness. Come close to Me and let My Light envelop you, driving out darkness and permeating you with Peace.

1 JOHN 1:7; ISAIAH 61:10; JOHN 8:12

I AM THE GATE; whoever enters through Me will be saved. I am not a locked barrier but an open door for you—for all My chosen followers. I came into the world so that you might *have Life and have it to the full.*

A full life means different things for different people. So in your quest to live abundantly, don't compare your circumstances with those of others. You don't need as much money or as many luxuries as your neighbor in order to live well.

Godliness with contentment is great gain. I want you to be satisfied with My provision for you. *If you have food and clothing*—the basic necessities of life—seek to *be content with that.* If I give you more, respond with Joy and thankfulness. But don't cling to what you have or covet things you do not have. The only thing you can cling to without harming your soul is *Me.* No matter what you possess in this world, remember: Little (or much) + Me = everything!

JOHN 10:9–10; 1 TIMOTHY 6:6–8;
PSALM 63:8; JOHN 3:16 ESV

I, THE CREATOR OF THE UNIVERSE, am with you and for you. What more could you need? When you feel some lack, it is because you are not connecting with Me at a deep level. I offer abundant Life; your part is to trust Me, refusing to worry about anything.

It is not so much adverse events that make you anxious as it is your thoughts about those events. Your mind engages in efforts to take control of a situation, to bring about the result you desire. Your thoughts close in on the problem like ravenous wolves. Determined to make things go your way, you forget that I am in charge of your life. The only remedy is to switch your focus from the problem to My Presence. Stop all your striving, and watch to see what I will do. *I am the Lord!*

ROMANS 8:31–32; MICAH 7:7;
1 CORINTHIANS 12:3

TREASURE ME ABOVE ALL ELSE. This will infuse Joy into your heart and mind. It will also glorify Me! To treasure something is to hold or keep it, esteeming it as precious. I am training you to hold securely onto *Me*, your Savior-God and constant Companion. Knowing that I never leave your side can increase your Joy and Peace immeasurably. Also, esteeming Me as your precious Savior strengthens your desire to keep Me "in your sights" and live according to My will.

When you prize Me above all else, other things lose their grip on you. One way to discern what you hold dearest is to examine your thoughts when your mind is at rest. If you don't like what you find, do not despair—you can teach yourself to think about Me more consistently. It's helpful to memorize Scripture, especially verses that draw you closer to Me. Try putting reminders of My loving Presence throughout your home and workplace. And remember to seek the help of My Spirit; He delights in pointing you back to Me.

MATTHEW 13:44; PHILIPPIANS 3:8–9;
JOHN 14:26 NKJV; JOHN 16:14 NKJV

WHEN THINGS DON'T GO AS YOU would like, accept the situation immediately. If you indulge in feelings of regret, they can easily spill over the line into resentment. Remember that I am sovereign over your circumstances, and *humble yourself under My mighty hand.* Rejoice in what I am doing in your life, even though it is beyond your understanding.

I am the Way, the Truth, and the Life. In Me you have everything you need, both for this life and for the life yet to come. Don't let the impact of the world shatter your thinking or draw you away from focusing on Me. The ultimate challenge is to keep fixing your eyes on Me, no matter what is going on around you. When I am central in your thinking, you are able to view circumstances from My perspective.

1 PETER 5:5–6; JOHN 14:6

I WANT YOU TO KNOW the depth and breadth of *My Love that surpasses knowledge.* There is an enormous difference between knowing Me and knowing *about* Me. Similarly, experiencing My loving Presence is vastly different from knowing facts about My character. To experience My Presence, you need the empowering work of My Spirit. Ask Him to *strengthen you with Power in your inner being* so that you can *know My Love* in full measure.

Since the moment of your salvation, I have been alive in your heart. The more room you make for Me there, the more I can fill you with My Love. There are several ways to expand this space in your heart. It's crucial to take time with Me—enjoying My Presence and studying My Word. It is also vital to stay in communication with Me. As the apostle Paul wrote, *pray continually.* This joyful practice will keep you close to Me. Finally, let My Love flow through you to others—in both your words and your actions. This *makes My Love in you complete.*

EPHESIANS 3:16–19; ACTS 4:12 NASB;
1 THESSALONIANS 5:17; 1 JOHN 4:11–12

APPROACH EACH NEW DAY with desire to find Me. Before you get out of bed, I have already been working to prepare the path that will get you through this day. There are hidden treasures strategically placed along the way. Some of the treasures are trials, designed to shake you free from earth-shackles. Others are blessings that reveal My Presence: sunshine, flowers, birds, friendships, answered prayer. I have not abandoned this sin-wracked world; I am still richly present in it.

Search for deep treasure as you go through this day. You will find Me all along the way.

PROVERBS 16:9 AMP; COLOSSIANS 2:2–3;
ISAIAH 33:6

WHEN THE WAY JUST AHEAD OF YOU seems too difficult, turn to Me and say: "I can't, but *we* (You and I together) *can*." Acknowledging your inability to handle things on your own is a healthy dose of reality. However, this is only one part of the equation, because a sense of inadequacy by itself can be immobilizing. The most important part of the equation is recognizing My abiding Presence with you and My desire to help you.

Pour out your heart to Me. Ask Me to carry your burdens and show you the way forward. Don't waste energy worrying about things that are beyond your control. Instead, use that energy to connect with Me. *Seek My Face continually.* Be ready to follow wherever I lead, trusting Me to open up the way before you as you go.

Dare to see your inadequacy as a door to My Presence. View your journey as an adventure that you share with Me. Remain in close communication with Me, enjoying My company as we journey together.

PHILIPPIANS 4:13 NKJV; PSALM 62:8;
PSALM 105:4 NASB

B RING ME YOUR MIND for rest and renewal. Let Me infuse My Presence into your thoughts. As your mind stops racing, your body relaxes and you regain awareness of Me. This awareness is vital to your spiritual well-being; it is your lifeline, spiritually speaking.

There are actually more than four dimensions in this world where you live. In addition to the three dimensions of space and the one of time, there is the dimension of openness to My Presence. This dimension transcends the others, giving you glimpses of heaven while you still reside on earth. This was part of My original design for mankind. Adam and Eve used to walk with Me in the garden, before their expulsion from Eden. I want you to walk with Me in the garden of your heart, where I have taken up permanent residence.

GENESIS 3:8; PSALM 89:15; PROVERBS 4:23

THERE IS PEACE AND FULLNESS OF JOY in My loving Presence. Look for Me as you go through this day—I am eager to be found by you. I never lose sight of you; I watch over you continually. However, there are many ways you can lose sight of Me. Most of these are just temporary distractions, which abound in the world. The remedy is simple: Remind yourself that I am with you.

A much more serious problem is *forsaking your First Love.* If you realize this has happened, repent and run back to Me. Confess the idols that have drawn you away from Me. Take time to receive My forgiveness with thanksgiving. Collaborate with Me in rearranging your priorities—making Me first in your life. As you spend time in My Presence, think about who I Am: King of the universe, *Light of the world.* Bask in this *Light of Life* so that you can reflect Me to others. While you are delighting in Me, I fill you up with *Love, Joy, and Peace.*

PSALM 121:8 NLT; REVELATION 2:4;
JOHN 8:12; GALATIANS 5:22–23

THE WORLD IS TOO MUCH WITH YOU, My child. Your mind leaps from problem to problem to problem, tangling your thoughts in anxious knots. When you think like that, you leave Me out of your worldview and your mind becomes darkened. Though I yearn to help, I will not violate your freedom. I stand silently in the background of your mind, waiting for you to remember that I am with you.

When you turn from your problems to My Presence, your load is immediately lighter. Circumstances may not have changed, but we carry your burdens together. Your compulsion to "fix" everything gives way to deep, satisfying connection with Me. Together we can handle whatever this day brings.

ISAIAH 41:10; ZEPHANIAH 3:17; PSALM 34:19

THANK ME FOR ALL THE CHALLENGES in your life. They are gifts from Me—opportunities to grow stronger and more dependent on Me. Most people think that the stronger they get, the less dependent they will be. But in *My* kingdom, strength and dependence go hand in hand. This is because you were designed to walk close to Me as you journey through your life. Challenging circumstances highlight your neediness and help you rely on My infinite sufficiency.

When circumstances are tough and you rise to the occasion, trusting in Me, you are blessed. It's exhilarating to get through challenges that you thought were too much for you. When you do so in reliance on Me, our relationship grows stronger.

Your success in handling difficulties also increases your sense of security. You gain confidence that you and I *together* can cope with whatever hard times the future may bring. *You are ready for anything and equal to anything through the One who infuses inner strength into you.* Rejoice in My sufficiency!

JAMES 1:2 MSG; PSALM 31:14–16;
PHILIPPIANS 4:13 AMP

I N   A   W O R L D   O F   U N R E L E N T I N G   C H A N G E S, I am the One who never changes. *I am the Alpha and the Omega, the First and the Last, the Beginning and the End.* Find in Me the stability for which you have yearned.

I created a beautifully ordered world: one that reflects My perfection. Now, however, the world is under the bondage of sin and evil. Every person on the planet faces gaping jaws of uncertainty. The only antidote to this poisonous threat is drawing closer to Me. In My Presence you can face uncertainty with perfect Peace.

REVELATION 22:13; ROMANS 5:12; JOHN 16:33 AMP

I AM GOD, YOUR JOY *and your delight.* I want you to find pleasure in Me and in My Word. I am the ever-living Word: *in the beginning* and forevermore. So you can find Me richly present in My written Word, the Bible. As more and more Scripture soaks into your inner being, you will experience the delight of My Presence more consistently. Make time to meditate on Bible passages—and to memorize some of them. They will help you get through sleepless nights and encounters with adversity.

Knowing that I am *your Joy* can protect you from bemoaning your circumstances or envying others whose situations seem better than yours. Because I am always with you, you have an ever-present source of Joy in your life. You can find pleasure in Me by *rejoicing in My Name all day long.* Simply uttering "Jesus" as a prayer can lift your spirits. An excellent way to *delight greatly in Me* is to *exult in My righteousness,* which I have lovingly bestowed on you. This *robe of righteousness* covers you perfectly—forever!

PSALM 43:4; JOHN 1:1 NKJV;
PSALM 89:16; ISAIAH 61:10

S EEK MY FACE at the beginning of your day. This practice enables you to "put Me on" and "wear Me" throughout the day. Most people put on clothes soon after arising from bed. Similarly, the sooner you "put Me on" by communicating with Me, the better prepared you are for whatever comes your way.

To "wear Me" is essentially to have My mind: to think My thoughts. Ask the Holy Spirit to control your thinking; be transformed by this renewal within you. Thus you are well-equipped to face whatever people and situations I bring your way. Clothing your mind in Me is your best preparation for each day. This discipline brings Joy and Peace to you and those around you.

PSALM 27:8 NKJV; ROMANS 13:14;
1 CORINTHIANS 2:16; COLOSSIANS 3:12

*M*Y KINGDOM IS NOT OF THIS WORLD; it is indestructible and eternal. When you see shocking evil and mismanagement all around you, do not despair. As I was being arrested, I told My disciples that *I could call on My Father and He would send more than twelve legions of angels* to rescue Me. However, this was not the plan We had chosen. It was necessary for Me to be crucified—to save *everyone who calls on My Name.*

Remember that you are part of My kingdom of everlasting Life and Light. The darker your planet becomes, the more you need to cling to the hope you have in Me. Despite the way things look, I am in control, and I'm accomplishing My purposes in ways you cannot understand. Though this world is deeply fallen, it's possible to live in it with Joy and Peace in your heart. As I told My disciples, so I say to you now: *Be of good cheer; I have overcome the world.* Because you belong to My kingdom, *in Me you may have Peace.*

JOHN 18:36; MATTHEW 26:53;
ACTS 2:21; JOHN 16:33 NKJV

L ET ME ANOINT YOU with My Presence. *I am King of kings and Lord of lords, dwelling in unapproachable Light. When you draw near to Me, I respond by coming closer to you.* As My Presence envelops you, you may feel overwhelmed by My Power and Glory. This is a form of worship: sensing your smallness in comparison to My Greatness.

Man has tended to make himself the measure of all things. But man's measure is too tiny to comprehend My majestic vastness. That is why most people do not see Me at all, even though *they live and move and have their being in Me.*

Enjoy the radiant beauty of My Presence. Declare My glorious Being to the world!

1 TIMOTHY 6:15–16; JAMES 4:8;
ACTS 17:28; PSALM 145:3–6

I *AM* *THE* *VINE; you are* one of *the branches. Whoever lives in Me and I in him bears abundant fruit. Apart from Me—cut off from vital union with Me—you can do nothing.*

Ponder this glorious truth: I am alive within you! Just as sap flows from a vine through its branches, so My Life flows through you. I am infinite and perfect, yet I choose to live inside you. This intimacy you have with Me is wondrously rich. I read your every thought. I'm aware of all your feelings. I know how weak you are, and I stand ready to infuse you with My strength.

When you cooperate with My indwelling Presence, asking Me to be in control, you can produce abundant fruit. If you try to do things in your own strength, ignoring your vital union with Me, you're likely to fall flat on your face. Anything you *do* produce apart from Me will have no value in My kingdom. So nourish well your intimacy with Me, beloved. Delight in My Life-giving Presence!

JOHN 15:5 AMP; COLOSSIANS 1:27;
2 CORINTHIANS 12:9 NKJV; DEUTERONOMY 33:12

I AM WITH YOU, watching over you constantly. I am Immanuel (*God with you*); My Presence enfolds you in radiant Love. Nothing, including the brightest blessings and the darkest trials, can separate you from Me. Some of My children find Me more readily during dark times, when difficulties force them to depend on Me. Others feel closer to Me when their lives are filled with good things. They respond with thanksgiving and praise, thus opening wide the door to My Presence.

I know precisely what you need to draw nearer to Me. Go through each day looking for what I have prepared for you. Accept every event as My hand-tailored provision for your needs. When you view your life this way, the most reasonable response is to be thankful. Do not reject any of My gifts; find Me in every situation.

MATTHEW 1:23; PSALM 34:5; COLOSSIANS 2:6–7

THANK ME JOYFULLY for forgiving *all* your sins—past, present, and future; known and unknown. Forgiveness is your greatest need, and I have met that need perfectly—forever! I am *the eternal Life that was with the Father and has appeared to you.* Because you believe in Me as your Savior-God, you have *everlasting Life.* Let this amazing promise fill you with Joy and drive out fear of the future. Your future is glorious and secure: *an inheritance that can never perish, spoil, or fade—kept in heaven for you.* The best response to this priceless, infinite gift is gratitude!

The more frequently you thank Me, the more joyful your life will be. So be on the lookout for things that fuel your gratitude. The very act of thanking Me—in spoken or written word, in silent prayers, whispers, shouts, or songs of praise—increases your Joy and lifts you above your circumstances. A delightful way to express your adoration is reading psalms out loud. Rejoice in Me, My redeemed one, for *nothing can separate you from My Love.*

1 JOHN 1:2; JOHN 3:16 NKJV;
1 PETER 1:3–4; ROMANS 8:38–39

TIME WITH ME cannot be rushed. When you are in a hurry, your mind flitters back and forth between Me and the tasks ahead of you. Push back the demands pressing in on you; create a safe space around you, a haven in which you can rest with Me. I also desire this time of focused attention, and I use it to bless you, strengthening and equipping you for the day ahead. Thus, spending time with Me is a wise investment.

Bring Me the sacrifice of your precious time. This creates sacred space around you—space permeated with My Presence and My Peace.

PSALM 119:27; 2 CHRONICLES 16:9;
HEBREWS 13:15 NKJV

I AM GOD, AND YOU ARE *NOT*. This may sound harsh, but it's actually a blessed dose of reality. In the Garden of Eden, Satan tempted Eve with the very same desire that had caused him to fall from heaven: to *be like God*, usurping My divine position. Eve succumbed to this temptation, as did Adam. Since that time, the sin-nature in people prompts them to act as if they are God—trying to control everything, judging Me when circumstances don't go as they'd like.

Remembering you are *not* God helps you live in freedom. You don't take responsibility for matters that are beyond your control—which includes *most* matters. If you let go of everything that is not your responsibility, you are freed from carrying unnecessary burdens. And you can be more effective in areas where you *do* have some control. Moreover, you can pray about all your concerns, trusting in My sovereignty. Bring Me your *prayers with thanksgiving; present your requests to Me.* Living this way will shield you from anxiety and bless you with *Peace that transcends all understanding.*

LUKE 10:18 NKJV;
GENESIS 3:5 NKJV; PHILIPPIANS 4:6–7

T HE PEACE THAT I GIVE YOU transcends your intellect. When most of your mental energy goes into efforts to figure things out, you are unable to receive this glorious gift. I look into your mind and see thoughts spinning round and round: going nowhere, accomplishing nothing. All the while, My Peace hovers over you, searching for a place to land.

Be still in My Presence, inviting Me to control your thoughts. Let My Light soak into your mind and heart until you are aglow with My very Being. This is the most effective way to receive My Peace.

2 THESSALONIANS 3:16; ZECHARIAH 2:13;
JOB 22:21

*C*ONTINUE TO LIVE IN ME, *rooted and built up in Me—and overflowing with thankfulness.* The relationship you have with Me is unlike any other. You live in Me, and I live in you. You never go anywhere without Me! This amazing degree of connectedness with Me provides a rock-solid foundation for your life. I want you to continue building on this foundation—living in joyful awareness of My Presence.

Thankfulness provides some of the most important building blocks for your life. The more of these blocks you use as you build, the better your life-experience will be. Thankfulness enlarges the capacity of your heart for abundant Joy. It also helps you endure suffering without falling into despair or self-pity. No matter what is happening, you can always thank Me for your eternal salvation and *My unfailing Love.* These are constant, unchangeable blessings. Other blessings—such as your relationships, your finances, your health—may change quite frequently. I encourage you to count *both* types of blessings until you overflow with thankfulness!

COLOSSIANS 2:6–7;
COLOSSIANS 1:27 NKJV; PSALM 13:5–6

June

*"For I am the LORD, your God, who
takes hold of your right hand and says
to you, Do not fear; I will help you."*

ISAIAH 41:13

June 1

I AM INVOLVED in each moment of your life. I have carefully mapped out every inch of your journey through this day, even though much of it may feel haphazard. Because the world is in a fallen condition, things always seem to be unraveling around the edges. Expect to find trouble in this day. At the same time, trust that *My way is perfect*, even in the midst of such messy imperfection.

Stay conscious of Me as you go through this day, remembering that I never leave your side. Let the Holy Spirit guide you step by step, protecting you from unnecessary trials and equipping you to get through whatever must be endured. As you trudge through the sludge of this fallen world, keep your mind in heavenly places with Me. Thus the Light of My Presence shines on you, giving you Peace and Joy that circumstances cannot touch.

PSALM 18:30; ISAIAH 41:13; PSALM 36:9

I APPROVE OF YOU, MY CHILD. Because you are Mine—adopted into My royal family—I see you through eyes of grace. *I chose you before the creation of the world to be holy and blameless in My sight.* I know you fall short of this perfect standard in your daily living. But I *view* you as holy and blameless because this is your permanent position in My kingdom. Of course, I don't endorse everything you do (or fail to do). Still, I approve of *you*—your true self, the one I created you to be.

I know how much you long for My affirmation—and how hard it is for you to accept it. I want you to learn to see yourself and others through grace-vision. Looking through eyes of grace, you can focus more on what is good and right than on what is bad and wrong. You learn to cooperate with Me and embrace what I'm doing in your life: *transforming you into My likeness with ever-increasing Glory.* I not only *approve* of you, I *delight* in you!

EPHESIANS 1:4; PHILIPPIANS 4:8 NCV;
2 CORINTHIANS 3:18; PSALM 149:4 NLT

Relax in My healing, holy Presence. *Be still* while I transform your heart and mind. *Let go* of cares and worries so that you can receive My Peace. *Cease striving, and know that I am God.*

Do not be like Pharisees who multiplied regulations, creating their own form of "godliness." They got so wrapped up in their own rules that they lost sight of Me. Even today, man-made rules about how to live the Christian life enslave many people. Their focus is on their performance, rather than on Me.

It is through knowing Me intimately that you become like Me. This requires spending time alone with Me. *Let go, relax, be still, and know that I am God.*

PSALM 46:10 NASB; MATTHEW 23:13; 1 JOHN 3:2

*F*IX YOUR EYES *not on what is seen but on what is unseen.* You spend too much time and mental energy thinking about trivial things—surface matters that have no value in My kingdom. The sense of sight is a wondrous gift from Me, but it can become a source of bondage if misused. You have such easy access to mirrors shining your reflection back to you in glaring accuracy. This, in conjunction with media images of people who look perfect, makes it tempting to be overly focused on your appearance. The same can be true of your home or family. This focus on appearances distracts you from the soul-satisfying pleasures of knowing Me.

When you seek *Me*, you enjoy the company of the only perfect Person who ever existed. However, My perfection was not in My appearance but in My divine, sinless character. I am the One who can love you with *unfailing Love* and give you *perfect Peace.* So don't waste time thinking about trivialities. Instead, *fix your thoughts on Me* and receive My Peace.

2 CORINTHIANS 4:18; PSALM 36:7;
ISAIAH 26:3 NLT

I WANT TO BE CENTRAL in your entire being. When your focus is firmly on Me, My Peace displaces fears and worries. They will encircle you, seeking entrance, so you must stay alert. Let trust and thankfulness stand guard, turning back fear before it can gain a foothold. *There is no fear in My Love*, which shines on you continually. Sit quietly in My Love-Light while I bless you with radiant Peace. Turn your whole being to trusting and loving Me.

2 THESSALONIANS 3:16; 1 JOHN 4:18;
NUMBERS 6:25–26 NKJV

I INVITE YOU TO GAZE UPON *My beauty and to seek Me* more and more. This is a most delightful invitation! You can get glimpses of My loveliness in the wonders of nature, but these are only tiny, weak reflections of My massive Glory. The best is indeed yet to come—when you will see Me face to Face in heaven. For now, gazing upon My beauty requires focusing on My unseen Presence through prayer and meditating on My Word.

Foundational to your search for Me is remembering that I am continually with you. I am always attuned to you, and I am training you to be increasingly aware of Me. Place reminders of My Presence in your home, car, and office. Whisper My Name to remind you of My nearness. Sing praises to Me. Read or recite Scripture passages out loud. Find others who desire to know Me more fully, and share this glorious quest with them. *Seek Me, and require Me as a vital necessity; search for Me with all your heart.*

PSALM 27:4; 1 CORINTHIANS 13:12;
JEREMIAH 29:13 AMP

WELCOME CHALLENGING TIMES as opportunities to trust Me. You have Me beside you and My Spirit within you, so no set of circumstances is too much for you to handle. When the path before you is dotted with difficulties, beware of measuring your strength against those challenges. That calculation is certain to riddle you with anxiety. Without Me, you wouldn't make it past the first hurdle!

The way to walk through demanding days is to grip My hand tightly and stay in close communication with Me. Let your thoughts and spoken words be richly flavored with trust and thankfulness. Regardless of the day's problems, *I can keep you in perfect Peace* as you stay close to Me.

JAMES 1:2; PHILIPPIANS 4:13 NKJV;
ISAIAH 26:3

I AM YOUR JOY! Let these words reverberate in your mind and sink into your innermost being. I—your Companion who *will never leave you*—am a boundless source of Joy. If you really believe this, you can rest in the truth that every day of your life is a good day. So refuse to use the label "a bad day," even when you're struggling deeply. Your circumstances may indeed be very hard, but I am nonetheless with you, *holding you by your right hand*. There is good to be found in this day—and every day—because of My constant Presence and steadfast Love.

You may not be rich by worldly standards, but *My unfailing Love is priceless!* This Love guarantees that you can *find refuge in the shadow of My wings* no matter what is happening. Also, it gives you access to *My river of delights*. When your world feels anything but delightful, turn to Me and drink deeply from this ravishing river: My loving Presence. *I am your Joy!*

DEUTERONOMY 31:8; PSALM 73:23 NKJV;
PSALM 36:7–8

REMEMBER THAT YOU LIVE IN a fallen world: an abnormal world tainted by sin. Much frustration and failure result from your seeking perfection in this life. There is nothing perfect in this world except Me. That is why closeness to Me satisfies deep yearnings and fills you with Joy.

I have planted longing for perfection in every human heart. This is a good desire, which I alone can fulfill. But most people seek this fulfillment in other people and earthly pleasures or achievements. Thus they create idols, before which they bow down. *I will have no other gods before Me!* Make Me the deepest desire of your heart. Let Me fulfill your yearning for perfection.

ROMANS 8:22; EXODUS 20:3; PSALM 37:4

D O W H A T Y O U C A N, and leave the rest to Me. When you're embroiled in a difficult situation, *pour out your heart to Me*, knowing that I listen and I care. Rely on Me, your *ever-present Help in trouble*. Refuse to let your problem become your main focus, no matter how anxious you are to solve it. When you've done all you can for the time being, the best thing is simply to wait—finding refreshment in My Presence. Don't fall for the lie that you can't enjoy life until the problem has been resolved. *In the world you have trouble*, but *in Me you may have Peace*—even in the midst of the mess!

Your relationship with Me is collaborative: you and I working together. Look to Me for help and guidance, doing whatever you can and trusting Me to do what you cannot do. Instead of trying to force things to a premature conclusion, relax and ask Me to *show you the way you should go*—in *My* timing. Hold My hand in confident trust, beloved, and enjoy the journey in My Presence.

PSALM 62:8; PSALM 46:1; JOHN 16:33 NET;
PSALM 143:8

S EEK MY FACE, and you will find fulfillment of your deepest longings. My world is filled with beautiful things; they are meant to be pointers to Me, reminders of My abiding Presence. The earth still declares My Glory to those who have eyes that see and ears that hear.

You had a darkened mind before you sought Me wholeheartedly. I chose to pour My Light into you so that you can be a beacon to others. There is no room for pride in this position. Your part is to reflect *My* Glory. I am the Lord!

PSALM 105:4; PSALM 19:1–2; ISAIAH 60:2

NURTURE WELL YOUR THANKFULNESS, for it is the royal road to Joy! In fact, no pleasure is really complete without expressing gratitude for it. It's good to thank the people through whom you receive blessings, but remember that I am *God from whom all blessings flow*. So praise and thank *Me* frequently each day. This nurtures your soul and completes your Joy. It also enhances your relationship with Me, providing an easy way for you to draw near Me.

As My cherished follower, you have received the glorious gift of grace—unearned, undeserved favor. No one and no set of circumstances can strip you of this lavish gift. You belong to Me forever! *Nothing in all creation will be able to separate you from My Love.*

When you awaken each morning, say, "Thank You, Jesus, for the gift of this new day." As you journey through the day, be on the lookout for blessings and pleasures I scatter along your path. The greatest treasure is My Presence with you, for I am the *indescribable Gift!*

PSALM 95:2 AMP; EPHESIANS 2:8–9;
ROMANS 8:38–39; 2 CORINTHIANS 9:15 NKJV

I AM ALL AROUND YOU, like a cocoon of Light. My Presence with you is a promise, independent of your awareness of Me. Many things can block this awareness, but the major culprit is worry. My children tend to accept worry as an inescapable fact of life. However, worry is a form of unbelief; it is anathema to Me.

Who is in charge of your life? If it is you, then you have good reason to worry. But since I am in charge, worry is both unnecessary and counterproductive. When you start to feel anxious about something, relinquish the situation to Me. Back off a bit, redirecting your focus to Me. I will either take care of the problem Myself or show you how to handle it. In this world you will have problems, but you need not lose sight of Me.

LUKE 12:22–31; JOHN 16:33

I F YOU HAVE *ME*—your Savior, Lord, and Friend— you have everything that really matters. You may not have riches, fame, or success, but don't let that discourage you. As I said to My disciples, *"What do you benefit if you gain the whole world but lose your own soul?"* Nothing can be compared with the priceless treasure of eternal Life! Consider *a jewel merchant on the hunt for excellent pearls. When he found one that was flawless, he sold everything and bought it.* My kingdom is like that: of inestimable worth! So learn to be content with having *Me*, beloved, regardless of what you may lack in this world.

The source of much discontentment is comparing oneself with others. I want you to make every effort to avoid this deadly trap. Remember that you are My unique creation— redeemed by My blood and exquisitely precious to Me. Stay in joyful communication with Me, the Savior who loves you immeasurably more than you can imagine. I will transform you more and more into the *masterpiece* I designed you to be.

MATTHEW 16:26 NLT; MATTHEW 13:45–46 MSG;
1 TIMOTHY 6:6; EPHESIANS 2:10 NLT

I WANT YOU TO BE ALL MINE, filled with the Light of My Presence. I gave everything for you by living as a man, then dying for your sins and living again. Hold back nothing from Me. Bring your most secret thoughts into the Light of My Love. Anything you bring to Me I transform and cleanse from darkness. I know everything about you, far more than you know of yourself. But I restrain My yearning to "fix" you, waiting instead for you to come to Me for help. Imagine the divine restraint this requires, for *I have all Power in heaven and on earth.*

Seek My Face with a teachable spirit. Come into My Presence with thanksgiving, desiring to be transformed.

JOHN 12:46 NKJV; PSALM 90:8;
MATTHEW 28:18; PSALM 100:4

M Y LOVE HAS CONQUERED YOU and *set you free*! The Power of My Love is so great that it has enslaved you to Me. *You are not your own. You were bought at a price*—My holy blood. The more you love Me, the more you will want to serve Me with every fiber of your being. This service can fill you with heavenly Joy as you yield yourself to Me more fully.

Because I am perfect in all My ways, you can give yourself wholeheartedly to Me without fear that I might take advantage of you. On the contrary, being conquered by Me is what makes you truly free. I have invaded the innermost core of your being, and My Spirit within you is taking over more and more territory. *Where the Spirit of the Lord is, there is freedom.* I want you *to reflect My Glory* to others, for I am *transforming you into My likeness with ever-increasing Glory.* Rejoice in the freedom you have found in Me, and surrender gladly to My victorious Love!

ROMANS 6:18 NKJV; 1 CORINTHIANS 6:19–20;
2 CORINTHIANS 3:17–18

S EEK TO LIVE IN MY LOVE, which *covers a multitude of sins*: both yours and others'. Wear My Love like a cloak of Light, covering you from head to toe. Have no fear, for *perfect Love decimates fear*. Look at other people through lenses of Love; see them from My perspective. This is how you walk in the Light, and it pleases Me.

I want My body of believers to be radiant with the Light of My Presence. How I grieve when pockets of darkness increasingly dim the Love-Light. Return to Me, your *First Love*! Gaze at Me in the splendor of holiness, and My Love will once again envelop you in Light.

1 PETER 4:8; 1 JOHN 4:18; REVELATION 2:4

*A*PART FROM *ME you can do nothing.* On days when the tasks before you seem overwhelming, remember this: I am with you, ready to help. Take a moment to rest in My loving Presence. Whisper: *"Surely the LORD is in this place."* Relax, knowing that you're not meant to be self-sufficient. I designed you to need Me and depend on Me. So *come to Me* just as you are—without shame or pretense. Talk with Me about the challenges you face and the inadequacy you feel. Entreat Me to show you the way forward. Instead of rushing ahead, take small steps of trust, staying in communication with Me.

I am the Vine; you are one of My branches. As you stay connected to Me, My Life flows through you, enabling you to *bear much fruit.* Don't worry about being successful in the eyes of the world. Bearing fruit in My kingdom means *doing the good things planned for you long ago.* So live close to Me— ready to do My will—and I will open up the way before you.

JOHN 15:5 NASB; GENESIS 28:16;
MATTHEW 11:28–29; EPHESIANS 2:10 NLT

REST IN ME, MY CHILD. Give your mind a break from planning and trying to anticipate what will happen. *Pray continually*, asking My Spirit to take charge of the details of this day. Remember that you are on a journey with Me. When you try to peer into the future and plan for every possibility, you ignore your constant Companion, who sustains you moment by moment. As you gaze anxiously into the distance, you don't even feel the strong grip of My hand holding yours. How foolish you are, My child!

Remembrance of Me is a daily discipline. Never lose sight of My Presence with you. This will keep you resting in Me all day, every day.

1 THESSALONIANS 5:17;
PSALM 139:9–10 NKJV; PSALM 62:5

R ECEIVE MY *GLORY-STRENGTH*. When ongoing problems require you to *stick it out over the long haul*, beware of responding by grimly *gritting your teeth*—just passing time in a gloomy frame of mind. This passive, negative attitude is *not* the way I want you to approach difficulties.

I am sovereign over the circumstances of your life, so there are always opportunities to be found in them. Don't be like the man who *hid his master's talent in the ground* because he was disgruntled with his circumstances. He gave up and took the easy way out, blaming his hard situation rather than making the most of his opportunity. Actually, the more difficult your circumstance, the more you can gain through it.

I gladly give you Glory-strength. It is exceedingly potent because the Spirit Himself empowers you—*strengthening you in your inner being*. Moreover, My limitless Glory-strength enables you to keep on *enduring the unendurable*. Since this Power is so vast, there is more than enough of it to *spill over into Joy*!

COLOSSIANS 1:11 MSG; ISAIAH 40:10;
MATTHEW 25:25 NKJV; EPHESIANS 3:16

T RUST ME *and don't be afraid, for I am your Strength and Song.* Do not let fear dissipate your energy. Instead, invest your energy in trusting Me and singing My Song. The battle for control of your mind is fierce, and years of worry have made you vulnerable to the enemy. Therefore, you need to be vigilant in guarding your thoughts. Do not despise this weakness in yourself since I am using it to draw you closer to Me. Your constant need for Me creates an intimacy that is well worth all the effort. You are not alone in this struggle for your mind. My Spirit living within you is ever ready to help in this striving. Ask Him to *control your mind*; He will bless you with *Life and Peace.*

ISAIAH 12:2; ROMANS 8:9; ROMANS 8:6

*M*Y PRESENCE WILL GO WITH YOU, *and I will give you rest.* Wherever you are, wherever you go, I am with you! This is an astonishing statement, yet it is true. My unseen Presence is more *real* than the flesh-and-blood people around you. But you must "see" Me with the eyes of your heart and communicate with Me through prayer, trusting that I really do hear and care.

I assure you that your prayers make a difference, though not always in ways you can see or in the timeframe you desire. I factor the prayers of believers into My sovereign governing of your world—in ways far too complex for finite minds to grasp. Remember: *As the heavens are higher than the earth, so are My ways and thoughts higher than yours.*

Since My methods of working in the world are often mysterious, it's important to take time to *be still and know that I am God.* Sit quietly in My Presence, breathing in My Peace, and I will give you rest.

EXODUS 33:14; ISAIAH 55:8–9 NKJV;
PSALM 46:10 NKJV; PSALM 29:11

L ET ME HELP YOU get through this day. There are many possible paths to travel between your getting up in the morning and your lying down at night. Stay alert to the many choice-points along the way, being continually aware of My Presence. You will get through this day one way or the other. One way is to moan and groan, stumbling along with shuffling feet. This will get you to the end of the day eventually, but there is a better way. You can choose to walk with Me along the path of Peace, leaning on Me as much as you need. There will still be difficulties along the way, but you can face them confidently in My strength. Thank Me for each problem you encounter, and watch to see how I transform trials into blessings.

1 CORINTHIANS 10:10; LUKE 1:79;
2 SAMUEL 22:29–30

*I*F *I AM FOR YOU, who can be against you?* Beloved, I most assuredly *am* for you since you are My follower. Of course, this doesn't mean that no one will ever oppose you. It means that having Me on your side is the most important fact of your existence. Regardless of what happens in your life, you are on the winning side! I already won the victory through My death and resurrection. I am the eternal Victor, and you share in My triumph—no matter how much adversity you encounter on your journey to heaven. Ultimately, nothing and no one can prevail against you because you belong to Me forever.

Knowing that your future is utterly secure can change your perspective dramatically. Instead of living in defensive mode—trying desperately to protect yourself from suffering—you learn to follow Me boldly, wherever I lead. I am training you not only to *seek My Face* and follow My lead but to enjoy this adventure of abandoning yourself to Me. Remember: I am your *ever-present Help in trouble*.

ROMANS 8:31; PSALM 27:8 NKJV; PSALM 46:1

I AM CREATING something new in you: a bubbling spring of Joy that spills over into others' lives. Do not mistake this Joy for your own or try to take credit for it in any way. Instead, watch in delight as My Spirit flows through you to bless others. Let yourself become a reservoir of the Spirit's fruit.

Your part is to live close to Me, open to all that I am doing in you. Don't try to control the streaming of My Spirit through you. Just keep focusing on Me as we walk through this day together. Enjoy My Presence, which permeates you with *Love, Joy, and Peace.*

JOHN 3:8; PROVERBS 4:11–12; GALATIANS 5:22

L ET MY PEACE PROTECT your mind and heart. Remember that *I am near*, and *rejoice* in My abiding Presence. Spend ample time with Me, *presenting your requests to Me with thanksgiving*. This is the way to receive *My Peace that transcends understanding*. This is how I *guard your heart and your mind*. It's a collaborative, you-and-I-together effort. You never face anything alone!

For Christians, aloneness is an illusion—a dangerous one that can lead to depression or self-pity. The devil and his underlings work hard to cloud your awareness of My Presence. It's crucial for you to recognize and resist their attacks. Fight back with My powerful Word, which is *living and active*. Read it; ponder it; memorize it; speak it.

Even if you're feeling alone, you can talk freely with Me—trusting that *I am with you always*. The longer you communicate with Me, the more convinced you'll become of My nearness. *Resist the devil, and he will flee from you. Come close to Me, and I will come close to you.*

PHILIPPIANS 4:4–7; HEBREWS 4:12 NASB;
MATTHEW 28:20; JAMES 4:7–8 NLT

I HAVE LOVED YOU *with an everlasting Love.* Before time began, I knew you. For years you swam around in a sea of meaninglessness, searching for Love, hoping for hope. All that time I was pursuing you, aching to embrace you in My compassionate arms.

When time was right, I revealed Myself to you. I lifted you out of that sea of despair and set you down on a firm foundation. Sometimes you felt naked—exposed to the revealing Light of My Presence. I wrapped an ermine robe around you: *My robe of righteousness.* I sang you a Love song, whose beginning and end are veiled in eternity. I infused meaning into your mind and harmony into your heart. Join Me in singing My song. Together we will draw others *out of darkness into My marvelous Light.*

JEREMIAH 31:3; ISAIAH 61:10; 1 PETER 2:9 NKJV

*L*OVE IS PATIENT. Notice that the very first adjective the apostle Paul uses to describe love is "patient." I treasure this quality in My followers, even though it is not highly visible in most twenty-first-century depictions of love.

Patient people can stay calm while enduring lengthy waits or dealing with difficult people and problems. I encourage you to examine your own life: to see how you respond to waiting and difficulties. This will give you a good measure of how patient—how loving—you are.

"Patience" is listed fourth in *the fruit of the Spirit*. My Spirit will help you grow in this important character trait, especially as you ask Him. Some Christians are afraid to pray for patience. They fear that I'll answer their prayer by subjecting them to severe suffering and trials. However, suffering serves an important purpose in My kingdom, and trials are not optional. They *come so that your faith may be proved genuine and may result in praise, glory, and honor* to Me!

1 CORINTHIANS 13:4;
GALATIANS 5:22–23 NASB; 1 PETER 1:6–7

WHEN YOU APPROACH ME in stillness and in trust, you are strengthened. You need a buffer zone of silence around you in order to *focus on things that are unseen.* Since I am invisible, you must not let your senses dominate your thinking. The curse of this age is overstimulation of the senses, which blocks out awareness of the unseen world.

The tangible world still reflects My Glory to those who have eyes that see and ears that hear. Spending time alone with Me is the best way to develop seeing eyes and hearing ears. The goal is to be aware of unseen things even as you live out your life in the visible world.

2 CORINTHIANS 4:18; ISAIAH 6:3;
PSALM 119:18 NKJV; PSALM 130:5

COME TO ME, BELOVED. I continually invite you to draw near Me. Be still in My Presence, and *fix your thoughts on Me.* Relax and listen to My Love whispering in your heart: *"I have loved you with an everlasting Love."* Meditate on the glorious truth that *I am with you always.* You can build your life on this rock-solid reality!

The world you inhabit is constantly in flux—you will find no solid ground there. So I challenge you to remain aware of *Me* as you go about your day. You won't be able to do this perfectly, but I'll help you when you ask. You can pray: "Jesus, keep me aware of Your Presence." Let these words echo through your heart and mind frequently. Though your thoughts will sometimes go elsewhere, this simple prayer can draw you back to Me.

The more of Me you have in your life—through staying close to Me—the more joyful you will be and the more I can bless others through you.

HEBREWS 3:1; JEREMIAH 31:3 NKJV;
MATTHEW 28:19–20

STAY ON THE HIGH ROAD WITH ME. Many voices clamor for your attention, trying to divert you to another path. But I have called you to walk ever so closely with Me, soaking in My Presence, living in My Peace. This is My unique design for you, planned before the world began.

I have called each of My children to a different path, distinctly designed for that one. Do not let anyone convince you that his path is the only right way. And be careful not to extol your path as superior to another's way. What I require of you is *to act justly, to love mercy, and to walk humbly with Me—*wherever I lead.

JOHN 14:27 NKJV; EPHESIANS 2:10;
MICAH 6:8

I HAVE GOOD INTENTIONS FOR YOU. They may be radically different from what you hoped or expected, but they are nonetheless good. *I am Light; in Me there is no darkness at all.* So look for My Light in all your circumstances. I am abundantly present in your moments. Your assignment is to be open to Me and My ways with you. Sometimes this requires relinquishing things you had planned or dreamed. You need to remember and wholeheartedly believe that *My way is perfect*, no matter how hard it is.

I am a shield for all who take refuge in Me. When you're feeling afflicted or afraid, come to Me and say: "Lord, I take refuge in *You*." I don't shield you from things I intend for you to deal with, for you have an important part to play in this world. However, I protect you from more dangers and troubles than you can imagine. So make every effort to *live the life I have assigned to you*. Do this in joyful dependence on Me, and *your soul will be richly satisfied*.

1 JOHN 1:5 NASB; PSALM 18:30;
1 CORINTHIANS 7:17 ESV; PSALM 63:5

June 17

L EARN TO LAUGH at yourself more freely. Don't take yourself or your circumstances so seriously. Relax and know that I am *God with you*. When you desire My will above all else, life becomes much less threatening. Stop trying to monitor My responsibilities—things that are beyond your control. Find freedom by accepting the boundaries of your domain.

Laughter lightens your load and lifts your heart into heavenly places. Your laughter rises to heaven and blends with angelic melodies of praise. Just as parents delight in the laughter of their children, so I delight in hearing My children laugh. I rejoice when you trust Me enough to enjoy your life lightheartedly.

Do not miss the Joy of My Presence by carrying the weight of the world on your shoulders. Rather, *take My yoke upon you and learn from Me. My yoke is comfortable and pleasant; My burden is light and easily borne.*

PROVERBS 17:22; PROVERBS 31:25;
MATTHEW 1:23; MATTHEW 11:29–30 AMP

S EEK TO BECOME increasingly receptive and responsive to Me. I am always actively involved in your life.
Instead of trying to force Me to do what you want, *when* you
want it, relax and look for what I'm already doing. Live in a
receptive mode—waiting for Me, trusting in My timing. *I am
good to those who wait hopefully and expectantly for Me.* Ask
Me to open your eyes to see all that I have for you. Such awareness helps you live responsively, ready to do My will.

My followers often fail to see the many blessings I shower
on them. They're so busy looking for other things that they
miss what is before them—*or* is on the way. They forget I am
sovereign God and the timing of events is My prerogative.

I want you to trust Me enough to let Me lead. When a
couple is dancing, one of them leads and the other follows.
Otherwise, there is confusion and awkwardness. Dance with
Me, beloved. Follow My lead as I guide you gracefully through
your life.

LAMENTATIONS 3:25 AMP;
EPHESIANS 5:17 NKJV;
PSALM 71:16; PSALM 28:7

YOU ARE MY BELOVED CHILD. *I chose you before the foundation of the world*, to walk with Me along paths designed uniquely for you. Concentrate on keeping in step with Me instead of trying to anticipate My plans for you. If you trust that My plans are *to prosper you and not to harm you*, you can relax and enjoy the present moment.

Your hope and your future are rooted in heaven, where eternal ecstasy awaits you. Nothing can rob you of your iheritance of unimaginable riches and well-being. Sometimes I grant you glimpses of your glorious future, to encourage you and spur you on. But your main focus should be staying close to Me. I set the pace in keeping with your needs and My purposes.

EPHESIANS 1:4 NASB; PROVERBS 16:9;
JEREMIAH 29:11; EPHESIANS 1:13–14

S TILLNESS IS INCREASINGLY HARD to come by in this restless, agitated world. You must fight to carve out time for Me. Distractions come at you from all sides when you try to sit quietly with Me. But our intimate connection is worth fighting for, so don't give up! Set aside uninterrupted time to spend with Me. Focus on a favorite scripture, and breathe deeply to help yourself unwind. Remember that I am *Immanuel—God with you*. Relax in My peaceful Presence, letting your concerns slip away. *Be still*, My loved one, *and know that I am God*.

The longer you gaze at Me, the more you can rejoice in My majestic splendors—and trust in My sovereign control. *Though the earth give way and the mountains fall into the heart of the sea*, I am *your Refuge*. There is transcendent stability in My Presence. As you ponder the vastness of My Power and Glory, your perspective will change, and your problems will look smaller. *In this world you will have trouble. But take heart! I have overcome the world.*

MATTHEW 1:23 NKJV; PSALM 46:10 NKJV;
PSALM 46:1–2; JOHN 16:33

I AM THE FIRM FOUNDATION on which you can dance and sing and celebrate My Presence. This is My high and holy calling for you; receive it as a precious gift. *Glorifying and enjoying Me* is a higher priority than maintaining a tidy, structured life. Give up your striving to keep everything under control—an impossible task and a waste of precious energy.

My guidance for each of My children is unique. That's why listening to Me is so vital for your well-being. Let me prepare you for the day that awaits you and point you in the right direction. I am with you continually, so don't be intimidated by fear. Though it stalks you, it cannot harm you, as long as you cling to My hand. Keep your eyes on Me, enjoying Peace in My Presence.

PSALM 5:11; EPHESIANS 3:20–21;
JUDE vv. 24–25; JOSHUA 1:5

I GUIDE YOU IN THE WAY OF WISDOM *and lead you along straight paths.* Wisdom can be defined as "the ability to make good decisions based on knowledge and experience." So it's important to learn what is true and apply that knowledge to your life—especially your decisions. Since *I am the Way, the Truth, and the Life,* I'm the best Guide imaginable. I am also *the Word* who *was with God and is God.* The way of wisdom found in the written Word guides you very effectively. So study My Word and stay near Me as you journey through this world.

Look for and follow the *straight paths* I have for you. I don't promise that these paths will always be easy. But if you walk close to Me, your journey will be much less circuitous. When you look ahead, you perceive confusing bends and turns. Yet when you look back at the ground you've already covered, you can see that I have been with you each step of the way—shielding you from dangers, removing obstacles, straightening out your path.

PROVERBS 4:11; JOHN 14:6 NKJV; JOHN 1:1

353

I SPEAK TO YOU CONTINUALLY. My nature is to communicate, though not always in words. I fling glorious sunsets across the sky, day after day after day. I speak in the faces and voices of loved ones. I caress you with a gentle breeze that refreshes and delights you. I speak softly in the depths of your spirit, where I have taken up residence.

You can find Me in each moment, when you have eyes that see and ears that hear. Ask My Spirit to sharpen your spiritual eyesight and hearing. I rejoice each time you discover My Presence. Practice looking and listening for Me during quiet intervals. Gradually you will find Me in more and more of your moments. *You will seek Me and find Me, when you seek Me above all else.*

PSALM 8:1–4; PSALM 19:1–2;
1 CORINTHIANS 6:19; JEREMIAH 29:13

*D*ON'T WORRY ABOUT EVIL PEOPLE *who pros-per; don't fret about their wicked schemes.* In this day of instant communication, you have access to so much information and news that it's easy to feel overwhelmed. Not only do you *hear* about evil people and their wicked schemes, you also *see* the graphic details. This visual imagery has a powerful impact on your brain chemistry. A steady diet of such carnage can make you anxious and fearful.

I want you to pray about world events and pursue peace as you are able. However, it's crucial to recognize what you can change and what you cannot. Fretting about things that are beyond your control will drain your energy and discourage you. Instead of this hurtful focus, endeavor to *fix your thoughts on Me.* I am with you and for you. *Delight yourself in Me!*

Remember that I am a God of justice and I know everything. Eventually I will right all wrongs. So *be still in My Presence—trusting in Me* with a steadfast heart while *waiting for Me to act.*

PSALM 37:7 NLT; HEBREWS 3:1; PSALM 37:3–4

WAIT PATIENTLY WITH ME while I bless you. Don't rush into My Presence with time-consciousness gnawing at your mind. I dwell in timelessness: *I am, I was, I will always be.* For you, time is a protection; you're a frail creature who can handle only twenty-four-hour segments of life. Time can also be a tyrant, ticking away relentlessly in your mind. Learn to master time, or it will be your master.

Though you are a time-bound creature, seek to meet Me in timelessness. As you focus on My Presence, the demands of time and tasks will diminish. *I will bless you and keep you, making My Face shine upon you graciously, giving you Peace.*

MICAH 7:7; REVELATION 1:8;
ECCLESIASTES 3:1; NUMBERS 6:24–26

I LIVE IN YOU! I am everything you could possibly need in a Savior-God, and I am alive within you. I fill you with radiant Life and Love. I want My Life in you to overflow and impact other people. As you interact with them, ask Me to live through you and love through you. When you collaborate with Me in this way, My Light will reflect from your face, and My Love will grace your words.

You are complete in Me. All that you need for your salvation and your spiritual growth is found in Me. Through *My divine Power* you have everything necessary to persevere in the eternal Life I have given you. I also give you intimate *knowledge of Me.* I invite you to open up and share with Me at the deepest levels—both your struggles and your delights.

Find rest in My finished work on the cross, and rejoice that you are eternally secure in Me. Enjoy rich soul-satisfaction through knowing *Me*, your loving Savior and forever-Friend.

GALATIANS 2:20 NLT; 2 CORINTHIANS 3:18;
COLOSSIANS 2:9–10 NKJV; 2 PETER 1:3

THANK ME for the very things that are troubling you. You are on the brink of rebellion, precariously close to shaking your fist in My Face. You are tempted to indulge in just a little complaining about My treatment of you. But once you step over that line, torrents of rage and self-pity can sweep you away. The best protection against this indulgence is thanksgiving. It is impossible to thank Me and curse Me at the same time.

Thanking Me for trials will feel awkward and contrived at first. But if you persist, your thankful words, prayed in faith, will eventually make a difference in your heart. Thankfulness awakens you to My Presence, which overshadows all your problems.

PSALM 116:17 NKJV;
PHILIPPIANS 4:4–6; PSALM 100:2 NKJV

Whenever you are feeling sad, I want you to anticipate feeling joyful again. This takes the sting out of your sorrow because you know it is only temporary. Sadness tends to duplicate itself along the timeline—convincing you that you'll always be unhappy. But this is a lie! The truth is, *all* My followers have infinite Joy ahead of them, guaranteed throughout eternity! *No one can take this away from you.*

Your path through this world has many ups and downs. Your down times are difficult, but they serve an important purpose. Pain and struggle help you change and grow stronger when you trust Me in the midst of adversity. Your troubles are comparable to a woman enduring labor pains. Her suffering is very real, and she may wonder how much longer she can bear the pain. However, this arduous struggle produces a wonderful result—a newborn baby. While *you* labor through your earthly struggles, keep your eyes on the promised reward: boundless Joy in heaven! Even now you can grow in awareness of My Presence, where there is *fullness of Joy.*

JOHN 16:22 NKJV; JOHN 16:21; PSALM 16:11 NKJV

L ET MY LOVE STREAM THROUGH YOU, washing away fear and distrust. A trusting response includes Me in your thoughts as you consider strategies to deal with a situation. My continual Presence is a promise, guaranteeing that you never have to face anything alone. My children teethe on the truth that I am always with them, yet they stumble around in a stupor, unaware of My loving Presence all around them. How that grieves Me!

When you walk through a day in trusting dependence on Me, My aching heart is soothed. Gently bring your attention back to Me whenever it wanders away. I look for persistence—rather than perfection—in your walk with Me.

PSALM 52:8; DEUTERONOMY 31:6;
EPHESIANS 4:30

*Y*OUR CITIZENSHIP IS IN HEAVEN. *Someday I will transform your lowly body so that it will be like My glorious body.* You will have an eternity to enjoy your perfect, glorified body. So don't be overly concerned about your physical condition now. Many of My followers cling desperately to their earthly lives when they are at the very portals of paradise. Yet once they let go and pass through that thin veil into heaven, they experience ecstatic Joy surpassing anything they've ever imagined!

Your times are in My hands. I have planned out all your days, and I know exactly how many you have left. Since *your body is a temple of the Holy Spirit,* I expect you to take care of it, but I don't want you to be too focused on its condition. This can make you anxious and distract you from My Presence. Instead, receive each day as a precious gift from Me. Look for both the pleasures and the responsibilities I've placed before you on your path. Hold My hand in joyful trust; I am always by your side.

PHILIPPIANS 3:20–21; 1 CORINTHIANS 2:9;
PSALM 31:15; 1 CORINTHIANS 6:19–20

H OLD MY HAND—AND TRUST. So long as you are conscious of My Presence with you, all is well. It is virtually impossible to stumble while walking in the Light with Me. I designed you to enjoy Me above all else. You find the deepest fulfillment of your heart in Me alone.

Fearful, anxious thoughts melt away in the Light of My Presence. When you turn away from Me, you are vulnerable to the darkness that is always at work in the world. Don't be surprised by how easily you sin when you forget to cling to My hand. In the world, dependency is seen as immaturity. But in My kingdom, dependence on Me is a prime measure of maturity.

ISAIAH 41:10; EPHESIANS 5:8 NKJV; PSALM 62:5–6

I AM MAKING YOU *NEW* *in the attitude of your mind.* Living close to Me is all about newness and change. I am transforming you *by the entire renewal of your mind.* This is a massive undertaking; you will be under construction till the day you die. However, unlike the inanimate materials that builders use to construct houses, *you* are living, breathing "material." I have given you the amazing ability to think things out and make important choices. I want you to use this godlike ability to cooperate with Me as I transform you. This involves *putting off your old self*—your old way of thinking and doing things—and *putting on the new self.*

To make good, godly choices, you need to know Me as I truly am. Search for Me in My Word; ask My Spirit to illuminate it—shining His Light so that Scripture comes alive to you. The more you choose to live according to My will, the more you will become *like Me*, and the more you can enjoy *walking in the Light of My Presence.*

EPHESIANS 4:22–24; 2 CORINTHIANS 5:17;
ROMANS 12:2 AMP; PSALM 89:15

OPEN YOUR HANDS and your heart to receive this day as a precious gift from Me. I begin each day with a sunrise, announcing My radiant Presence. By the time you rise from your bed, I have already prepared the way before you. I eagerly await your first conscious thought. I rejoice when you glance My way.

Bring Me the gift of thanksgiving, which opens your heart to rich communion with Me. Because I am God, from whom all blessings flow, thankfulness is the best way to draw near Me. Sing praise songs to Me; tell of My wondrous works. Remember that *I take great delight in you; I rejoice over you with singing.*

PSALM 118:24; PSALM 95:1–2; ZEPHANIAH 3:17

REFUSE TO WORRY, MY CHERISHED ONE. Displace those worry-thoughts with trusting and thankful thoughts. Affirm your faith in Me while praising Me for all that I am and all I have done. This combination of praise and trust is potent. It drives away anxiety and powers of darkness. Also, it strengthens your relationship with Me. You may still have legitimate concerns to deal with, but I will help you with them. As you become more peaceful, you can look at your problems in the Light of My Presence and seek My counsel. Let Scripture inform your thinking so that I can communicate with you more clearly.

Take time to thank Me for the many good things in your life. I want you to express gratefulness in your prayers, in your conversations with others, and in your private thoughts. I read your thoughts continually, and I rejoice when they contain gratitude. You can thank Me even for things you wish were different. This act of faith helps you break free from negative thinking. *In everything give thanks; this is My will for you.*

PSALM 31:14; PSALM 32:8;
1 THESSALONIANS 5:18 NKJV

S TAY CALMLY CONSCIOUS OF ME today, no matter what. Remember that I go before you as well as with you into the day. Nothing takes Me by surprise. I will not allow circumstances to overwhelm you so long as you look to Me. I will help you cope with whatever the moment presents. Collaborating with Me brings *blessings that far outweigh all your troubles*. Awareness of My Presence contains Joy that can endure all eventualities.

PSALM 23:1–4 NKJV;
2 CORINTHIANS 4:16–17; PSALM 28:7

*I*F *I AM FOR YOU, who can be against you?* It is essential for you to grasp that I truly *am* for you. This is a promise for all of My followers. When things are not going your way and people you trusted turn against you, it's easy to feel as if I've abandoned you. At such times it's vital to tell yourself the truth: I am not only *with* you always, I am also *for* you all the time. This is true on days when you perform well and on days when you don't, when people treat you well and when they don't.

If you really understand and fully believe that I am *for you*, then fear will diminish and you can face adversity more calmly. Knowing that I will never turn against you gives you confidence to persevere in tough times. I approve of you, beloved, because you are Mine! It is *My* opinion of you that prevails—and will continue to prevail throughout eternity. No person and no thing *will be able to separate you from My loving Presence*!

ROMANS 8:31; NUMBERS 6:26 AMP; ROMANS 8:39

REST WITH ME A WHILE. You have journeyed up a steep, rugged path in recent days. The way ahead is shrouded in uncertainty. Look neither behind you nor before you. Instead, focus your attention on Me, your constant Companion. Trust that I will equip you fully for whatever awaits you on your journey.

I designed time to be a protection for you. You couldn't bear to see all your life at once. Though I am unlimited by time, it is in the present moment that I meet you. Refresh yourself in My company, breathing deep draughts of My Presence. The highest level of trust is to enjoy Me moment by moment. *I am with you, watching over you wherever you go.*

MATTHEW 11:28 NKJV; PSALM 143:8; GENESIS 28:15

I AM RICHLY PRESENT in the world around you, in the Word, and in your heart through My Spirit. Ask Me to open the eyes of your heart so that you can "see" Me—for I am lovingly present in all your moments. It's vital to set aside blocks of time for *seeking My Face*. This requires sustained mental discipline: pulling your thoughts back from the idols that entice you and choosing to think about Me. I am the living Word, so you will find Me vibrantly present when you search for Me in the Scriptures.

I created breathtaking beauty in the world, to point you to the One who made everything. *Without Me, nothing was made that has been made.* Whenever you are enjoying something beautiful, thank Me. This pleases Me, and it also increases your pleasure. When you encounter difficult, ugly things in this broken world, trust Me then too. Keep looking for Me in the midst of your good times *and* your hard times. Find hope and comfort through knowing that *all your times are in My hands.*

1 CHRONICLES 16:11; JOHN 1:3;
PSALM 31:14–15 NKJV

T ASTE AND SEE THAT I AM GOOD. This command contains an invitation to experience My living Presence. It also contains a promise. The more you experience Me, the more convinced you become of My goodness. This knowledge is essential to your faith-walk. When adversities strike, the human instinct is to doubt My goodness. My ways are mysterious, even to those who know Me intimately. *As the heavens are higher than the earth, so are My ways and thoughts higher than your ways and thoughts.* Do not try to fathom My ways. Instead, spend time enjoying Me and experiencing My goodness.

PSALM 34:8; ISAIAH 55:8–9; PSALM 100:5 NKJV

E VERYTHING YOU HAVE IS A GIFT from Me, including each breath you breathe. I shower so many blessings on you that it's easy to take some of My precious gifts for granted. Most people don't recognize the wonder of inhaling My Life continually. Yet it was only when I breathed *the breath of Life* into Adam that he *became a living being*.

As you sit quietly in My Presence, try thanking Me silently each time you inhale. As you exhale, affirm your trust in Me. The longer you do this, the more relaxed you will become. While you are taking time with Me, I help you appreciate and thank Me for blessings you often overlook: skies and trees, light and colors, loved ones and daily comforts. The list is endless! The more you look for good things in your life, the clearer your vision becomes.

Of course, your greatest gratitude should be for *eternal Life*, which is yours because you *believe in Me*. This is a price-less forever-gift that will fill you with ever-increasing *Joy in My Presence*!

GENESIS 2:7 NKJV; JOHN 3:16; PSALM 16:11

June 29

A s you get out of bed in the morning, be aware of My Presence with you. You may not be thinking clearly yet, but I am. Your early morning thoughts tend to be anxious ones until you get connected with Me. Invite Me into your thoughts by whispering My Name. Suddenly your day brightens and feels more user-friendly. You cannot dread a day that is vibrant with My Presence.

You gain confidence through knowing that I am with you—that you face nothing alone. Anxiety stems from asking the wrong question: "If such and such happens, can I handle it?" The true question is not whether you can cope with whatever happens, but whether you and I together can handle anything that occurs. It is this you-and-I-together factor that gives you confidence to face the day cheerfully.

PSALM 5:3; PSALM 63:1 NKJV; PHILIPPIANS 4:13

*T*HOSE WHO SOW IN TEARS *will reap with songs of Joy.* So do not despise your tears, My child; they are precious to Me. Someday *I will wipe every tear from your eyes,* but for now you inhabit a vale of tears. Just as water is necessary for seeds to grow into plants, your tears help you grow into a stronger, more joyful Christian. Your willingness to share in the sorrow of this deeply fallen world gives you depth and compassion. It also enlarges your capacity for Joy—your ability to enjoy Me in good times and tough times.

Songs of Joy have been your birthright ever since you became My follower. Do not neglect this delightful way of worshiping Me and lifting your spirits. Even though it is counterintuitive to sing praises when you're feeling sad, this is a powerful way to lift your heart to Me. As your Joy in Me encounters My delight in you, you can frolic in the Light of My Presence. This is *the Joy of the Lord*!

PSALM 126:5–6; REVELATION 21:4;
ISAIAH 62:4 NKJV; NEHEMIAH 8:10

I AM THE TRUTH: the One who came to *set you free.* As the Holy Spirit controls your mind and actions more fully, you become free in Me. You are increasingly released to become the one I created you to be. This is a work that I do in you as you yield to My Spirit. I can do My best handiwork when you sit in the stillness of My Presence, focusing your entire being on Me.

Let My thoughts burst freely upon your consciousness, stimulating abundant Life. *I am the Way and the Truth and the Life.* As you follow Me, I lead you along paths of newness: ways you have never imagined. Don't worry about what is on the road up ahead. I want you to find your security in knowing Me, the One who died to *set you free.*

JOHN 8:32; PHILIPPIANS 2:13; JOHN 14:6

*T*RUST ME AND DON'T BE AFRAID. Do not be frightened by world events or news reports. These reports are biased—presented as if I do not exist. News clips show tiny bits of world events from which the most important factor has been carefully removed: *My Presence in the world*. As journalists sift through massive amounts of information, they strain out everything about Me and what I'm accomplishing on the earth.

Whenever your world is feeling like a scary place, turn to Me and encourage yourself in My Presence. Follow the example of David, who *strengthened himself in the Lord* when his men were threatening to stone him. You also can find courage through remembering who I am. Ponder My awesome Glory and Power; delight in My unfailing Love. Rejoice that you are on an adventurous journey with Me and your ultimate destination is heaven. As you keep focusing on Me and enjoying the rich relationship I offer you, fear will subside and Joy will rise up within you. Trust in Me wholeheartedly, beloved, for *I am your Strength and your Song.*

ISAIAH 12:2; EXODUS 33:14; 1 SAMUEL 30:6 NKJV

July

Therefore, there is now no condemnation for those who are in Christ Jesus.

ROMANS 8:1

I AM LIFE AND LIGHT IN ABUNDANCE. As you spend time "soaking" in My Presence, you are energized and lightened. Through communing with Me, you transfer your heavy burdens to My strong shoulders. By gazing at Me, you gain My perspective on your life. This time alone with Me is essential for unscrambling your thoughts and smoothing out the day before you.

Be willing to fight for this precious time with Me. Opposition comes in many forms: your own desire to linger in bed; the evil one's determination to distract you from Me; the pressure of family, friends, and your own inner critic to spend your time more productively. As you grow in your desire to please Me above all else, you gain strength to resist these opponents. *Delight yourself in Me, for I am the deepest Desire of your heart.*

PSALM 48:9; DEUTERONOMY 33:12; PSALM 37:4

I HAVE ENGRAVED YOU *on the palms of My hands,* and this is an eternal commitment. Nothing could ever scrape off or corrode this inscription, for you are My treasured, blood-bought possession.

Engraving on precious metals is a practice that is meant to be permanent. However, the etching may wear off over the years, and sometimes these objects are lost or stolen or melted down. So, put first things first, beloved. Precious metals like gold and silver have *some* value in the world. But they are as worthless as *rubbish compared to the surpassing greatness of knowing Me* forever!

Since you are written on the palms of My hands, you can be assured that you are always visible to Me. People sometimes jot notes on their palms to remind themselves of something important. I have engraved you on *My* palms because you are eternally precious to Me. Rejoice in the wonder of knowing that I—the King of the universe—consider you a priceless treasure! Respond by treasuring *Me* above all else.

ISAIAH 49:15–16; PHILIPPIANS 3:8–9; PSALM 43:4

L ET ME SHOW YOU My way for you this day. I guide you continually so you can relax and enjoy My Presence in the present. Living well is both a discipline and an art. Concentrate on staying close to Me, the divine Artist. Discipline your thoughts to trust Me as I work My ways in your life. Pray about everything; then leave outcomes up to Me. Do not fear My will, for through it I accomplish what is best for you. Take a deep breath and dive into the depths of absolute trust in Me. *Underneath are the everlasting arms!*

PSALM 5:2–3; ISAIAH 26:4 AMP;
DEUTERONOMY 33:27

*W*HEN YOUR SPIRIT GROWS FAINT *within you, it is I who know your way.* This is one of the benefits of weakness. It highlights the fact that you cannot find your way without help from Me. If you are feeling weary or confused, you can choose to look away from those feelings and turn wholeheartedly toward Me. Pour out your heart freely, and then rest in the Presence of the One who *knows your way* perfectly—all the way to heaven.

Continue this practice of gazing at Me even during the times you're feeling strong and confident. In fact, this is when you are most at risk of going the wrong direction. Instead of assuming that you know the next step of your journey, train yourself to make your plans in My Presence—asking Me to guide you. Remember that *My ways and thoughts are higher than yours, as the heavens are higher than the earth.* Let this remembrance draw you into worshiping Me, *the High and Lofty One who inhabits eternity* and who reaches down to help you.

PSALM 142:3; ISAIAH 55:9;
ISAIAH 57:15 NKJV

M Y CHILDREN make a pastime of judging one another—and themselves. But I am the only capable Judge, and I have acquitted you through My own blood. Your acquittal came at the price of My unparalleled sacrifice. That is why I am highly offended when I hear My children judge one another or indulge in self-hatred.

If you live close to Me and absorb My Word, the Holy Spirit will guide and correct you as needed. There is *no condemnation* for those who belong to Me.

LUKE 6:37; 2 TIMOTHY 4:8;
TITUS 3:5; ROMANS 8:1

I AM THE LORD YOUR GOD, *who takes hold of your right hand and says to you, Do not fear; I will help you.* It is essential for you to recognize—and believe—that I am not only your Savior, I am also *your God.* Many people try to cast Me as a great human model, a martyr who sacrificed everything for others. But if I were only human, you would still be *dead in your sins.* The One who takes hold of your hand and calms your fears is the living God! Rejoice as you ponder this astonishing truth. Delight in the mysterious wonder of the Trinity—Father, Son, and Spirit—one God.

Take time to wait in My Presence. Tell Me your troubles; *pour out your heart before Me.* Hear Me saying, "Do not be afraid, beloved. I am here—ready to help you." I don't condemn you for your fears, but I do want you to displace them with hope and trust in Me. As you trustingly *put your hope in Me, My unfailing Love rests upon you.*

ISAIAH 41:13; EPHESIANS 2:1;
PSALM 62:8 NKJV; PSALM 33:22

W HEN YOU WORSHIP ME *in spirit and truth,* you join with choirs of angels who are continually before My throne. Though you cannot hear their voices, your praise and thanksgiving are distinctly audible in heaven. Your petitions are also heard, but it is your gratitude that clears the way to My Heart. With the way between us wide open, My blessings fall upon you in rich abundance. The greatest blessing is nearness to Me—abundant Joy and Peace in My Presence. Practice praising and thanking Me continually throughout this day.

JOHN 4:23–24; COLOSSIANS 3:16; PSALM 100:4

*T*O EVERYONE WHO IS VICTORIOUS, *I will give fruit from the Tree of Life in paradise.* Beloved, there is one sense in which you are already victorious. For *those I predestined, I also called; those I called, I also justified; those I justified, I also glorified.* I brought you out of darkness into My kingdom of Light; this means that you are on your way to Glory! The victory has been won—accomplished through My finished work on the cross.

There is another sense in which you must struggle throughout your lifetime to be victorious. In this world you will encounter fiery trials and temptations that highlight your sinfulness and weaknesses. This can lead to discouragement as you view your multiple failures. You may even feel as if you no longer belong to Me, but do not be deceived by feelings. Instead, cling tenaciously to My hand, trusting that the joyous wonders of paradise are indeed your promised inheritance. The Light in the heavenly city is dazzlingly bright, for *the Glory of God illumines it and the Lamb is its Light.*

REVELATION 2:7 TLB; ROMANS 8:30;
REVELATION 21:23 NKJV

D RAW NEAR TO ME with a thankful heart, aware that your cup is overflowing with blessings. Gratitude enables you to perceive Me more clearly and to rejoice in our Love-relationship. *Nothing can separate you from My loving Presence!* That is the basis of your security. Whenever you start to feel anxious, remind yourself that your security rests in Me alone, and I am totally trustworthy.

You will never be in control of your life circumstances, but you can relax and trust in My control. Instead of striving for a predictable, safe lifestyle, seek to know Me in greater depth and breadth. I long to make your life a glorious adventure, but you must stop clinging to old ways. I am always doing something new within My beloved ones. Be on the lookout for all that I have prepared for you.

ROMANS 8:38–39; PSALM 56:3–4; ISAIAH 43:19

WALK IN THE LIGHT of My Presence. This delightful way to live involves *acclaiming Me, rejoicing in My Name*, and *exulting in My righteousness*. To acclaim Me is to praise Me in a very strong and enthusiastic way, sometimes with shouts and applause. When you rejoice in My Name, you find Joy in all that I am—your Savior and Shepherd, your Lord and God, your Sovereign King, your Friend who loves you with *unfailing Love*. You can exult in My righteousness because I have shared it with you. Though you will continue to sin in this life, My perfect righteousness is already credited to your account.

When you walk in My glorious Light, *My blood continually cleanses you from all sin*. As you seek to live near Me, acknowledging that you're a sinner in need of forgiveness, My holy illumination purifies you. This blessing is for all believers, making it possible for My followers to *have rich fellowship with one another*. So walk in the Light with Me, My friend. Spend time enjoying My bright, loving Presence.

PSALM 89:15–16; PSALM 31:16;
ROMANS 3:22; 1 JOHN 1:7 NKJV

I AM YOUR FATHER-GOD. Listen to Me! Learn what it means to be a child of the everlasting King. Your richest duty is devotion to Me. This duty is such a joyous privilege that it feels like a luxury. You tend to feel guilty about pushing back the boundaries of your life to make space for time alone with Me. The world is waiting to squeeze you into its mold and to crowd out time devoted to Me. The ways of the world have also warped your conscience, which punishes you for doing the very thing that pleases Me most: seeking My Face. Listen to Me above the clamor of voices trying to distract you. Ask My Spirit to control your mind, for He and I work in perfect harmony. Be still and attentive in My Presence. *You are on holy ground.*

ISAIAH 9:6; ZECHARIAH 9:9 NKJV;
ROMANS 8:15–16; EXODUS 3:5

I AM BEFORE ALL THINGS, and in Me all things hold together. I have always been and will always be. *All things were created by Me: things in heaven and on earth, visible and invisible.* I am Lord over creation, over the church, over everything! Worship Me as your vibrant Lord, *the living God.* I want My loved ones to thirst for Me—*as the deer pants for streams of water.*

Do not be satisfied with only thinking about Me or knowing Me intellectually. Thirst for experiential knowledge of Me, grounded in sound biblical truth. Seek to *know My Love that far surpasses mere knowledge.* You will need the help of My Spirit to accomplish this.

You must *be strengthened with mighty Power by the Holy Spirit, who indwells your innermost being and personality.* Invite Him to empower and guide you in this amorous adventure. But remember that *I* am the goal of your searching—make Me central in your quest. *You will seek Me and find Me when you search for Me with all your heart!*

COLOSSIANS 1:16–17; PSALM 42:1–2;
EPHESIANS 3:16–19 AMP; JEREMIAH 29:13 NKJV

T RUST ME IN ALL YOUR THOUGHTS. I know that some thoughts are unconscious or semiconscious, and I do not hold you responsible for those. But you can direct conscious thoughts much more than you may realize. Practice thinking in certain ways—trusting Me, thanking Me—and those thoughts become more natural. Reject negative or sinful thoughts as soon as you become aware of them. Don't try to hide them from Me; confess them and leave them with Me. Go on your way lightheartedly. This method of controlling your thoughts will keep your mind in My Presence and your feet on the *path of Peace.*

PSALM 20:7; 1 JOHN 1:9; LUKE 1:79

I AM THE GATE; whoever enters through Me will be saved. I am the only Entrance to *the path of Life*—to eternal Life. If you do not enter through Me, you will never find salvation from your sins.

Some people compare the spiritual journey to climbing a mountain: There are many paths that lead to the summit, and all the successful climbers will end up at the same place. People often use this analogy to claim that all paths to God are equally effective. Nothing could be further from the truth! You can enter salvation only through *Me*, the one true Gate.

Once you have come through this Gate, you can enjoy walking along the path of Life. I don't guarantee you an easy journey, but I *do* promise to be with you every moment. No matter what difficulties you may encounter along the way, *there is Joy to be found in My Presence.* Moreover, each step you take brings you closer to your goal—your heavenly home.

JOHN 10:9; PSALM 16:11 NKJV;
MATTHEW 1:21; 2 TIMOTHY 4:18 AMP

July 8

W HEN YOU SEEK MY FACE, put aside thoughts of everything else. I am above all, as well as in all; your communion with Me transcends both time and circumstances. Be prepared to be blessed bountifully by My Presence, for I am a God of unlimited abundance. Open wide your heart and mind to receive more and more of Me. When your Joy in Me meets My Joy in you, there are fireworks of heavenly ecstasy. This is eternal life here and now: a tiny foretaste of what awaits you in the life to come. *Now you see only a poor reflection as in a mirror, but then you will see face to Face.*

PSALM 27:8 NKJV; JOHN 15:11;
1 CORINTHIANS 13:12

I DRAW NEAR YOU in the present moment. Seek to enjoy My Presence in the present; trust and thankfulness are your best allies in this quest.

When you wallow in the past or worry about the future, your awareness of Me grows dim. But the more you trust Me, the more fully you can live in the present, where My Presence awaits you always. Speak to Me frequently: "I trust You, Jesus." "*I love You, O LORD, my strength*." These short prayers keep you close to Me—confident that I'm lovingly watching over you.

It's important for you to grow not only more trusting but more thankful. A grateful attitude is essential for living near Me. Ingratitude is offensive to Me, and it drags you down both spiritually and emotionally. Remember that *you are receiving a kingdom that cannot be shaken*—no matter what is happening in your life or in the world. This means that you have a constant, unshakable reason to *be thankful*. Stay anchored to Me and enjoy My Presence by *giving thanks in all circumstances*.

PSALM 18:1 NASB; HEBREWS 12:28–29;
1 THESSALONIANS 5:18 ESV

S TOP WORRYING LONG ENOUGH to hear My voice. I speak softly to you, in the depths of your being. Your mind shuttles back and forth, hither and yon, weaving webs of anxious confusion. As My thoughts rise up within you, they become entangled in those sticky webs of worry. Thus, My voice is muffled, and you hear only white noise.

Ask My Spirit to quiet your mind so that you can think My thoughts. This ability is an awesome benefit of being My child, patterned after My own image. Do not be deafened by the noise of the world or that of your own thinking. Instead, *be transformed by the renewing of your mind.* Sit quietly in My Presence, letting My thoughts reprogram your thinking.

DEUTERONOMY 30:20; GENESIS 1:27;
ROMANS 12:2

A S YOU *LOOK TO ME* more and more, I become your joyful Focus. When you look at the world today, many disturbing things call out for your attention. If you concentrate too much on those things, you will become deeply discouraged. Meanwhile, the One who is *continually with you* calls out: "I am here! Look to Me, beloved, and find Joy in Me!"

My Presence can bless you always—even when it's only in the background of your mind. You can learn to stay conscious of Me while you are engaged in other matters. The magnificent brain I gave you can function on several tracks at once. When you're doing something that involves a lot of brainpower, your awareness of My Presence will be subtle. Nonetheless, it can be comforting and encouraging.

Making Me your joyous Focus is *not* escapism. On the contrary, your attentiveness to Me strengthens you and gives you courage to cope with the difficulties in your life. The more persistently you look to Me, the more effective and joyful you will be.

PSALM 105:4; PSALM 73:23 NKJV;
DEUTERONOMY 31:6 ESV

Relax in My peaceful Presence. Do not bring performance pressures into our sacred space of communion. When you are with someone you trust completely, you feel free to be yourself. This is one of the joys of true friendship. Though I am *Lord of lords and King of kings*, I also desire to be your intimate Friend. When you are tense or pretentious in our relationship, I feel hurt. I know the worst about you, but I also see the best in you. I long for you to trust Me enough to be fully yourself with Me. When you are real with Me, I am able to bring out the best in you: the very gifts I have planted in your soul. Relax and enjoy our friendship.

2 THESSALONIANS 3:16 NKJV;
REVELATION 17:14; JOHN 15:13–15

*Y*OU OVERWHELMINGLY CONQUER *through Me,* the King of Glory who loves you. No matter what is happening in this fractured, fallen world or in your own life, you are victorious. I won the Victory once for all time through My sacrificial death and miraculous resurrection. *My unfailing Love* has accomplished this wondrous conquest and made you much, much more than a conqueror. You're an heir of the kingdom of eternal Life and Light!

Nothing will be able to separate you from My Love! Ponder what it means to have *Me* as the Lover of your soul every moment, forever and ever. Your soul is the eternal part of you, the part that can never be separated from Me. It is not what you see in the mirror or what other people reflect back to you. It is the essence of who you are—the "real you" that is *being transformed from Glory to Glory*. Therefore, do not be discouraged by the defects you see in yourself. Instead, remember that you are continually being *transformed into My image*—and rejoice!

ROMANS 8:37–39 NASB;
PSALM 13:5–6; 2 CORINTHIANS 3:18 NKJV

WORSHIP ME ONLY. Idolatry has always been the downfall of My people. I make no secrets about being *a jealous God*. Current idols are more subtle than ancient ones because today's false gods are often outside the field of religion. People, possessions, status, and self-aggrandizement are some of the most popular deities today. Beware of bowing down before these things. False gods never satisfy; instead, they stir up lust for more and more.

When you seek Me instead of the world's idols, you experience My Joy and Peace. These intangibles slake the thirst of your soul, providing deep satisfaction. The glitter of the world is tinny and temporal. The Light of My Presence is brilliant and everlasting. Walk in the Light with Me. Thus you become a beacon through whom others are drawn to Me.

EXODUS 20:4–5; ISAIAH 55:12; 2 SAMUEL 22:29

YOUR COMPETENCE COMES FROM ME. This means there is no place for pride in your achievements. It also means you are capable of much more than you think possible. The combination of your natural abilities and My supernatural empowerment is very effective. I have called you to live in joyful dependence on Me, so don't hesitate to ask Me for help. Make every effort to discern My will for you—searching the Scriptures and *seeking My Face*. Also, seek wise counsel from other Christians. I will show you the way to go forward according to My wisdom and will.

Ask My Spirit to guide you along the pathway I have chosen for you. This Holy Helper will equip and empower you to achieve My purposes in your life. Thank Me for everything: the abilities I have given you, the opportunities before you, and My Spirit's enabling you to accomplish important things in My kingdom. Stay in communication with Me, enjoying My Company as you journey along *the path of Life. In My Presence is fullness of Joy*!

2 CORINTHIANS 3:5; 1 CHRONICLES 16:10–11;
1 THESSALONIANS 5:16–18 NKJV; PSALM 16:11 NKJV

WHENEVER YOU FEEL DISTANT from Me, whisper My Name in loving trust. This simple prayer can restore your awareness of My Presence.

My Name is constantly abused in the world, where people use it as a curse word. This verbal assault reaches all the way to heaven; every word is heard and recorded. When you trustingly whisper My Name, My aching ears are soothed. The grating rancor of the world's blasphemies cannot compete with a trusting child's utterance: "Jesus." The power of My Name to bless both you and Me is beyond your understanding.

PROVERBS 18:10; ACTS 4:12; JOHN 16:24

I WANT YOU TO DRAW WATER *from the wells of salvation with Joy.* These wells are unfathomably deep, and they are filled to the brim with My blessings. The worth of your salvation is inestimable, far greater than all of earth's fortunes—past, present, and future. When your life in this world ends, you will live with Me *forever* in a perfect environment filled with dazzling Glory. You will worship Me with untold numbers of My followers, all of whom will relate to one another with wondrous Love—and respond to Me with even *greater* Love. Moreover, you will be able to receive Love from Me in unimaginably great measure!

The assurance of forevermore-pleasures awaiting you in heaven can help you endure your struggles in this world. I understand the difficulties you're facing, but remember: I am *your Strength and Song.* I am strong enough to carry you when you feel as if you can go no further. I even enable you to sing with Me—on good days *and* hard days. I, *your Song,* can fill you with Joy!

ISAIAH 12:2–3; 2 CORINTHIANS 8:9;
PSALM 16:11 NKJV

I WANT YOU TO EXPERIENCE the riches of your salvation: the Joy of being loved constantly and perfectly. You make a practice of judging yourself, based on how you look or behave or feel. If you like what you see in the mirror, you feel a bit more worthy of My Love. When things are going smoothly and your performance seems adequate, you find it easier to believe you are My beloved child. When you feel discouraged, you tend to look inward so you can correct whatever is wrong.

Instead of trying to "fix" yourself, *fix your gaze on Me, the Lover of your soul*. Rather than using your energy to judge yourself, redirect it to praising Me. Remember that I see you clothed in My righteousness, radiant in My perfect Love.

EPHESIANS 2:7–8; HEBREWS 3:1; PSALM 34:5

SOMETIMES YOU NEED HELP even to ask for My help. As you try to do several things at once, you find yourself moving faster and faster—interrupting one thing to do another. If your phone rings at such a time, your stress level rises even higher. The best way out of this turmoil is to STOP everything. Take a few deep breaths and whisper My Name. Acknowledge your need for My guidance through the moments of this day. I will lovingly lead you along *paths of righteousness—for My Name's sake.*

When you are preparing to do something challenging, you usually take time to enlist My help. But when you're facing everyday tasks, you tend to dive in unassisted—as if you can handle these matters alone. How much better it is to approach *everything* in humble dependence on Me! Whenever you find yourself in "diving" mode, ask Me to help you stop and seek Me—letting Me show you the way to go forward. *I will guide you along the best pathway for your life.*

PSALM 23:3; ACTS 17:27; PSALM 32:8 NLT

KEEP WALKING with Me along the path I have chosen for you. Your desire to live close to Me is a delight to My heart. I could instantly grant you the spiritual riches you desire, but that is not My way for you. Together we will forge a pathway up the high mountain. The journey is arduous at times, and you are weak. Someday you will dance light-footed on the high peaks; but for now your walk is often plodding and heavy. All I require of you is to take the next step, clinging to My hand for strength and direction. Though the path is difficult and the scenery dull at the moment, there are sparkling surprises just around the bend. Stay on the path I have selected for you. It is truly the *path of Life*.

ISAIAH 40:31 NKJV; PSALM 37:23–24;
PSALM 16:11 NKJV

*B*E STILL IN MY PRESENCE, *and wait patiently for Me to act.* Stillness is a rare commodity in this world. Many people judge themselves and their day by how much they have accomplished. Resting in My Presence is usually not one of those accomplishments. Yet how much blessing can be found in this holy rest!

Peace and Joy abound in My Presence, but it takes time for them to soak into your inner being. It also takes trust. Instead of fussing and fuming when your plans are thwarted, wait patiently for Me to act. You can *watch in hope for Me* because I am *God your Savior.* Be assured that *I will hear you.* I may not answer as soon as you would like, but I always respond to your prayers in the best way.

Don't worry about evil people or fret about their wicked schemes. I laugh at the wicked, for I know their day is coming. Rest in Me, beloved. *Be still, and know that I am God.*

PSALM 37:7 NLT; MICAH 7:7;
PSALM 37:13; PSALM 46:10 NKJV

D O NOT WORRY ABOUT TOMORROW! This is not a suggestion but a command. I divided time into days and nights so that you would have manageable portions of life to handle. *My grace is sufficient for you*, but its sufficiency is for only one day at a time. When you worry about the future, you heap day upon day of troubles onto your flimsy frame. You stagger under this heavy load, which I never intended you to carry.

Throw off this oppressive burden with one quick thrust of trust. Anxious thoughts meander about and crisscross in your brain, but trusting Me brings you directly into My Presence. As you thus affirm your faith, shackles of worry fall off instantly. Enjoy My Presence continually by trusting Me at all times.

MATTHEW 6:34; 2 CORINTHIANS 12:9;
PSALM 62:8 NKJV

*M*Y UNFAILING LOVE IS BETTER *than life itself!* There is no limit to My Love—in quality, quantity, or duration. It is infinitely better than anything this world offers, and it will never run out. *How priceless is My unfailing Love!*

Consider the parable of *the merchant looking for fine pearls. When he found one of great value, he sold everything he had and bought it.* My Love is like that pearl: so valuable that it is worth losing everything else to secure it forever.

Though gaining My Love is worth losing your life, it actually enriches your life. This glorious gift provides a foundation for you to build on, and it improves your relationships with other people. Knowing that you are perfectly and eternally loved helps you grow into the one I designed you to be. *Grasping how wide and long and high and deep is My Love* for you leads you into worship. *This* is where your intimacy with Me grows by leaps and bounds—as you joyously celebrate My magnificent Presence!

PSALM 63:3 NLT; PSALM 36:7;
MATTHEW 13:45–46; EPHESIANS 3:17–18

SELF-PITY IS A SLIMY, BOTTOMLESS PIT. Once you fall in, you tend to go deeper and deeper into the mire. As you slide down those slippery walls, you are well on your way to depression, and the darkness is profound.

Your only hope is to look up and see the Light of My Presence shining down on you. Though the Light looks dim from your perspective, deep in the pit, those rays of hope can reach you at any depth. While you focus on Me in trust, you rise ever so slowly out of the abyss of despair. Finally, you can reach up and grasp My hand. I will pull you out into the Light again. I will gently cleanse you, washing off the clinging mire. I will cover you with My righteousness and walk with you down the path of Life.

PSALM 40:2–3; PSALM 42:5 NASB; PSALM 147:11

*P*ROCLAIM *MY SALVATION day after day.* You need to recall the truth of the gospel every single day: *By grace you have been saved through faith, and this is not your own doing; it's a gift—not a result of works.* This truth is very countercultural. The world tells you that you have to work at being good enough. Your own fallen mind and heart will agree with these messages unless you are vigilant. That's why Scripture warns you to *be alert.* The devil is *the accuser* of My followers. His accusations discourage and defeat many Christians, so remind yourself of gospel-truth frequently.

The best response to the glorious gift of grace is a thankful heart that delights in doing My will. It is vital to proclaim the gospel not only to yourself but to the world. *Declare My Glory to the nations!* Seek to share this good news—both near (to family, friends, coworkers) and far (to the nations). *All peoples* need to know the truth about Me. Let your thankfulness motivate you, energize you, and fill you with Joy!

PSALM 96:2–3; EPHESIANS 2:8–9 ESV;
1 PETER 5:8; REVELATION 12:10

C OME AWAY WITH M E for a while. The world, with its nonstop demands, can be put on hold. Most people put *Me* on hold, rationalizing that someday they will find time to focus on Me. But the longer people push Me into the background of their lives, the harder it is for them to find Me.

You live among people who glorify busyness; they have made time a tyrant that controls their lives. Even those who know Me as Savior tend to march to the tempo of the world. They have bought into the illusion that more is always better: more meetings, more programs, more activity.

I have called you to follow Me on a solitary path, making time alone with Me your highest priority and deepest Joy. It is a pathway largely unappreciated and often despised. However, *you have chosen the better thing, which will never be taken away from you*. Moreover, as you walk close to Me, I can bless others through you.

SONG OF SONGS 2:13; LUKE 10:41–42

*B*LESSED ARE THOSE *who have learned to acclaim Me.* The word "acclaim" means to express enthusiastic approval. This is not the natural inclination of mankind. It is something you need to learn—and practice. Begin with your thoughts. Instead of thinking of Me in boring, repetitive ways, ponder My glorious greatness! I spoke the world into existence. I formed people in My own image and gave them eternal souls. I created beauty in the world and throughout the universe. I am infinitely more brilliant than the greatest genius imaginable. My wisdom is *unsearchable,* and My Love is unfailing. Learn to think great thoughts of Me and to express them enthusiastically. The Psalms provide excellent instruction in this quest.

To acclaim Me also means to acknowledge My excellence publicly. *You are the light of the world* because you know Me as your Savior-God. I want you to *let your light shine before men;* tell them the wonders of who I am—and all I have done. *Proclaim the excellencies of Him who called you out of darkness into His marvelous Light.*

PSALM 89:15; ROMANS 11:33;
MATTHEW 5:14–16 NASB; 1 PETER 2:9 NASB

411

July 18

I AM NEARER than you think, richly present in all your moments. You are connected to Me by Love-bonds that nothing can sever. However, you may sometimes feel alone because your union with Me is invisible. Ask Me to open your eyes so that you can find Me everywhere. The more aware you are of My Presence, the safer you feel. This is not some sort of escape from reality; it is tuning in to *ultimate reality*. I am far more Real than the world you can see, hear, and touch. *Faith is the confirmation of things we do not see and the conviction of their reality, perceiving as real fact what is not revealed to the senses.*

PSALM 90:14; ACTS 17:27–28; HEBREWS 11:1 AMP

*R*EJOICE ALWAYS! This is one of the shortest verses in the Bible, but it is radiant with heavenly Light. I made you in My image, and I crafted you with the ability to choose Joy in the moments of your life. When your mind is going down an unpleasant, gloomy path, stop it in its tracks with this glorious command. See how many times each day you can remind yourself to rejoice.

It is important not only to be joyful but to think about specific reasons for rejoicing. They can be as simple as My daily provisions for you—food, shelter, clothing. Relationships with loved ones can also be a rich source of Joy. Since you are My beloved, your relationship with Me is an ever-present wellspring of gladness. These joyful thoughts will light up both your mind and your heart, enabling you to find more pleasure in your life.

Choosing to rejoice will bless you and those around you. It will also strengthen your relationship with Me.

1 THESSALONIANS 5:16 NKJV;
GENESIS 1:27 NKJV; PHILIPPIANS 4:4

B RING ME ALL YOUR FEELINGS, even the ones you wish you didn't have. Fear and anxiety still plague you. Feelings per se are not sinful, but they can be temptations to sin. Blazing missiles of fear fly at you day and night; these attacks from the evil one come at you relentlessly. Use your *shield of faith to extinguish those flaming arrows.* Affirm your trust in Me, regardless of how you feel. If you persist, your feelings will eventually fall in line with your faith.

Do not hide from your fear or pretend it isn't there. Anxiety that you hide in the recesses of your heart will give birth to fear of fear: a monstrous mutation. Bring your anxieties out into the Light of My Presence, where we can deal with them together. Concentrate on trusting Me, and fearfulness will gradually lose its foothold within you.

EPHESIANS 6:16; 1 JOHN 1:5–7; ISAIAH 12:2

I AM YOUR HELP AND YOUR SHIELD. Pay special attention to the possessive pronoun *your*. I am not just *a* Help and *a* Shield. I am *yours*—for all time and throughout eternity. Let this forever-commitment strengthen and encourage you as you walk with Me through this day. *I will never leave you or forsake you.* You can depend on Me!

Because I am your Help, you don't need to fear your inadequacy. When the task ahead of you looks daunting, rejoice that I stand ready to assist you. Openly acknowledge your insufficiency, and trust in My infinite sufficiency. You and I *together* can accomplish anything, as long as it is My will.

You definitely need Me as your Shield. I protect you from many dangers—physical, emotional, and spiritual. Sometimes you're aware of My protective work on your behalf, but I also shield you from perils you never even suspect. Find comfort in this assurance of My powerful Presence watching over you. *Fear no evil*, My cherished one, *for I am with you.*

PSALM 33:20; DEUTERONOMY 31:8;
PHILIPPIANS 4:13 NKJV; PSALM 23:4

S EEK MY FACE, and you will find all that you have longed for. The deepest yearnings of your heart are for intimacy with Me. I know because I designed you to desire Me. Do not feel guilty about taking time to be still in My Presence. You are simply responding to the tugs of divinity within you. I made you in My image, and I hid heaven in your heart. Your yearning for Me is a form of homesickness: longing for your true home in heaven.

Do not be afraid to be different from other people. The path I have called you to travel is exquisitely right for you. The more closely you follow My leading, the more fully I can develop your gifts. To follow Me wholeheartedly, you must relinquish your desire to please other people. However, your closeness to Me will bless others by enabling you to shine brightly in this dark world.

PSALM 42:1–2; PSALM 34:5; PHILIPPIANS 2:15

CLING TO ME, BELOVED, for *My right hand supports you*. When you hold onto Me in childlike dependence, you are demonstrating your commitment to Me. I use difficult times to refine your faith and prove that it is genuine. As you cling to Me in the midst of adversity, your faith grows stronger and you are comforted. Having endured various trials, you gain confidence that you can cope with future hardships—with My help. You realize more and more that I will always be available to help you.

In the middle of the night or in the midst of tough times, remember that My right hand supports you. This hand that holds you up is strong and righteous; there's no limit to how much support it can provide. So when you're feeling overwhelmed, don't give up. Instead, *look to Me and My Strength*. Be assured that My powerful hand is also righteous; what it provides is good. *Do not fear, for I will strengthen you and help you. I will uphold you with My righteous right hand.*

PSALM 63:8; 1 PETER 1:7;
PSALM 105:4; ISAIAH 41:10

R EST IN MY PRESENCE WHEN you need refreshment. Resting is not necessarily idleness, as people often perceive it. When you relax in My company, you are demonstrating trust in Me. *Trust* is a rich word, laden with meaning and direction for your life. I want you to *lean on, trust, and be confident in Me*. When you lean on Me for support, I delight in your trusting confidence.

Many people turn away from Me when they are exhausted. They associate Me with duty and diligence, so they try to hide from My Presence when they need a break from work. How this saddens Me! As I spoke through My prophet Isaiah: *In returning to Me and resting in Me you shall be saved; in quietness and trust shall be your strength.*

PSALM 91:1; PROVERBS 3:5 AMP;
ISAIAH 30:15 AMP

*T*HOSE WHO LOOK TO *ME* ARE RADIANT. I am the Sun that shines on continually, even when your circumstances are difficult and the way ahead looks dark. Because you know Me as Savior, you have a source of Light that overcomes the darkness. I designed you to *reflect My Glory*, and you do so by looking to Me—turning your face toward the Light. Take time to be still in My Presence, with your face upturned to absorb My radiance. The longer you stay in this Light-drenched atmosphere, the more I can bless and strengthen you.

While you are resting with Me, you may want to whisper the words of Jacob: *"Surely the Lord is in this place."* I am everywhere at every time, so this statement is always true—whether or not you sense My nearness.

Taking time to bask in My Love-Light, soaking in My radiance, can enhance your awareness of My Presence. Also, time spent with Me helps you to be a light in the world—radiating My Love to those around you.

PSALM 34:5; 2 CORINTHIANS 3:18;
GENESIS 28:16; MATTHEW 5:16 NKJV

F IND FREEDOM through seeking to please Me above all else. *You can have only one Master.* When you let others' expectations drive you, you scatter your energy to the winds. Your own desire to look good can also drain your energy. I am your Master, and I do not drive you to be what you are not. Your pretense displeases Me, especially when it is in My "service." Concentrate on staying close to Me at all times. It is impossible to be inauthentic while you are focusing on My Presence.

EPHESIANS 5:8–10; MATTHEW 23:8; MATTHEW 6:1

Y OU HAVE RECEIVED *NEW BIRTH into a living hope through My resurrection from the dead.* I died on the cross to pay the penalty for the sins of all My followers. However, if I had remained dead, *your faith would be useless* and you would forever be spiritually dead—*still guilty of your sins.* Of course, it was impossible for My death to be permanent because I am God! As I stated clearly to those who questioned Me, *I and My Father are One.*

My resurrection is an extremely well-documented historical fact. This miraculous event opened the way for you to experience *new birth.* By confessing your sinfulness and trusting Me as your Savior, you have become one of My own—walking along a pathway to heaven. Because I am your living Savior, you walk along a way of *living hope!* The Light of My loving Presence shines upon you always, even in your darkest, most difficult moments. Look up to Me, beloved. Let My brilliant Love-Light pierce the darkness and fill your heart with Joy.

1 PETER 1:3; 1 CORINTHIANS 15:17 NLT;
EPHESIANS 2:1; JOHN 10:30 NKJV

I AM THE LIGHT OF THE WORLD. Men crawl through their lives cursing the darkness, but all the while I am shining brightly. I desire each of My followers to be a Light-bearer. The Holy Spirit who lives in you can shine from your face, making Me visible to people around you. Ask My Spirit to live through you as you wend your way through this day. Hold My hand in joyful trust, for I never leave your side. The Light of My Presence is shining upon you. Brighten up the world by reflecting who I AM.

JOHN 8:12; MATTHEW 5:14–16;
2 CORINTHIANS 3:18; EXODUS 3:14

I AM GOD YOUR SAVIOR. No matter what is happening in the world, you can *be joyful in Me.* Your planet has been in a terribly fallen condition ever since Adam and Eve first disobeyed Me. They lost their first two sons in a heartbreaking way. Cain killed his younger brother Abel because he was jealous of him. Then God punished Cain by sentencing him to a life of *restless wandering on the earth.*

Ongoing effects of the Fall continue to make the world a dangerous, uncertain place. So the challenge before you each day is to be joyful in the midst of brokenness. Remind yourself often: "Jesus is with me and for me. *Nothing can separate me from His Love.*" Pour your energies into enjoying My Presence and looking for the good that remains on the earth. Use your gifts to shine My Light into places where I have given you access. *Have no fear of bad news,* for I am able to bring good out of evil. Train your heart to be *steadfast, trusting in Me,* your Savior.

HABAKKUK 3:18; GENESIS 4:12;
ROMANS 8:39; PSALM 112:7

T HANKFULNESS OPENS THE DOOR to My Presence. Though I am always with you, I have gone to great measures to preserve your freedom of choice. I have placed a door between you and Me, and I have empowered you to open or close that door. There are many ways to open it, but a grateful attitude is one of the most effective.

Thankfulness is built on a substructure of trust. When thankful words stick in your throat, you need to check up on your foundation of trust. When thankfulness flows freely from your heart and lips, let your gratitude draw you closer to Me. I want you to learn the art of *giving thanks in all circumstances*. See how many times you can thank Me daily; this will awaken your awareness to a multitude of blessings. It will also cushion the impact of trials when they come against you. Practice My Presence by practicing the discipline of thankfulness.

PSALM 100:4; PSALM 31:14;
1 THESSALONIANS 5:18

*D*O NOT BE AFRAID; *do not be discouraged.* You are looking ahead at uncertainties, letting them unnerve you. Fear and discouragement are waiting alongside your pathway into the future—ready to accompany you if you let them. *Yet I am always with you, holding you by your right hand.* Because I live beyond time, I am also on the path up ahead—shining brightly, beckoning you on, encouraging you to fix your gaze on Me. Cling tightly to My hand, and walk resolutely past those dark presences of fearfulness and despair. Keep looking toward My radiant Presence that beams out rays of *unfailing Love* and endless encouragement.

Your confidence comes from knowing I am continually with you *and* I am already in your future, preparing the way before you. Listen as I call back to you—words of warning and wisdom, courage and hope: *Do not fear, for I am with you. Do not be dismayed, for I am your God. I will strengthen you and help you; I will uphold you with My righteous right hand.*

DEUTERONOMY 31:8; PSALM 73:23;
PSALM 119:76; ISAIAH 41:10

A S YOU LISTEN to birds calling to one another, hear also My Love-call to you. I speak to you continually: through sights, sounds, thoughts, impressions, scriptures. There is no limit to the variety of ways I can communicate with you. Your part is to be attentive to My messages, in whatever form they come. When you set out to find Me in a day, you discover that the world is vibrantly alive with My Presence. You can find Me not only in beauty and birdcalls, but also in tragedy and faces filled with grief. I can take the deepest sorrow and *weave it into a pattern for good*.

Search for Me and My messages as you go through this day. *You will seek Me and find Me when you seek Me with your whole being*.

JOHN 10:27; ROMANS 8:28 AMP; JEREMIAH 29:13

I T I S I N T H E P R E S E N T M O M E N T that you find Me ever near you. My Presence in the present is an endless source of Joy—*a continual feast*! I am training you to *rejoice in Me always*. This is a moment-by-moment choice. It is possible to find Joy in Me even during your most difficult times. I am always near, so I am constantly available to help you. I can even carry you through your hardest times.

Imagine a woman who has become engaged to a man she deeply loves and admires. Her heart overflows with pleasure whenever she thinks about her beloved. While he is on her mind, problems fade into the background, unable to dampen her enthusiasm and excitement. Similarly, when you remember that I am your Betrothed and you are promised to Me forever, you can find pleasure in Me even though you face many difficulties. The soul-satisfaction you find in Me helps you relate well to other people. As you enjoy My loving Presence, you are able to bless others with your Joy.

PROVERBS 15:15 NKJV; PHILIPPIANS 4:4–5;
PSALM 63:5; DEUTERONOMY 33:12

R ELAX AND LET ME LEAD YOU through this day. I have everything under control: *My* control. You tend to peer anxiously into the day that is before you, trying to figure out what to do and when. Meanwhile, the phone or the doorbell rings, and you have to reshuffle your plans. All that planning ties you up in knots and distracts you from Me. Attentiveness to Me is not only for your quiet time, but for all your time. As you look to Me, I show you what to do *now* and *next*.

Vast quantities of time and energy are wasted in obsessive planning. When you let *Me* direct your steps, you are set free to enjoy Me and to find what I have prepared for you this day.

PSALM 32:8; PSALM 119:35; PSALM 143:8

I BROADEN THE PATH BENEATH YOU *so that your ankles do not turn.* This shows how intricately I am involved in your life-journey. I know exactly what is before you, and I can alter the path ahead of you to make your way easier. Sometimes I enable you to see what I have done on your behalf. At other times you are blissfully unaware of the hardship I have spared you. Either way, My work to widen the way before you demonstrates how lovingly I am involved in your life.

From your perspective, My workings are often mysterious. I do not protect you—or anyone—from *all* adversity. Neither was *I* shielded from hardship during my thirty-three years of living in your world. On the contrary, I willingly suffered unimaginable pain, humiliation, and agony on the cross—for your sake! When My Father turned away from Me, I experienced unspeakable suffering. But because I was willing to endure that excruciating isolation from Him, you will *never* have to suffer alone. I have promised: *I am with you always!*

PSALM 18:36; MATTHEW 27:46 NKJV;
MATTHEW 28:20

HOPE IS A GOLDEN CORD connecting you to heaven. This cord helps you hold your head up high, even when multiple trials are buffeting you. I never leave your side, and I never let go of your hand. But without the cord of hope, your head may slump and your feet may shuffle as you journey uphill with Me. Hope lifts your perspective from your weary feet to the glorious view you can see from the high road. You are reminded that the road we're traveling together is ultimately a highway to heaven. When you consider this radiant destination, the roughness or smoothness of the road ahead becomes much less significant. I am training you to hold in your heart a dual focus: My continual Presence and the hope of heaven.

ROMANS 12:12; 1 THESSALONIANS 5:8;
HEBREWS 6:18–19

*W*HOEVER BELIEVES IN *ME* *does not believe in Me only, but in the One who sent Me. When you look at Me, you see the One who sent Me.* I came into the world not only to be your Savior but also to help you see the Father more clearly. He and I always work in perfect unity. As I proclaimed when I was teaching in the temple in Jerusalem: *"I and My Father are one."* So when you strive to live close to Me—*fixing your eyes on Me*—you are by no means ignoring My Father.

The Trinity, comprised of Father, Son, and Holy Spirit, is a great gift to you; it is also a mystery far beyond your comprehension. This blessing of three Persons in one greatly enriches your prayer life. You can pray to the Father in My Name; you can also speak directly to Me. And the Holy Spirit is continually available to help you with your prayers. Do not be perturbed by mysteries of the Godhead. Instead, respond to these wonders with joyous praise and adoration!

JOHN 12:44–45; JOHN 10:30 NKJV;
HEBREWS 12:2; PSALM 150:6

L ET MY LOVE seep into the inner recesses of your being. Do not close off any part of yourself from Me. I know you inside and out, so do not try to present a "cleaned-up" self to Me. Wounds that you shut away from the Light of My Love will fester and become wormy. Secret sins that you "hide" from Me can split off and develop lives of their own, controlling you without your realizing it.

Open yourself fully to My transforming Presence. Let My brilliant Love-Light search out and destroy hidden fears. This process requires time alone with Me, as My Love soaks into your innermost being. Enjoy *My perfect Love, which expels every trace of fear.*

PSALM 139:1–4, 23–24; 1 JOHN 4:18 AMP

I AM *THE LIVING ONE who sees you* always. I see into the very depths of your being. Not even one of your thoughts escapes My notice. My intimate awareness of everything about you means that you are never alone—in good times or in struggles. It also means that I want to cleanse your thoughts from their sinful tendencies.

When you find yourself thinking in a loveless, hurtful way, confess it to Me immediately. Ask Me not only to forgive you but to change you. You don't need to belabor your confession, as if you had to convince Me to extend grace to you. I went through torturous execution and utter separation from My Father so that I could *remove your sins as far from you as the east is from the west.* I delight in forgiving you!

Remember that even now I view you clothed in radiant garments—My perfect righteousness. And I can already see in you the glorious vision you will be when heaven becomes your home.

GENESIS 16:14 AMP; PSALM 139:1–2;
2 CORINTHIANS 5:21; PSALM 103:12 NLT

C OME TO ME CONTINUALLY. I am meant to be the Center of your consciousness, the *Anchor of your soul.* Your mind will wander from Me, but the question is how far you allow it to wander. An anchor on a short rope lets a boat drift only slightly before the taut line tugs the boat back toward the center. Similarly, as you drift away from Me, My Spirit within you gives a tug, prompting you to return to Me. As you become increasingly attuned to My Presence, the length of rope on your soul's Anchor is shortened. You wander only a short distance before feeling that inner tug—telling you to return to your true Center in Me.

HEBREWS 6:19; 1 JOHN 2:28; MATTHEW 22:37

I AM TRAINING YOU in *patient endurance.* This lesson is not for the faint-hearted. However, it is a rich blessing— one aspect of sharing in My kingdom and My suffering.

Since My kingdom is eternal, it is of infinite value. And I have made it clear that *sharing in My sufferings* is necessary for *sharing in My Glory.* Moreover, this experience produces real benefits in the here and now—character.

Patient endurance can be developed only through hardship. So make every effort to welcome the very problem you dread. Bring it into My Presence with thanksgiving, and acknowledge your willingness to endure it as long as I deem necessary. Ask Me to take this dark, ugly thing and transform it into something lovely. I can weave bright, golden strands of Glory into the most heart-wrenching situation. It may take a long time for the lovely pattern to emerge, but this waiting can build patience. Rejoice, beloved, for I am polishing your character till it shines with the Light of My Glory!

REVELATION 1:9; ROMANS 8:17;
PHILIPPIANS 2:14–15

WORSHIP ME *in the beauty of holiness.* I created beauty to declare the existence of My holy Being. A magnificent rose, a hauntingly glorious sunset, oceanic splendor—all these things were meant to proclaim My Presence in the world. Most people rush past these proclamations without giving them a second thought. Some people use beauty, especially feminine loveliness, to sell their products.

How precious are My children who are awed by nature's beauty; this opens them up to My holy Presence. Even before you knew Me personally, you responded to My creation with wonder. This is a gift, and it carries responsibility with it. Declare My glorious Being to the world. *The whole earth is full of My radiant beauty—My Glory!*

PSALM 29:2 NKJV; 1 SAMUEL 2:2; ISAIAH 6:3

B ELOVED, *My compassions never fail. They are new every morning.* So you can begin each day confidently, knowing that My vast reservoir of blessings is full to the brim. This knowledge helps you *wait for Me*, entrusting your long-unanswered prayers into My care and keeping. I assure you that not one of those petitions has slipped past Me unnoticed. I want you to drink deeply from My fountain of limitless Love and unfailing compassion. As you wait in My Presence, these divine nutrients are freely available to you.

Although many of your prayers are not yet answered, you can find hope in *My great faithfulness.* I keep all My promises in My perfect way and timing. I have promised to *give you Peace* that can displace the trouble and fear in your heart. If you become weary of waiting, remember that I also wait— *that I may be gracious to you and have mercy on you.* I hold back till you're ready to receive the things I have lovingly prepared for you. *Blessed are all those who wait for Me.*

LAMENTATIONS 3:22–24;
JOHN 14:27; ISAIAH 30:18 NKJV

July 31

Trust Me in the depths of your being. It is there that I live in constant communion with you. When you feel flustered and frazzled on the outside, do not get upset with yourself. You are only human, and the swirl of events going on all around you will sometimes feel overwhelming. Rather than scolding yourself for your humanness, remind yourself that I am both with you and within you.

I am with you at all times, encouraging and supportive rather than condemning. I know that deep within you, where I live, My Peace is your continual experience. Slow down your pace of living for a time. Quiet your mind in My Presence. Then you will be able to hear Me bestowing the resurrection blessing: *Peace be with you.*

COLOSSIANS 1:27; MATTHEW 28:20; JOHN 20:19

*B*EFORE YOU CALL *I* WILL ANSWER; *while you are still speaking I will hear.* I know you sometimes feel as if you're alone—in the dark. You continue praying because it's the right thing to do, but you wonder if your prayers make any difference. When you are feeling this way, it's good to stop and remember who I AM—*the King of Glory!* I transcend time. Past, present, and future all are alike to Me. This is why I can answer before you even call out to Me.

No prayer of yours is ever unheard or unanswered. However, sometimes My answer is "No" or "Not yet." At other times your prayers are answered in ways you cannot see. *My wisdom is unsearchable*—immeasurably beyond your understanding. Take time to think about the wonders of My infinite intelligence and to delight in My endless Love for you. If you persist in this intimate adoration, you will know beyond any doubt that you are *never* alone. You are Mine!

ISAIAH 65:24; PSALM 24:10; ROMANS 11:33 NKJV

August

"Whoever believes in me, as the
Scripture has said, streams of living
water will flow from within him."

JOHN 7:38

August 1

N OTHING CAN SEPARATE YOU *from My Love.* Let this divine assurance trickle through your mind and into your heart and soul. Whenever you start to feel fearful or anxious, repeat this unconditional promise: "Nothing can separate me from Your Love, Jesus."

Most of mankind's misery stems from feeling unloved. In the midst of adverse circumstances, people tend to feel that love has been withdrawn and they have been forsaken. This feeling of abandonment is often worse than the adversity itself. Be assured that I never abandon any of My children, not even temporarily. *I will never leave you or forsake you!* My Presence watches over you continually. *I have engraved you on the palms of My hands.*

ROMANS 8:38–39; JOSHUA 1:5; ISAIAH 49:15–16

COME EAGERLY INTO MY ARDENT PRESENCE, inviting Me to *satisfy you with My unfailing Love*. The best time to seek My Face is *in the morning*, soon after you awaken. Connecting with Me early sets the tone for the rest of the day. My endless Love is immensely satisfying: It helps you know you are treasured and significant. It reminds you that *together* you and I can handle the circumstances of your day. Knowing you are forever loved energizes you and gives you courage to persevere through difficulties.

Encountering My loving Presence in the morning equips you to *sing for Joy and be glad*. Think about the astonishing privilege of meeting with the One who is *King of kings and Lord of lords* in the privacy of your home. Rejoice that your name is written in *the Lamb's Book of Life*—with indelible ink! Take time to enjoy My Presence. Speak or sing praises; read Scripture and pray. Delight yourself in the wondrous truth that *nothing in all creation can separate you from My Love*!

PSALM 90:14; REVELATION 19:16 NASB;
REVELATION 21:27; ROMANS 8:39

B RING ME THE SACRIFICE OF YOUR TIME: a most precious commodity. In this action-addicted world, few of My children take time to sit quietly in My Presence. But for those who do, blessings flow like *streams of living water*. I, the One from whom all blessings flow, am also blessed by our time together. This is a deep mystery; do not try to fathom it. Instead, glorify Me by delighting in Me. Enjoy Me now and forever!

PSALM 21:6; JOHN 7:37–38;
PSALM 103:11; PSALM 34:3

I AM YOUR LIVING LORD, your Rock, your Savior-God. Spend time pondering My greatness and My endless commitment to you. You live in a culture where vast numbers of people are leery of making commitments. Even those who say "I do" often change their minds later and leave. I, however, am your forever-Friend and the eternal Lover of your soul. You are utterly secure in My Love!

Instead of focusing on troubles in your life and in your world, remember who I Am. Not only am I your living Lord and unchanging Rock, I am also *God your Savior*. Because I am the everlasting God, my death on the cross for your sins *saves you to the uttermost*! So you don't need to worry that I'll stop loving you because your performance isn't good enough. It is *My* goodness and *My* righteousness that keep you secure in My Love. Let My unending commitment to you be a comfort as you journey through this trouble-filled world. Someday you will live with Me in paradise.

PSALM 18:46; HEBREWS 7:25 NKJV;
2 CORINTHIANS 5:21 NKJV

WATCH YOUR WORDS DILIGENTLY. Words have such great power to bless or to wound. When you speak carelessly or negatively, you damage others as well as yourself. This ability to verbalize is an awesome privilege, granted only to those I created in My image. You need help in wielding this mighty power responsibly.

Though the world applauds quick-witted retorts, My instructions about communication are quite different: *Be quick to listen, slow to speak, and slow to become angry.* Ask My Spirit to help you whenever you speak. I have trained you to pray—"Help me, Holy Spirit"—before answering the phone, and you have seen the benefits of this discipline. Simply apply the same discipline to communicating with people around you. If they are silent, pray before speaking to them. If they are talking, pray before responding. These are split-second prayers, but they put you in touch with My Presence. In this way, your speaking comes under the control of My Spirit. As positive speech patterns replace your negative ones, the increase in your Joy will amaze you.

PROVERBS 12:18; JAMES 1:19; EPHESIANS 4:29

WAIT IN MY PRESENCE. There are so many benefits—spiritual, emotional, and physical—to spending time with Me. Yet many of My children think this is a luxury they cannot afford. Even though they crave rest and quietness, they continue in their fast-paced lifestyle. I want *you* to arrange your priorities in such a way that you can have some restful times with Me. I will refresh your soul and strengthen you for the journey that lies ahead.

Be of good courage. Living in this very broken world requires bravery on your part. Since bravery is not the default setting in most human hearts, you will need My help to *be strong and courageous.* In spite of all the alarming events in the world, you don't have to be terrified or discouraged. Discipline yourself to *fix your thoughts on Me* again and again—and again! Find comfort in My promise to *be with you wherever you go.*

Continue your efforts to be courageous, and look to Me for help. *I will strengthen your heart.*

PSALM 27:14 NKJV; JOSHUA 1:9; HEBREWS 3:1

HOLD MY HAND, and walk joyously with Me through this day. Together we will savor the pleasures and endure the difficulties it brings. Be on the lookout for everything I have prepared for you: stunning scenery, bracing winds of adventure, cozy nooks for resting when you are weary, and much more. I am your Guide, as well as your constant Companion. I know every step of the journey ahead of you, all the way to heaven.

You don't have to choose between staying close to Me and staying on course. Since *I am the Way*, staying close to Me is staying on course. As you focus your thoughts on Me, I will guide you carefully along today's journey. Don't worry about what is around the next bend. Just concentrate on enjoying My Presence and staying in step with Me.

PHILIPPIANS 4:13 NKJV; ISAIAH 58:11;
JOHN 14:6; COLOSSIANS 4:2

NEVER UNDERESTIMATE the power of prayer! People who are feeling discouraged and hopeless often say something like, "There's nothing left to do but pray." The implication is that this is their last resort—and a feeble one at that. Nothing could be further from the truth!

I created mankind with the ability to communicate with Me. Since I am *the eternal, immortal, invisible King* of the universe, this is an astonishing privilege. Even when the human race became tainted with sin through Adam and Eve's disobedience, I did not withdraw this glorious privilege. And when I lived in your world as a flesh-and-blood man, I relied heavily on praying to My Father. I was keenly aware of how continuously I needed His help.

Persistent, heartfelt prayer will bless not only you but also your family, friends, church—even your country. Ask the Holy Spirit to help you pray effectively. Find others to join you in this venture of seeking My Face in humility and repentance. Beseech Me to *heal your land*.

COLOSSIANS 1:16 NKJV; 1 TIMOTHY 1:17;
MATTHEW 14:23 NKJV; 2 CHRONICLES 7:14

S IT QUIETLY IN MY PRESENCE while I bless you. Make your mind like a still pool of water, ready to receive whatever thoughts I drop into it. Rest in My sufficiency as you consider the challenges this day presents. Do not wear yourself out by worrying about whether you can cope with the pressures. Keep looking to Me and communicating with Me as we walk through this day together.

Take time to rest by the wayside, for I am not in a hurry. A leisurely pace accomplishes more than hurried striving. When you rush, you forget who you are and Whose you are. Remember that you are royalty in My kingdom.

PSALM 37:7; ROMANS 8:16–17; 1 PETER 2:9

*L*OOK TO *ME AND MY STRENGTH*; *seek My Face always*. I encourage you to *let your heart rejoice* whenever you are seeking Me.

Imagine an engaged couple—passionately in love. When the man goes to visit his betrothed, she doesn't open the door and blithely say, "Oh, it's you." Nor does he look past her as if she were invisible and ask, "Do you have anything to eat?" Instead, their hearts leap for joy because they are together. You are My betrothed, and I am the forever-Lover of your soul. Rejoice in the astonishing affection I have for you!

Glory in My holy Name; it's holy because it represents *Me*. This Name is *above every name*, yet you may use it freely to commune with Me and worship Me joyously. You are privileged to have such easy access to Me. Some people glory in their wealth, achievements, beauty, or fame. But I invite you to exult in *Me*—your Savior, Lord, and Lover. Glorifying Me will strengthen and delight you, bringing Power to your prayers and Joy to your heart.

1 CHRONICLES 16:10–11; 2 CORINTHIANS 11:2;
JOHN 15:13; PHILIPPIANS 2:9–10 NKJV

WHEN THINGS SEEM to be going all wrong, stop and affirm your trust in Me. Calmly bring these matters to Me, and leave them in My capable hands. Then, simply do the next thing. Stay in touch with Me through thankful, trusting prayers, resting in My sovereign control. Rejoice in Me—exult in the God of your salvation! As you trust in Me, *I make your feet like the feet of a deer. I enable you to walk and make progress upon your high places of trouble, suffering, or responsibility.*

JOB 13:15 NKJV; PSALM 18:33;
HABAKKUK 3:17–19 AMP

WHEN PLANNING AND PROBLEMS are preoccupying your mind, turn to Me and whisper My Name. Let the Light of My Presence shine on you as you rejoice in *My unfailing Love*. Thank Me for watching over you always and loving you eternally. Affirm your trust in Me; express your devotion to Me. Then ask Me to illuminate the way forward—helping you sort out what needs to be done today and what does not. Deal with problems as you must, but refuse to let worry or fear become central in your thoughts.

Keep returning your focus to Me as often as you can, and I will light up your perspective. Saturate your mind and heart with Scripture—reading it, studying it, and memorizing verses that are especially helpful to you. *My Word is a lamp to your feet and a Light for your path.*

If you follow these guidelines, your preoccupation with planning and problems will diminish. This leaves room in your life for more of *Me*. Delight in *the Joy of My Presence*!

PSALM 107:21–22; 1 PETER 5:7 AMP;
PSALM 119:105; ACTS 2:28 NLT

U NDERSTANDING WILL NEVER BRING YOU PEACE. That's why I have instructed you to *trust in Me, not in your understanding.* Human beings have a voracious appetite for trying to figure things out in order to gain a sense of mastery over their lives. But the world presents you with an endless series of problems. As soon as you master one set, another pops up to challenge you. The relief you had anticipated is short-lived. Soon your mind is gearing up again: searching for understanding (mastery) instead of seeking Me (your Master).

The wisest of all men, Solomon, could never think his way through to Peace. His vast understanding resulted in feelings of futility rather than in fulfillment. Finally, he lost his way and succumbed to the will of his wives by worshiping idols.

My Peace is not an elusive goal, hidden at the center of some complicated maze. Actually, you are always enveloped in Peace, which is inherent in My Presence. As you look to Me, you gain awareness of this precious Peace.

PROVERBS 3:5–6; ROMANS 5:1;
2 THESSALONIANS 3:16

I AM THE ONE who *keeps your lamp burning. I turn your darkness into Light.* Sometimes, when you are *weary and burdened*, you may feel as if your lamp is about to go out. It seems to be flickering and sputtering—on the verge of running out of fuel. Whenever this happens, call out to Me for help. Take some deep breaths in My Presence, and remember that *I* am the One who fuels your lamp. I am *your Strength!*

I am also your Light. Keep turning toward Me, letting the Glory of My Presence soak into you. My radiant beauty brightens your life and changes your perspective. When you turn away from Me and forget that I am with you, your world looks very dark. Indeed, there is much darkness in this deeply fallen world you inhabit. However, I am *the Light that shines on in the darkness.* So do not be afraid, My child. Trust Me wholeheartedly—no matter how gloomy things may appear— and I will *transform your darkness into Light.*

PSALM 18:28; MATTHEW 11:28;
PSALM 18:1; JOHN 1:5 AMP

I SPEAK TO YOU from deepest heaven. You hear Me in the depths of your being. *Deep calls unto deep.* You are blessed to hear Me so directly. Never take this privilege for granted. The best response is a heart overflowing with gratitude. I am training you to cultivate a thankful mind-set. This is like *building your house on a firm rock, where life's storms cannot shake you.* As you learn these lessons, you are to teach them to others. I will open up the way before you, one step at a time.

PSALM 42:7–8 NKJV; PSALM 95:1–2;
MATTHEW 7:24–25

*T*HE FEAR OF MAN IS A SNARE. A snare is a kind of trap—something that entangles you, making it difficult for you to escape. "Fear of man" involves being overly concerned about what others think of you. It's an unhealthy, ungodly focus—seeing yourself through the eyes of others. This fear can be crippling, and it is full of distortions. Other people's views of you are distorted by their sinful nature. Furthermore, it's almost impossible to know what they really think about you. When you view yourself from others' perspectives, you add your own distortions to theirs. As you strive to present an acceptable "persona," you become trapped.

When you realize that fear of man is motivating you—controlling your thoughts and behavior—come to Me. At your request, I will forgive you for making others' views of you into an idol; I will help you break free from these entanglements. Affirm your trust in Me and take time to enjoy My Presence. As you forget about yourself and focus on Me, your loving Lord, you grow increasingly free!

PROVERBS 29:25 HCSB; 1 JOHN 1:9 NKJV;
2 CORINTHIANS 3:17

WEAR MY ROBE OF RIGHTEOUSNESS with ease. I custom-made it for you, to cover you from head to toe. The price I paid for this covering was astronomical—My own blood. You could never purchase such a royal garment, no matter how hard you worked. Sometimes you forget that My righteousness is a gift, and you feel ill at ease in your regal robe. I weep when I see you squirming under the velvety fabric, as if it were made of scratchy sackcloth.

I want you to trust Me enough to realize your privileged position in My kingdom. Relax in the luxuriant folds of your magnificent robe. Keep your eyes on Me as you practice walking in this garment of salvation. When your behavior is unfitting for one in My kingdom, do not try to throw off your royal robe. Instead, throw off the unrighteous behavior. Then you will be able to feel at ease in this glorious garment, enjoying the gift I fashioned for you before the foundation of the world.

ISAIAH 61:10; 2 CORINTHIANS 5:21;
EPHESIANS 4:22–24

COME REST WITH ME, BELOVED. Though many tasks are calling to you, urging you to put them first, *I* know what you need most: to *be still* in My Presence. Take some deep breaths, and fix your gaze on Me. As you return your attention to Me, let your concerns roll off—like water off a duck's back. This enables you to relax and enjoy My nearness. I am never far from you!

Meditate on Scripture; search for Me in the Bible. Let these words of grace and truth soak into the depths of your soul and draw you closer to Me. *My Word is living and active*, so it can infuse fresh life into you.

When it is time to return to your tasks, bring Me into those activities. Include Me in your plans and problem-solving. I am relevant to everything you do, say, and think. Whisper My Name, "Jesus," in sweet remembrance of My nearness. *In everything you do, put Me first*, for I am the Lord of your life.

PSALM 46:10; HEBREWS 4:12 ESV;
PROVERBS 3:6 TLB

R ELAX IN MY HEALING, holy Presence. Allow Me to transform you through this time alone with Me. As your thoughts center more and more on Me, trust displaces fear and worry. Your mind is somewhat like a seesaw. As your trust in Me goes up, fear and worry automatically go down. Time spent with Me not only increases your trust; it also helps you discern what is important and what is not.

Energy and time are precious, limited entities. Therefore, you need to use them wisely, focusing on what is truly important. As you walk close to Me, saturating your mind with Scripture, I will show you how to spend your time and energy. *My Word is a lamp to your feet; My Presence is a Light for your path.*

ROMANS 12:2 NKJV; PSALM 52:8;
EPHESIANS 5:15–16 NKJV; PSALM 119:105

I AM TRAINING YOU to be an overcomer—to find Joy in the midst of circumstances that previously would have defeated you. Your ability to transcend trouble is based on this rock-solid fact: *I have overcome the world*; I have already won the ultimate victory! Nonetheless, as I taught, *you will have trouble in this world*. So expect to encounter many difficulties as you journey through life. You inhabit a planet that is always at war, and the enemy of your soul never rests. But don't be afraid, because *He who is in you is greater than he who is in the world*. This is good reason to rejoice!

When you are in the midst of challenging circumstances, it is crucial to keep trusting Me. Whisper "I trust You, Jesus" as often as you need—remembering I am always near. Ask Me to help you learn all that I have for you in this trial. Look for flowers of Joy growing in the rich soil of adversity. The sunlight of *My Face is shining upon you*, beloved.

JOHN 16:33; 1 JOHN 4:4 NKJV;
PSALM 145:18; NUMBERS 6:25

C OME TO ME. *Come to Me. Come to Me.* This is My continual invitation to you, proclaimed in holy whispers. When your heart and mind are quiet, you can hear Me inviting you to draw near. Coming close to Me requires no great effort on your part; it is more like ceasing to resist the magnetic pull of My Love. Open yourself to My loving Presence so that I may fill you with My fullness. I want you to experience *how wide and long and high and deep is My Love for you so that you can know My Love that surpasses knowledge.* This vast ocean of Love cannot be measured or explained, but it can be experienced.

REVELATION 22:17; JOHN 6:37;
EPHESIANS 3:16–19

M Y FACE IS SHINING UPON YOU, beloved. Take time to linger in My joyous Light, and seek to know Me as I truly am. I am always near you, closer than the air you're breathing. Awareness of My loving Presence is a rich blessing. However, the most important thing is to *trust* that I am with you regardless of what you are experiencing.

I am immanent—present throughout the entire universe. I am also transcendent—existing above and independent from the universe. I am *the King eternal, immortal, invisible, the only God. As the heavens are higher than the earth, so are My ways higher than your ways and My thoughts than your thoughts.* Therefore, don't expect to fully understand Me or My ways. When things don't go as you think they should, be willing to bow before My infinite *wisdom and knowledge. My judgments are unsearchable and My paths beyond tracing out,* but they are good. Remember the example of Job. When his family experienced multiple disasters, *he fell to the ground in worship.* I transcend all your troubles!

1 TIMOTHY 1:17; ISAIAH 55:9 NKJV;
ROMANS 11:33; JOB 1:20

August 12

COME TO ME when you are weak and weary. Rest snugly in My everlasting arms. I do not despise your weakness, My child. Actually, it draws Me closer to you because weakness stirs up My compassion—My yearning to help. Accept yourself in your weariness, knowing that I understand how difficult your journey has been.

Do not compare yourself with others who seem to skip along their life-paths with ease. Their journeys have been different from yours, and I have gifted them with abundant energy. I have gifted you with fragility, providing opportunities for your spirit to blossom in My Presence. Accept this gift as a sacred treasure: delicate, yet glowing with brilliant Light. Rather than struggling to disguise or deny your weakness, allow Me to bless you richly through it.

ISAIAH 42:3; ISAIAH 54:10; ROMANS 8:26

WHEN YOU BUMP INTO massive difficulties on your life-path, I want you to *consider it pure Joy*. As you bounce off these "impossibilities," *My everlasting arms* are wide open—ready to catch you, calm you, and help you do what does not seem possible. You can be joyful in the midst of perplexing problems because I am *God your Savior*—and I have already accomplished the greatest miracle in your life: saving you from your sins. If you keep looking to Me, your resurrected Lord and King, your pessimism will eventually give way to courage. Though you are an earthbound creature, your soul shares in My eternal victory.

I have infinite Power, so "impossibilities" are My specialty. I delight in them because they display My Glory so vividly. They also help you live the way I intended: in joyful, trusting dependence on Me. The next time you face an "impossible" situation, turn to Me immediately with a hopeful heart. Acknowledge your total inadequacy and cling to Me—relying on My infinite sufficiency. *All things are possible with Me*!

JAMES 1:2–3; DEUTERONOMY 33:27 NKJV;
HABAKKUK 3:17–18; MATTHEW 19:26

L EARN TO ENJOY LIFE MORE. Relax, remember-
ing that I am *God with you*. I crafted you with enormous
capacity to know Me and enjoy My Presence. When My people
wear sour faces and walk through their lives with resigned
rigidity, I am displeased. When you walk through a day with
childlike delight, savoring every blessing, you proclaim your
trust in Me, your ever-present Shepherd. The more you focus
on My Presence with you, the more fully you can enjoy life.
Glorify Me through your pleasure in Me. Thus you proclaim
My Presence to the watching world.

MATTHEW 1:23; JOHN 10:10–11;
JUDE vv. 24–25

N O MATTER HOW YOU'RE FEELING, remember that you are *not* on trial. *There is no condemnation for those who belong to Me*—those who know Me as Savior. You have already been judged "Not guilty!" in the courts of heaven.

I came to earth to set you free from bondage to sin. I long to see you living joyfully in that freedom. Learn to enjoy your guilt-free position in My kingdom, refusing to be weighed down or shackled. The world is in a fallen condition where sin and evil abound, but *I have overcome the world*!

The best response to the grace lavished on you is thankfulness—gratitude that fuels a desire to live according to My will. The closer you live to Me, the better you can discern My will; also, the more you can experience My Peace and Joy. Knowing Me intimately helps you trust Me enough to receive Peace from Me even in the midst of trouble. *Overflowing with thankfulness* has the delightful "side effect" of increasing your Joy. Live freely and joyously in My Presence, beloved!

ROMANS 8:1; JOHN 8:36 ESV;
JOHN 16:33; COLOSSIANS 2:6–7

I AM YOURS FOR ALL ETERNITY. *I am the Alpha and the Omega: the One who is and was and is to come.* The world you inhabit is a place of constant changes—more than your mind can absorb without going into shock. Even the body you inhabit is changing relentlessly in spite of modern science's attempts to prolong youth and life indefinitely. *I, however, am the same yesterday and today and forever.*

Because I never change, your relationship with Me provides a rock-solid foundation for your life. I will never leave your side. When you move on from this life to the next, My Presence beside you will shine brighter with each step. You have nothing to fear because I am with you for all time and throughout eternity.

REVELATION 1:8; HEBREWS 13:8;
PSALM 102:25–27; PSALM 48:14

I WILL RESTORE TO YOU *the Joy of My salvation.* When you confess your sins to Me with a humble heart, I gladly forgive you. But there is more: I restore *you. The salvation of your soul* is the source of *inexpressible and glorious Joy*! I want you to experience once again the rich, deep pleasure of a close relationship with Me. I desire to be your *First Love.*

Many people and things compete for your attention, so keeping Me first in your heart requires diligence. You have developed ways of seeking Me that are familiar and easy for you. But the danger of relying too much on routine is that it can become a tedious duty. When you realize this has happened, you need to stop—and try something new. Remember who I am: King of kings, Lord of lords, Creator-Sustainer of this vast, awesome universe! Take extra time to worship and adore Me before bringing Me your other prayers and petitions. This will awaken your heart to *My Glory*—and to the Joy of My Presence.

PSALM 51:12 NKJV; 1 PETER 1:8–9;
REVELATION 2:4; JOHN 17:24 NKJV

I AM THE GOD OF ALL TIME and all that is. Seek Me not only in morning quietness but consistently throughout the day. Do not let unexpected problems distract you from My Presence. Instead, talk with Me about everything, and watch confidently to see what I will do.

Adversity need not interrupt your communion with Me. When things go "wrong," you tend to react as if you're being punished. Instead of this negative response, try to view difficulties as blessings in disguise. *Make Me your Refuge by pouring out your heart to Me, trusting in Me at all times.*

PSALM 105:3 NKJV; PSALM 55:17;
PSALM 32:6; PSALM 62:8

*Y*OU WILL SEEK ME AND FIND ME *when you search for Me with all your heart.* This is a delightful assignment, but it is also quite challenging. Spending time enjoying My Presence is a privilege reserved for those who know Me as Savior and Lord. To maximize the benefits of this precious experience, you need to seek Me wholeheartedly. However, your mind is often a tangled, unfocused mess. Enlist My Spirit to protect your mind and heart from distractions, distortions, deception, anxiety, and other entanglements. This will help you unscramble your thoughts and calm your heart—freeing you *to search for Me* unhindered.

I want you to seek Me not only in quiet times but also when you are engaged in other matters. Your astonishing brain is able to focus on Me even when you are busy. The simple prayer "Jesus, keep me aware of your Presence" can be like soft background music in your mind—playing continuously underneath your other mental activities. When *your mind is stayed on Me, I keep you in perfect Peace.*

JEREMIAH 29:13 NKJV; PSALM 112:7;
ISAIAH 26:3 NKJV

MEET ME in early morning splendor. I eagerly await you here. In the stillness of this holy time with Me, I *renew your strength* and saturate you with Peace. While others turn over for extra sleep or anxiously tune in to the latest news, you commune with the Creator of the universe. I have awakened in your heart strong desire to know Me. This longing originated in Me, though it now burns brightly in you.

When you seek My Face in response to My Love-call, both of us are blessed. This is a deep mystery, designed more for your enjoyment than for your understanding. I am not a dour God who discourages pleasure. I delight in your enjoyment of *everything that is true, noble, right, pure, lovely, admirable. Think on these things*, and My Light in you will shine brighter day by day.

ISAIAH 40:31; PSALM 27:4;
PHILIPPIANS 4:8

I WILL BLESS MY PEOPLE with Peace. This biblical promise is for everyone who trusts Me as Savior. So when you're feeling anxious, try praying: "Jesus, bless me with Your Peace." This short, simple prayer connects you with Me and opens you up to My help.

Peace and trust in Me are richly intertwined in My kingdom. The more you lean on Me in confident dependence, the less fearful you will be. If your *heart is steadfastly trusting in Me*, you need not be *afraid of bad news*. Because I am both sovereign and good, you can be confident that this world isn't spinning out of control. There *is* plenty of bad news in the world, but I'm not wringing My hands impotently. I am continually at work—even in the most devastating situations— bringing good out of evil.

My kingdom is about transformation, and I invite you to join Me in this endeavor. *Live as a child of the Light.* Together we will draw others out of darkness into the Light of My transforming Presence.

PSALM 29:11 NKJV; PSALM 112:7;
EPHESIANS 5:8–10

FIND ME in the midst of the maelstrom. Sometimes events whirl around you so quickly that they become a blur. Whisper My Name in recognition that I am still with you. Without skipping a beat in the activities that occupy you, you find strength and Peace through praying My Name. Later, when the happenings have run their course, you can talk with Me more fully.

Accept each day just as it comes to you. Do not waste your time and energy wishing for a different set of circumstances. Instead, trust Me enough to yield to My design and purposes. Remember that nothing can separate you from My loving Presence; *you are Mine.*

PHILIPPIANS 2:9–11; PSALM 29:11; ISAIAH 43:1

M Y CHOSEN PEOPLE are *holy and dearly loved*. I know that you are neither perfect nor sinless, but you are indeed *holy in My sight*. This is because I see you wrapped in the radiance of My righteousness. As My follower, you are covered with perfect righteousness forever!

You are also dearly loved. Let this transformational truth seep into the inner recesses of your heart, mind, and spirit. *Beloved* is your deepest, truest identity. When you look in the mirror, say to yourself, *"I am my Beloved's."* Repeat these four words throughout the day and just before you fall asleep.

Remembering you are perfectly loved by *the King of Glory* provides a solid foundation for your life. With your identity secure in Me, you can relate better to others. I want you to *clothe yourself with compassion, kindness, humility, gentleness, and patience.* Work on developing these qualities in your relationships with other people. The Holy Spirit will help you. He lives in you and delights to live through you—blessing others *and* you.

COLOSSIANS 3:12; EPHESIANS 1:4;
SONG OF SOLOMON 6:3 NKJV; PSALM 24:10 NKJV

EXPECT TO ENCOUNTER ADVERSITY in your life, remembering that you live in a deeply fallen world. Stop trying to find a way that circumvents difficulties. The main problem with an easy life is that it masks your need for Me. When you became a Christian, I infused My very Life into you, empowering you to live on a supernatural plane by depending on Me.

Anticipate coming face to face with impossibilities: situations totally beyond your ability to handle. This awareness of your inadequacy is not something you should try to evade. It is precisely where I want you—the best place to encounter Me in *My Glory and Power*. When you see armies of problems marching toward you, cry out to Me! Allow Me to fight for you. Watch Me working on your behalf, as you *rest in the shadow of My Almighty Presence*.

JOB 5:7; REVELATION 19:1; PSALM 91:1

Y OU ARE FEELING WEIGHED DOWN by yesterday's failures. You wish you could undo decisions you made that you now regret. However, the past is beyond the realm of change and cannot be undone. Even *I*, though I live in timelessness, respect the boundaries of time that exist in your world. So don't waste your energy bemoaning bad choices you have made. Instead, ask Me to forgive your sins and help you learn from your mistakes.

I hate to see My children weighed down by past failures, dragging them around like heavy chains attached to their legs. When you're feeling this way, try to imagine Me cutting the chains from your legs. I came to set My loved ones free. You are *free indeed*!

Rejoice that I redeem your failures—forgiving you and leading you along paths of newness. Talk with Me about your mistakes and be ready to *learn from Me*. Ask Me to show you the changes I want you to make. I will *guide you along right paths*.

MATTHEW 11:28–29; JOHN 8:36 NKJV;
PSALM 23:3 NLT

I CONTINUALLY CALL YOU to closeness with Me. I know the depth and breadth of your need for Me. I can read the emptiness of your thoughts when they wander away from Me. I offer rest for your soul, as well as refreshment for your mind and body. As you increasingly find fulfillment in Me, other pleasures become less important. Knowing Me intimately is like having a private wellspring of Joy within you. This spring flows freely from My throne of grace, so your Joy is independent of circumstances.

Waiting in My Presence keeps you connected to Me, aware of all that I offer you. If you feel any deficiency, you need to refocus your attention on Me. This is how you trust Me in the moments of your life.

PSALM 131:2; PSALM 21:6;
PSALM 37:7; JEREMIAH 17:7 NKJV

REJOICE IN YOUR DEPENDENCE on Me. This is a place of wonderful security! People who depend on themselves, others, or circumstances are building their lives on a foundation of sand. When storms come, they will realize how flimsy their foundation is; it will not be adequate to support them. You, on the other hand, are building your life *on the rock*. Your foundation will be more than sufficient to support you during life's storms.

I want you to depend on Me not only in stormy circumstances but when the skies of your life are calm. This is a daily discipline—preparing you for whatever lies ahead. It is also a source of great Joy. Relying on Me involves staying in communication with Me: an extraordinary privilege. This rich blessing provides you with strength, encouragement, and guidance. When you stay in touch with Me, you know you are not alone. As you *walk in the Light of My Presence*, I help you *rejoice in Me all day long*. Depending on Me is a most joyful way to live.

MATTHEW 7:24–27; PSALM 89:15–16;
1 THESSALONIANS 5:16–17

I AM A GOD WHO HEALS. I heal broken bodies, broken minds, broken hearts, broken lives, and broken relationships. My very Presence has immense healing powers. You cannot live close to Me without experiencing some degree of healing. However, it is also true that *you have not because you ask not.* You receive the healing that flows naturally from My Presence, whether you seek it or not. But there is more—much more—available to those who ask.

The first step in receiving healing is to live ever so close to Me. The benefits of this practice are too numerous to list. As you grow more and more intimate with Me, I reveal My will to you more directly. When the time is right, I prompt you to ask for healing of some brokenness in you or in another person. The healing may be instantaneous, or it may be a process. That is up to Me. Your part is to trust Me fully and to thank Me for the restoration that has begun.

I rarely heal all the brokenness in a person's life. Even My servant Paul was told, *"My grace is sufficient for you,"* when he sought healing for the *thorn in his flesh.* Nonetheless, much healing is available to those whose lives are intimately interwoven with Mine. *Ask, and you will receive.*

JAMES 4:2 KJV; 2 CORINTHIANS 12:7–9;
MATTHEW 7:7

FIND YOUR SECURITY IN ME. As the world you inhabit seems increasingly unsafe, turn your attention to Me more and more often. Remember that I am with you at *all* times, and I have already won the ultimate victory. Because *I am in you and you are in Me*, you have an eternity of perfect, stress-free life awaiting you. There will be no trace of fear or worry in heaven. Reverential worship of *the King of Glory* will flood you with unimaginable Joy!

Let this *future hope* strengthen and encourage you while you're living in this deeply fallen world. When you start to feel anxious about something you have seen, heard, or thought, bring that concern to Me. Remind yourself that *I* am the One who makes you secure—in all circumstances! If you find your mind gravitating toward an idolatrous way of feeling safe, tell yourself: "*That's* not what makes me safe." Then look trustingly to Me, and think about who I am: the victorious Savior-God who is your Friend forever. In Me you are absolutely secure!

JOHN 14:20; PSALM 24:7 NKJV;
PROVERBS 23:18

Wait with Me for a while. I have much to tell you. You are walking along the path I have chosen for you. It is both a privileged and a perilous way: experiencing My glorious Presence and heralding that reality to others. Sometimes you feel presumptuous to be carrying out such an assignment.

Do not worry about what other people think of you. The work I am doing in you is hidden at first. But eventually blossoms will burst forth, and abundant fruit will be born. Stay on the path of Life with Me. Trust Me wholeheartedly, letting My Spirit fill you with Joy and Peace.

ISAIAH 30:18; 1 KINGS 8:23;
GALATIANS 5:22–23

*P*UT YOUR TRUST IN ME so you can discover *My unfailing Love* shining on in the midst of your troubles. When you are struggling with discouragement, you need to assert your trust in Me over and over again. It is vital to remember who I am: Creator and Sustainer of the universe, as well as your Savior, Lord, and Friend. You can count on Me because My Love for you is unfailing. It never runs out or grows dim, and it is not dependent on how well you're performing. Just as *I am the same yesterday, today, and forever,* so is My perfect Love.

Lift up your soul to Me—waiting in My Presence with no pretense and no demands. As you dedicate time to waiting and worshiping, I gradually transform you and open up the way before you. I will not necessarily reveal future things to you, but I will *show you the way* through this day—step by step. So trust Me wholeheartedly, beloved, for I am taking care of you wonderfully well!

PSALM 143:8; HEBREWS 1:1–2;
HEBREWS 13:8 NKJV

T RUST ME, *and don't be afraid.* I want you to view trials as exercises designed to develop your trust-muscles. You live in the midst of fierce spiritual battles, and fear is one of Satan's favorite weapons. When you start to feel afraid, affirm your trust in Me. Speak out loud, if circumstances permit. *Resist the devil in My Name, and he will slink away from you.* Refresh yourself in My holy Presence. Speak or sing praises to Me, and My Face will shine radiantly upon you.

Remember that there is *no condemnation for those who belong to Me.* You have been judged NOT GUILTY for all eternity. *Trust Me, and don't be afraid; for I am your Strength, Song, and Salvation.*

JAMES 4:7; ROMANS 8:1–2; ISAIAH 12:2

I AM LIGHT; in Me there is no darkness at all. I, your God, am perfect in every way. There's not even an iota of badness in Me. You live in a world where evil and ungodliness run rampant. But remember: I am *the Light that keeps on shining in the darkness*! Nothing can extinguish—or even diminish— the perfection of My everlasting radiance. Someday you will be able to see My brilliance in all its Glory, and you will experience unimaginable Joy. For now, though, you must *live by faith, not by sight.*

When events in the world or in your private life are threatening to unnerve you, grasp My hand in trusting determination. Refuse to be intimidated by evil; instead, *overcome evil with good.* I am with you, and I have won the ultimate victory through My crucifixion and resurrection. *Nothing* will be able to undo these awesome events that punctured the darkness so that My dazzling brightness could break through and pour into the hearts of My followers. Spend time basking in this holy Light, for My Face is shining upon you.

1 JOHN 1:5; JOHN 1:5 AMP;
2 CORINTHIANS 5:7; ROMANS 12:21

ENTRUST YOUR LOVED ONES TO ME; release them into My protective care. They are much safer with Me than in your clinging hands. If you let a loved one become an idol in your heart, you endanger that one—as well as yourself. Joseph and his father, Jacob, suffered terribly because *Jacob loved Joseph more than any of his other sons* and treated him with special favor. So Joseph's brothers hated him and plotted against him. Ultimately, I used that situation for good, but both father and son had to endure years of suffering and separation from one another.

I detest idolatry, even in the form of parental love, so beware of making a beloved child your idol. When you release loved ones to Me, you are free to cling to My hand. As you entrust others into My care, I am free to shower blessings on them. *My Presence will go with them wherever they go, and I will give them rest.* This same Presence stays with you as you relax and place your trust in Me. Watch to see what I will do.

GENESIS 37:3–4; EPHESIANS 3:20; EXODUS 33:14

WHEN TESTS AND CHALLENGES *come at you from all sides,* consider it a joyful opportunity. Don't waste energy regretting the way things are or wishing you could go back to yesterday. Remember that I am sovereign, powerful, and loving; moreover, I am with you to help. Instead of being overwhelmed by all the difficulties, grasp My hand with confident trust. Though you are insufficient to handle your troubles by yourself, you and I *together* can handle anything! If you view your circumstances from this big-picture perspective, you can be joyful even in the midst of your struggles.

You have not only My Presence with you but My Spirit within you. He is always ready to help; seek His assistance as often as you need. One of the hardest parts of dealing with multiple trials is waiting for their resolution. Since patience is part of the Spirit's fruit, He can help you endure the waiting. Don't try to get out of hard times prematurely. Instead, persevere patiently, knowing that *perseverance must finish its work*—making you *mature and complete.*

JAMES 1:2 MSG; GALATIANS 5:22–23;
ROMANS 12:12; JAMES 1:4

I AM ALL AROUND YOU, hovering over you even as you seek My Face. I am nearer than you dare believe, closer than the air you breathe. If My children could only recognize My Presence, they would never feel lonely again. *I know every thought before you think it, every word before you speak it.* My Presence impinges on your innermost being. Can you see the absurdity of trying to hide anything from Me? You can easily deceive other people, and even yourself, but I read you like an open, large-print book.

Deep within themselves, most people have some awareness of My imminent Presence. Many people run from Me and vehemently deny My existence because My closeness terrifies them. But My own children have nothing to fear, for I have cleansed them by My blood and clothed them in My righteousness. Be blessed by My intimate nearness. Since I live in you, let Me also live through you, shining My Light into the darkness.

PSALM 139:1–4; EPHESIANS 2:13;
2 CORINTHIANS 5:21

*C*OME TO ME, MY WEARY ONE, *and I will give you rest.* I know the depth and breadth of your weariness. Nothing is hidden from Me. There is a time to keep pushing yourself—when circumstances require it—and a time to rest. Even I, who have infinite energy, rested on the seventh day after completing My work of creation.

Seek My Face, and then just linger in My loving Presence while I shine upon you. Let favorite scriptures amble through your brain, refreshing your heart and spirit. If something comes to mind that you don't want to forget, jot it down; then return your attention to Me. As you relax with Me, My Love will soak into the depths of your being. You may want to express your love for Me—in whispers, in spoken words, in song.

I want you to know that I approve of you and I approve of rest. When you relax in My Presence, trusting in My finished work on the cross, both you and I are refreshed.

MATTHEW 11:28; GENESIS 2:2 NKJV;
NUMBERS 6:25

I AM THE ETERNAL I AM; I always have been, and I always will be. In My Presence you experience Love and Light, Peace and Joy. I am intimately involved in all your moments, and I am training you to be aware of Me at all times. Your assignment is to collaborate with Me in this training process.

I have taken up residence within you; I am central in your innermost being. Your mind goes off in tangents from its holy Center, time after time. Do not be alarmed by your inability to remain focused on Me. Simply bring your thoughts gently back to Me each time they wander. The quickest way to redirect your mind to me is to whisper My Name.

EXODUS 3:14; 1 CORINTHIANS 3:16;
PSALM 25:14–15

I LIVE IN YOU! This four-word truth changes everything, wondrously improving your life both now and forever. Don't worry about whether you're an adequate home for Me. I joyfully move into believers' humble hearts, where I work patiently on renovating them. But I refuse to dwell in people who think they are "good enough" without Me. I have called such hypocrites *whitewashed tombs: beautiful on the outside* but putrid on the inside.

As you ponder the miraculous truth that *I live in you*, let your heart overflow with Joy! I am not a short-term tenant, indwelling you only as long as your behavior pleases Me. I have come to stay—permanently. I warn you, though, that My renovations can be quite painful at times. When My transforming work in you causes intense discomfort, cling trustingly to Me. *Live by faith in the One who loved you and gave Himself for you.* As you continue yielding to the changes I'm making, you'll become more and more fully the masterpiece I designed you to be.

GALATIANS 2:20; MATTHEW 23:27;
EPHESIANS 2:10 NKJV

T RUST ME in the midst of a messy day. Your inner calm—your Peace in My Presence—need not be shaken by what is going on around you. Though you live in this temporal world, your innermost being is rooted and grounded in eternity. When you start to feel stressed, detach yourself from the disturbances around you. Instead of desperately striving to maintain order and control in your little world, relax and remember that circumstances cannot touch My Peace.

Seek My Face, and I will share My mind with you, opening your eyes to see things from My perspective. *Do not let your heart be troubled, and do not be afraid.* The Peace I give is sufficient for you.

JOHN 16:33; PSALM 105:4; JOHN 14:27

No matter what is happening in your life, you can *be joyful in Me* because I am *your Savior.* When Habakkuk wrote about this, he was awaiting the invasion of his country by the Babylonians—*a ruthless, feared, and dreaded people.* Even as he pondered this terrifying prophecy, he was able to rejoice in his relationship with Me. This sort of Joy is supernatural—powered by the Holy Spirit, who lives in all My followers.

Joy and thankfulness are closely connected. *Give thanks to Me for My unfailing Love; tell of My wonderful works with songs of Joy.* My Love for you will never fail because I have already paid the full penalty for your sins. It doesn't depend on you! The more you thank Me—for your salvation, My Love, and other blessings—the more you will realize how blessed you really are. And a grateful attitude increases your Joy. You can nourish this gladness by thanking Me in your silent prayers, in your written, spoken, or whispered words, and through music. *Come before Me with joyful songs*!

HABAKKUK 3:18; HABAKKUK 1:6–7;
PSALM 107:21–22; PSALM 100:2 HCSB

August 27

S PEND TIME WITH ME for the pure pleasure of being in My company. I can brighten up the dullest of gray days; I can add sparkle to the routines of daily life. You have to repeat so many tasks day after day. This monotony can dull your thinking until your mind slips into neutral. A mind that is unfocused is vulnerable to the world, the flesh, and the devil, all of which exert a downward pull on your thoughts. As your thinking processes deteriorate, you become increasingly confused and directionless. The best remedy is to refocus your mind and heart on Me, your constant Companion.

Even the most confusing day opens up before you as you go step by step with Me. My Presence goes with you wherever you go, providing *Light for your path*.

PSALM 43:4; PSALM 63:7–8; PSALM 119:105

I GIVE STRENGTH TO THE WEARY *and increase the power of the weak.* So do not be discouraged by your weakness. There are many kinds of weaknesses, and no one is exempt from all of them. I use them to keep My loved ones humble and to train them to wait on Me in trusting dependence. I have promised that *those who wait on Me will gain new strength.*

This waiting is not meant to be practiced only *sometimes.* I designed you to look to Me continually, knowing Me as *the Living One who sees you* always. Waiting on Me is closely related to trusting Me. The more time you spend focusing on Me, the more you will trust Me. And the more you trust Me, the more you will want to spend time with Me. Waiting on Me in the midst of your moments also increases your hope in Me. This hope blesses you in countless ways—lifting you above your circumstances, enabling you to *praise Me for the help of My Presence.*

ISAIAH 40:29; ISAIAH 40:30–31 NASB;
GENESIS 16:14 AMP; PSALM 42:5 NASB

G ROW STRONG in the Light of My Presence. As My Face shines upon you, you receive nutrients that enhance your growth in grace. I designed you to commune with Me face to Face, and this interaction strengthens your soul. Such communion provides a tiny glimpse of what awaits you in heaven, where all barriers between you and My Glory will be removed. This meditative time with Me blesses you doubly: You experience My Presence here and now, and you are refreshed by the hope of heaven, where you will know Me in ecstatic Joy.

PSALM 4:6–8; REVELATION 21:23; 2 PETER 3:13

I AM WITH YOU and will watch over you wherever you go. There is an adventurous journey awaiting you, and you're anticipating it with mixed feelings. In some ways you are eager to step into this new adventure. You're even expecting to find abundant blessings along the way. However, part of you fears leaving your comfortable, predictable routine. When fearful thoughts assail you, remind yourself that I will be watching over you constantly—wherever you are. The comfort of My Presence is a forever-promise!

Your best preparation for the journey ahead is practicing My Presence each day. Tell yourself frequently: "Jesus is with me, taking good care of me." Visualize yourself holding onto My hand as you walk. Trust Me—your Guide—to show you the way forward as you go step by step. I have a perfect sense of direction, so don't worry about getting lost. Relax in My Presence, and rejoice in the wonder of sharing your whole life with Me.

GENESIS 28:15; JOSHUA 1:9 ESV; PSALM 48:14

D EMONSTRATE YOUR TRUST IN ME by sitting quietly in My Presence. Put aside all that is waiting to be done, and refuse to worry about anything. This sacred time together strengthens you and prepares you to face whatever the day will bring. By waiting with Me before you begin the day's activities, you proclaim the reality of My living Presence. This act of faith—waiting before working—is noted in the spirit world, where your demonstration of trust weakens *principalities and powers of darkness.*

The most effective way to resist evil is to draw near Me. When you need to take action, I will guide you clearly through My Spirit and My Word. The world is so complex and over-stimulating that you can easily lose your sense of direction. Doing countless unnecessary activities will dissipate your energy. When you spend time with Me, I restore your sense of direction. As you look to Me for guidance, I enable you to do less but accomplish more.

LUKE 12:22–25; EPHESIANS 6:12 NKJV;
PROVERBS 16:3

THE LIGHT OF MY PRESENCE SHINES on every situation in your life—past, present, and future. I knew you *before the creation of the world*, and *I have loved you with an everlasting Love.* You are never alone, so look for Me in your moments. Search for Me as for hidden treasure.

Seek to "see" Me in the midst of all your circumstances; don't let them obscure your view of Me. Sometimes I display My Presence in grand, glorious ways. At other times I show Myself in simple, humble ways that make sense only to you. Ask Me to open your eyes and your heart to discern *all* My communications to you, beloved.

As you go through this day, remind yourself to look for the Light of My Presence shining on your life. Don't have such a narrow focus that you see only responsibilities and worldly concerns. Instead, expand your focus to include *Me* in your perspective. *You will seek Me and find Me when you search for Me with all your heart.*

EPHESIANS 1:4; JEREMIAH 31:3;
PSALM 89:15; JEREMIAH 29:13 NKJV

THERE IS NO PLACE so desolate that you cannot find Me there. When Hagar fled from her mistress, Sarah, into the wilderness, she thought she was utterly alone and forsaken. But Hagar encountered Me in that desolate place. There she addressed Me as *the Living One who sees me*. Through that encounter with My Presence, she gained courage to return to her mistress.

No set of circumstances could ever isolate you from My loving Presence. Not only do I see you always; I see you as a redeemed saint, gloriously radiant in My righteousness. That is why *I take great delight in you and rejoice over you with singing*!

GENESIS 16:13–14 AMP;
PSALM 139:7–10; ZEPHANIAH 3:17

I MAKE YOUR FEET LIKE THE FEET OF A DEER. *I enable you to stand on the heights.* I created deer with the ability to climb steep mountains with ease and to stand on the heights with confidence. Your trust in Me can give you confidence to *walk and make progress upon your high places of trouble, responsibility, or suffering.*

It's crucial to remember that you live in a world where your spiritual enemies never declare a truce. So you need to stay alert and be ready for battle. Unlike warriors with servants to help them put on their gear, you must make the effort to armor yourself each day. No matter what happens, I want you to *be able to stand your ground, and after you have done everything, to stand.* When you're in the thick of battle, declare your trust in Me—your confidence that I am with you, helping you. You may feel as if you're losing the battle, but don't give up! Hold tightly to My hand, and just keep standing. This is victory.

2 SAMUEL 22:34; HABAKKUK 3:19 AMP;
EPHESIANS 6:13

GROW STRONG IN YOUR WEAKNESS. Some of My children I've gifted with abundant strength and stamina. Others, like you, have received the humble gift of frailty. Your fragility is not a punishment, nor does it indicate lack of faith. On the contrary, weak ones like you must live by faith, depending on Me to get you through the day. I am developing your ability to trust Me, to lean on Me rather than on your understanding. Your natural preference is to plan out your day, knowing what will happen when. My preference is for you to depend on Me continually, trusting Me to guide you and strengthen you as needed. This is how you grow strong in your weakness.

JAMES 4:13–15; PROVERBS 3:5 AMP;
ISAIAH 40:28–31

I AM YOUR TREASURE. I am immeasurably more valuable than anything you can see, hear, or touch. *Knowing Me* is the Prize above every other prize.

Earthly treasures are frequently hoarded, insured, worried over, or hidden for safekeeping. But the riches you have in Me can never be lost or stolen or damaged. On the contrary, as you freely share Me with others, you gain more of Me. Since I am infinite, there will always be more of Me to discover—and to love.

Your world often feels fragmented, with countless things—both large and small—vying for your attention. So much "stuff" keeps getting in the way of enjoying My Presence. *You are worried and troubled about many things, but only one thing is needed.* When you make Me that *one thing*, you choose what *will never be taken away from you.* Rejoice in My continual nearness, and let your knowledge of Me put everything else in perspective. I am the Treasure that can brighten all your moments!

PHILIPPIANS 3:10; MATTHEW 6:19;
LUKE 10:41–42 NKJV

September

"*I am the light of the world. Whoever follows me will never walk in darkness, but will have the light of life.*"

JOHN 8:12

S EEK ME with your whole being. I desire to be found by you, and I orchestrate the events of your life with that purpose in mind. When things go well and you are blessed, you can feel Me smiling on you. When you encounter rough patches along your life-journey, trust that My Light is still shining upon you. My reasons for allowing these adversities may be shrouded in mystery, but My continual Presence with you is an absolute promise. Seek Me in good times; seek Me in hard times. You will find Me watching over you all the time.

DEUTERONOMY 4:29; HEBREWS 10:23;
PSALM 145:20; PSALM 121:7–8

I AM YOUR STRENGTH. This truth about Me is especially precious on days when your inadequacies are screaming at you, telling you that you just can't go on. Knowing Me as your Strength is like having a guide who is always with you—showing you the way forward, clearing away obstacles, empowering you to take the next step. *I hold you by your right hand*, and *I guide you with My counsel.* Since I am omniscient, knowing everything, My counsel provides the best wisdom imaginable.

So don't fret about your weaknesses. They are training you to depend on My loving Presence—confident that I am with you and I will help you. Your world becomes less threatening when you throw off the pretense of being able to handle things by yourself. Furthermore, I meet you in your weaknesses and use them to draw other people to Me. My Light shines in and through your inadequacies when you keep looking to Me, your Strength. Let this Love-Light flow freely through you, filling you with Joy that overflows into others' lives.

PSALM 59:17 ESV; PSALM 73:23–24 NKJV;
2 CORINTHIANS 11:30; ROMANS 12:12

L IVING IN DEPENDENCE ON ME is a glorious adventure. Most people scurry around busily, trying to accomplish things through their own strength and ability. Some succeed enormously; others fail miserably. But both groups miss what life is meant to be: living and working in collaboration with Me.

When you depend on Me continually, your whole perspective changes. You see miracles happening all around, while others see only natural occurrences and "coincidences." You begin each day with joyful expectation, watching to see what I will do. You accept weakness as a gift from Me, knowing that *My Power plugs in most readily to consecrated weakness.* You keep your plans tentative, knowing that My plans are far superior. *You consciously live, move, and have your being in Me*, desiring that I live in you. I in you and you in Me. This is the intimate adventure I offer you.

2 CORINTHIANS 12:9–10; ACTS 17:28;
COLOSSIANS 2:6–7; JOHN 14:20

W HEN PEOPLE BARE THEIR SOULS to you, you are *on holy ground*. Your responsibility is to listen and love. If you jump in with both feet—trying to fix their problems—you pollute the holy terrain. Some people will retreat when this happens; others may be too wounded to realize they've been violated. Either way, you have spoiled a splendid opportunity.

To function effectively on holy ground, you need the help of the Holy Spirit. Ask Him to think through you, listen through you, love through you. As the Spirit's Love shines through you, My healing Presence goes to work in the other person. While you continue listening, your main role is to direct the person toward Me and My bountiful resources.

If you follow these guidelines, both you and others will be blessed. They will connect with *My unfailing Love* at soul-level, and I will *show them the way they should go*. As you listen and love in dependence on Me, My Spirit will flow through you like *streams of living water*, refreshing your soul.

EXODUS 3:5; PSALM 143:8;
JOHN 7:38–39 HCSB

L ET THE DEW OF MY PRESENCE refresh your mind and heart. So many, many things vie for your attention in this complex world of instant communication. The world has changed enormously since I first gave the command to *be still, and know that I am God*. However, this timeless truth is essential for the well-being of your soul. As dew refreshes grass and flowers during the stillness of the night, so My Presence revitalizes you as you sit quietly with Me.

A refreshed, revitalized mind is able to sort out what is important and what is not. In its natural condition, your mind easily gets stuck on trivial matters. Like the spinning wheels of a car trapped in mud, the cogs of your brain spin impotently when you focus on a trivial thing. As soon as you start communicating with Me about the matter, your thoughts gain traction, and you can move on to more important things. Communicate with Me continually, and I will put My thoughts into your mind.

PSALM 46:10; LUKE 10:39–42;
1 CORINTHIANS 14:33 NKJV

IF ANYTHING IS EXCELLENT or praiseworthy, think about such things. This may sound easy, but it's actually quite countercultural. People who work in the media almost always shine their spotlights on what is wrong. They rarely bother to report good things that are happening—especially the many good things My people are doing.

Having a positive focus is not only countercultural; it's contrary to human nature. Your mind is a magnificent creation, but it is deeply fallen. When Adam and Eve rebelled against Me in the Garden of Eden, everything was damaged by the Fall. As a result, seeking to focus on excellent things does not come naturally to you. It requires persistent effort—making the right choice over and over again. Daily, moment by moment, you choose to look for what is good.

In spite of the massive problems in your world, much remains that is worthy of praise. Moreover, the One who is *most* praiseworthy is the One who is right beside you—closer than your thoughts. Rejoice in *Me*, beloved!

PHILIPPIANS 4:8; GENESIS 3:6;
PROVERBS 16:16; PSALM 73:23 NKJV

I N CLOSENESS TO ME, you are safe. In the intimacy of My Presence, you are energized. No matter where you are in the world, you know you belong when you sense My nearness. Ever since the Fall, man has experienced a gaping emptiness that only My Presence can fill. I designed you for close communication with your Creator. How I enjoyed walking in the garden with Adam and Eve before the evil one deceived them!

When you commune with Me in the garden of your heart, both you and I are blessed. This is My way of living in the world—through you! Together we will push back the darkness, for *I am the Light of the world.*

PSALM 32:7; ROMANS 1:6;
GENESIS 3:8–9; JOHN 8:12

*I*DISCIPLINE THE ONE *I* LOVE. Discipline is instruction intended to train; it's a course of action leading to a greater goal than immediate satisfaction. In fact, effective discipline can be unpleasant—even painful. So it's easy for you to feel unloved when I am leading you along a way that is difficult or confusing. In such a situation you have an important choice: to cling to Me in trusting dependence or to back away from Me and seek to go your own way.

When you are able to recognize My discipline as a facet of My Love for you, you can go through tough times joyfully—just as the early disciples did. You can come boldly into My Presence, asking Me to show you what I want you to learn and what changes you need to make. Tell Me also of your desire for reassurance of My Love. Take time to bask in the Light of My loving Presence. As you gaze at My Face, *the Light of the knowledge of My Glory* shines upon you!

HEBREWS 12:6, 11 ESV;
ACTS 5:41 NKJV; 2 CORINTHIANS 4:4

I AM YOUR BEST FRIEND, as well as your King. Walk hand in hand with Me through your life. Together we will face whatever each day brings: pleasures, hardships, adventures, disappointments. Nothing is wasted when it is shared with Me. *I can bring beauty out of the ashes* of lost dreams. I can glean Joy out of sorrow, Peace out of adversity. Only a Friend who is also the King of kings could accomplish this divine alchemy. There is no other like Me!

The friendship I offer you is practical and down-to-earth, yet it is saturated with heavenly Glory. Living in My Presence means living in two realms simultaneously: the visible world and unseen, eternal reality. I have equipped you to stay conscious of Me while walking along dusty, earthbound paths.

JOHN 15:13–15; ISAIAH 61:3;
2 CORINTHIANS 6:10

J OY IS A CHOICE. You may not have much control over your circumstances, but you can still choose to be joyful. I created you *a little lower than the heavenly beings*, and I gave you an amazing mind. Your ability to think things through and make decisions derives from your elevated position in My kingdom. Your thoughts are extremely important because emotions and behavior flow out of them. So endeavor to make good thought-choices.

Whenever you are feeling joyless, you need to pause and remember: *I am with you. I am watching over you* continuously. I love you with perfect, *unfailing Love.* I have given you My Spirit, and this Holy Helper within you has infinite Power. He can help you line up your thinking with the absolute truths of Scripture. My continual Presence is a biblical promise, so seek to see *Me* in the midst of your circumstances. At first you may perceive only your problems. But keep on looking till you can discern the Light of My Presence shining upon your difficulties, reflecting sparkles of Joy back to you.

PSALM 8:5 ESV; GENESIS 28:15;
PSALM 107:8; ROMANS 8:9

D O EVERYTHING IN DEPENDENCE ON ME. The desire to act independently—apart from Me—springs from the root of pride. Self-sufficiency is subtle, insinuating its way into your thoughts and actions without your realizing it. But *apart from Me, you can do nothing*: that is, nothing of eternal value. My deepest desire for you is that you learn to depend on Me in every situation. I move heaven and earth to accomplish this purpose, but you must collaborate with Me in this training. Teaching you would be simple if I negated your free will or overwhelmed you with My Power. However, I love you too much to withdraw the godlike privilege I bestowed on you as My image-bearer. Use your freedom wisely by relying on Me constantly. Thus you enjoy My Presence and My Peace.

JOHN 15:5; EPHESIANS 6:10; GENESIS 1:26–27

I BROADEN THE PATH BENEATH YOU *so that your ankles do not turn.* I don't want you to focus overly much on what is ahead of you—wondering whether you'll be able to cope with it. Only *I* know what your future really holds. Moreover, I am the only One who fully understands what you are capable of. Finally, I can alter your circumstances— gradually or dramatically. In fact, I can widen the path you are walking on right now.

I want you to realize how intricately involved in your life I am. I delight in taking care of you—"tweaking" the situation you are in, to spare you from unnecessary hardship. Remember that I am *a shield for all who take refuge in Me.* Your part in this adventurous journey is to trust Me, communicate with Me, and walk with Me in steps of joyful dependence. I will not remove all adversity from your life, but I will widen the path you are traveling on—to *bless you and keep you* from harm.

PSALM 18:36; PSALM 18:30; NUMBERS 6:24 NKJV

ENJOY THE WARMTH OF MY PRESENCE shining upon you. Feel your face tingle as you bask in My Love-Light. I delight in you more than you can imagine. I approve of you continuously, for I see you cloaked in My Light, *arrayed in My righteousness. There is no condemnation for those who are clothed in Me!* That is why I abhor the use of guilt as a means of motivation among Christians.

Some pastors try to whip their people into action with guilt-inducing sermons. This procedure can drive many people to work harder, but the end does not justify the means. Guilt-evoking messages can undermine the very foundation of grace in a believer's heart. A pastor may feel successful when his people are doing more, but I look at their hearts. I grieve when I see grace eroding, with weeds of anxious works creeping in. I want you to relax in the assurance of My perfect Love. *The law of My Spirit of Life has set you free from the law of sin and death.*

ISAIAH 61:10; ROMANS 8:1–2

I HAVE SEARCHED YOU *and known you. I am inti-mately acquainted with all your ways. Even before there is a word on your tongue, I know it all.* Beloved, you are indeed *fully known*! I have complete knowledge of everything about you—including your most secret thoughts and feelings. This transparency could be terrifying for you if you were not My follower. But you have nothing to fear because My perfect righteousness has been credited to you through your *faith in Me*. You're a cherished member of My family!

My intimate relationship with you is a powerful antidote to feelings of loneliness. Whenever you feel alone or afraid, voice your prayers to Me. I hear your silent prayers too, but whispering your words or uttering them out loud helps you think more clearly. Because I understand you perfectly, you don't have to explain things to Me. You can dive right in, seeking My help in your "here and now" circumstances. Spend a few moments relaxing with Me—breathing in *the Joy of My Presence*.

PSALM 139:1–4 NASB; 1 CORINTHIANS 13:12 HCSB;
ROMANS 3:22; PSALM 21:6

A CCEPT EACH DAY exactly as it comes to you. By that, I mean not only the circumstances of your day but also the condition of your body. Your assignment is to trust Me absolutely, resting in My sovereignty and faithfulness.

On some days, your circumstances and your physical condition feel out of balance: The demands on you seem far greater than your strength. Days like that present a choice between two alternatives—giving up or relying on Me. Even if you wrongly choose the first alternative, I will not reject you. You can turn to Me at any point, and I will help you crawl out of the mire of discouragement. I will infuse My strength into you moment by moment, giving you all that you need for this day. Trust Me by relying on My empowering Presence.

PSALM 42:5; 2 CORINTHIANS 13:4; JEREMIAH 31:25

WHILE YOU WAIT WITH ME, I work on *renewing your mind*. As the Light of My Presence shines into your mind, darkness flees and deception is unmasked. However, there are many crevices where old thought patterns try to hide. My Spirit can search out and destroy those enemies, but He awaits your cooperation. Habitual ways of thinking do not die easily. When the Spirit's Light illuminates a hurtful thought, capture it by writing it down. Then bring it to Me so we can examine it together. I will help you identify the distortions and replace them with biblical truth.

The more you focus on Me and My Word, the more you can break free from painful, irrational thoughts. They usually have their roots in distressing experiences that wounded you, so the distortions are deeply etched into your brain. You may need to recapture the same thought multiple times before you can gain mastery over it. But all that effort leads to a marvelous result: increased ability to live freely and enjoy My Presence.

PSALM 130:5; ROMANS 12:2;
JOHN 8:12 ESV; 2 CORINTHIANS 10:5

WALK WITH ME ALONG PATHS OF TRUST. The most direct route between point A and point B on your life-journey is the path of unwavering trust in Me. When your faith falters, you choose a trail that meanders and takes you well out of your way. You will get to point B eventually, but you will have lost precious time and energy. As soon as you realize you have wandered from your trust-path, look to Me and whisper, "I trust You, Jesus." This affirmation will help you get back on track.

The farther you roam along paths of unbelief, the harder it is to remember that I am with you. Anxious thoughts branch off in all directions, taking you farther and farther from awareness of My Presence. You need to voice your trust in Me frequently. This simple act of faith will keep you walking along straight paths with Me. *Trust in Me with all your heart, and I will make your paths straight.*

ISAIAH 26:4; PSALM 9:10;
PSALM 25:4–5; PROVERBS 3:5–6

Y OUR PRAYERS ARE NOT CRIES IN THE DARK; they rise to My kingdom of glorious Light. *Call to Me, and I will answer you and show you great and mighty things.* Mankind has long been plagued with eyes that do not see what is most important. People often fail to perceive the most obvious things. I can perform miracles before their very eyes, yet they see only mundane occurrences—or label them coincidences. Only *the eyes of your heart* can perceive spiritual realities.

I delight in people who have a *teachable* attitude. When you come to Me eager to learn *great things which you do not know*, I rejoice. A good teacher takes pleasure in a student who puts forth extra effort to discover new things. I am pleased with your desire to learn wondrous things from Me. Your openness to My teaching helps you understand *the hope to which I have called you, the riches of My glorious inheritance* in which you share. You can look forward to living with Me in the Holy City, where *the Glory of God provides Light.*

JEREMIAH 33:3 NKJV; EPHESIANS 1:18;
PSALM 143:10; REVELATION 21:23

I AM ALWAYS AVAILABLE TO YOU. Once you have trusted Me as your Savior, I never distance Myself from you. Sometimes you may *feel* distant from Me. Recognize that as feeling; do not confuse it with reality. The Bible is full of My promises to be with you always. As I assured Jacob, when he was journeying away from home into unknown places, *I am with you and will watch over you wherever you go.* After My resurrection, I made this promise to My followers: *Surely I am with you always, to the very end of the age.* Let these assurances of My continual Presence fill you with Joy and Peace. No matter what you may lose in this life, you can never lose your relationship with Me.

ISAIAH 54:10; GENESIS 28:15;
MATTHEW 28:19–20

A S THE WORLD GROWS INCREASINGLY DARK, remember that *you are the light of the world*. Don't waste energy lamenting bad things over which you have no control. Pray about these matters, but refuse to let them haunt your thoughts. Instead, focus your energies on doing what you can to brighten the place where I have put you. Use your time, talents, and resources to push back the darkness. Shine *My* Light into the world!

I am *the true Light that shines on in the darkness*—even in the most terrible conditions. Your light originates in Me and reflects from you. I have called you to *reflect My Glory*! You do this most effectively by becoming more and more fully the one I designed you to be. Spend ample time seeking My Face, beloved. Focusing on My Presence and My Word helps you to grow in grace and discern My will. Your time spent with Me nourishes your soul, providing comfort and encouragement. Thus I strengthen you and enable you to be a source of strength for others.

MATTHEW 5:14 NKJV; JOHN 1:9;
JOHN 1:5 AMP; 2 CORINTHIANS 3:18

R EJOICE IN ME ALWAYS! No matter what is going on, you can rejoice in your Love-relationship with Me. This is *the secret of being content in all circumstances.* So many people dream of the day when they will finally be happy: when they are out of debt, when their children are out of trouble, when they have more leisure time, and so on. While they daydream, their moments are trickling into the ground like precious balm spilling wastefully from overturned bottles.

Fantasizing about future happiness will never bring fulfillment because fantasy is unreality. Even though I am invisible, I am far more Real than the world you see around you. My reality is eternal and unchanging. Bring your moments to Me, and I will fill them with vibrant Joy. *Now* is the time to rejoice in My Presence!

PHILIPPIANS 4:4, 12; PSALM 102:27; 1 PETER 1:8

WITH THE THREAT OF TERRORISM looming over planet Earth, some people are saying—and feeling—that no place is really safe. In one sense, this is true. Evil people, especially terrorists, are unpredictable and ruthless. However, for Christian believers, there is no place that is actually *unsafe*. Your ultimate home is heaven, and no one can rob you of this glorious *inheritance that can never perish, spoil, or fade.* Furthermore, I am *sovereign* over everything, including your life and your loved ones. Nothing can happen to you—or to them—except what I allow.

The truth is, the world has been at war ever since Adam and Eve first sinned. The Fall in the Garden of Eden rendered the earth a dangerous place where good and evil contend against each other continually. So it's crucial to *be alert and self-controlled*. Remember that your ultimate enemy, the devil, has already been defeated. *I have overcome the world*, and you are on the winning side—*My* side. *In Me you have Peace*. In Me you are always safe.

1 PETER 1:3–4; PSALM 71:16;
1 PETER 5:8; JOHN 16:33 NKJV

Receive My Peace. It is My continual gift to you. The best way to receive this gift is to sit quietly in My Presence, trusting Me in every area of your life. *Quietness and trust* accomplish far more than you can imagine: not only in you, but also on earth and in heaven. When you trust Me in a given area, you release that problem or person into My care.

Spending time alone with Me can be a difficult discipline because it goes against the activity addiction of this age. You may appear to be doing nothing, but actually you are participating in battles going on within spiritual realms. You are waging war—not with *the weapons of the world*, but with heavenly weapons, which *have divine power to demolish strongholds*. Living close to Me is a sure defense against evil.

John 14:27; Isaiah 30:15; 2 Corinthians 10:4

*Y*OUR TIMES ARE IN *MY HANDS*. So *trust in Me*, beloved. I am training you to feel secure in the midst of change and uncertainty. It can actually be a relief to realize you are not in control of your life. When you accept this human condition while resting in My sovereignty, you become increasingly free.

I am not telling you to be passive or fatalistic. It's important to use your energy and abilities, but I want you to do so prayerfully. Pray about everything, and search for Me in your moments. I am a God of surprises, so look for Me in unexpected places.

I invite you to *rejoice in this day that I have made*, asking Me to orchestrate its details and events. Since I am in control of *your times*, you don't have to be anxious about making things happen faster. Rushing and anxiety go hand in hand, and I have instructed you not to be anxious. If you let *Me* set the pace, I will bless you with *Peace that transcends all understanding*.

PSALM 31:14–15; PSALM 118:24 NKJV;
PHILIPPIANS 4:6–7

COME TO ME AND REST. Give your mind a break from its habitual judging. You form judgments about this situation, that situation, this person, that person, yourself, even the weather—as if judging were your main function in life. But I created you first and foremost to *know Me* and to live in rich communication with Me. When you become preoccupied with passing judgment, you usurp My role.

Relate to Me as creature to Creator, sheep to Shepherd, subject to King, clay to Potter. Allow Me to have My way in your life. Rather than evaluating My ways with you, accept them thankfully. The intimacy I offer you is not an invitation to act as if you were My equal. Worship Me as *King of kings* while walking hand in hand with Me down the path of Life.

MATTHEW 7:1; JOHN 17:3;
ROMANS 9:20–21; 1 TIMOTHY 6:15

Y OUR LIFE IS A PRECIOUS GIFT from Me. Open your hands and your heart to receive this day gratefully. Relate to Me as your Savior and Friend, but remember I am also your Creator-God: *All things were created by Me.* As you go through this day that I've gifted to you, look for signs of My abiding Presence. *I am with you, watching over you* continually. On bright, joyful days, speak to Me about the pleasures I provide; as you thank Me for them, your Joy will expand abundantly. On dark, difficult days, grasp My hand in trusting dependence. *I will help you*, beloved.

Your physical life is an amazing gift, but your spiritual life is a treasure of infinite value! People who don't know Me as Savior will spend an eternity in terrible separation from Me. But because you belong to Me, you will live with Me forever, enjoying a glorified body that will never get sick or tired. Since I have saved you *by grace through faith*, let thankfulness for this indescribable gift fill you with overflowing Joy!

COLOSSIANS 1:16 NKJV; GENESIS 28:15;
ISAIAH 41:13; EPHESIANS 2:8 NKJV

531

WORSHIP ME by living close to Me. This was My original design for man, into whom *I breathed My very breath of Life.* This is My desire for you: that you stay near Me as you walk along your life-path. Each day is an important part of that journey. Although you may feel as if you are going nowhere in this world, your spiritual journey is another matter altogether, taking you along steep, treacherous paths of adventure. That is why *walking in the Light of My Presence* is essential to keep you from stumbling. By staying close to Me, you present yourself as a *living sacrifice.* Even the most routine part of your day can be *a spiritual act of worship, holy and pleasing to Me.*

GENESIS 2:7; PSALM 89:15; ROMANS 12:1–2

A LONG-TERM PROBLEM can become an idol. When you are troubled by a situation that just won't go away, it's important to monitor your thoughts. An ongoing difficulty can occupy more and more of your thinking, until it looms in idolatrous proportions—casting ugly shadows on the landscape of your mind. When you realize this has happened, confess it to Me. Pour out your feelings as you seek to break free from the hurtful preoccupation. Acknowledge your weakness in the face of this hardship, and *humble yourself under My mighty hand.*

A problem-preoccupation makes you anxious. So I urge you to *cast all your anxiety on Me*—trusting that *I care for you.* You may have to do this thousands of times daily, but don't give up! Each time you cast your worrisome concerns on Me, you are redirecting your attention from problems to My loving Presence. To strengthen these transactions, you can thank Me for caring so much for you. Remember that I not only died for you, *I live to make intercession for you.*

1 JOHN 5:21; 1 PETER 5:6–7; HEBREWS 7:25 NKJV

REST IN ME, MY CHILD. This time devoted to Me is meant to be peaceful, not stressful. You don't have to perform in order to receive My Love. I have boundless, unconditional Love for you. How it grieves Me to see My children working for Love: trying harder and harder, yet never feeling good enough to be loved.

Be careful that your devotion to Me does not become another form of works. I want you to come into My Presence joyfully and confidently. You have nothing to fear, for you wear My own righteousness. Gaze into My eyes, and you will see no condemnation, only Love and delight in the one I see. Be blessed as *My Face shines radiantly upon you, giving you Peace.*

JOHN 15:13; 2 CORINTHIANS 5:21 NKJV;
ZEPHANIAH 3:17; NUMBERS 6:25–26

I CAN SMOOTH OUT all the tangled-up places, including those in your mind and heart. So come to Me just as you are, with all your knotty problems and loose ends. Many of your difficulties are complicated by other people's perplexities. It can be hard to sort out how much of the mess is yours and how much is theirs. Be willing to take responsibility for your own mistakes and sin without feeling responsible for the sinful failures of others. I am here to help you untangle your complex problems and find the best way to go forward.

Christianity is all about transformation—a lifelong process. Some of the knots from your past are hard to untie, especially when they involve people who continue to hurt you. Beware of getting stuck in introspection or obsessing about how to fix things. Instead, keep turning toward Me, seeking My Face *and* My will. Wait with Me, trusting in My timing for unscrambling things and making your way clear. Be willing to live with unresolved problems, but don't let them be your focus. My Presence in the present is *your portion*—and your boundless blessing.

2 CORINTHIANS 3:18; 1 CHRONICLES 16:10–11;
LAMENTATIONS 3:24

I DESIGNED YOU to live in union with Me. This union does not negate who you are; it actually makes you more fully yourself. When you try to live independently of Me, you experience emptiness and dissatisfaction. You may *gain the whole world* and yet lose everything that really counts.

Find fulfillment through living close to Me, yielding to My purposes for you. Though I may lead you along paths that feel alien to you, trust that I know what I am doing. If you follow Me wholeheartedly, you will discover facets of yourself that were previously hidden. I know you intimately—far better than you know yourself. In union with Me, you are complete. In closeness to Me, you are transformed more and more into the one I designed you to be.

MARK 8:36; PSALM 139:13–16;
2 CORINTHIANS 3:17–18

*D*EVOTE YOURSELF TO PRAYER *with an alert mind and a thankful heart.* For My followers, praying is a way of life—a way of staying connected with Me. But it's not easy. The evil one disdains your devotion to Me; his demonic underlings work to interrupt and weaken your communications with Me. So it's crucial for you to be committed to this discipline—determined to stay in touch with Me.

You can train yourself to call on Me even while you're engaging in other activities. This invites Me into your world, helping your work to go better and your life to be more fulfilling. It's also important to set aside some time to focus just on communicating with Me. This can be quite challenging! To pray effectively, you need an alert mind and a thankful heart. Ask My Spirit, *the Helper*, to empower your prayers—increasing your mental alertness and your thankfulness.

A wide-awake mind and a grateful heart will help you not only pray better but also live better. *Give thanks to Me and praise My Name.*

COLOSSIANS 4:2 NLT; JOHN 15:26 NKJV; PSALM 100:4

YOU WILL NOT FIND MY PEACE by engaging in excessive planning, attempting to control what will happen to you in the future. That is a commonly practiced form of unbelief. When your mind spins with multiple plans, Peace may sometimes seem to be within your grasp; yet it always eludes you. Just when you think you have prepared for all possibilities, something unexpected pops up and throws things into confusion.

I did not design the human mind to figure out the future. That is beyond your capability. I crafted your mind for continual communication with Me. Bring Me all your needs, your hopes and fears. Commit everything into My care. Turn from the path of planning to the path of Peace.

1 PETER 5:6–7; PROVERBS 16:9; PSALM 37:5 NKJV

I DELIGHT IN THOSE WHO FEAR ME, *who put their hope in My unfailing Love.* "Fear of the Lord" is often misunderstood, but it is the foundation of spiritual wisdom and knowledge. It consists of reverential awe, adoration, and submission to My will. You submit to Me by exchanging *your* attitudes and goals for *Mine.* Since I am your Creator, aligning yourself with Me is the best way to live. When your lifestyle exhibits this biblical fear, I take delight in you. Seek to feel My pleasure shining on you at such times.

Living according to My will is not easy; there will be many ups and downs as you journey with Me. But no matter what is happening, you can find hope in My unfailing Love. In your world today, many people are feeling desperate. They've become disillusioned and cynical because they put their confidence in the wrong thing. But *My steadfast Love* will never let you down—it will never let you go! Cling to hope, beloved. It's a golden cord connecting you to Me.

PSALM 147:11; PROVERBS 1:7 NKJV;
LAMENTATIONS 3:22–23 ESV

S EEK TO PLEASE ME above all else. Let that goal be your focal point as you go through this day. Such a mind-set will protect you from scattering your energy to the winds. The free will I bestowed on you comes with awesome responsibility. Each day presents you with choice after choice. Many of these decisions you ignore and thus make by default. Without a focal point to guide you, you can easily lose your way. That's why it is so important to stay in communication with Me, living in thankful awareness of My Presence.

You inhabit a fallen, disjointed world, where things are constantly unraveling around the edges. Only a vibrant relationship with Me can keep you from coming unraveled too.

MATTHEW 6:33; JOHN 8:29; COLOSSIANS 3:23–24

To infuse more Joy into your day, seek to increase your awareness that I am with you. An easy way to do this is to say: "Thank You, Jesus, for Your Presence." This is such a short, simple prayer that you can pray it frequently; it beautifully connects you to Me, expressing your gratitude. You don't have to *feel* My nearness in order to pray this way. However, the more you thank Me for My Presence, the more real I become to you. You align yourself—mind, heart, and spirit—with the reality that *in Me you live and move and have your being.*

You also increase your awareness by looking for signs of My unseen Presence around you. The beauties of nature and the pleasures of loved ones are reminders, pointing you to Me. You can also find Me in My Word, for I am the living Word. Ask My Spirit to illuminate Scripture to you—shining His Light in your heart, helping you see the Glory of My Presence.

ACTS 17:28; JOHN 1:1–2 NKJV; 2 CORINTHIANS 4:6

THERE IS A MIGHTY BATTLE going on for control of your mind. Heaven and earth intersect in your mind; the tugs of both spheres influence your thinking. I created you with the capacity to experience foretastes of heaven. When you shut out the world and focus on My Presence, you can enjoy sitting with Me *in heavenly realms.* This is an incredible privilege reserved for precious ones who belong to Me and seek My Face. Your greatest strength is your desire to spend time communing with Me. As you concentrate on Me, *My Spirit fills your mind with Life and Peace.*

The world exerts a downward pull on your thoughts. Media bombard you with greed, lust, and cynicism. When you face these things, pray for protection and discernment. Stay in continual communication with Me whenever you walk through the wastelands of this world. Refuse to worry, because this form of worldliness will weigh you down and block awareness of My Presence. Stay alert, recognizing the battle being waged against your mind. Look forward to an eternity of strife-free living, reserved for you in heaven.

EPHESIANS 2:6; ROMANS 8:6; 1 JOHN 2:15, 17

WHEN YOU ARE FEELING *DOWNCAST*, the best remedy is to *remember Me*. Think about who I am—*your Lord and your God*, your Savior and Shepherd, the Friend who *will never leave you*. I am fully aware of your every circumstance as well as all your thoughts and feelings. Everything about you is important to Me because you are so precious to Me. Remember the many ways I have taken care of you and helped you. Thank Me for each one that comes to mind, and relax in My loving Presence.

Tell Me about the things that are weighing you down. Though I know all about them, your voicing them to Me provides relief from the heavy load you've been carrying. In the Light of My Presence, you will see things more clearly. Together, you and I can sort out what is important and what is not. Moreover, as you linger with Me, My Face shines upon you—blessing, encouraging, and comforting you. I assure you that *you will again praise Me for the help of My Presence*.

PSALM 42:6; JOHN 20:28 NKJV;
DEUTERONOMY 31:8; PSALM 42:5 NASB

T RY TO SEE THINGS more and more from My perspective. Let the Light of My Presence so fully fill your mind that you view the world through Me. When little things don't go as you had hoped, look to Me lightheartedly and say, "Oh, well." This simple discipline can protect you from being burdened with an accumulation of petty cares and frustrations. If you practice this diligently, you will make a life-changing discovery: You realize that most of the things that worry you are not important. If you shrug them off immediately and return your focus to Me, you will walk through your days with lighter steps and a joyful heart.

When serious problems come your way, you will have more reserves for dealing with them. You will not have squandered your energy on petty problems. You may even reach the point where you can agree with the apostle Paul that all your troubles are *light and momentary* compared with *the eternal glory* being achieved by them.

PSALM 36:9 NKJV, PROVERBS 20:24;
2 CORINTHIANS 4:17–18

I AM GRACIOUS AND COMPASSIONATE, *slow to anger and rich in Love.* Explore the wonders of grace: unmerited favor lavished on you through My finished work on the cross. *By grace you have been saved through faith, and that not of yourself; it is the gift of God.* What's more, *My compassions never fail. They are new every morning.* So begin your day expectantly, ready to receive fresh compassions. Don't let yesterday's failures weigh you down. Learn from your mistakes and confess known sins, but don't let those become your focus. Instead, keep your eyes on Me.

I am *slow to anger.* So don't be quick to judge yourself—or others. Rather, rejoice that I am *rich in Love.* In fact, Love is at the very core of who I am. Your growth in grace involves learning to be more attentive to Me, more receptive to My loving Presence. This requires vigilant effort because the evil one despises your closeness to Me. Strive to stay alert, and remember: *There is no condemnation for those who belong to Me!*

PSALM 145:8–9; EPHESIANS 2:8 NKJV;
LAMENTATIONS 3:22–23; ROMANS 8:1

WAIT QUIETLY IN MY PRESENCE while My thoughts form silently in the depths of your being. Do not try to rush this process, because hurry keeps your heart earthbound. I am the Creator of the entire universe, yet I choose to make My humble home in your heart. It is there where you know Me most intimately; it is there where I speak to you in holy whispers. Ask My Spirit to quiet your mind so that you can hear *My still small voice* within you. I am speaking to you continually: words of Life . . . Peace . . . Love. Tune your heart to receive these messages of abundant blessing. *Lay your requests before Me, and wait in expectation.*

COLOSSIANS 1:16 NKJV;
1 KINGS 19:12 NKJV; PSALM 5:3

*C*OME TO ME, and rest in My Presence. I am *constantly thinking about you*, and I want you to become increasingly mindful of Me. Awareness of My Presence can *give you rest* even when you are quite busy. An inner peacefulness flows out of knowing *I am with you always*. This knowledge of Me permeates your heart, mind, and spirit—and it can fill you with deep Joy.

Many of My followers are so focused on the problems they see and the predictions they hear that they lose their Joy. It becomes buried under multiple layers of worry and fear. When you realize this has happened in your life, bring all your concerns to Me. Talk with Me about each one, seeking My help and guidance. Ask Me to remove the anxious layers that have buried your Joy. As you entrust your concerns into My care and keeping, your Joy will begin to emerge again. Nurture this gladness by speaking or singing praises to Me— *the King of Glory* who loves you eternally.

MATTHEW 11:28; PSALM 139:17 TLB;
MATTHEW 28:20; PSALM 24:7 NKJV

TRUST ME AND REFUSE TO WORRY, for *I am your Strength and Song.* You are feeling wobbly this morning, looking at difficult times looming ahead, measuring them against your own strength. However, they are not today's tasks—or even tomorrow's. So leave them in the future and come home to the present, where you will find Me waiting for you. Since *I am your Strength*, I can empower you to handle each task as it comes. Because *I am your Song*, I can give you Joy as you work alongside Me.

Keep bringing your mind back to the present moment. Among all My creatures, only humans can anticipate future events. This ability is a blessing, but it becomes a curse whenever it is misused. If you use your magnificent mind to worry about tomorrow, you cloak yourself in dark unbelief. However, when the hope of heaven fills your thoughts, the Light of My Presence envelops you. Though heaven is future, it is also present tense. As you walk in the Light with Me, you have one foot on earth and one foot in heaven.

EXODUS 15:2; 2 CORINTHIANS 10:5;
HEBREWS 10:23

Don't worry about your inadequacy; instead, accept and embrace it. It's the perfect link to My limitless sufficiency. When your resources seem lacking, your natural inclination is to worry. The best way to resist this temptation is to openly acknowledge your insufficiencies and thank Me for them. This frees you from trying to be what you are not—your own Savior and Provider. Because you are weak and sinful, you need a Savior who is strong and perfect—a Provider who can *meet all your needs.*

You gain access to My boundless resources by being both still *and* active. Spending time alone with Me, waiting in My Presence, enhances your connection with Me. *I work for those who wait for Me,* doing for you what you cannot do for yourself. But there are many things you *can* do. When you go about your activities relying on *the strength that I supply, I am glorified* and you are blessed.

The next time you're feeling inadequate, turn to Me immediately. I lovingly meet you in the place of your neediness.

PHILIPPIANS 4:19; ISAIAH 64:4 NLT;
1 PETER 4:11 ESV

WALK WITH ME in the freedom of forgiveness. The path we follow together is sometimes steep and slippery. If you carry a burden of guilt on your back, you are more likely to stumble and fall. At your request, I will remove the heavy load from you and bury it at the foot of the cross. When I unburden you, you are undeniably free! Stand up straight and tall in My Presence so that no one can place more burdens on your back. Look into My Face and feel the warmth of My Love-Light shining upon you. It is this unconditional Love that frees you from both fears and sins. Spend time basking in the Light of My Presence. As you come to know Me more and more intimately, you grow increasingly free.

PSALM 68:19; 1 JOHN 1:7–9;
1 JOHN 4:18

A BRUISED REED *I WILL NOT BREAK*, *and a dimly burning wick I will not extinguish.* I know you sometimes feel as weak and helpless as a bent reed or a faintly burning flame. Accept your weakness and brokenness, beloved; let them open your heart to Me. You can be fully yourself with Me because I understand you perfectly. As you tell Me your troubles, I refresh you and offer you *Peace that surpasses all comprehension.* Instead of trying to figure everything out, *lean on Me* in confident trust. Go off-duty for a while, trusting that I'm watching over you and working on your behalf.

My healing work within you is most effective when you are resting in My watchful care. *Though the mountains be shaken and the hills be removed, yet My unfailing Love for you will not be shaken nor My covenant of Peace be removed—for I have compassion on you.* Whenever you're feeling weak and wounded, come confidently into My Presence to receive abundant Love and Peace.

ISAIAH 42:3 NASB; PHILIPPIANS 4:6–7 NASB;
PROVERBS 3:5 AMP; ISAIAH 54:10

L IVE FIRST AND FOREMOST in My Presence. Gradually you will become more aware of Me than of people and places around you. This awareness will not detract from your relationships with others. Instead, it will increase your ability to give love and encouragement to them. My Peace will permeate your words and demeanor. You will be active in the world, yet one step removed from it. You will not be easily shaken because My enveloping Presence buffers the blow of problems.

This is the path I have set before you. As you follow it wholeheartedly, you experience abundant Life and Peace.

PSALM 89:15–16; PSALM 16:8;
2 PETER 1:2; JOHN 10:28 NKJV

*Y*OU ARE A LETTER FROM *ME, written not with ink but with the Spirit of the living God—on the tablet of your heart.* Because you are one of My followers, the Holy Spirit is in you. He equips and empowers you to do far more than you could ever do on your own. So don't be intimidated by challenging circumstances or tough times. The third Person of the Godhead lives *inside* you! Ponder the implications of this glorious truth. You can do much more than you think possible when you walk in My ways, asking *the Helper* to strengthen you as you go step by step with Me.

The Spirit writes on the tablet of your heart not only to bless you but also to draw others to Me. When you are with people who don't know Me, He can make you a living letter from Me. One of the shortest but most effective prayers is: "Help me, Holy Spirit." Use this prayer as often as you need, inviting Him to bring gospel truths alive through you.

2 CORINTHIANS 3:3; ROMANS 8:9;
JOHN 15:26 NKJV

P OUR ALL OF YOUR ENERGY into trusting Me. It is through trust that you stay connected to Me, aware of My Presence. Every step on your life-journey can be a step of faith. Baby steps of trust are simple for you; you can take them with almost unconscious ease. Giant steps are another matter altogether: leaping across chasms in semidarkness, scaling cliffs of uncertainty, trudging *through the valley of the shadow of death*. These feats require sheer concentration, as well as utter commitment to Me.

Each of My children is a unique blend of temperament, giftedness, and life experiences. Something that is a baby step for you may be a giant step for another person, and vice versa. Only I know the difficulty or ease of each segment of your journey. Beware of trying to impress others by acting as if your giant steps are only baby ones. Do not judge others who hesitate in trembling fear before an act that would be easy for you. If each of My children would seek to please Me above all else, fear of others' judgments would vanish, as would attempts to impress others. Focus your attention on the path just ahead of you and on the One who never leaves your side.

PSALM 23:4; MATTHEW 7:1–2; PROVERBS 29:25

*I*F IT IS POSSIBLE, *as far as it depends on you, live at peace with everyone.* At times there will be someone who is determined to oppose you—without good cause. In this case, I don't hold you accountable for the conflict. More often, however, you have contributed something to the dissension. When this happens, you should repent of your part in the conflict and do whatever you can to restore a peaceful relationship. In *either* situation, you need to forgive the person who offended you. You may also need to forgive yourself.

Beloved, *be quick to listen, slow to speak, and slow to become angry.* Take time—not only to think through what you want to say but to *listen* to the other person. If you listen carefully and pause before responding, you will be much less likely to become angry.

Whenever you have failed to live at peace with others and you are at fault, do not despair. I paid the penalty for *all* your sins so you could have permanent Peace with Me.

ROMANS 12:18; JAMES 1:19; ROMANS 5:1

COME TO ME AND LISTEN! Attune yourself to My voice, and receive My richest blessings. Marvel at the wonder of communing with the Creator of the universe while sitting in the comfort of your home. Kings who reign on earth tend to make themselves inaccessible; ordinary people almost never gain an audience with them. Even dignitaries must plow through red tape and protocol in order to speak with royalty.

Though I am King of the universe, I am totally accessible to you. I am with you wherever you are. Nothing can separate you from My Presence! When I cried out from the cross, *"It is finished!"* the curtain of the temple was torn in two from top to bottom.* This opened the way for you to meet Me face to Face, with no need of protocol or priests. I, the King of kings, am your constant Companion.

ISAIAH 50:4; ISAIAH 55:2–3;
JOHN 19:30; MATTHEW 27:50–51

D ON'T BE SURPRISED by the many loose ends in your life. They will always be part of your experience in this fallen world. When I created Adam and Eve, I placed them in a perfect environment: the Garden of Eden. Since you are one of their descendants, your longing for perfection is natural. It is also supernatural. Because you are My follower, your ultimate destination is heaven—magnificent and glorious beyond anything you can imagine! Your longings will be completely satisfied there.

When the loose ends of this broken world are getting you down, stop and look up to Me. Remember that I, the Perfect One, am with you. Tell Me your troubles, and let Me help you with them. Seek My guidance in setting good priorities—according to My will for you. Take time to rest in My Presence and to worship Me. Praising Me directs your attention away from the world with all its brokenness, toward Me in all My Glory. While you're engaged in worshiping Me, you are participating in My Glory.

GENESIS 2:15; PSALM 73:23–24;

PSALM 29:2 NKJV

RELAX IN MY EVERLASTING ARMS. Your weakness is an opportunity to grow strong in awareness of My Almighty Presence. When your energy fails you, do not look inward and lament the lack you find there. Look to Me and My sufficiency; rejoice in My radiant riches that are abundantly available to help you.

Go gently through this day, leaning on Me and enjoying My Presence. Thank Me for your neediness, which is building trust-bonds between us. If you look back on your journey thus far, you can see that days of extreme weakness have been some of your most precious times. Memories of these days are richly interwoven with golden strands of My intimate Presence.

DEUTERONOMY 33:27; ROMANS 8:26;
PSALM 27:13–14

*T*O ALL WHO RECEIVE ME, *to those who believe in My Name, I give the right to become children of God.* There is a close connection between receiving Me and believing in My Name—the essence of who I am. Receiving a gift requires some measure of openness, and I am the best Gift imaginable! Recognizing Me as your Savior-God, you can believe that My offer of everlasting Life is real—and that it is for you.

Being a child of God is indescribably glorious! I am both your Savior and your constant Companion. As you journey through life in this dark world, I am with you each step of the way. I provide Light not only for your path but also for your mind and heart. I delight in giving you Joy—now and throughout eternity. Your brightest moment on earth will one day look quite dim in comparison with the Glory-Light of heaven! There you will *see My Face* in its brilliant splendor, and you will *be satisfied* with endless oceans of Love.

JOHN 1:10–12; JOHN 3:16 NKJV;
PSALM 17:15

O PEN YOUR MIND AND HEART —your entire being—to receive My Love in full measure. So many of My children limp through their lives starved for Love because they haven't learned the art of receiving. This is essentially an act of faith: believing that I love you with boundless, everlasting Love. The art of receiving is also a discipline: training your mind to trust Me, coming close to Me with confidence.

Remember that the evil one is the *father of lies.* Learn to recognize his deceptive intrusions into your thoughts. One of his favorite deceptions is to undermine your confidence in My unconditional Love. Fight back against these lies! Do not let them go unchallenged. *Resist the devil in My Name, and he will slink away from you. Draw near to Me*, and My Presence will envelop you in Love.

EPHESIANS 3:16–19; HEBREWS 4:16;
JOHN 8:44; JAMES 4:7–8 NKJV

WHEN YOUR WORLD LOOKS DARK and threatening, come to Me. *Pour out your heart to Me*, knowing that I'm listening—and I care. Find comfort in My sovereignty: I'm in control even when global events look terribly out of control. Actually, many things are *not* as they should be, *not* as they were created to be. You do well to yearn for perfect goodness—someday those longings will be wondrously satisfied.

Consider the prophet Habakkuk as he awaited the Babylonian invasion of Judah. He knew the attack would be brutal, and he wrestled deeply with this prophetic knowledge. Finally, though, he wrote a hymn of absolute confidence in Me. After describing utterly desperate circumstances, he concluded: *"Yet I will rejoice in the Lord, I will be joyful in God my Savior."*

Feel free to wrestle with Me about your concerns. But remember that the goal is to come to a place of confident trust and transcendent Joy. You won't understand My mysterious ways, but you can find hope and help in My Presence. *I am your Strength*!

PSALM 62:8 NLT; REVELATION 22:5;
HABAKKUK 3:17–19; PSALM 42:5 NASB

I AM WITH YOU and all around you, encircling you in golden rays of Light. I always behold you Face to face. Not one of your thoughts escapes My notice. Because I am infinite, I am able to love you as if you and I were the only ones in the universe.

Walk with Me in intimate Love-steps, but do not lose sight of My Majesty. I desire to be your closest Friend, yet I am also your sovereign Lord. I created your brain with capacity to know Me as Friend and Lord simultaneously. The human mind is the pinnacle of My creation, but so few use it for its primary purpose—knowing Me. I communicate continually through My Spirit, My Word, and My creation. Only humans are capable of receiving Me and responding to My Presence. You are indeed *fearfully and wonderfully made*!

PSALM 34:4–6; 2 PETER 1:16–17;
JOHN 17:3; PSALM 139:14

IF YOUR PRIMARY GOAL is pleasing yourself, your life will be filled with frustrations. The attitude that things should go your way is based on a faulty premise: that you are the center of your world. The truth is, *I* am the Center, and everything revolves around Me. So make your plans tentatively, *seeking My Face* and My will in all you do. This is a win-win situation: If things go according to your plans, rejoice and thank Me. When your desires are thwarted, communicate with Me and be ready to subordinate your will to Mine.

Remember that you belong to Me, beloved; *you are not your own.* This awareness that you belong to Another can be a great relief. It shifts your focus away from yourself and what you want. Instead of striving to make things go your way, your primary goal becomes pleasing *Me.* You might think this would be burdensome, but it is actually quite freeing. *My yoke is easy, and My burden is light.* Knowing that you belong to Me provides deep, satisfying *rest for your soul.*

PSALM 105:4 NASB; 1 CORINTHIANS 6:19 HCSB;
2 CORINTHIANS 5:9; MATTHEW 11:29–30

I AM PERPETUALLY WITH YOU, taking care of you. That is the most important fact of your existence. I am not limited by time or space; My Presence with you is a forever-promise. You need not fear the future, for I am already there. When you make that quantum leap into eternity, you will find Me awaiting you in heaven. Your future is in My hands; I release it to you day by day, moment by moment. Therefore, *do not worry about tomorrow.*

I want you to live this day abundantly, seeing all there is to see, doing all there is to do. Don't be distracted by future concerns. Leave them to Me! Each day of life is a glorious gift, but so few people know how to live within the confines of today. Much of their energy for abundant living spills over the timeline into tomorrow's worries or past regrets. Their remaining energy is sufficient only for limping through the day, not for living it to the full. I am training you to keep your focus on My Presence in the present. This is how to receive abundant Life, which flows freely from My throne of grace.

MATTHEW 6:34; JOHN 10:10; JAMES 4:13–15

T HE RICHEST TREASURE I offer you is *the Light of the gospel of My Glory.* This is what makes the gospel such amazingly good news. It opens the way to My Glory!

When you trusted Me as your Savior, I set your feet on a pathway to heaven. Forgiveness of sins and a future in heaven are wondrous blessings, but I have even more for you. I have *made My Light shine in your heart to give you the Light of the knowledge of the Glory of My Face.* I want you to *seek My Face* wholeheartedly, so you can enjoy the radiant knowledge of My glorious Presence.

"Knowledge" is a very rich word. Some of its meanings are: *awareness acquired by experience or study* and *the sum of what has been perceived, discovered, or learned.* So knowing Me involves *awareness* of Me—experiencing My Presence. It also involves *perceiving* Me. *The god of this age has blinded the minds of unbelievers,* but you can know Me through perceiving the Light of My Glory!

2 CORINTHIANS 4:4;

2 CORINTHIANS 4:6; PSALM 27:8 NKJV

October

"Come to me, all you who are weary and burdened, and I will give you rest."

Matthew 11:28

October 1

W ORSHIP ME ONLY. *I am King of kings and Lord of lords, dwelling in unapproachable Light.* I am taking care of you! I am not only committed to caring for you, but I am also absolutely capable of doing so. Rest in Me, My weary one, for this is a form of worship.

Though self-flagellation has gone out of style, many of My children drive themselves like racehorses. They whip themselves into action, ignoring how exhausted they are. They forget that I am sovereign and that *My ways are higher* than theirs. Underneath their driven service, they may secretly resent Me as a harsh taskmaster. Their worship of Me is lukewarm because I am no longer their *First Love.*

My invitation never changes: *Come to Me, all you who are weary, and I will give you rest.* Worship Me by resting peacefully in My Presence.

1 TIMOTHY 6:15–16; ISAIAH 55:8–9;
REVELATION 2:4; MATTHEW 11:28

I WANT YOU TO RELAX and enjoy this day. It's easy for you to get so focused on your goals that you push yourself too hard—and neglect your need for rest. You tend to judge yourself on the basis of how much you've accomplished. There is certainly a time and place for being productive, using the opportunities and abilities I provide. Nonetheless, I want you to be able to like yourself as much when you're relaxing as when you're achieving.

Rest in the knowledge that you're a child of God, *saved by grace through faith* in Me. This is your ultimate—and foundational—identity. You hold a position of royalty in My eternal kingdom. Remember who you are!

When you're comfortable enough in your true identity to balance work with relaxation, you are more effective in My kingdom. A refreshed mind is able to think more clearly and biblically. A *restored soul* is more winsome and loving in interactions with others. So take time with Me, and let Me *lead you beside waters of rest.*

GENESIS 2:2–3; EPHESIANS 2:8 NKJV;
PSALM 23:2–3 NASB

NEVER TAKE FOR GRANTED My intimate nearness. Marvel at the wonder of My continual Presence with you. Even the most ardent human lover cannot be with you always. Nor can another person know the intimacies of your heart, mind, and spirit. *I know everything about you—even the number of hairs on your head.* You don't need to work at revealing yourself to Me.

Many people spend a lifetime or a small fortune searching for someone who understands them. Yet I am freely available to all who call upon My Name, who open their hearts to receive Me as Savior. This simple act of faith is the beginning of a lifelong love story. I, the Lover of your soul, understand you perfectly and love you eternally.

PSALM 145:18 NKJV; LUKE 12:7;
JOHN 1:12; ROMANS 10:13

I WILL JUDGE THE WORLD *in righteousness and the peoples in My truth.* This promise is full of blessing and encouragement. It means that someday evil will be judged; My perfect justice will finally—and forever—prevail! Because you are My follower, clothed in My own righteousness, you have nothing to fear. But those who refuse to trust Me as Savior have *everything* to fear. Someday time will run out, and My wrath will be terrifying to all who persist in unbelief. They will even *call to the mountains and the rocks, "Fall on us and hide us from the face of Him who sits on the throne and from the wrath of the Lamb!"*

I will judge everyone in My truth. The concept of absolute truth is widely opposed, yet it is nonetheless rock-solid reality. Unbelievers will eventually bump up against this certainty whether they believe in it or not. For you—and all believers—My truth is a firm foundation on which you can live and work, play and praise. This is good reason to *sing for Joy*!

PSALM 96:13; ISAIAH 61:10 NKJV;
REVELATION 6:16; PSALM 95:1

WHEN MANY THINGS SEEM to be going wrong, trust Me. When your life feels increasingly out of control, thank Me. These are supernatural responses, and they can lift you above your circumstances. If you do what comes naturally in the face of difficulties, you may fall prey to negativism. Even a few complaints can set you on a path that is a downward spiral, by darkening your perspective and mind-set. With this attitude controlling you, complaints flow more and more readily from your mouth. Each one moves you steadily down the slippery spiral. The lower you go, the faster you slide; but it is still possible to apply brakes. Cry out to Me in My Name! Affirm your trust in Me, regardless of how you feel. Thank Me for everything, though this seems unnatural—even irrational. Gradually you will begin to ascend, recovering your lost ground.

When you are back on ground level, you can face your circumstances from a humble perspective. If you choose supernatural responses this time—trusting and thanking Me—you will experience My unfathomable Peace.

PSALM 13:5; EPHESIANS 5:20; PSALM 34:10

*M*Y JUDGMENTS ARE UNSEARCHABLE, *and My paths are beyond tracing out!* This is why trusting Me is your best response to My ways with you. My *wisdom and knowledge* are too deep for Me to explain Myself to you. This should not be surprising, since I am infinite and eternal. I have always existed—*from everlasting to everlasting I am God.*

I am also *the Word who became flesh and dwelt among you.* I identified with mankind to the full extent—taking on a human body and dying a terrible death to save sinners who believe in Me. My sacrificial life and death provide ample reason for you to trust Me even when you don't understand My ways. You can rejoice that your loving Savior and sovereign Lord is infinitely wise! And you can draw near Me at any time by lovingly whispering My Name. I am always within whispering-distance: now, throughout your lifetime, and for all eternity. I am *Immanuel—God with you*—and I will never leave you.

ROMANS 11:33; PSALM 90:2;
JOHN 1:14 ESV; MATTHEW 1:23

I AM THE CREATOR OF HEAVEN AND EARTH: Lord of all that is and all that will ever be. Although I am unimaginably vast, I choose to dwell within you, permeating you with My Presence. Only in the spirit realm could Someone so infinitely great live within someone so very small. Be awed by the Power and the Glory of My Spirit within you!

Though the Holy Spirit is infinite, *He deigns to be your Helper.* He is always ready to offer assistance; all you need to do is ask. When the path before you looks easy and straightforward, you may be tempted to *go it alone* instead of relying on Me. This is when you are in the greatest danger of stumbling. Ask My Spirit to help you as you go each step of the way. Never neglect this glorious Source of strength within you.

JOHN 14:16–17 NKJV; JOHN 16:7; ZECHARIAH 4:6

D O NOT LET FEAR OF MISTAKES immobilize you or make you anxious. In this life you *will* err sometimes because you're only human, with limited knowledge and understanding. When you're facing a major decision, learn as much as you can about the matter. *Seek My Face*— and My help. I will *guide you with My counsel* as you think things out in My Presence. When the time is right, go ahead and make the decision, even though the outcome is uncertain. Pray for My will to be done in this matter, and release the results to Me.

Fear has to do with punishment. If you have been punished unjustly or severely mistreated, it is natural for you to dread making mistakes. When choices need to be made, anxiety can cloud your thinking—perhaps even immobilizing you. The remedy is to remember that *I am with you* and for you—that you don't have to perform well for Me to keep loving you. Absolutely nothing, including your worst mistakes, *can separate you from My Love*!

PSALM 27:8 NKJV; PSALM 73:23–24;
1 JOHN 4:18 ESV; ROMANS 8:38–39

R EMEMBER THAT JOY is not dependent on your circumstances. Some of the world's most miserable people are those whose circumstances seem the most enviable. People who reach the top of the ladder career-wise are often surprised to find emptiness awaiting them. True Joy is a by-product of living in My Presence. Therefore you can experience it in palaces, in prisons . . . anywhere.

Do not judge a day as devoid of Joy just because it contains difficulties. Instead, concentrate on staying in communication with Me. Many of the problems that clamor for your attention will resolve themselves. Other matters you must deal with, but I will help you with them. If you make problem solving secondary to the goal of living close to Me, you can find Joy even in your most difficult days.

HABAKKUK 3:17–19; 1 CHRONICLES 16:27

I WANT YOU TO *HAVE NO FEAR* *of bad news.* The only way to accomplish this feat is to have a *steadfast heart, trusting in Me.* There is an abundance of bad news in the world, but you don't need to be afraid of it. Instead, confidently rely on Me—*believe* in Me. Find encouragement in My sacrificial death on the cross and My miraculous resurrection. I, your living Savior, am Almighty God! I am *sovereign* over global events; I am still in control.

When things around you or in the world seem to be spinning out of control, come to Me and *pour out your heart.* Instead of fretting and fuming, put your energy into praying. Come to Me, not only for comfort but also for direction; I will help you find the way forward. Moreover, I take your prayers into account as I govern your planet—in ways far, far beyond your understanding.

Don't dread bad news or let it spook you. Instead, keep your heart steadfast and calm through confident trust in Me.

PSALM 112:7; ISAIAH 40:10 NLT;
PSALM 62:8 NKJV; ISAIAH 9:6

B E WILLING TO FOLLOW wherever I lead. Follow Me wholeheartedly, with glad anticipation quickening your pace. Though you don't know what lies ahead, I know; and that is enough! Some of My richest blessings are just around the bend: out of sight, but nonetheless very real. To receive these gifts, you must *walk by faith—not by sight.* This doesn't mean closing your eyes to what is all around you. It means subordinating the visible world to the invisible Shepherd of your soul.

Sometimes I lead you up a high mountain with only My hand to support you. The higher you climb, the more spectacular the view becomes; also, the more keenly you sense your separation from the world with all its problems. This frees you to experience exuberantly the joyous reality of My Presence. Give yourself fully to these Glory-moments, awash in dazzling Light. I will eventually lead you down the mountain, back into community with others. Let My Light continue to shine within you as you walk among people again.

2 CORINTHIANS 5:7; PSALM 96:6;
JOHN 8:12; PSALM 36:9

A SK ME FOR WISDOM, BELOVED. I know how much you need it! King Solomon requested *a discerning heart*, and he received wisdom in magnificent abundance. This precious gift is also essential for you, especially when you're making plans and decisions. So come to Me for what you need, and *trust Me* to provide it in full measure.

One aspect of wisdom is recognizing your need for My help in all that you do. When your mind is sluggish, it's easy to forget about Me and simply dive into your tasks and activities. But eventually you bump into an obstacle. Then you face an important choice: to push ahead full throttle or to stop and ask Me for insight, understanding, and guidance. The closer to Me you live, the more readily and frequently you will seek My help.

The fear of the Lord is the beginning of wisdom. Though I am your Friend, remember who I am in My *great Power and Glory*! Godly fear—reverential awe and worshipful admiration—provides the best foundation for wisdom.

JAMES 1:5–6; 1 KINGS 3:9, 4:29;
PROVERBS 1:7; MARK 13:26 NKJV

IN ORDER TO HEAR MY VOICE, you must release all your worries into My care. Entrust to Me everything that concerns you. This clears the way for you to seek My Face unhindered. Let Me free you from fear that is hiding deep inside you. Sit quietly in My Presence, allowing My Light to soak into you and drive out any darkness lodged within you.

Accept each day just as it comes to you, remembering that I am sovereign over your life. *Rejoice in this day that I have made,* trusting that I am abundantly present in it. Instead of regretting or resenting the way things are, *thank Me in all circumstances.* Trust Me and don't be fearful; thank Me and rest in My sovereignty.

1 PETER 5:6–7; PSALM 118:24;
1 THESSALONIANS 5:18

T RAIN YOUR MIND to think great thoughts of Me! Many Christians are defeated by focusing mainly on less important things—the news, the weather, the economy, loved ones' problems, their own problems, and so on. Granted, *in this world you will have trouble*, but don't let troubles become your primary focus. Remind yourself that I am with you and *I have overcome the world*. I am nearer than the air you breathe, yet I am infinite God—*King of kings and Lord of lords*. I am also your loving Savior and faithful Friend.

One of the best ways to enhance awareness of My greatness is to worship Me. This connects you with the Godhead (Father, Son, and Spirit) in a glorious way. True worship expands My kingdom of Light in the world, pushing back the darkness. An exquisite way to praise Me is to read or sing the Psalms. Filling your mind with biblical truth will help you resist discouragement. When troubles assail you, exert yourself to think about who I am—your Savior and Friend who is Almighty God!

JOHN 16:33; REVELATION 19:16 NASB;
REVELATION 1:8 NKJV

I LOVE YOU WITH *an everlasting Love*. The human mind cannot comprehend My constancy. Your emotions flicker and falter in the face of varying circumstances, and you tend to project your fickle feelings onto Me. Thus you do not bene-fit fully from My unfailing Love.

You need to look beyond the flux of circumstances and discover Me gazing lovingly back at you. This awareness of My Presence strengthens you as you receive and respond to My Love. *I am the same yesterday, today, and forever!* Let My Love flow into you continually. Your need for Me is as constant as the outflow of My Love to you.

JEREMIAH 31:3; EXODUS 15:13; HEBREWS 13:8

I WANT YOU TO BECOME increasingly preoccupied with Me. The default mode of most people is self-absorption. My followers are not immune to this affliction, and it hinders their growth in grace.

When a man and woman are deeply in love, they tend to be preoccupied with each other. So the way to become preoccupied with *Me* is to love Me more fully—*with all your heart and soul and mind.* This is *the greatest commandment,* and it is a most worthy goal. Of course, you cannot do it perfectly in this life. But the more you comprehend and delight in the wondrous, *unfailing Love* I have for you, the more ardently you can respond to Me. Ask My Spirit to help you in this glorious quest!

There are two parts to this adventure: learning to receive My Love in greater depth, breadth, and constancy; and responding by loving Me more and more. Thus you break free from the bondage of self-absorption and grow increasingly preoccupied with Me. I delight in setting you free!

MATTHEW 22:37–39; PSALM 52:8;
1 JOHN 4:19 NKJV; JOHN 8:36 NKJV

Y OU HAVE BEEN on a long, uphill journey, and your energy is almost spent. Though you have faltered at times, you have not let go of My hand. I am pleased with your desire to stay close to Me. There is one thing, however, that displeases Me: your tendency to complain. You may talk to Me as much as you like about the difficulty of the path we are following. I understand better than anyone else the stresses and strains that have afflicted you. You can ventilate safely to Me because talking with Me tempers your thoughts and helps you see things from My perspective.

Complaining to others is another matter altogether. It opens the door to deadly sins such as self-pity and rage. Whenever you are tempted to grumble, come to Me and talk it out. As you open up to Me, I will put My thoughts in your mind and My song in your heart.

JEREMIAH 31:25; PHILIPPIANS 2:14–15;
PSALM 40:3

B E CAREFUL not to attach your sense of worth to your performance. When you're dissatisfied with something you have said or done, talk with Me about it. Ask Me to help you sort out what is truly sinful and what is not. Confess any sins you're aware of, and receive My forgiveness gratefully. Then live in the freedom of being My beloved believer. Don't let your mistakes and sins diminish your sense of worth. Remember that you have been declared "Not Guilty" forever! *There is no condemnation for those who are in Me*—who belong to Me. You are precious to Me, and *I take delight in you*, so refuse to condemn yourself.

Your imperfect performance reminds you that you are human. It humbles you and helps you identify with flawed humanity. Since pride is such a deadly sin—the one that ultimately led to Satan's expulsion from heaven—being humbled is really a blessing. So thank Me for the circumstances that have diminished your pride, and draw nearer to Me. Receive *My priceless, unfailing Love* in full measure!

1 JOHN 1:9 NKJV; ROMANS 8:1 ESV;
ZEPHANIAH 3:17; PSALM 36:7

T RUST ME ENOUGH to let things happen without striving to predict or control them. Relax, and refresh yourself in the Light of My everlasting Love. My Love-Light never dims, yet you are often unaware of My radiant Presence. When you project yourself into the future, rehearsing what you will do or say, you are seeking to be self-sufficient: to be adequate without My help. This is a subtle sin—so common that it usually slips by unnoticed.

The alternative is to live fully in the present, depending on Me each moment. Rather than fearing your inadequacy, rejoice in My abundant supply. Train your mind to seek My help continually, even when you feel competent to handle something by yourself. Don't divide your life into things you can do by yourself and things that require My help. Instead, learn to rely on Me in every situation. This discipline will enable you to enjoy life more and to face each day confidently.

PSALM 37:3–6; PHILIPPIANS 4:19 NKJV

A TROUBLESOME PROBLEM can become an idol in your mind. If you consistently think about something—pleasant or unpleasant—more than you think about Me, you are practicing a subtle form of idolatry. So it is wise to examine your thoughts.

Most people view idols as things that bring pleasure. But a chronic difficulty can captivate your mind, taking over increasingly more of your mental activity. Becoming aware of this bondage is a huge step toward breaking free from it. When you find yourself dwelling on a persistent problem, bring it to Me and confess the mental bondage you're experiencing. Request My help and My forgiveness, which I freely give. I will help you *take captive every thought to make it obedient to Me.*

I am teaching you to *fix your thoughts on Me* more and more. To achieve this goal, you need both discipline and desire. It's vital that you find pleasure in thinking of Me—rejoicing in My loving Presence. *Delight yourself in Me,* beloved; make Me the Desire of your heart.

ACTS 10:43 NCV; 2 CORINTHIANS 10:5;
HEBREWS 3:1; PSALM 37:4 NASB

I AM THE CULMINATION of all your hopes and desires. *I am the Alpha and the Omega, the first and the last: who is and was and is to come.* Before you knew Me, you expressed your longing for Me in hurtful ways. You were ever so vulnerable to the evil around you in the world. But now My Presence safely shields you, enfolding you in My loving arms. *I have lifted you out of darkness into My marvelous Light.*

Though I have brought many pleasures into your life, not one of them is essential. Receive My blessings with open hands. Enjoy My good gifts, but do not cling to them. Turn your attention to *the Giver of all good things*, and rest in the knowledge that you are complete in Me. The one thing you absolutely need is the one thing you can never lose: My Presence with you.

PSALM 62:5–8; REVELATION 1:8;
1 PETER 2:9 NKJV; JAMES 1:17

I AM YOUR STRENGTH AND YOUR SHIELD. I continually work—sometimes in wondrous ways—to invigorate you and protect you. The more fully you trust in Me, the more your heart can *leap for Joy*!

I want you to trust Me wholeheartedly—resting in My sovereign control over the universe. When circumstances seem to be spinning out of control, grab onto Me, believing that I know what I'm doing. I orchestrate every event of your life to benefit you in this world and the next.

While you are in the throes of adversity, your greatest challenge is to keep on trusting that I am both sovereign and good. Do not expect to understand My ways; *for as the heavens are higher than the earth, so are My ways and thoughts higher than yours*. When you respond to trouble with thanksgiving— convinced that I can bring good out of the most difficult situations—I am pleased. This act of faith encourages you and glorifies Me. I rejoice when My struggling children *give thanks to Me in song*!

PSALM 28:7; PSALM 18:1–2;
ISAIAH 55:9 NKJV

BEWARE OF SEEING YOURSELF through other people's eyes. There are several dangers to this practice. First of all, it is nearly impossible to discern what others actually think of you. Moreover, their views of you are variable: subject to each viewer's spiritual, emotional, and physical condition. The major problem with letting others define you is that it borders on idolatry. Your concern to please others dampens your desire to please Me, your Creator.

It is much more real to see yourself through *My eyes*. My gaze upon you is steady and sure, untainted by sin. Through My eyes you can see yourself as one who is deeply, eternally loved. Rest in My loving gaze, and you will receive deep Peace. Respond to My loving Presence by *worshiping Me in spirit and in truth*.

HEBREWS 11:6; ROMANS 5:5; JOHN 4:23–24

L EARN TO LEAN ON ME more and more. I know the full extent of your weakness, and that is where My powerful Presence meets you! My strength and your weakness fit together perfectly—in a wonderful synergy designed long before your birth. Actually, *My Power is most effective in weakness.* This is counterintuitive and mysterious, yet it is true.

It's important to lean on Me when you're feeling inadequate or overwhelmed. Remind yourself that you and I *together* are more than adequate. To sense my nearness, try closing your hand as if you're holding onto Mine. *For I take hold of your right hand and say to you, "Do not fear; I will help you."*

I want you to depend on Me even when you feel competent to handle things yourself. This requires awareness of both My Presence and your neediness. I am infinitely wise, so let Me guide your thinking as you make plans and decisions. Leaning on Me produces warm intimacy with Me—the One who *will never leave you or forsake you.*

2 CORINTHIANS 12:9 AMP; PHILIPPIANS 4:13 NKJV;
ISAIAH 41:13; DEUTERONOMY 31:6

October 13

T AKE TIME TO BE STILL in My Presence. The more hassled you feel, the more you need this sacred space of communion with Me. Breathe slowly and deeply. Relax in My holy Presence while *My Face shines upon you*. This is how you receive My Peace, which I always proffer to you.

Imagine the pain I feel when My children tie themselves up in anxious knots, ignoring My gift of Peace. I died a criminal's death to secure this blessing for you. Receive it gratefully; hide it in your heart. My Peace is an inner treasure, growing within you as you trust in Me. Therefore, circumstances cannot touch it. Be still, enjoying Peace in My Presence.

PSALM 46:10; NUMBERS 6:25–26; JOHN 14:27

*S*TAY ALERT AND BE PERSISTENT *in your prayers.* With My Spirit's help, you can learn to be increasingly wide-awake to Me. This is not an easy assignment, because the world is rigged to pull your attention away from Me. Excessive noise and visual stimulation make it hard for you to find Me in the midst of your moments. Yet I am always nearby—as near as a whispered prayer.

People who are in love yearn to be alone together so they can concentrate intently on each other. I am the Lover of your soul, and I long for you to spend time alone with Me. When you shut out distractions to focus only on Me, I awaken your soul to *the Joy of My Presence*! This increases your love for Me and helps you stay spiritually alert. Praying becomes easier when you're aware of My radiant Presence.

Praying not only blesses you but provides an avenue for serving Me. Rejoice that you can collaborate with Me through prayer as I establish My kingdom on earth.

EPHESIANS 6:18 NLT; ACTS 17:27–28;
PSALM 21:6; MATTHEW 6:10 NKJV

BE PREPARED TO SUFFER FOR ME, in My Name. All suffering has meaning in My kingdom. Pain and problems are opportunities to demonstrate your trust in Me. Bearing your circumstances bravely—even thanking Me for them—is one of the highest forms of praise. This sacrifice of thanksgiving rings golden-toned bells of Joy throughout heavenly realms. On earth also, your patient suffering sends out ripples of good tidings in ever-widening circles.

When suffering strikes, remember that I am sovereign and that I can bring good out of everything. Do not try to run from pain or hide from problems. Instead, accept adversity in My Name, offering it up to Me for My purposes. Thus your suffering gains meaning and draws you closer to Me. Joy emerges from the ashes of adversity through your trust and thankfulness.

JAMES 1:2–4; PSALM 107:21–22; PSALM 33:21

I WILL BE YOUR GUIDE *even to the end.* Rejoice that the One who leads you through each day will never abandon you. I am the Constant you can always count on—the One who goes before you yet remains close beside you. I never let go of your hand. *I guide you with My counsel, and afterward I will take you into Glory.*

Many people are overly dependent on human leaders because they want someone to make their decisions for them. Unscrupulous people can manipulate their followers to do things they wouldn't freely choose to do. But everyone who trusts Me as Savior has a Leader who is completely trustworthy and dependable.

I guide you with My truth and teach you My precepts so that you can make good decisions. I've provided you with a wonderfully reliable map: the Bible. *My Word is a lamp to your feet and a light to your path.* Follow this Light, and follow *Me*—for I am the One who knows the best way for you to go.

PSALM 48:14; PSALM 73:23–24;
PSALM 25:5; PSALM 119:105 NKJV

October 15

T RY TO STAY CONSCIOUS OF ME as you go step by step through this day. My Presence with you is both a promise and a protection. After My resurrection, I assured My followers: *Surely I am with you always.* That promise was for all of My followers, without exception.

The promise of My Presence is a powerful protection. As you journey through your life, there are numerous pitfalls along the way. Many voices clamor for your attention, enticing you to go their way. A few steps away from your true path are pits of self-pity and despair, plateaus of pride and self-will. If you take your eyes off Me and follow another's way, you are in grave danger. Even well-meaning friends can lead you astray if you let them usurp My place in your life. The way to stay on the path of Life is to keep your focus on Me. Awareness of My Presence is your best protection.

MATTHEW 28:20; HEBREWS 12:1–2

I GIVE YOU MY SHIELD OF VICTORY, *and My right hand sustains you.* I won the ultimate victory through My sacrificial crucifixion and My miraculous resurrection! I did this for *you*, for all who trust Me as Savior-God. I accomplished everything! Your part is just to *believe*: that you need a Savior to pay the penalty for your sins and that *I* am the only Way of salvation.

Your saving faith sets you on a path to heaven. Meanwhile, My victorious shield protects you as you journey through this world. Use *the shield of faith to stop the fiery arrows of the devil.* When you're in the thick of battle, call out to Me: "Help me, Lord! I trust in *You*."

As you live in close dependence on Me, My right hand does indeed sustain you, holding you up. I have indescribably great Power! Yet I use My mighty right hand not only to protect you but to tenderly lead you and help you keep going. Sometimes I even *gather you in My arms and carry you close to My heart.*

PSALM 18:35; JOHN 14:6 NKJV;
EPHESIANS 6:16 NLT; ISAIAH 40:11

Look to Me continually for help, comfort, and companionship. Because I am always by your side, the briefest glance can connect you with Me. When you look to Me for help, it flows freely from My Presence. This recognition of your need for Me, in small matters as well as in large ones, keeps you spiritually alive.

When you need comfort, I love to enfold you in My arms. I enable you not only to feel comforted but also to be a channel through whom I comfort others. Thus you are doubly blessed, because a living channel absorbs some of whatever flows through it.

My constant Companionship is the *pièce de résistance*: the summit of salvation blessings. No matter what losses you experience in your life, no one can take away this glorious gift.

PSALM 34:4–6; PSALM 105:4;
2 CORINTHIANS 1:3–4

CHALLENGING CIRCUMSTANCES come and go, but I am constantly with you. I'm writing the storyline of your life through good times *and* hard times. I can see the big picture: from before your birth to beyond the grave. I know exactly what you will be like when heaven becomes your forever-home, and I'm continually working to transform you into this perfect creation. You are royalty in My kingdom!

The constancy of My Presence is a glorious treasure that is underrated by most Christians. They've been taught that *I am continually with them*, but they often think and act as if they're alone. How this grieves Me!

When you lovingly whisper My Name—drawing near Me even in tough times—both you and I are blessed. This simple prayer demonstrates your trust that I am indeed with you and I am taking care of you. The reality of My Presence outweighs the difficulties you are facing, no matter how heavy they seem. So *come to Me* when you're feeling *weary and heavy-laden. I will give you rest.*

2 THESSALONIANS 2:13;
PSALM 73:23 NKJV; MATTHEW 11:28 NASB

A NXIETY IS A RESULT OF envisioning the future without Me. So the best defense against worry is staying in communication with Me. When you turn your thoughts toward Me, you can think much more positively. Remember to listen as well as to speak, making your thoughts a dialogue with Me.

If you must consider upcoming events, follow these rules: 1) Do not linger in the future, because anxieties sprout up like mushrooms when you wander there. 2) Remember the promise of My continual Presence; include Me in any imagery that comes to mind. This mental discipline does not come easily because you are accustomed to being god of your fantasies. However, the reality of My Presence with you, now and forevermore, outshines any fantasy you could ever imagine.

LUKE 12:22–26; EPHESIANS 3:20–21

I AM THE CHAMPION *who perfects your faith*. The more problem-filled your life becomes, the more important it is to *keep your eyes on Me*. If you gaze too long at your problems or at the troubles in this world, you will become discouraged. Whenever you're feeling weighed down or disheartened, break free by looking to Me. I am always with you, so you can communicate with Me at any time, in any situation. Instead of just letting your thoughts run freely, direct them to Me. This gives traction to your thinking and draws you closer to Me.

Rest in My embrace for a while, enjoying the nurturing protection of My Presence. As you survey the landscape of this broken world, rejoice that *nothing can separate you from My Love*! This promise applies to *anything* you could ever encounter. No matter how bleak things may look to you at this time, I am still in control. I—your Champion who fights for you—*scoff at* those who think they can defeat Me. Remember: *My unfailing Love surrounds you*!

HEBREWS 12:1–2 NLT; ROMANS 8:38–39;
PSALM 2:4; PSALM 32:10

G O GENTLY THROUGH THIS DAY, keeping your eyes on Me. I will open up the way before you as you take steps of trust along your path. Sometimes the way before you appears to be blocked. If you focus on the obstacle or search for a way around it, you will probably go off course. Instead, focus on Me, the Shepherd who is leading you along your life-journey. Before you know it, the "obstacle" will be behind you and you will hardly know how you passed through it.

That is the secret of success in My kingdom. Although you remain aware of the visible world around you, your primary awareness is of Me. When the road before you looks rocky, you can trust Me to get you through that rough patch. My Presence enables you to face each day with confidence.

JOHN 10:14–15; ISAIAH 26:7;
PROVERBS 3:25–26

T RUST IN *MY UNFAILING LOVE*—thanking Me for the good you do not see. When evil seems to be flourishing in the world around you, it can look as if things are spinning out of control. But rest assured: I'm not wringing My hands helplessly, wondering what to do next. I am still in control, and there is behind-the-scenes goodness in the midst of the turmoil. So I urge you to thank Me not only for the blessings you can see but for the ones you cannot see.

My *wisdom and knowledge* are deeper and richer than words can express. *My judgments are unsearchable, and My paths beyond tracing out!* This is why trusting Me *at all times* is so crucial. You must not let confusing circumstances shake your faith in Me. When your world feels unsteady, the disciplines of trusting and thanking Me serve to stabilize you. Remember: *I am always with you. I guide you with My counsel, and afterward I will take you into Glory.* Let this hidden treasure—your heavenly inheritance—lead you into joyous thanksgiving!

ISAIAH 54:10; ROMANS 11:33;
PSALM 62:8 NKJV; PSALM 73:23–24

October 19

COME TO ME with your defenses down, ready to be blessed and filled with My Presence. Relax and feel the relief of being totally open and authentic with Me. You have nothing to hide and nothing to disclose because I know everything about you already. You can have no other relationship like this one. Take time to savor its richness, basking in My golden Light.

One of the worst consequences of the Fall is the elaborate barriers people erect between themselves and others. Facades abound in the world, even in My body, the church. Sometimes, church is the last place where people feel free to be themselves. They cover up with Sunday clothes and Sunday smiles. They feel relief when they leave because of the strain of false fellowship. The best antidote to this artificial atmosphere is practicing My Presence at church. Let your primary focus be communing with Me, worshiping Me, glorifying Me. Then you will be able to smile at others with My Joy and love them with My Love.

1 JOHN 1:5–7; EXODUS 33:14; PHILIPPIANS 4:8

I WANT YOU TO LIVE CLOSE to Me, open to Me—aware of, attentive to, trusting, and thanking Me. I am always near you, so open yourself fully—heart, mind, and spirit—to My living Presence. Feel free to ask the Holy Spirit to help you in this endeavor.

Seek to stay aware of Me as you follow your path through this day. There is never a moment when I am not fully aware of you. Attentiveness involves being alert, listening carefully, and observing closely. I encourage you to be attentive not only to Me but to the people I bring into your life. Listening to others with full, prayerful attention blesses both them and you.

The Bible is full of instruction to trust Me and thank Me. Remember: I am totally trustworthy! So it is always appropriate to believe Me and My promises. I understand your weakness, and I will *help you overcome your unbelief.* Finally, thank Me throughout the day. This discipline of gratitude helps you receive My Joy in full measure!

REVELATION 1:18; JAMES 1:19;
MARK 9:24 NLT; PSALM 28:7

I AM YOUR LIVING GOD, far more abundantly alive than the most vivacious person you know. The human body is wonderfully crafted, but gravity and the inevitable effects of aging weigh it down. Even the most superb athlete cannot maintain his fitness over many decades. Lasting abundant life can be found in Me alone. Do not be anxious about the weakness of your body. Instead, view it as the prelude to My infusing energy into your being.

As you identify more and more fully with Me, My Life becomes increasingly intertwined with yours. Though the process of aging continues, inwardly you grow stronger with the passing years. Those who live close to Me develop an inner aliveness that makes them seem youthful in spite of their years. Let My Life shine through you as you *walk in the Light* with Me.

REVELATION 1:18; PSALM 139:14;
COLOSSIANS 1:29; ISAIAH 2:5

WHEN THE TASK BEFORE YOU looks daunting, refuse to be intimidated. Discipline your thinking to view the challenge as a privilege rather than a burdensome duty. Make the effort to replace your "I have to" mentality with an "I get to" approach. This will make all the difference in your perspective—transforming drudgery into delight. This is not a magic trick; the work still has to be done. But the change in your viewpoint can help you face the challenging chore joyfully and confidently.

As you go about your work, perseverance is essential. If you start to grow weary or discouraged, remind yourself: "I *get* to do this!" Then thank Me for giving you the ability and strength to do what needs to be done. Thankfulness clears your mind and draws you close to Me. Remember that My Spirit who lives in you is *the Helper*; ask Him to help you when you're perplexed. As you ponder problems and seek solutions, He will guide your mind. *Whatever you do, work at it with all your heart—as working for Me.*

COLOSSIANS 4:2; JOHN 14:16 NKJV;
COLOSSIANS 3:23

To live in My Presence consistently, you must expose and expel your rebellious tendencies. When something interferes with your plans or desires, you tend to resent the interference. Try to become aware of each resentment, however petty it may seem. Don't push those unpleasant feelings down; instead, let them come to the surface where you can deal with them. Ask My Spirit to increase your awareness of resentful feelings. Bring them boldly into the Light of My Presence so that I can free you from them.

The ultimate solution to rebellious tendencies is submission to My authority over you. Intellectually, you rejoice in My sovereignty, without which the world would be a terrifying place. But when My sovereign will encroaches on your little domain of control, you often react with telltale resentment.

The best response to losses or thwarted hopes is praise: *The LORD gives and the LORD takes away. Blessed be the name of the LORD.* Remember that all good things—your possessions, your family and friends, your health and abilities, your time—are gifts from Me. Instead of feeling entitled to all these blessings, respond to them with gratitude. Be prepared to let go of anything I take from you, but never let go of My hand!

PSALM 139:23–24; 1 PETER 5:6; JOB 1:21 NKJV

HOLD THINGS WITH LOOSE HANDS, but cling tightly and always to *My* hand. To be spiritually healthy, you must not be overly attached to your possessions. These are all blessings from Me, so receive them *with thankfulness*. But don't forget that ultimately *I* am the Owner of everything.

It's also important to hold *people* with open hands. Cherish your family and friends, yet beware of making them idols. If your life revolves around someone other than Me, you need to repent—changing your ways. Return to Me, beloved. Make Me *your First Love*, seeking to please Me above all else.

Another thing to hold loosely is control over your circumstances. When your life is flowing smoothly, it's easy to feel as if you're in control. Enjoy these peaceful times, but don't cling to them or think they are the norm. Instead, cling tightly to My hand—in good times, in hard times, at all times. Good times are better and hardship is more bearable when you're trustingly depending on Me. My abiding Presence is *your portion forever*!

COLOSSIANS 2:6–7 NLT;
REVELATION 2:4–5 NASB; PSALM 73:23–26

N O MATTER WHAT your circumstances may be, you can find Joy in My Presence. On some days, Joy is generously strewn along your life-path, glistening in the sunlight. On days like that, being content is as simple as breathing the next breath or taking the next step. Other days are overcast and gloomy; you feel the strain of the journey, which seems endless. Dull gray rocks greet your gaze and cause your feet to ache. Yet Joy is still attainable. *Search for it as for hidden treasure.*

Begin by remembering that I have created this day; it is not a chance occurrence. Recall that I am present with you whether you sense My Presence or not. Then, start talking with Me about whatever is on your mind. Rejoice in the fact that I understand you perfectly and I know exactly what you are experiencing. As you continue communicating with Me, your mood will gradually lighten. Awareness of My marvelous Companionship can infuse Joy into the grayest day.

PSALM 21:6; PROVERBS 2:4;
COLOSSIANS 1:16 NKJV

D ON'T BE AFRAID to tell Me how weak and weary—even overwhelmed—you feel at times. I am fully aware of the depth and breadth of your difficulties; nothing is hidden from Me.

Although I know everything, I wait to hear from you. *Pour out your heart to Me, for I am your Refuge.* There can be a peaceful intimacy in sharing your struggles with Me. You let down your guard and your pretense; you get real with Me—and with yourself. Then you rest in the safety of My Presence, trusting that I understand you perfectly and *love you with an everlasting Love.*

Relax deeply with Me; release yourself from striving to perform. *Be still,* letting My Presence refresh and renew you. When you are ready, ask Me to show you the way forward. Remember that I never leave your side; *I am holding you by your right hand.* This gives you courage and confidence to continue your journey. As you go along your path, hear Me saying, *"Do not fear; I will help you."*

PSALM 62:8; JEREMIAH 31:3;
PSALM 46:10 NKJV; ISAIAH 41:13

A s you turn your attention to Me, feel the Light of My Presence shining upon you. Open your mind and heart to receive My heavenly smile of approval. Let My gold-tinged Love wash over you and soak into the depths of your being. As you are increasingly filled with My Being, you experience joyous union with Me: *I in you and you in Me.* Your Joy-in-Me and My Joy-in-you become intertwined and inseparable. I suffuse your soul with Joy in My Presence; *at My right hand there are pleasures forevermore.*

NUMBERS 6:26 AMP; JOHN 17:20–23;
PSALM 16:11 NKJV

D O NOT DESPISE SUFFERING. It reminds you that you are on a pilgrimage to a far better place. I do provide some pleasures and comforts along the way, but they are temporary. When you reach your final destination—your home in heaven—I will shower you with *pleasures forevermore*. In that glorious place *there will be no more death or mourning or crying or pain*. The *fullness of Joy* you experience there will be permanent, never-ending.

Because you are My treasured follower, I can promise that your suffering will come to an end someday. Therefore, try to view your trouble as *momentary and light—producing for you an eternal weight of Glory beyond all measure and surpassing all comparisons!*

While you continue your journey through this world, be thankful for the comforts and pleasures I bless you with. And reach out to others who are suffering. *I comfort you in all your troubles so that you can comfort others.* Offering help to hurting people gives meaning to your suffering—and Glory to Me!

PSALM 16:11 NKJV; REVELATION 21:4;
2 CORINTHIANS 4:17 AMP; 2 CORINTHIANS 1:4 NLT

L IE DOWN IN GREEN PASTURES of Peace. Learn to unwind whenever possible, resting in the Presence of your Shepherd. This electronic age keeps My children "wired" much of the time, too tense to find Me in the midst of their moments. I built into your very being the need for rest. How twisted the world has become when people feel guilty about meeting this basic need! How much time and energy they waste by being always on the go rather than taking time to seek My direction for their lives.

I have called you to walk with Me down *paths of Peace.* I want you to blaze a trail for others who desire to live in My peaceful Presence. I have chosen you less for your strengths than for your weaknesses, which amplify your need for Me. Depend on Me more and more, and I will shower Peace on all your paths.

PSALM 23:1–3; GENESIS 2:2–3; LUKE 1:79

LASTING JOY CAN BE FOUND only in Me. There are many sources of happiness in this world, and sometimes they spill over into Joy—especially when you share your pleasures with Me. I shower blessings into your life, and I rejoice when you respond to them with a glad, thankful heart. So come frequently to Me with thanksgiving, and the Joy of My Presence will multiply the pleasures of My blessings.

On days when Joy seems a distant memory, you need to *seek My Face* more than ever. Don't let circumstances or feelings weigh you down. Instead, tell yourself the ultimate truth: *I am continually with you, holding you by your right hand. I guide you with My counsel, and afterward I will receive you into Glory.* As you make your way through the debris of this broken world, hold onto these truths with all your might. Remember that I Myself am *the Truth.* Cling to Me; follow Me, for I am also *the Way.* The Light of My Presence is shining on you, illumining the path before you.

PSALM 105:4; PSALM 73:23–24 NKJV; JOHN 14:6

I AM GOD WITH YOU, for all time and throughout eternity. Don't let the familiarity of that concept numb its impact on your consciousness. My perpetual Presence with you can be a continual source of Joy, springing up and flowing out in streams of abundant Life. Let your mind reverberate with meanings of My Names: Jesus, *the Lord saves*; and Immanuel, *God with us*. Strive to remain conscious of My Presence even in your busiest moments. Talk with Me about whatever delights you, whatever upsets you, whatever is on your mind. These tiny steps of daily discipline, taken one after the other, will keep you close to Me on the path of Life.

MATTHEW 1:21, 23; JOHN 10:10 NKJV; ACTS 2:28

*L*ET MY UNFAILING LOVE *be your comfort.* "Comfort" eases grief and trouble; it also gives strength and hope. The best source of these blessings is My constant Love that will never, ever fail you. No matter what is happening in your life, this Love can console you and cheer you up. However, you must make the effort to turn to Me for help. I am always accessible to you, and I delight in giving you everything you need.

I have complete, perfect understanding of you and your circumstances. My grasp of your situation is far better than yours. So beware of being overly introspective—trying to figure things out by looking inward, leaving Me out of the equation. When you realize you have done this, turn to Me with a brief prayer: "Help me, Jesus." Remind yourself that *I* am the most important part of the equation of your life! Relax with Me awhile, letting My loving Presence comfort you. *In the world you will have trouble; but be of good cheer, I have overcome the world.*

PSALM 119:76; PSALM 29:11;
PSALM 42:5 NASB; JOHN 16:33 NKJV

C OME TO ME when you are hurting, and I will soothe your pain. Come to Me when you are joyful, and I will share your Joy, multiplying it many times over. I am All you need, just when you need it. Your deepest desires find fulfillment in Me alone.

This is the age of self-help. Bookstores abound with books about "taking care of number one," making oneself the center of all things. The main goal of these methodologies is to become self-sufficient and confident. You, however, have been called to take a "road less traveled": continual dependence on Me. True confidence comes from knowing you are complete in My Presence. Everything you need has its counterpart in Me.

ISAIAH 49:13; JOHN 15:5; JAMES 1:4

L EARN TO BE JOYFUL when things don't go as you would like. Do not begin your day determined to make everything go your way. Each day you will bump up against at least one thing that doesn't yield to your will. It could be as trivial as the reflection you see in the mirror or as massive as a loved one's serious illness or injury. My purpose for you is *not* to grant your every wish or to make your life easy. My desire is that you learn to trust Me in all circumstances.

If you are intent upon having your way in everything, you will be frustrated much of the time. I don't want you to waste energy regretting things that have happened. The past cannot be changed, but you have My help in the present and My hope for the future. So try to relax—trusting in My control over your life. Remember: I am always close to you, and there is abundant *Joy in My Presence.* In fact, *My Face radiates with Joy* that shines upon you!

PSALM 62:8; PROVERBS 23:18;
ACTS 2:28; NUMBERS 6:25 TLB

A S YOU BECOME increasingly aware of My Presence, you find it easier to discern the way you should go. This is one of the practical benefits of living close to Me. Instead of wondering about what is on the road ahead or worrying about what you should do if . . . or when . . . , you can concentrate on staying in communication with Me. When you actually arrive at a choice-point, I will show you which direction to go.

Many people are so preoccupied with future plans and decisions that they fail to see choices they need to make today. Without any conscious awareness, they make their habitual responses. People who live this way find a dullness creeping into their lives. They sleepwalk through their days, following well-worn paths of routine.

I, the Creator of the universe, am the most creative Being imaginable. I will not leave you circling in deeply rutted paths. Instead, I will lead you along fresh trails of adventure, revealing to you things you did not know. Stay in communication with Me. Follow My guiding Presence.

PSALM 32:8; GENESIS 1:1; ISAIAH 58:11 NKJV

COME TO ME, My weary one. Find rest in My refreshing Presence. I am always by your side, eager to help you—but sometimes you are forgetful of Me.

You are easily distracted by the demands of other people. Their expectations can be expressed in ways that are harsh or gentle, guilt-inducing or kind. But if these demands are numerous and weighty, they eventually add up to a crushing load.

When you find yourself sinking under *heavy burdens*, turn to Me for help. Ask Me to lift those weights from your shoulders and carry them for you. Talk with Me about the matters that concern you. Let the Light of My Presence shine on them so you can see the way forward. This same Light soothes and strengthens you as it soaks into the depths of your being.

Open your heart to My healing, holy Presence. *Lift up your hands* in joyful adoration, letting My blessings flow freely into you. Take time to rest with Me, beloved; relax while I *bless you with Peace.*

MATTHEW 11:28 NLT; PSALM 134:2; PSALM 29:11

D O N O T E X P E C T to be treated fairly in this life. People will say and do hurtful things to you, things that you don't deserve. When someone mistreats you, try to view it as an opportunity to grow in grace. See how quickly you can forgive the one who has wounded you. Don't be concerned about setting the record straight. Instead of obsessing about other people's opinions of you, keep your focus on Me. Ultimately, it is My view of you that counts.

As you concentrate on relating to Me, remember that I have clothed you in My righteousness and holiness. I see you attired in these radiant garments, which I bought for you with My blood. This also is not fair; it is pure gift. When others treat you unfairly, remember that My ways with you are much better than fair. My ways are Peace and *Love, which I have poured out into your heart by My Spirit.*

COLOSSIANS 3:13; ISAIAH 61:10;
EPHESIANS 1:7–8; ROMANS 5:5

MANY PEOPLE ARE SELECTIVE about which parts of themselves they bring to Me in prayer. Some hesitate to approach Me about traits they consider shameful or embarrassing. Others are so used to living with painful feelings—loneliness, fear, guilt, shame—that it never occurs to them to ask for help in dealing with those things. Still others get so preoccupied with their struggles that they forget I'm even here. This is not My way for you, beloved.

There are hurting parts of you that I desire to heal. Some of them have been with you so long that you consider them facets of your identity. You carry them with you wherever you go, barely aware of their impact on your life. I want to help you learn to walk in freedom. However, you are so addicted to certain painful patterns that it will take time to break free from them. Only repeatedly exposing them to My loving Presence will bring you long-term healing. As you grow increasingly free, you'll be released to experience My Joy in greater and greater measure!

ROMANS 8:1; PSALM 118:5; PSALM 126:3

L INGER IN MY PRESENCE A WHILE. Rein in your impulses to plunge into the day's activities. Beginning your day alone with Me is essential preparation for success. A great athlete takes time to prepare himself mentally for the feat ahead of him before he moves a muscle. Similarly, your time of being still in My Presence equips you for the day ahead of you. Only I know what will happen to you this day. I have arranged the events you will encounter as you go along your way. If you are not adequately equipped for the journey, you will *grow weary and lose heart*. Relax with Me while I ready you for action.

ZECHARIAH 2:13; EPHESIANS 2:10; HEBREWS 12:3

*D*O NOT BE OVERCOME BY EVIL, *but overcome evil with good.* Sometimes you feel bombarded with all the bad things happening in the world. News reports are alarming, and people are *calling evil good and good evil.* All of this can be overwhelming unless you stay in communication with Me. I am saddened but not surprised by the horrors you see around you. I know fully the deceitful, wicked condition of human hearts. Unless people are redeemed through saving faith in Me, their potential for doing wrong is unlimited.

Instead of being disheartened by the condition of the world, I want My followers to be lights shining in the darkness. When evil appears to be winning, be more determined than ever to accomplish *something* good. Sometimes this will involve working directly against the bad things that upset you. At other times it will be a matter of doing whatever you can to promote biblical goodness—according to your gifts, abilities, and circumstances. Either way, you focus less on bemoaning evil and more on working to create something that is good.

ROMANS 12:21; ISAIAH 5:20; JEREMIAH 17:9 NKJV

I AM WITH YOU. *I am with you. I am with you.* Heaven's bells continually peal with that promise of My Presence. Some people never hear those bells because their minds are earthbound and their hearts are closed to Me. Others hear the bells only once or twice in their lifetimes, in rare moments of seeking Me above all else. My desire is that My "sheep" hear My voice continually, for *I am the ever-present Shepherd.*

Quietness is the classroom where you learn to hear My voice. Beginners need a quiet place in order to still their minds. As you advance in this discipline, you gradually learn to carry the stillness with you wherever you go. When you step back into the mainstream of life, strain to hear those glorious bells: *I am with you. I am with you. I am with you.*

ISAIAH 41:10 NKJV; JEREMIAH 29:12–13;
JOHN 10:14, 27–28

WALK WITH ME in close, trusting Love-bonds of joyful dependence. The companionship I offer you sparkles with precious promises from the Bible. I love you with perfect, *everlasting Love*. I am always with you—every nanosecond of your life. I know everything about you, and I have already paid the penalty for all your sins. Your inheritance—*kept in heaven for you—can never perish, spoil, or fade*. I guide you through your life, and *afterward I will take you into Glory*!

Dependence is an inescapable trait of the human condition. Many people despise their neediness and work hard to create the illusion of self-sufficiency in their lives. However, I designed you to need Me constantly and to be joyful about your reliance on Me. Recognizing and accepting your dependence increases your awareness of My loving Presence. This draws you closer to Me and helps you enjoy My company.

I invite you to commune with Me, your devoted Companion, in more and more of your moments. Walk joyfully with Me along the pathway of your life.

JEREMIAH 31:3 NKJV; 1 PETER 1:3–4; PSALM 73:24

L EARN TO LISTEN TO ME even while you are listening to other people. As they open their souls to your scrutiny, *you are on holy ground*. You need the help of My Spirit to respond appropriately. Ask Him to think through you, live through you, love through you. My own Being is alive within you in the Person of the Holy Spirit. If you respond to others' needs through your unaided thought processes, you offer them dry crumbs. When the Spirit empowers your listening and speaking, *My streams of living water flow* through you to other people. Be a channel of My Love, Joy, and Peace by listening to Me as you listen to others.

EXODUS 3:5; 1 CORINTHIANS 6:19; JOHN 7:38–39

I AM A *SHIELD FOR ALL who take refuge in Me.* When your world is feeling unsafe and threatening, ponder this precious promise. I personally shield and protect *all* who make Me their refuge—their safe place in the midst of trouble.

Finding shelter in Me involves *trusting in Me* and *pouring out your heart to Me.* No matter what is going on in your life, it is always the right time to tell Me that you trust Me. However, sometimes it will be necessary to attend to the demands of your circumstances before you pause to pour out your heart. Whisper your trust—and wait till you find the right time and place for expressing your deep emotions to Me. Then, when circumstances permit, speak freely in My Presence. This rich communication will provide real relief; it will also strengthen your relationship with Me and help you find the way forward.

My shielding Presence is continually available to you. Whenever you're feeling fearful, turn to Me and say: "Jesus, I take refuge in You."

2 SAMUEL 22:31; PSALM 46:1 NLT; PSALM 62:8

November

And my God will meet all your needs according to his glorious riches in Christ Jesus.

Philippians 4:19

November 1

D O N O T B E D I S C O U R A G E D by the difficulty of keeping your focus on Me. I know that your heart's desire is to be aware of My Presence continually. This is a lofty goal; you aim toward it but never fully achieve it in this life. Don't let feelings of failure weigh you down. Instead, try to see yourself as I see you. First of all, I am delighted by your deep desire to walk closely with Me through your life. I am pleased each time you initiate communication with Me. In addition, I notice the progress you have made since you first resolved to live in My Presence.

When you realize that your mind has wandered away from Me, don't be alarmed or surprised. You live in a world that has been rigged to distract you. Each time you plow your way through the massive distractions to communicate with Me, you achieve a victory. Rejoice in these tiny triumphs, and they will increasingly light up your days.

ROMANS 8:33–34; HEBREWS 4:14–16

November 1

I AM THE GOD WHO MAKES YOU STRONG, who makes your pathway safe. Come to Me just as you are—with all your sins and weaknesses. Confess your sins, and ask Me to remove them from you *as far as the east is from the west.* Then stay in My Presence with your inadequacies in full view. Ask Me to infuse strength into you, seeing your weaknesses as "jars" that are ready to be filled with My Power. Thank Me for your insufficiency that helps you keep depending on Me. Rejoice in My infinite sufficiency!

I am the One who makes your pathway safe. This includes protection from worry and excessive planning. Instead of gazing into the unknown future, try to be mindful of Me as you journey through this day. Remain in communication with Me, letting My guiding Presence keep you on course. I will go before you as well as beside you—clearing away obstacles on the path up ahead. Trust Me to make conditions on your pathway the very best for you.

PSALM 18:32 GNT; PSALM 103:12;
2 CORINTHIANS 12:9; 2 CORINTHIANS 4:7

GROW STRONG in the Light of My Presence. Your weakness does not repel Me. On the contrary, it attracts My Power, which is always available to flow into a yielded heart. Do not condemn yourself for your constant need of help. Instead, come to Me with your gaping neediness; let the Light of My Love fill you.

A yielded heart does not whine or rebel when the going gets rough. It musters the courage to thank Me even during hard times. Yielding yourself to My will is ultimately an act of trust. *In quietness and trust is your strength.*

PSALM 116:5–7; EPHESIANS 5:20; ISAIAH 30:15

WHEN ANXIETY IS GREAT WITHIN YOU, turn to Me for *consolation*. Other words for "consolation" are *comfort, compassion, empathy, help, encouragement, reassurance,* and *relief*. I gladly provide all of this—and much more—for My children. Yet your natural tendency when you're feeling anxious is to focus on yourself or your problems. The more you do this, the more you forget about Me and all the help I can supply. This worldly focus only increases your anxiety! Let the discomfort you feel at such times alert you to your neglect of Me. Whisper My Name, and invite Me into your difficulties.

Seek My Face, finding comfort in My compassion and empathy. Look to Me for encouragement, reassurance, and help. I know all about your problems, and I also know the best way to deal with them. As you relax in My loving Presence, I strengthen you and provide relief from your anxiety. I reassure you that *nothing in all creation can separate you from My Love*. My consolation is full of blessings, beloved; *it brings Joy to your soul.*

PSALM 94:19; PSALM 27:8 NKJV; ROMANS 8:38–39

EVERY TIME SOMETHING THWARTS YOUR PLANS or desires, use that as a reminder to communicate with Me. This practice has several benefits. The first is obvious: Talking with Me blesses you and strengthens our relationship. Another benefit is that disappointments, instead of dragging you down, are transformed into opportunities for good. This transformation removes the sting from difficult circumstances, making it possible to be joyful in the midst of adversity.

Begin by practicing this discipline in all the little disappointments of daily life. It is often these minor setbacks that draw you away from My Presence. When you reframe *setbacks as opportunities*, you find that you gain much more than you have lost. It is only after much training that you can accept major losses in this positive way. But it is possible to attain the perspective of the apostle Paul, who wrote: *Compared to the surpassing greatness of knowing Christ Jesus, I consider everything I once treasured to be as insignificant as rubbish.*

PROVERBS 19:21; COLOSSIANS 4:2;
PHILIPPIANS 3:7–8

G IVE UP THE ILLUSION of being in control of your life. When things are going smoothly, it's easy to feel as if you're in charge. The more you perceive yourself as your own master, and the more comfortable you become in this role, the harder you will fall.

I want you to enjoy times of smooth sailing and be thankful for them. But don't become addicted to this sense of mastery over your life, and don't consider it the norm. Storms *will* come, and uncertainties will loom on the horizon. If you cling to control and feel entitled to having things go your way, you are likely to sink when difficulties come.

I am training you to *trust in Me at all times—for I am your Refuge*. I use adversity to set you free from the illusion of being in control. When your circumstances and your future are full of uncertainties, look to Me. Find your security in *knowing Me*, the Master who is sovereign over the storms of your life—over everything.

JAMES 4:13–14; PSALM 62:8; JOHN 17:3 NKJV

WALK PEACEFULLY WITH ME through this day. You are wondering how you will cope with all that is expected of you. You must traverse this day like any other: one step at a time. Instead of mentally rehearsing how you will do this or that, keep your mind on My Presence and on taking the next step. The more demanding your day, the more help you can expect from Me. This is a training opportunity, since I designed you for deep dependence on your Shepherd-King. Challenging times wake you up and amplify your awareness of needing My help.

When you don't know what to do, wait while I open the way before you. Trust that I know what I'm doing, and be ready to follow My lead. *I will give strength to you, and I will bless you with Peace.*

EXODUS 33:14; DEUTERONOMY 33:25; HEBREWS 13:20–21; PSALM 29:11

LIVING IN CLOSE COMMUNICATION with Me can be a foretaste of heaven. It is wonderful, but it requires a level of spiritual and mental concentration that is extremely challenging. In the Psalms, David wrote about this wonderful way of living, declaring that *he had set Me always before him.* As a shepherd, he had plenty of time to seek My Face and enjoy My Presence. He discovered the beauty of days lived with Me always before him and beside him. I am training you to live this way too. It is an endeavor that requires persistent effort and determination. Yet rather than detracting from what you are doing, your closeness to Me will fill your activities with vibrant Life.

Whatever you do, do it for Me—with Me, through Me, in Me. Even menial tasks glow with the Joy of My Presence when you do them for Me. Ultimately, *nothing in all creation will ever be able to separate you from Me.* So this delightful you-and-I-together adventure can continue throughout eternity!

PSALM 16:8; COLOSSIANS 3:23–24;
ROMANS 8:39 NLT

639

Y OU CAN LIVE as close to Me as you choose. I set up no barriers between us; neither do I tear down barriers that you erect.

People tend to think their circumstances determine the quality of their lives. So they pour their energy into trying to control those situations. They feel happy when things are going well and sad or frustrated when things don't turn out as they'd hoped. They rarely question this correlation between their circumstances and feelings. Yet it is possible *to be content in any and every situation.*

Put more energy into trusting Me and enjoying My Presence. Don't let your well-being depend on your circumstances. Instead, connect your joy to My precious promises:

I am with you and will watch over you wherever you go. I will meet all your needs according to My glorious riches. Nothing in all creation will be able to separate you from My Love.

PHILIPPIANS 4:12; GENESIS 28:15;
PHILIPPIANS 4:19; ROMANS 8:38–39

*D*O NOT BE AFRAID, *for I am close beside you, guarding, guiding all the way.* Though I am always with you, you are often unaware of My Presence.

Fear can provide a wake-up call to your heart, alerting you to reconnect with Me. When you feel your anxiety rising, take time to relax and let the Light of My Presence shine upon you—and within you. As you rest in the warmth of My Love-Light, that cold, hard fear will start to melt away. Respond to My Love by affirming your love for Me and your trust in Me.

Remember that I am a *guarding, guiding* God. If you knew how much harm I protect you from, you would be astonished! The most important protection I provide is to guard your soul, which is eternal. Because you are My follower, your soul is secure in Me; *no one can snatch you out of My hand.* Moreover, I lead you as you go along your pathway toward heaven. *I will be your Guide even to the end.*

PSALM 23:4 TLB; JOHN 10:28; PSALM 48:14

S EEK TO PLEASE ME above all else. As you journey through today, there will be many choice-points along your way. Most of the day's decisions will be small ones you have to make quickly. You need some rule of thumb to help you make good choices. Many people's decisions are a combination of their habitual responses and their desire to please themselves or others. This is not My way for you. Strive to please Me in everything, not just in major decisions. This is possible only to the extent that you are living in close communion with Me. When My Presence is your deepest delight, you know almost instinctively what will please Me. A quick *glance* at Me is all you need to make the right choice. *Delight yourself in Me* more and more; seek My pleasure in all you do.

JOHN 8:29; HEBREWS 11:5–6; PSALM 37:4

*L*OVE IS PATIENT. In the apostle Paul's long list of characteristics of Christian love, the very first one is "patience." This is the ability to endure adversity calmly—not becoming upset when waiting a long time or dealing with difficult people or problems. Paul's emphasis on patience is countercultural, and it is often overlooked by My followers. This vital virtue rarely comes first in people's minds when they think about love. However, there is one common exception to this rule: a devoted mother or father. The demands of babies and young children help develop patience in good parents. They put aside their own needs to focus on their children—tenderly taking care of their needs.

I want My followers to lace their love for one another with plenty of patience. This virtue is the fourth trait listed in the fruit of the Spirit. Therefore, My Spirit can equip you to succeed in this challenging endeavor. Remember that I love you with perfect, *unfailing Love*. Ask the Holy Spirit to help you care for others with My bountiful, patient Love.

1 CORINTHIANS 13:4; ROMANS 12:12 HCSB;
GALATIANS 5:22–23 NASB; PSALM 147:11

Worship Me *in the beauty of holiness.* All true beauty reflects some of who I AM. I am working My ways in you: the divine Artist creating loveliness within your being. My main work is to clear out debris and clutter, making room for My Spirit to take full possession. Collaborate with Me in this effort by being willing to let go of anything I choose to take away. I know what you need, and I have promised to provide all of that—abundantly!

Your sense of security must not rest in your possessions or in things going your way. I am training you to depend on Me alone, finding fulfillment in My Presence. This entails being satisfied with much or with little, accepting *either* as My will for the moment. Instead of grasping and controlling, you are learning to release and receive. Cultivate this receptive stance by trusting Me in every situation.

PSALM 29:2 NKJV; PSALM 27:4; PSALM 52:8

*E*ACH DAY HAS ENOUGH TROUBLE *of its own.* A logical implication of this truth is that you can expect to encounter *some* trouble every day. I want to help you handle calmly and confidently the difficulties that come your way. Events that surprise you do *not* surprise Me, because I know everything. I am *the Beginning and the End.* Moreover, I am fully available to you—to guide and comfort you as you go through turbulent times.

Having *enough* trouble in each day can help you live in the present. Your active mind seeks challenges to chew on. Without enough to occupy your mind today, you are more likely to worry about the future. I am training you to keep your focus on My Presence in the present.

Difficulties need not deter you from enjoying My Presence. On the contrary, they draw you closer to Me when you collaborate with Me in handling them. As we deal with your problems *together*, you gain confidence in your ability to cope. And the pleasure of My Company greatly increases your Joy!

MATTHEW 6:34; REVELATION 21:6 NKJV;
ROMANS 12:12

L EARN TO APPRECIATE difficult days. Be stimulated by the challenges you encounter along your way. As you journey through rough terrain with Me, gain confidence from your knowledge that together we can handle anything. This knowledge is comprised of three parts: your relationship with Me, promises in the Bible, and past experiences of coping successfully during hard times.

Look back on your life, and see how I have helped you through difficult days. If you are tempted to think, "Yes, but that was then, and this is now," remember who I AM! Although you and your circumstances may change dramatically, *I remain the same* throughout time and eternity. This is the basis of your confidence. In My Presence *you live and move and have your being.*

ISAIAH 41:10; PSALM 102:27; ACTS 17:27–28

*B*EWARE OF LOVING PRAISE FROM MEN *more than praise from Me.* One of the effects of the Fall is that people are overly concerned about what others think of them—their social or professional performance, their physical attractiveness. Advertisements for cosmetics and fashionable clothes can feed this hurtful tendency to be focused on one's image.

I don't want you to be preoccupied with how other people view you. I have lovingly shielded you from being able to read the minds of others. What they think of you is really "none of your business." People's thoughts are unreliable—distorted by their sinfulness, weaknesses, and insecurities. Even if they praise you to your face, some of their thoughts about you will be quite different.

I am the only One who sees you as you truly are. Although you are far from perfect, I view you radiantly clothed in My perfect righteousness. Instead of seeking *praise from men*, seek to see Me looking at you. My loving approval of you is shining from My Face.

JOHN 12:43; ISAIAH 61:10;
NUMBERS 6:25–26 AMP

S IT QUIETLY WITH ME, letting all your fears and worries bubble up to the surface of your consciousness. There, in the Light of My Presence, the bubbles pop and disappear. However, some fears surface over and over again, especially fear of the future. You tend to project yourself mentally into the next day, week, month, year, decade; and you visualize yourself coping badly in those times. What you are seeing is a false image, because it doesn't include Me. Those gloomy times that you imagine will not come to pass, since My Presence will be with you at *all* times.

When a future-oriented worry assails you, capture it and disarm it by suffusing the Light of My Presence into that mental image. Say to yourself, "Jesus will be with me then and there. With His help, I can cope!" Then, come home to the present moment, where you can enjoy Peace in My Presence.

LUKE 12:22–25; DEUTERONOMY 31:6;
2 CORINTHIANS 10:5

TRUST ME TO LEAD YOU step by step through this day. I provide sufficient Light for only one day at a time. If you try to look into the future, you will find yourself peering into darkness. *My Face shines upon you* only in the present! This is where you find My unfailing, unquenchable Love. My Love for you is even stronger than the bond between a mother and her baby. *Though she may forget the baby at her breast, I will not forget you!* You are so precious to Me that *I have engraved you on the palms of My hands.* Forgetting you is out of the question.

I want you to *really come to know—practically, through experience—My Love, which far surpasses mere knowledge.* The Holy Spirit, who lives in your innermost being, will help you. Ask Him to fill you up completely with My fullness so that you may have *the richest measure of the divine Presence*: becoming *a body wholly filled and flooded* with Me! Thus you can experience My Love in full measure.

NUMBERS 6:25 NKJV; SONG OF SOLOMON 8:7 NKJV; ISAIAH 49:15–16; EPHESIANS 3:19 AMP

FOCUS YOUR ENTIRE BEING on My living Presence. I am most assuredly with you, enveloping you in My Love and Peace. While you relax in My Presence, I am molding your mind and cleansing your heart. I am re-creating you into the one I designed you to be.

As you move from stillness into the activities of your day, do not relinquish your attentiveness to Me. If something troubles you, talk it over with Me. If you get bored with what you are doing, fill the time with prayers and praise. When someone irritates you, don't let your thoughts linger on that person's faults. Gently nudge your mind back to Me. Every moment is precious if you keep your focus on Me. Any day can be a good day because My Presence permeates all time.

PSALM 89:15–16; 1 JOHN 3:19–20;
JUDE vv. 24–25; PSALM 41:12

I WANT YOU TO COMFORT OTHERS *with the comfort you have received from Me.* No matter what circumstances you are enduring, My Presence and comfort are sufficient for your needs. As a Christian, everything you endure has meaning and purpose. Suffering can build your character and prepare you to help others who are struggling. So talk freely with Me about the difficulties in your life, and ask Me to use them for My purposes. Of course, you can seek relief from hardship, but be careful not to overlook the blessings hidden in it.

When you draw closer to Me during tough times— seeking My help—you grow in maturity and wisdom. This equips you to help others as they endure adversity. Your empathy for hurting people will spill over into their lives. You will find that you're the most effective at comforting those who are enduring trials you've already been through.

You can grow in peacefulness through the discipline of hardship. Though it is painful at the time, *later it yields the peaceful fruit of righteousness.*

2 CORINTHIANS 1:3–4;
PHILIPPIANS 4:19; HEBREWS 12:11 ESV

D O N O T L E T any set of circumstances intimidate you. The more challenging your day, the more of My Power I place at your disposal. You seem to think that I empower you equally each day, but this is not so. Your tendency upon awakening is to assess the difficulties ahead of you, measuring them against your average strength. This is an exercise in unreality.

I know what each of your days will contain, and I empower you accordingly. The degree to which I strengthen you on a given day is based mainly on two variables: the difficulty of your circumstances, and your willingness to depend on Me for help. Try to view challenging days as opportunities to receive more of My Power than usual. Look to Me for all that you need, and watch to see what I will do. *As your day, so shall your strength be.*

EPHESIANS 1:18–20; PSALM 105:4;
DEUTERONOMY 33:25 NKJV

T HANKFULNESS IS THE BEST ANTIDOTE to a sense of entitlement—the poisonous attitude that "the world owes me." This misconception is epidemic in the work world, and it is contrary to biblical teaching. The apostle Paul commanded Christians to "keep away from every brother who is idle." Paul also taught by example—*working day and night to make himself a model for others to follow.* He even gave this rule: "If a man will not work, he shall not eat."

One definition of entitlement is *the feeling or belief that you deserve to be given something.* Thankfulness is the opposite: a grateful attitude for what you *already* have. If I gave you what you deserved, your ultimate destination would be hell—you would have no hope of salvation. So be thankful that I am *rich in mercy; it is by grace you have been saved.*

Thinking that you deserve more than you currently have will make you miserable, but a grateful attitude will fill you with Joy. Moreover, when you are thankful, you *worship Me acceptably with reverence and awe.*

2 THESSALONIANS 3:6–10; EPHESIANS 2:4–5;
PSALM 107:1 NKJV; HEBREWS 12:28

THIS IS A TIME OF ABUNDANCE in your life. *Your cup runneth over* with blessings. After plodding uphill for many weeks, you are now traipsing through lush meadows drenched in warm sunshine. I want you to enjoy to the full this time of ease and refreshment. I delight in providing it for you.

Sometimes My children hesitate to receive My good gifts with open hands. Feelings of false guilt creep in, telling them they don't deserve to be so richly blessed. This is nonsense-thinking because no one deserves anything from Me. My kingdom is not about earning and deserving; it's about believing and receiving.

When a child of Mine balks at accepting My gifts, I am deeply grieved. When you receive My abundant blessings with a grateful heart, I rejoice. My pleasure in giving and your pleasure in receiving flow together in joyous harmony.

PSALM 23:5 KJV; JOHN 3:16;
LUKE 11:9–10; ROMANS 8:32

I AM *FULL OF GRACE AND TRUTH*. "Grace" refers to the undeserved favor and Love I have for you. Receiving something you don't deserve is humbling, and that's a good thing—protecting you from pride. Grace is a gift of boundless worth, for it secures your eternal salvation. Because you know Me as Savior, I will always be favorable toward you, beloved. My Love for you is undeserved, unearned, and unfailing; so you can't lose it! Just *trust in My unfailing Love, and rejoice in My salvation.*

I am not only full of truth, but *I am the Truth*. People today are barraged by news and messages laced with spin and lies. As a result, cynicism abounds in the world. But in Me and in the Bible, you find absolute, unchanging Truth! Knowing Me *sets your feet on a rock and gives you a firm place to stand.* This secure foundation for your life makes you a bright beacon in a dark, relativistic world. *Let your light shine* so that *many will see and put their trust in Me.*

JOHN 1:14 ESV; PSALM 13:5–6; JOHN 14:6 NKJV;
PSALM 40:2; MATTHEW 5:16

I AM CHRIST IN YOU, *the hope of Glory.* The One who walks beside you, holding you by your hand, is the same One who lives within you. This is a deep, unfathomable mystery. You and I are intertwined in an intimacy involving every fiber of your being. The Light of My Presence shines within you, as well as upon you. I am in you, and you are in Me; therefore nothing in heaven or on earth can separate you from Me!

As you sit quietly in My Presence, your awareness of My Life within you is heightened. This produces the *Joy of the Lord, which is your strength. I, the God of hope, fill you with all Joy and Peace as you trust in Me, so that you may bubble over with hope by the power of the Holy Spirit.*

COLOSSIANS 1:27; ISAIAH 42:6;
NEHEMIAH 8:10; ROMANS 15:13 AMP

I WANT YOU TO HAVE QUIET CONFIDENCE in Me, your living God. As the prophet Isaiah wrote: *In quietness and confidence is your strength.* Sometimes people use loud voices or preposterous promises to gain power over others. These noisy speakers may appear to be strong—offering health and wealth to people who give them money—but they are actually just parasites. They survive by sucking precious resources out of others.

True strength comes from quietly trusting in *Me* and *My* promises. Rejoice that I am a *living* God—not a lifeless idol. *I am the Living One; I was dead, and behold I am alive for ever and ever.* My Power is infinite, yet I approach you gently and lovingly. Spend time with Me, cherished one, relating to Me in confident trust. As you relax with Me, I strengthen you—preparing you for challenges you will encounter on the road ahead. While you are focusing on My Presence, use Scripture to help you pray. You can draw near Me by whispering: *"I love You, O Lord, my strength."*

ISAIAH 30:15 NLT; REVELATION 1:18;
PSALM 18:1 NASB

B ASK IN THE LUXURY of being fully understood and unconditionally loved. Dare to see yourself as I see you: radiant in My righteousness, cleansed by My blood. I view you as the one I created you to be, the one you will be in actuality when heaven becomes your home. It is My Life within you that is changing you *from glory to glory*. Rejoice in this mysterious miracle! Thank Me continually for the amazing gift of My Spirit within you.

Try to depend on the help of the Spirit as you go through this day of life. Pause briefly from time to time so you can consult with this Holy One inside you. He will not force you to do His bidding, but He will guide you as you give Him space in your life. Walk along this wondrous way of collaboration with My Spirit.

PSALM 34:5; 2 CORINTHIANS 5:21:
2 CORINTHIANS 3:18 NKJV; GALATIANS 5:25

I AM ALWAYS WITH YOU, beloved, whether you're aware of My Presence or not. Sometimes the place you are in seems desolate—devoid of My loving companionship. But you can call out to Me and *know* that I am by your side, eager to help. *I am near to all who call on Me.* Whisper My Name in tender trust, casting your doubts to the wind. Tell Me your troubles and seek My guidance; then change the subject. Praise Me for My greatness and glory, My power and majesty! Thank Me for the good things I have done and am doing in your life. You will find Me richly present in your praise and thanksgiving.

Taste and see that I am good! The more you focus on Me and My blessings, the better you can taste My goodness. Delight in the sweetness of *My unfailing Love.* Savor the hearty flavor of My strength. Satisfy the hunger of your heart with the Joy and Peace of My Presence. *I am with you and will watch over you wherever you go.*

PSALM 145:18; PSALM 34:8 NKJV;
ISAIAH 54:10; GENESIS 28:15

A PPROACH PROBLEMS with a light touch. When your mind moves toward a problem area, you tend to focus on that situation so intensely that you lose sight of Me. You pit yourself against the difficulty as if you had to conquer it immediately. Your mind gears up for battle, and your body becomes tense and anxious. Unless you achieve total victory, you feel defeated.

There is a better way. When a problem starts to overshadow your thoughts, bring this matter to Me. Talk with Me about it and look at it in the Light of My Presence. This puts some much-needed space between you and your concern, enabling you to see from My perspective. You will be surprised at the results. Sometimes you may even laugh at yourself for being so serious about something so insignificant.

You will always face trouble in this life. But more importantly, you will always have Me with you, helping you to handle whatever you encounter. Approach problems with a light touch by viewing them in My revealing Light.

LUKE 12:25 ESV; PSALM 89:15; JOHN 16:33

*C*OME TO ME, and rest in My Presence. I am the *Prince of Peace.* You need My Peace continually, just as you need *Me* at all times. When things are going smoothly in your life, you tend to forget how dependent on Me you really are. Later, when you encounter bumps in the road, you become anxious and upset. Eventually you return to Me and seek My Peace. I gladly give you this glorious gift, though it's hard for you to receive it till you calm down. How much better it is to stay close to Me at *all* times.

Remember that I, your Prince, am royalty! *All authority in heaven and on earth has been given to Me.* When you're experiencing hard times in your life, come to Me and tell Me your troubles. But remember who I Am! Don't shake your fist at Me or demand that I do things your way. Instead, pray these encouraging words of David: *"But I trust in You, O Lord; I say, 'You are my God.' My times are in Your hands."*

MATTHEW 11:28; ISAIAH 9:6;
MATTHEW 28:18; PSALM 31:14–15

A S YOU LOOK at the day before you, you see a twisted, complicated path, with branches going off in all directions. You wonder how you can possibly find your way through that maze. Then you remember the One who is *with you always, holding you by your right hand.* You recall My promise to *guide you with My counsel*, and you begin to relax. As you look again at the path ahead, you notice that a peaceful fog has settled over it, obscuring your view. You can see only a few steps in front of you, so you turn your attention more fully to Me and begin to enjoy My Presence.

The fog is a protection for you, calling you back into the present moment. Although I inhabit all of space and time, you can communicate with Me only here and now. Someday the fog will no longer be necessary, for you will have learned to keep your focus on Me and on the path just ahead of you.

PSALM 73:23–24; PSALM 25:4–5;
1 CORINTHIANS 13:12

Y OU ARE SAFE, secure, and complete in Me. So stop your anxious striving, and come to Me with the things that concern you. Trust Me enough to be open and honest as you talk about these matters that weigh you down. *Give all your worries and cares to Me, for I care about you*—I am taking care of you! Then rest for a while *in the shelter of My Presence.*

When you wander away and leave Me out of your life, you no longer feel complete. The restlessness you experience at such times is a gift from Me, reminding you to return to your *First Love.* I want to be central in your thoughts and feelings, your plans and actions. This helps you live meaningfully, according to My will.

You are on a pathway to heaven, and I am your constant Companion. You *will* encounter trouble as you journey with Me, *but take heart! I have overcome the world.* In Me you are indeed safe, secure, and complete.

1 PETER 5:7 NLT; PSALM 31:19–20;
REVELATION 2:4; JOHN 16:33

THERE IS NO CONDEMNATION for those who are in Me. *The law of the Spirit of Life has set you free from the law of sin and death.* Not many Christians know how to live in this radical freedom, which is their birthright. I died to set you free; live freely in Me!

To walk along the path of freedom, you must keep your mind firmly fixed on Me. Many voices proclaim, "This is the way for you to go," but only My voice tells you the true way. If you follow the way of the world with all its glitter and glamour, you will descend deeper and deeper into an abyss. Christian voices also can lead you astray: "Do this!" "Don't do that!" "Pray this way!" "Don't pray that way!" If you listen to all those voices, you will become increasingly confused.

Be content to be a simple sheep, listening for My voice and following Me. *I will lead you into restful green pastures and guide you along paths of righteousness.*

ROMANS 8:1–2; ISAIAH 30:21;
JOHN 10:27; PSALM 23:1–3

*T*HE VERY ESSENCE OF MY WORDS *is truth—*
absolute, unchanging, eternal Truth! More and more
people are falling for the lie that truth is either relative or non-
existent. They are too cynical or too wounded to see things
that are *true, noble, right, pure, lovely, admirable.* They tend
to focus on what is false, wrong, impure, and ugly. This hurtful focus leads many to despair and self-destructive behavior.
*The god of this age has blinded the minds of unbelievers so that
they cannot see the Light of the gospel of My Glory.*

The gospel radiates pure, powerful Light that illuminates
My Glory—the wonder of who I am and what I have done!
This good news has unlimited Power to transform lives from
despair to delight. All My children, filled with My Spirit, are
well equipped to be Light-bearers, shining gospel brightness
into the lives of others. I want *you* to join in this glorious venture, using your gifts and the opportunities I provide. I know
you are weak, but that fits My purposes perfectly. My Power is
most effective in your weakness.

PSALM 119:160 NLT; PHILIPPIANS 4:8;
2 CORINTHIANS 4:4; 2 CORINTHIANS 12:9 AMP

C OME TO ME, and rest in My Peace. My Face is shining upon you, in rays of *Peace transcending understanding.* Instead of trying to figure things out yourself, you can relax in the Presence of the One who knows everything. As you lean on Me in trusting dependence, you feel peaceful and complete. This is how I designed you to live: in close communion with Me.

When you are around other people, you tend to cater to their expectations—real or imagined. You feel enslaved to pleasing them, and your awareness of My Presence grows dim. Your efforts to win their approval eventually exhaust you. You offer these people dry crumbs rather than the *living water* of My Spirit flowing through you. This is not My way for you! Stay in touch with Me, even during your busiest moments. Let My Spirit give you words of grace as you live in the Light of My Peace.

PHILIPPIANS 4:6–7; JOHN 7:38;
EPHESIANS 5:18–20

I, THE LORD, AM *YOUR STRENGTH*. **On days when you are feeling strong, this truth may not speak powerfully to you. However, it is a lifeline full of encouragement and hope, and it is always available to you. Whenever you're feeling weak, your lack of strength can help you look to Me and cling to this secure lifeline. You may call out to Me at any time, *"Lord, save me!"***

Let *My unfailing Love be your comfort*. When you seem to be sinking in your struggles, it's crucial to hold onto something that will not fail you, something you can trust with your very life. My powerful Presence not only strengthens you; it holds you close and doesn't let go. I have a firm grip on you, beloved.

Because I am always near, there's no need to fear being weak. In fact, *My Strength comes into its own in your weakness*; the two fit together perfectly. So, thank Me for your weaknesses—trusting in My ever-present Strength.

PSALM 59:17; MATTHEW 14:30;
PSALM 119:76; 2 CORINTHIANS 12:9 MSG

L EAVE OUTCOMES UP TO ME. Follow Me wherever I lead, without worrying about how it will all turn out. Think of your life as an adventure, with Me as your Guide and Companion. Live in the now, concentrating on staying in step with Me. When our path leads to a cliff, be willing to climb it with My help. When we come to a resting place, take time to be refreshed in My Presence. Enjoy the rhythm of life lived close to Me.

You already know the ultimate destination of your journey: your entrance into heaven. So keep your focus on the path just before you, leaving outcomes up to Me.

JOHN 10:4; PSALM 27:13–14;
EXODUS 15:13

D ON'T BE AFRAID to face your sins. Except for Me, there has never been a sinless person. *If you claim to be without sin, you deceive yourself* and evade *the truth*. It's actually quite freeing to *confess your sins*, knowing that *I will forgive you and purify you from all unrighteousness*. The good news is that I have redeemed you—paid the full penalty for all your sins. When you confess your wrongdoings, you are aligning yourself with the truth. Since I Myself *am the Truth*, your confession draws you closer to Me. It also *sets you free* from nagging guilt feelings.

When you realize you have sinned in your thoughts, words, or actions, admit it immediately. Your confession need not be lengthy or eloquent. It can be as simple as: "Forgive me and cleanse me, Lord." I have already done the hard part—dying on the cross for your sins. Your part is to live in the Light of the Truth. I, your Savior, *am the Light of the world*.

1 JOHN 1:8–9; JOHN 14:6 NKJV;
JOHN 8:32; JOHN 8:12

I AM PLEASED WITH YOU, MY CHILD. Allow yourself to become fully aware of My pleasure shining upon you. You don't have to perform well in order to receive My Love. In fact, a performance focus will pull you away from Me, toward some sort of Pharisaism. This can be a subtle form of idolatry: worshiping your own good works. It can also be a source of deep discouragement when your works don't measure up to your expectations.

Shift your focus from your performance to My radiant Presence. The Light of My Love shines on you continually, regardless of your feelings or behavior. Your responsibility is to be receptive to this unconditional Love. Thankfulness and trust are your primary receptors. Thank Me for everything; *trust in Me at all times.* These simple disciplines will keep you open to My loving Presence.

EPHESIANS 2:8–9; EPHESIANS 3:16–19;
PSALM 62:8

L ET ME TEACH YOU how to spend more of your time in the present. The future, as most people conceptualize it, does not really exist. When you gaze into your tomorrows, making predictions, you are simply exercising your imagination. I alone have access to what is "not yet" because I am not limited by time. As you go step by step through each day, I unfurl the future before you. However, while you're moving forward through time, you never set foot on anything but the present moment. Recognizing the futility of gazing into yet-to-come times can set you free to live more fully in the present.

Becoming free is a demanding process because your mind is accustomed to wandering into the future at will. When you find yourself caught up in such thoughts, recognize that you are roaming in a fantasyland. Awakening yourself to this truth helps you return to the present, where I eagerly await you, ready to enfold you in *My unfailing Love*.

ECCLESIASTES 8:7; REVELATION 1:8;
PSALM 32:10

THANK ME THROUGHOUT THIS DAY for My Presence and My Peace. These are gifts of supernatural proportions. Ever since the resurrection, I have comforted My followers with these messages: *Peace be with you*, and *I am with you always*. Listen as I offer you My Peace and Presence in full measure. The best way to receive these glorious gifts is to thank Me for them.

It is impossible to spend too much time thanking and praising Me. I created you first and foremost to glorify Me. Thanksgiving and praise put you in proper relationship with Me, opening the way for My riches to flow into you. As you thank Me for My Presence and Peace, you appropriate My richest gifts.

LUKE 24:36; MATTHEW 28:20;
HEBREWS 13:15; 2 CORINTHIANS 9:15 NKJV

WHEN YOU ARE THANKFUL, you *worship Me acceptably—with reverence and awe.* Thanksgiving is not just a holiday celebration once a year. It's an attitude of the heart that produces Joy; it is also a biblical command. You cannot worship Me acceptably with an ungrateful heart. You may go through the motions, but your ingratitude will hold you back.

Whenever you're struggling spiritually or emotionally, pause and check your "thankfulness gauge." If the reading is low, ask Me to help you increase your level of gratefulness. Search for reasons to thank Me; jot them down if you like. Your perspective will gradually shift from focusing on all that is wrong to rejoicing in things that are right.

No matter what is happening, you can *be joyful in God your Savior.* Because of My finished work on the cross, you have a glorious future that is guaranteed forever! Rejoice in this free gift of salvation—for you, for *all* who trust Me as Savior. Let your heart overflow with thankfulness, and I will fill you with My Joy.

HEBREWS 12:28; PSALM 100:4 NKJV;
1 CORINTHIANS 13:6; HABAKKUK 3:17–18

A THANKFUL ATTITUDE opens windows of heaven. Spiritual blessings fall freely onto you through those openings into eternity. Moreover, as you look up with a grateful heart, you get glimpses of Glory through those windows. You cannot yet live in heaven, but you can experience foretastes of your ultimate home. Such samples of heavenly fare revive your hope. Thankfulness opens you up to these experiences, which then provide further reasons to be grateful. Thus your path becomes an upward spiral: ever increasing in gladness.

Thankfulness is not some sort of magic formula; it is the language of Love, which enables you to communicate intimately with Me. A thankful mind-set does not entail a denial of reality with its plethora of problems. Instead, it *rejoices in Me, your Savior,* in the midst of trials and tribulations. *I am your refuge and strength, an ever-present and well-proved help in trouble.*

EPHESIANS 1:3; HABAKKUK 3:17–18;
PSALM 46:1 AMP

THANK ME for the glorious gift of grace! *For by grace you have been saved through faith. And this is not your own doing; it is the gift of God, not a result of works, so that no one may boast.* Through My finished work on the cross and your belief in Me as your Savior, you have received the greatest gift of all: *eternal Life.* Even the faith needed to receive salvation is a gift. The best response to such amazing generosity is a grateful heart. You can never thank Me too much or too frequently for grace.

During this Thanksgiving season, ponder what it means to have all your sins forgiven. It means you are no longer on a pathway to hell; your destination is *a new heaven and a new earth.* It also means that every day of your life is valuable. As you go through this day, thank Me often for the amazing gift of grace. Let this gratitude for grace fill you with Joy and increase your thankfulness for the many *other* blessings I provide.

EPHESIANS 2:8–9 ESV; JOHN 3:16;
MATTHEW 10:28; REVELATION 21:1 NKJV

A s you sit quietly in My Presence, let Me fill your heart and mind with thankfulness. This is the most direct way to achieve a thankful stance. If your mind needs a focal point, gaze at My Love poured out for you on the cross. Remember that *nothing in heaven or on earth can separate you from that Love*. This remembrance builds a foundation of gratitude in you, a foundation that circumstances cannot shake.

As you go through this day, look for tiny treasures strategically placed along the way. I lovingly go before you and plant little pleasures to brighten your day. Look carefully for them, and pluck them one by one. When you reach the end of the day, you will have gathered a lovely bouquet. Offer it up to Me with a grateful heart. Receive My Peace as you lie down to sleep, with thankful thoughts playing a lullaby in your mind.

ROMANS 8:38–39; 1 CORINTHIANS 3:11;
PSALM 4:7–8

GIVE THANKS TO ME, for I am good; My Love endures forever. I want you to set aside time to think about the many blessings I have provided for you. Thank Me for the gift of life—yours and those you love. Be grateful also for everyday provisions: food and water, shelter, clothing, and so on. Then remember the greatest gift of all: everlasting Life for everyone who knows Me, the Savior.

As you ponder all I have done for you, delight also in who *I AM*. I am one hundred percent Good! There has never been, and there will never be, even a speck of darkness in Me. *I am the Light of the world!* Moreover, My Love for you will go on and on—throughout eternity.

Even now, you are enveloped in My loving Presence. Regardless of what is happening, I am always close to My followers. So don't worry about whether or not you can sense My Presence. Simply *trust* that I am with you, and find comfort in *My unfailing Love.*

PSALM 107:1; JOHN 8:58 AMP;
JOHN 8:12 NASB; PSALM 107:8

T HANKFULNESS takes the sting out of adversity. That is why I have instructed you to *give thanks for everything*. There is an element of mystery in this transaction: You give Me thanks (regardless of your feelings), and I give you Joy (regardless of your circumstances). This is a spiritual act of obedience—at times, blind obedience. To people who don't know Me intimately, it can seem irrational and even impossible to thank Me for heartrending hardships. Nonetheless, those who obey Me in this way are invariably blessed, even though difficulties may remain.

Thankfulness opens your heart to My Presence and your mind to My thoughts. You may still be in the same place, with the same set of circumstances, but it is as if a light has been switched on, enabling you to see from My perspective. It is this *Light of My Presence* that removes the sting from adversity.

EPHESIANS 5:20; PSALM 118:1;
PSALM 89:15

RECEIVE JOYFULLY AND THANKFULLY the blessings I shower on you, but do not cling to them. Hold them loosely—ready to release them back to Me. At the same time, I want you to enjoy fully the good things I give you. The best way to do this is to live in the present, refusing to worry about tomorrow. *Today* is the time to delight in the blessings I have provided. Since you don't know what tomorrow will bring, make the most of what you have today: family, friends, talents, possessions. And look for opportunities to be a blessing to others.

When I remove from you something or someone you treasure, it's healthy to grieve your loss. It is also important to draw closer to Me during this time. Cling to Me, beloved, for your relationship with Me will never be taken away from you. Let Me be *your Rock, in whom you take refuge.* Often I provide unexpected *new* blessings to comfort you and lead you forward. Be on the lookout for all that I have for you!

MATTHEW 6:34 NKJV; LUKE 10:41–42;
PSALM 18:2; ISAIAH 43:19

T HANK ME FREQUENTLY as you journey through today. This practice makes it possible to *pray without ceasing*, as the apostle Paul taught. If you are serious about learning to pray continually, the best approach is to thank Me in every situation. These thankful prayers provide a solid foundation on which you can build all your other prayers. Moreover, a grateful attitude makes it easier for you to communicate with Me.

When your mind is occupied with thanking Me, you have no time for worrying or complaining. If you practice thankfulness consistently, negative thought patterns will gradually grow weaker and weaker. *Draw near to Me* with a grateful heart, and My Presence will *fill you with Joy and Peace*.

1 THESSALONIANS 5:16–18 KJV;
JAMES 4:8; ROMANS 15:13

I CREATED YOU TO GLORIFY ME. Make this precept your focal point as you find your way through this day. Thanksgiving, praise, and worship are means of glorifying Me. Thank Me frequently; be on the lookout for My blessings, searching for them as for hidden treasure. Praise Me not only in prayer and song but in your words to other people. Tell them about My marvelous deeds; declare how great I am! Join with others to worship Me at church, where the weight of My Glory can be palpable.

When you need to make decisions, consider what would glorify Me and bring Me pleasure. This can help you to choose wisely and stay more aware of My Presence. Instead of getting stuck in introspection, ask Me to guide your mind as you think things out. I know everything about you and your situation. The better you know Me, the more effectively I can guide your choices; so endeavor to enhance your knowledge of Me. *My Word is a lamp to your feet and a light for your path.*

1 THESSALONIANS 5:18 ESV; PSALM 96:3;
2 CORINTHIANS 4:17–18 NKJV; PSALM 119:105

T HIS IS THE DAY THAT I HAVE MADE! As you rejoice in this day of life, it will yield up to you precious gifts and beneficial training. Walk with Me along the high road of thanksgiving, and you will find all the delights I have made ready for you.

To protect your thankfulness, you must remember that you reside in a fallen world, where blessings and sorrows intermingle freely. A constant focus on adversity defeats many Christians. They walk through a day that is brimming with beauty and brightness, seeing only the grayness of their thoughts. Neglecting the practice of giving thanks has darkened their minds. How precious are My children who remember to thank Me at all times. They can walk through the darkest days with Joy in their hearts because they know that the Light of My Presence is still shining on them. *Rejoice in this day that I have made*, for I am your steadfast Companion.

PSALM 118:24; PSALM 116:17;
PSALM 118:28

T HANKING ME AWAKENS YOUR HEART and sharpens your mind, helping you enjoy My Presence. So when you're feeling out of focus or out of touch with Me, make the effort to thank Me for *something*. There is always an abundance of things to choose from: eternal gifts—such as salvation, grace, and faith—as well as ordinary, everyday blessings. Think back over the past twenty-four hours, and make note of all the good things I've provided in that short block of time. Not only will this lift your spirits, it will wake up your mind so you can think more clearly.

Remember that *your enemy the devil prowls around like a roaring lion, looking for someone to devour.* This is why it's so important to *be self-controlled and alert!* When you let your mind drift out of focus, you are much more vulnerable to the evil one. However, the remedy is simple. As soon as you realize what has happened, you can drive away the enemy by thanking and praising Me. This is worship warfare—and it works!

EPHESIANS 2:8–9; 1 PETER 5:8;
2 CORINTHIANS 9:15 NKJV

L ET THANKFULNESS RULE in your heart. As you thank Me for blessings in your life, a marvelous thing happens. It is as if *scales fall off your eyes*, enabling you to see more and more of My glorious riches. With your eyes thus opened, you can help yourself to whatever you need from My treasure house. Each time you receive one of My golden gifts, let your thankfulness sing out praises to My Name. "Hallelujahs" are the language of heaven, and they can become the language of your heart.

A life of praise and thankfulness becomes a life filled with miracles. Instead of trying to be in control, you focus on Me and what I am doing. This is the power of praise: centering your entire being in Me. This is how I created you to live, for I made you in My own image. Enjoy abundant life by overflowing with praise and thankfulness.

COLOSSIANS 3:15; ACTS 9:18;
REVELATION 19:3–6; PSALM 100:4

THANKFULNESS AND TRUST are like close friends who are always ready to help you. When your day looks bleak and the world seems scary, it's time to rely on these faithful friends. Stop for a moment and take some deep breaths. Look around you—searching for beauty and blessings—and thank Me for what you find. This connects you with Me in a wonderful way. Speak to Me in glowing terms about the many good gifts I've provided. Make the effort to thank Me with enthusiasm, regardless of how you're feeling. As you persist in expressing your gratitude, you'll find yourself becoming joyful.

It's also helpful to frequently voice your trust in Me. This reminds you that I am with you and I am absolutely reliable! There are always areas of your life where you need to trust Me more fully. When hard times come, view them as opportunities to expand the scope of your trust—*living by faith* in these challenging seasons. Don't waste the opportunities; use them to come closer to Me. I welcome you warmly, with open arms!

PSALM 92:1–2 NKJV; PSALM 118:28;
2 CORINTHIANS 5:7; JAMES 4:8

R EST IN THE DEEP ASSURANCE of My unfailing Love. Let your body, mind, and spirit relax in My Presence. Release into My care anything that is troubling you so that you can focus your full attention on Me. Be awed by the vast dimensions of My Love for you: *wider, longer, higher, and deeper* than anything you know. Rejoice that this marvelous Love is yours forever!

The best response to this glorious gift is a life steeped in thankfulness. Every time you thank Me, you acknowledge that I am your Lord and Provider. This is the proper stance for a child of God: receiving with thanksgiving. Bring Me the sacrifice of gratitude, and watch to see how much I bless you.

1 PETER 5:7; EPHESIANS 3:16–19;
PSALM 107:21–22

*Y*OU LOVE *M*E BECAUSE *I* FIRST LOVED YOU. The truth is that *you were dead in your sins*—completely unable to love Me—until My Spirit worked in the depths of your being to make you spiritually alive. This enabled you to repent of your sinfulness and receive not only eternal Life but also everlasting Love. As you ponder this miraculous gift of salvation, let gratitude rise up within you and fill you with Joy.

Thankfulness is so very important for your growth in grace. It opens your heart and mind to My Word, enabling you to increase in wisdom and understanding. A thankful attitude helps you discover the myriad blessings I shower upon you—even in the midst of hard times. A grateful heart protects you from discouragement and self-pity. It heightens your awareness of My continual Presence and helps you grasp more fully the vast dimensions of My Love for you. So nurture well your thankfulness, beloved. Your gratitude will nourish your love for Me—making it grow bright and strong!

1 JOHN 4:19 NKJV; EPHESIANS 2:1;
EPHESIANS 3:16–18

L ET ME INFUSE MY PEACE into your innermost being. As you sit quietly in the Light of My Presence, you can sense Peace growing within you. This is not something that you accomplish through self-discipline and willpower; it is opening yourself to receive My blessing.

In this age of independence, people find it hard to acknowledge their neediness. However, I have taken you along a path that has highlighted your need for Me, placing you in situations where your strengths were irrelevant and your weaknesses were glaringly evident. Through the aridity of those desert marches, I have drawn you closer and closer to Myself. You have discovered flowers of Peace blossoming in the most desolate places. You have learned to thank Me for hard times and difficult journeys, trusting that through them I accomplish My best work. You have realized that needing Me is the key to knowing Me intimately, which is the gift above all gifts.

JOHN 14:27 NKJV; ISAIAH 58:11;
ISAIAH 40:11

*T*HE PROSPECT OF THE RIGHTEOUS IS JOY. This means your prospects are excellent, for I have clothed you with My *robe of righteousness*. So begin each day eager to receive the Joy I have in store for you.

Some of My followers fail to find the pleasures I have prepared for them because they focus too much on problems in their lives and trouble in the world. Instead of living *to the full*, they live cautiously, seeking to minimize pain and risk. In doing so, they also minimize their Joy and their effectiveness in My kingdom. This is *not* My way for you.

As you awaken each morning, seek My Face with hopeful anticipation. Invite Me to prepare you not only for any difficulties on the road ahead but also for the pleasures I've planted alongside your path. Then take My hand as you begin your journey through the day, and let Me share in everything you encounter along the way—including all the Joy!

PROVERBS 10:28; ISAIAH 61:10 NKJV;
JOHN 10:10

November 30

PROBLEMS ARE PART OF LIFE. They are inescapable, woven into the very fabric of this fallen world. You tend to go into problem-solving mode all too readily, acting as if you have the capacity to fix everything. This is a habitual response, so automatic that it bypasses your conscious thinking. Not only does this habit frustrate you, it also distances you from Me.

Do not let fixing things be your top priority. You are ever so limited in your capacity to correct all that is wrong in the world around you. Don't weigh yourself down with responsibilities that are not your own. Instead, make your relationship with Me your primary concern. Talk with Me about whatever is on your mind, seeking My perspective on the situation. Rather than trying to fix everything that comes to your attention, ask Me to show you what is truly important. Remember that you are *en route* to heaven, and let your problems fade in the Light of eternity.

PSALM 32:8; LUKE 10:41–42;
PHILIPPIANS 3:20–21

J OY IS A CHOICE—one that you face many times each day as long as you live in this world. When you graduate to heaven, indescribably glorious Joy will be yours—effortlessly. You won't have to exert your will to be joyful. It will come naturally and be constant.

While you journey through this fallen world, I want to help you make increasingly wise choices. You need to become aware—and stay aware—that you can choose to be positive and hopeful moment by moment. Make it your goal to find Joy in the midst of your day. If you notice that you're experiencing discouragement, frustration, or other negative feelings, let those prickly emotions prod you into remembering Me. *Seek My Face* and talk with Me. You can pray something like, "Jesus, I choose to be joyful because You are *God My Savior* and *nothing can separate me from Your loving Presence.*"

Live victoriously, beloved, by seeking to find Me in more and more of your moments.

PSALM 27:8 NKJV; HABAKKUK 3:18;
ROMANS 8:38–39

December

"For to us a child is born. . . . And he will be called Wonderful Counselor, Mighty God, Everlasting Father, Prince of Peace."

I LOVE YOU *with an everlasting Love*, which flows out from the depths of eternity. Before you were born, I knew you. Ponder the awesome mystery of a Love that encompasses you from before birth to beyond the grave.

Modern man has lost the perspective of eternity. To distract himself from the gaping jaws of death, he engages in ceaseless activity and amusement. The practice of being still in My Presence is almost a lost art, yet it is this very stillness that enables you to experience My eternal Love. You need the certainty of My loving Presence in order to weather the storms of life. During times of severe testing, even the best theology can fail you if it isn't accompanied by experiential knowledge of Me. The ultimate protection against sinking during life's storms is devoting time to develop your friendship with Me.

JEREMIAH 31:3; LAMENTATIONS 3:22–26

*W*HATEVER YOU DO, *work at it with all your heart, as working for Me, not for men.* Half-heartedness is not pleasing to Me, nor is it good for you. It's tempting to rush through routine tasks and do them sloppily, just to get them done. But this negative attitude will pull you down and lower your sense of worth. If you do the same tasks with a thankful heart, you can find pleasure in them and do a much better job.

It's helpful to remember that every moment of your life is a gift from Me. Instead of feeling entitled to better circumstances, make the most of whatever I provide—including your work. When I put Adam and Eve in the Garden of Eden, I instructed them to *work it and take care of it.* Even though it was a perfect environment, it was not a place of idleness or total leisure.

Whatever you do, beloved, you are *working for Me.* So give Me your best efforts, and I will give you Joy.

COLOSSIANS 3:23; GENESIS 2:15;
2 THESSALONIANS 3:11–12

December 2

I AM THE PRINCE OF PEACE. As I said to My disciples, I say also to you: *Peace be with you.* Since I am your constant Companion, My Peace is steadfastly with you. When you keep your focus on Me, you experience both My Presence and My Peace. Worship Me as King of kings, Lord of lords, and Prince of Peace.

You need My Peace each moment to accomplish My purposes in your life. Sometimes you are tempted to take shortcuts in order to reach your goal as quickly as possible. But if the shortcut requires turning your back on My peaceful Presence, you must choose the longer route. Walk with Me along paths of Peace; enjoy the journey in My Presence.

ISAIAH 9:6; JOHN 20:19–21; PSALM 25:4 NKJV

*T*O THE ONE WHO IS THIRSTY *I will give water free of charge from the spring of the water of Life.* Drink deeply from this spring so that I can live abundantly in you. Let the water of Life soak into the depths of your being, refreshing and renewing you. Since this Life-water is free, you can have as much of it as you want—as much of *Me* as you want. I am *Christ in you, the hope of Glory*!

I long for you to *thirst for Me, your God*, more and more. Thirst is a very powerful appetite; this is necessary because drinking sustains life even more than eating. Pure water is a much healthier choice than canned drinks full of sugar or chemicals. Similarly, thirsting for Me first and foremost is crucial for your spiritual health. Though other things may seem to satisfy you for a while, they will not slake the thirst of your soul.

Rejoice that what you need most is free of charge! *Joyously draw water from the springs of salvation.*

REVELATION 21:6 NET; COLOSSIANS 1:27;
PSALM 63:1 ESV; ISAIAH 12:3 NASB

D<small>O NOT BE SURPRISED</small> by the fiery attacks on your mind. When you struggle to find Me and to live in My Peace, don't let discouragement set in. You are engaged in massive warfare, spiritually speaking. The evil one abhors your closeness to Me, and his demonic underlings are determined to destroy our intimacy. When you find yourself in the thick of battle, call upon My Name: "Jesus, help me!" At that instant, the battle becomes Mine; your role is simply to trust Me as I fight for you.

My Name, properly used, has unlimited Power to bless and protect. At the end of time, *every knee will bow (in heaven, on earth, and under the earth) when My Name is proclaimed.* People who have used "Jesus" as a shoddy swear word will fall down in terror on that awesome day. But all those who have drawn near Me through trustingly uttering My Name will be filled with *inexpressible and glorious Joy.* This is your great hope as you await My return.

E<small>PHESIANS</small> 6:12; P<small>HILIPPIANS</small> 2:9–10;
1 P<small>ETER</small> 1:8–9

*E*VEN THOUGH YOU DO NOT SEE ME, *you believe in Me.* I am far more real—complete, unchanging, unlimited—than the things you can see. When you believe in Me, you are trusting in rock-solid Reality. I am the indestructible *Rock* on which you can keep standing, no matter what your circumstances may be. And because you belong to Me, I am devoted to you. Beloved, I encourage you to *take refuge in Me.*

Believing in Me has innumerable benefits. The most precious one is *the salvation of your soul*—forever and ever. Your belief in Me also enhances your present life immensely, making it possible for you to know who you are and Whose you are. As you stay in communication with Me, I help you find your way through this fallen world with hope in your heart. All of this enlarges your capacity for Joy. The more you seek Me and the more fully you know Me, the more I can fill you with *inexpressible and glorious Joy*!

1 PETER 1:8–9; PSALM 18:2;
ROMANS 8:25 NKJV

M Y THOUGHTS *are not your thoughts; neither are your ways My ways. As the heavens are higher than the earth, so are My ways and thoughts higher than yours.* Remember who I AM when you spend time with Me. Marvel at the wonder of being able to commune with the King of the universe—any time, any place. Never take this amazing privilege for granted!

Though I am vastly higher and greater than you, I am training you to think My thoughts. As you spend time in My Presence, My thoughts gradually form in your mind. My Spirit is the Director of this process. Sometimes He brings Bible verses to mind. Sometimes He enables you to hear Me "speak" directly to you. These communications strengthen you and prepare you for whatever is before you on your life-path. Take time to listen to My voice. Through your sacrifice of precious time, I bless you far more than you dare to ask.

ISAIAH 55:8–9; COLOSSIANS 4:2; PSALM 116:17

I WANT YOU TO TRUST ME enough to relax and enjoy My Presence. I did not design you to live in a state of hyper-vigilance—feeling and acting as if you are constantly in the midst of an emergency. Your body is wonderfully crafted to "gear up" when necessary and then to "gear down" when the crisis is over. But because you live in such a broken world, you find it difficult to let down your guard and relax. I want you to remember that I am with you all the time and that I am totally worthy of your confidence. *Pour out your heart to Me*, committing all the things that are troubling you into My sovereign care.

The more you *lean on Me*, the more fully you can enjoy My Presence. As you relax in My healing Light, I shine Peace into your mind and heart. Your awareness of My Presence with you grows stronger, and *My unfailing Love* soaks into your inner being. *Trust in Me*, beloved, *with all your heart and mind.*

PSALM 62:8; PSALM 52:8; PROVERBS 3:5 AMP

December 5

L ET MY PRESENCE override everything you experience. Like a luminous veil of Light, I hover over you and everything around you. I am training you to stay conscious of Me in each situation you encounter.

When the patriarch Jacob ran away from his enraged brother, he went to sleep on a stone pillow in a land that seemed desolate. But after dreaming about heaven and angels and promises of My Presence, he awoke and exclaimed: "Surely the LORD is in this place, and I was not aware of it." His discovery was not only for him but for all who seek Me. Whenever you feel distant from Me, say, "Surely the Lord is in this place!" Then ask Me to give you awareness of My Presence. This is a prayer that I delight to answer.

PSALM 31:20; GENESIS 28:11–16

I CREATED YOU *IN MY IMAGE*—with the amazing capacity to communicate with Me. As My image-bearer, you are capable of choosing the focus of your mind. Many of your thoughts come and go unbidden, but you can control them more than you realize. The Holy Spirit inspired Paul to write, *"Whatever is true, whatever is noble, whatever is right . . . think about such things."* I wouldn't instruct you to think in this way unless it was possible for you to do so.

Because the world contains both good and evil, you can choose to focus on *excellent, praiseworthy* things or on terrible, upsetting matters. Sometimes you have to deal with the brokenness around you, but each day offers moments when you are free to ponder *pure, lovely* things. When your mind is idle, it often moves toward a negative focus—regretting things in the past, worrying about the future. Meanwhile, I am *with you* in the present, waiting for you to recall My Presence. Train yourself to turn toward Me frequently. This brightens even your hardest times, increasing your Joy.

GENESIS 1:27; PHILIPPIANS 4:8;
MATTHEW 1:23 NKJV; ACTS 2:28

S TAY EVER SO CLOSE TO ME, and you will not deviate from the path I have prepared for you. This is the most efficient way to stay on track; it is also the most enjoyable way. Men tend to multiply duties in their observance of religion. This practice enables them to give Me money, time, and work without yielding up to Me what I desire the most— their hearts. Rules can be observed mechanically. Once they become habitual, they can be followed with minimal effort and almost no thought. These habit-forming rules provide a false sense of security, lulling the soul into a comatose condition.

What I search for in My children is an awakened soul that thrills to the Joy of My Presence! I created mankind to glorify Me and enjoy Me forever. I provide the Joy; your part is to glorify Me by living close to Me.

DEUTERONOMY 6:5; COLOSSIANS 3:23;
PSALM 16:11; PSALM 86:12 NKJV

T RUST ME, BELOVED. Every time you have an anxious, fearful thought, you need to take multiple looks at Me. Speak My Name to remind yourself I am near, ready to help you. Quote Scripture back to Me: *"I trust in You, O Lord; I say, 'You are my God.' My times are in Your hands."* Express your love to Me, saying: *"I love You, O Lord, my Strength."* Remember that I—your Savior and King—*take great delight in you.* You're a cherished member of My royal family forever!

Connecting with Me interrupts the negative thoughts that tend to course through your mind. So the more consistently you communicate with Me, the freer you will become. Since *I am the Truth*, living close to Me helps you recognize and break free from distortions and lies.

Trusting and loving Me are at the very core of your relationship with Me. These beautiful ways of drawing near Me protect you from being too focused on yourself and your fears. Turn to Me over and over again—secure in My sheltering Presence.

PSALM 31:14–15; PSALM 18:1;
ZEPHANIAH 3:17 NET; JOHN 14:6 NKJV

I AM WITH YOU IN ALL THAT YOU DO, even in the most menial task. I am always aware of you, concerned with every detail of your life. Nothing escapes My notice—not even *the number of hairs on your head*. However, your awareness of My Presence falters and flickers; as a result, your life experience feels fragmented. When your focus is broad enough to include Me in your thoughts, you feel safe and complete. When your perception narrows so that problems or details fill your consciousness, you feel empty and incomplete.

Learn to look steadily at Me in all your moments and all your circumstances. Though the world is unstable and in flux, you can experience continuity through your uninterrupted awareness of My Presence. *Fix your gaze on what is unseen*, even as the visible world parades before your eyes.

MATTHEW 10:29–31;

HEBREWS 11:27; 2 CORINTHIANS 4:18

December 7

EVENING

JESUS ALWAYS

I WANT YOU TO LEARN to *be joyful always* by connecting your Joy to Me first and foremost. One way of doing this is to remember that I love you at all times and in all circumstances. *Though the mountains be shaken and the hills be removed, My unfailing Love for you will* not *be shaken.* So don't give in to the temptation to doubt My Love when things don't go as you would like or when you have failed in some way. My loving Presence is the solid rock on which you can always stand—knowing that in *Me* you are eternally secure. I am *the Lord who has compassion on you!*

Another way of increasing your Joy is to *give thanks in all circumstances.* Ask My Spirit to help you view your life through the lens of gratitude. Search for blessings scattered along your pathway—even during your hardest times—and thank Me for each one. I encourage you to look steadily through your lens of gratefulness by *thinking about things that are excellent and worthy of praise.*

1 THESSALONIANS 5:16–18;
ISAIAH 54:10; PHILIPPIANS 4:8 NLT

Y OUR NEEDS AND MY RICHES are a perfect fit. I never meant for you to be self-sufficient. Instead, I designed you to need Me not only for daily bread but also for fulfillment of deep yearnings. I carefully crafted your longings and feelings of incompleteness to point you to Me. Therefore, do not try to bury or deny these feelings. Beware also of trying to pacify these longings with lesser gods: people, possessions, power.

Come to Me in all your neediness, with defenses down and with desire to be blessed. As you spend time in My Presence, your deepest longings are fulfilled. Rejoice in your neediness, which enables you to find intimate completion in Me.

PHILIPPIANS 4:19; COLOSSIANS 2:2–3;
PSALM 84:11–12 NKJV

I AM *THE LORD OF PEACE*—the only source of genuine Peace. I give you this gift, not as something separate from Myself, but as part of who I am. You cannot just grab this blessing on the run. You need to set aside time for focusing on Me and enjoying My Presence.

You live in the midst of intense spiritual warfare, and My Peace is an essential part of your armor. To stay on your feet during the battles, you must wear sturdy combat boots—*the Gospel of Peace*. This good news assures you that I love you and I am *for you*.

Many of My followers forfeit Peace because they think I am always scrutinizing them through critical eyes. On the contrary, I gaze at you through eyes of perfect Love. Instead of punishing yourself when you've failed, remember that My death on the cross covers *all* your sins. I love you *with unfailing Love*—simply because you're Mine! Rejoice in this Gospel-Peace; it is yours to enjoy *at all times and in every way*.

2 THESSALONIANS 3:16; EPHESIANS 6:15 AMP;
ROMANS 8:31 NKJV; PSALM 90:14

B E WILLING TO GO OUT on a limb with Me. If that is where I am leading you, it is the safest place to be. Your desire to live a risk-free life is a form of unbelief. Your longing to live close to Me is at odds with your attempts to minimize risk. You are approaching a crossroads in your journey. In order to follow Me wholeheartedly, you must relinquish your tendency to play it safe.

Let Me lead you step by step through this day. If your primary focus is on Me, you can walk along perilous paths without being afraid. Eventually, you will learn to relax and enjoy the adventure of our journey together. As long as you stay close to Me, My sovereign Presence protects you wherever you go.

PSALM 23:4; PSALM 9:10; JOHN 12:26

A S YOU JOURNEY THROUGH LIFE with Me, see the hope of heaven shining on your path—lighting up your perspective. Remember that you are one of My *chosen people, belonging to Me. I called you out of darkness into My wonderful Light.* Savor the richness of these concepts: *I chose you before the creation of the world,* so nothing can separate you from Me. You belong to Me forever! I drew you out of the darkness *of sin and death* into the exquisite Light of eternal Life.

The brightness of My Presence helps you in multiple ways. The closer to Me you live, the more clearly you can see the way forward. As you soak in this Love-drenched Light, *I give you strength and bless you with Peace.* My radiance blesses not only you but also other people as it permeates your whole being. This time spent focusing on Me helps you become more like Me, enabling you to shine into the lives of others. I'm continually drawing My loved ones out of darkness into My glorious Light.

1 PETER 2:9; EPHESIANS 1:4;
ROMANS 8:2 ESV; PSALM 29:11 NKJV

711

M AKE ME THE FOCAL POINT of your search for
security. In your private thoughts, you are still trying
to order your world so that it is predictable and feels safe. Not
only is this an impossible goal, but it is also counterproductive
to spiritual growth. When your private world feels unsteady
and you grip My hand for support, you are living in conscious
dependence on Me.

Instead of yearning for a problem-free life, rejoice that
trouble can highlight your awareness of My Presence. In the
darkness of adversity, you are able to see more clearly the
radiance of My Face. Accept the value of problems in this life,
considering them pure joy. Remember that you have an eternity of trouble-free living awaiting you in heaven.

ISAIAH 41:10; PSALM 139:10; JAMES 1:2

*B*E STILL IN MY PRESENCE, *and wait patiently for Me to act.* Spending quality time with Me is so good for you, beloved. I rejoice when you push back the many things clamoring for your attention and focus wholeheartedly on Me. I know how hard it is for you to sit quietly with Me, and I don't expect perfection from you. Instead, I treasure your persistence in seeking My Face. My loving approval shines on you as you *seek Me with all your heart.* This intimate connection between us helps you wait trustingly for Me to act.

Don't worry about evil people who prosper or fret about their wicked schemes. Trust that I'm still in control and that justice will ultimately prevail. *I will judge the world in righteousness and the peoples in My truth.* Meanwhile, look for ways to advance My kingdom in this world. Keep your eyes on Me as you go through today, and be willing to follow wherever I lead. *Do not be overcome* or discouraged *by evil, but overcome evil with good*!

PSALM 37:7 NLT; JEREMIAH 29:13;
PSALM 96:12–13; ROMANS 12:21 NKJV

I AM WORKING ON YOUR BEHALF. Bring Me all your concerns, including your dreams. Talk with Me about everything, letting the Light of My Presence shine on your hopes and plans. Spend time allowing My Light to infuse your dreams with life, gradually transforming them into reality. This is a very practical way of collaborating with Me. I, the Creator of the universe, have deigned to co-create with you. Do not try to hurry this process. If you want to work with Me, you have to accept My time frame. Hurry is not in My nature. Abraham and Sarah had to wait many years for the fulfillment of My promise, a son. How their long wait intensified their enjoyment of this child! *Faith is the assurance of things hoped for, perceiving as real fact what is not revealed to the senses.*

PSALM 36:9; GENESIS 21:1–7;
HEBREWS 11:1 AMP

I AM *THE ROCK* *that is higher than you* and your circumstances. I am *your* Rock in whom you can take refuge—any time, any place. Come to Me, beloved; rest in the Peace of My Presence. Take a break from trying to figure everything out. Admit that many, many things are beyond your understanding—and your control. *My ways and thoughts are higher than yours, as the heavens are higher than the earth.*

When the world around you looks confusing and evil appears to be winning, remember this: I am the Light that keeps on shining in all situations. And light *always* overcomes darkness whenever these two opposites meet face to face.

Since you are My follower, I want you to shine brightly in this troubled world. Whisper My Name; sing songs of praise. Tell others *good tidings of great Joy*—that I am the *Savior, who is Christ the Lord*! I am also the One who is with you continually. Keep looking to Me, and My Presence will illuminate your path.

PSALM 61:2; PSALM 18:2;
ISAIAH 55:9; LUKE 2:10–11 NKJV

I AM TAKING CARE OF YOU. Feel the warmth and security of being enveloped in My loving Presence. Every detail of your life is under My control. Moreover, *everything fits into a pattern for good, to those who love Me and are called according to My design and purpose.*

Because the world is in an abnormal, fallen condition, people tend to think that chance governs the universe. Events may seem to occur randomly, with little or no meaning. People who view the world this way have overlooked one basic fact: the limitations of human understanding. What you know of the world you inhabit is only the tip of the iceberg. Submerged beneath the surface of the visible world are mysteries too vast for you to comprehend. If you could only see how close I am to you and how constantly I work on your behalf, you would never again doubt that I am wonderfully caring for you. This is why you must *live by faith, not by sight*, trusting in My mysterious, majestic Presence.

ROMANS 8:28 AMP; JOB 42:1–3;
1 PETER 5:7; 2 CORINTHIANS 5:7

W HEN I ENTERED YOUR WORLD as the God-Man, *I came to that which was My own.* Everything belongs to Me! Most people think their possessions are their own, but the truth is, you—and everything you possess—belong to Me. Though you may feel isolated and alone at times, this is only an illusion. I bought you at an astronomical price, so you are Mine—My treasure. The colossal price I paid shows how precious you are to Me! Ponder this powerful truth whenever you start to doubt your worth. You are My cherished one, *saved by grace through faith* in Me, your Savior.

Because you are precious to Me, I want you to take good care of yourself: spiritually, emotionally, and physically. Make time for pondering Scripture in your mind and heart. Protect yourself, both emotionally and physically, from those who would take advantage of you. Remember that *your body is the Holy Spirit's temple.* I also want you to help others discover the glorious good news—the free gift of *eternal Life for all who believe in Me.*

JOHN 1:11; EPHESIANS 2:8–9;
1 CORINTHIANS 6:19–20; JOHN 3:16

TAKE TIME TO BE HOLY. The word *holy* does not mean *goody-goody*; it means *set apart for sacred use*. That is what these quiet moments in My Presence are accomplishing within you. As you focus your mind and heart on Me, you are being transformed: re-created into the one I designed you to be. This process requires blocks of time set aside for communion with Me.

The benefits of this practice are limitless. Emotional and physical healing are enhanced by your soaking in the Light of My Presence. You experience a nearness to Me that strengthens your faith and fills you with Peace. You open yourself up to receive the many blessings that I have prepared for you. You become a cleansed *temple of My Holy Spirit*, who is able to do in and through you *immeasurably more than you ask or imagine*. These are just some of the benefits of being still in My Presence.

2 THESSALONIANS 1:10; PSALM 27:4;
1 CORINTHIANS 6:19; EPHESIANS 3:20

*E*VERYONE ON THE SIDE OF TRUTH *listens to Me.* I am Truth incarnated. The reason I was born and came into your world was *to testify to the truth.*

Many people believe that there are no absolutes and that everything is relative. Unscrupulous people capitalize on this prevailing view by manipulating information in false ways—to promote their own agendas. They present evil things as good, and vice versa. This is abhorrent to Me! As I said about all unrepentant liars, *their place will be in the fiery lake of burning sulfur.*

Remember that *the devil is a liar and the father of lies.* The more you listen to Me, especially through the reading of Scripture, the more you will treasure truth and take delight in Me—the living Truth. The Holy Spirit is *the Spirit of Truth*; ask Him to give you discernment. He will help you navigate your way through this world where spin and outright lies are commonplace. Strive to stay *on the side of truth* so you can live close to Me and enjoy My Presence.

JOHN 18:37; REVELATION 21:8;
JOHN 8:44; JOHN 16:13 NKJV

REST IN ME, MY CHILD, forgetting about the worries of the world. Focus on Me—Immanuel—and let My living Presence envelop you in Peace. Tune in to My eternal security, for *I am the same yesterday, today, and forever.* If you live on the surface of life by focusing on ever-changing phenomena, you will find yourself echoing the words of Solomon: *"Meaningless! Meaningless! Everything is meaningless!"*

Living in collaboration with Me is the way to instill meaning into your days. Begin each day alone with Me so that you can experience the reality of My Presence. As you spend time with Me, the way before you opens up step by step. Arise from the stillness of our communion, and gradually begin your journey through the day. Hold My hand in deliberate dependence on Me, and I will smooth out the path before you.

MATTHEW 1:22–23; HEBREWS 13:8;
ECCLESIASTES 1:2; PROVERBS 3:6

*D*O NOT GROW WEARY AND LOSE HEART. When you are dealing with difficulties that go on and on, it's easy to get so tired that you feel like giving up. Chronic problems can wear you out and wear you down. If you focus too much on these troubles, you're in danger of sliding into a black hole of self-pity or despair.

There are several kinds of weariness. Unrelieved physical tiredness makes you vulnerable to emotional exhaustion and spiritual fatigue—losing heart. However, I have equipped you to transcend your troubles by *fixing your eyes on Me*. I paid dearly for this provision by *enduring the cross* for you. Pondering My willingness to suffer so much can strengthen you to endure your own hardships.

Worshiping Me is a wonderful way to renew your strength in My Presence. When you take steps of faith by praising Me in the midst of difficulties, My glorious Light shines upon you. As you persevere in focusing on Me, you *reflect My Glory* to others, and you're *transformed into My likeness with ever-increasing Glory*.

HEBREWS 12:2–3; 2 CORINTHIANS 5:7 NKJV;
2 CORINTHIANS 3:18

Y OUR LONGING for heaven is good because it is an extension of your yearning for Me. The hope of heaven is meant to strengthen and encourage you, filling you with wondrous Joy. Many Christians have misunderstood this word *hope*, believing that it denotes wishful thinking. Nothing could be farther from the truth! As soon as I became your Savior, heaven became your ultimate destination. The phrase *hope of heaven* highlights the benefits you can enjoy even while remaining on earth. This hope keeps you spiritually alive during dark times of adversity; it brightens your path and heightens your awareness of My Presence. My desire is *that you may overflow with hope by the power of the Holy Spirit.*

ROMANS 8:23–25; HEBREWS 6:18–19;
ROMANS 15:13

IN ISAIAH'S PROPHECY ABOUT MY BIRTH, he referred to Me as *Eternal Father.* There is unity of essence in the Trinity, even though it is comprised of three Persons. When the Jews were questioning Me in the temple, I went so far as to say: *"I and the Father are one."* Later, when Philip asked Me to show the Father to the disciples, I said: *"Anyone who has seen Me has seen the Father."* So never think of Me as just a great teacher. I am God, and the Father and I live in perfect unity.

As you come to know Me in greater depth and breadth, realize that you are also growing closer to the Father. Don't let the mysterious richness of the Trinity confuse you. Simply come to Me, recognizing that I am everything you could ever need Me to be. I—your only Savior—am sufficient for you.

In the midst of this busy Advent season, keep bringing your focus back to My holy Presence. Remember that *Immanuel* has come, and rejoice!

ISAIAH 9:6 NASB; JOHN 10:30;
JOHN 14:9; MATTHEW 1:23 NKJV

I AM SPEAKING in the depths of your being. Be still so that you can hear My voice. I speak in the language of Love; My words fill you with Life and Peace, Joy and Hope. I desire to talk with all of My children, but many are too busy to listen. The "work ethic" has them tied up in knots. They submit wholeheartedly to this taskmaster, wondering why they feel so distant from Me.

Living close to Me requires making Me your *First Love*—your highest priority. As you seek My Presence above all else, you experience Peace and Joy in full measure. I also am blessed when you make Me first in your life. While you journey through life in My Presence, *My Glory brightens the world around you.*

PSALM 119:64; ISAIAH 50:4;
REVELATION 2:4; ISAIAH 60:2

WHEN AN ANGEL ANNOUNCED MY BIRTH to *shepherds living out in the fields* near Bethlehem, he told them: *Do not be afraid. I bring you good news of great Joy.* The instruction to not be afraid is repeated in the Bible more than any other command. It is a tender, merciful directive—and it is for you! I know how prone to fear you are, and I do not condemn you for it. However, I *do* want to help you break free from this tendency.

Joy is a powerful antidote to fear! And the greater the Joy, the more effective an antidote it is. The angel's announcement to the shepherds was one of *great* Joy. Don't ever lose sight of what amazingly *good news* the gospel is! You repent of your sins and trust Me as Savior. I forgive *all* your sins, changing your ultimate destination from hell to heaven. Moreover, I give you *Myself*—lavishing My Love upon you, promising you My Presence forever. Take time to ponder the angel's glorious proclamation to the shepherds. *Rejoice in Me*, beloved.

LUKE 2:8–10; 1 JOHN 3:1; PHILIPPIANS 4:4 NKJV

COME TO ME with your gaping emptiness, knowing that in Me you are complete. As you rest quietly in My Presence, My Light within you grows brighter and brighter. Facing the emptiness inside you is simply the prelude to being filled with My fullness. Therefore, rejoice on those days when you drag yourself out of bed, feeling sluggish and inadequate. Tell yourself that this is a perfect day to depend on Me in childlike trust. If you persevere in this dependence as you go through the day, you will discover at bedtime that Joy and Peace have become your companions. You may not realize at what point they joined you on your journey, but you will feel the beneficial effects of their presence. The perfect end to such a day is a doxology of gratitude. I am He from whom all blessings flow!

2 CORINTHIANS 4:6; MATTHEW 5:3, 6;
COLOSSIANS 2:9–10; PSALM 150:6

*S*ING FOR JOY TO ME, *your Strength.* Christmas music is one of the best blessings of the season, and it doesn't have to cost you anything. You can sing the carols at church or in the privacy of your home—or even in your car. As you are making a joyful noise, pay close attention to the words. They are all about Me and My miraculous entrance into your world through the virgin birth. Singing from your heart increases both your Joy and your energy. It also blesses Me.

I created you to glorify Me and enjoy Me forever. So it's not surprising that you feel more fully alive when you glorify Me through song. I want you to learn to enjoy Me in more and more aspects of your life. Before you arise from your bed each morning, try to become aware of My Presence with you. Say to yourself: *"Surely the* LORD *is in this place."* This will awaken your awareness to the wonders of My continual nearness. *I will fill you with Joy in My Presence.*

PSALM 5:11 NLT; GENESIS 28:16; ACTS 2:28

WHEN YOU ARE PLAGUED by a persistent problem—one that goes on and on—view it as a rich opportunity. An ongoing problem is like a tutor who is always by your side. The learning possibilities are limited only by your willingness to be teachable. In faith, thank Me for your problem. Ask Me to open your eyes and your heart to all that I am accomplishing through this difficulty. Once you have become grateful for a problem, it loses its power to drag you down. On the contrary, your thankful attitude will lift you up into heavenly places with Me. From this perspective, your difficulty can be seen as *a slight, temporary distress that is producing for you a transcendent Glory never to cease*!

ISAIAH 30:20–21; EPHESIANS 5:19–20;
2 CORINTHIANS 4:17 AMP

I, YOUR SAVIOR, AM *MIGHTY GOD*! Much of the focus during Advent is on the Baby in the manger. I did indeed begin My life on earth in this humble way. I set aside My Glory and took on human flesh. But I continued to be God—able to live a perfect, sinless life and perform mighty miracles. *I, your God, am with you—mighty to save!* Be blessed by this combination of My tender nearness and My majestic Power.

When I entered the world, *I came to that which was My own*, because everything was made through Me. *But My own did not receive Me. Yet to all who received Me, to those who believed in My Name, I gave the right to become children of God.* This gift of salvation is of infinite value. It gives meaning and direction to your life—and makes heaven your final destination. During this season of giving and receiving presents, remember that the ultimate present is eternal Life. Respond to this glorious gift by *rejoicing in Me always!*

ISAIAH 9:6 NKJV; ZEPHANIAH 3:17;
JOHN 1:11–12; PHILIPPIANS 4:4

D O N O T B E W E I G H E D D O W N by the clutter in your life: lots of little chores to do sometime, in no particular order. If you focus too much on these petty tasks, trying to get them all out of the way, you will discover that they are endless. They can eat up as much time as you devote to them.

Instead of trying to do all your chores at once, choose the ones that need to be done today. Let the rest slip into the background of your mind so I can be in the forefront of your awareness. Remember that your ultimate goal is living close to Me, being responsive to My initiatives. I can communicate with you most readily when your mind is uncluttered and turned toward Me. Seek My Face continually throughout this day. Let My Presence bring order to your thoughts, infusing Peace into your entire being.

PROVERBS 16:3; MATTHEW 6:33;
PSALM 27:8 NKJV; ISAIAH 26:3 NKJV

I AM *IMMANUEL*—*God with you* at all times. This promise provides a solid foundation for your Joy. Many people try to pin their pleasure to temporary things, but My Presence with you is eternal. Rejoice greatly, beloved, knowing that your Savior *will never leave you or forsake you.*

The nature of time can make it difficult for you to enjoy your life. On rare days when everything is going well, your awareness that the ideal conditions are fleeting can dampen your enjoyment of them. Even the most delightful vacation must eventually come to an end. Seasons of life also come and go, despite your longing at times to "stop the clock" and keep things just as they are.

Do not look down on temporary pleasures, but *do* recognize their limitations—their inability to quench the thirst of your soul. Your search for lasting Joy will fail unless you make *Me* the ultimate goal of your quest. *I will show you the path of Life. In My Presence is fullness of Joy.*

MATTHEW 1:23; DEUTERONOMY 31:8;
PSALM 16:11 NKJV

WHEN I JOINED THE RANKS of humanity, born into the humblest conditions, My Glory was hidden from all but a few people. Occasionally, streaks of Glory shone out of Me, especially when I began to do miracles. Toward the end of My life, I was taunted and tempted to display more of My awesome Power than My Father's plan permitted. I could have called down legions of angels to rescue Me at any point. Imagine the self-control required of a martyr who could free Himself at will! All of this was necessary to provide the relationship with Me that you now enjoy. Let your life become a praise song to Me by proclaiming My glorious Presence in the world.

JOHN 2:11; LUKE 23:35–36; PSALM 92:1–5

N O MATTER HOW LONELY you may feel, you are never alone. Christmas can be a hard time for people who are separated from loved ones. The separation may be a result of death, divorce, distance, or other causes. The holiday merriment around you can intensify your sense of aloneness. But all My children have a resource that is more than adequate to help them: My continual Presence.

Remember this prophecy about Me: *The virgin . . . will give birth to a Son, and they will call Him Immanuel—which means* "God with us." Long before I was born, I was proclaimed to be the God who is *with you*. This is rock-solid truth that nobody and no circumstance can take away from you.

Whenever you're feeling lonely, take time to enjoy My Presence. Thank Me for *wrapping you with a robe of righteousness* to make you righteous. Ask Me—*the God of hope*—to *fill you with Joy and Peace*. Then, through the help of My Spirit, you can *overflow with hope* into the lives of other people.

ISAIAH 7:14; ISAIAH 61:10 NASB;
2 CORINTHIANS 5:21 NKJV; ROMANS 15:13

M Y PLAN FOR YOUR LIFE is unfolding before you. Sometimes the road you are traveling seems blocked, or it opens up so painfully slowly that you must hold yourself back. Then, when time is right, the way before you suddenly clears—through no effort of your own. What you have longed for and worked for I present to you freely, as pure gift. You feel awed by the ease with which I operate in the world, and you glimpse *My Power and My Glory.*

Do not fear your weakness, for it is the stage on which My Power and Glory perform most brilliantly. As you persevere along the path I have prepared for you, depending on My strength to sustain you, expect to see miracles—and you will. Miracles are not always visible to the naked eye, but those who *live by faith* can see them clearly. *Living by faith, rather than sight,* enables you to see My Glory.

PSALM 63:2–5; 2 CORINTHIANS 5:7; JOHN 11:40

I BECAME POOR *so that you might become rich.* My incarnation—the essence of Christmas—was a gift of infinitely great value. However, it impoverished Me immeasurably! I gave up the majestic splendors of heaven to become a helpless baby. My parents were poor, young, and far away from home when I was born in a stable in Bethlehem.

I performed many miracles during My lifetime, but they were for the benefit of others, not Myself. After fasting forty days and nights in the wilderness, I was tempted by the devil to *turn stones into bread.* But I refused to do this miracle, even though I was so hungry. I lived as a homeless man for years.

Because I was willing to experience a life of poverty, you are incredibly rich! My life, death, and resurrection opened the way for My followers to become *children of God* and heirs of glorious, eternal riches. My abiding Presence is also a precious gift. Celebrate all these amazing gifts with gratitude and overflowing Joy!

2 CORINTHIANS 8:9; MATTHEW 4:1–4 NKJV;
JOHN 1:12; LUKE 2:10 ESV

COME TO ME, and rest in My Presence. As you ponder the majestic mystery of the Incarnation, relax in My everlasting arms. I am the only Person who was ever *sired* by the Holy Spirit. This is beyond your understanding. Instead of trying to comprehend My Incarnation intellectually, learn from the example of the wise men. They followed the leading of a spectacular star, then fell down in humble worship when they found Me.

Praise and worship are the best responses to the wonder of My Being. Sing praises to My holy Name. Gaze at Me in silent adoration. Look for a star of guidance in your own life, and be willing to follow wherever I lead. *I am the Light from on high that dawns upon you, to guide your feet into the way of Peace.*

LUKE 1:35; JOHN 1:14;
MATTHEW 2:10–11 NKJV;
LUKE 1:78–79 AMP

I AM THE LIGHT OF THE WORLD! **Many people** celebrate Advent season by illuminating their homes with candles and decorated trees. This is a way of symbolizing My coming into the world—eternal Light breaking through the darkness and opening up the way to heaven. Nothing can reverse this glorious plan of salvation. All who trust Me as Savior are adopted into My royal family forever!

My Light shines on in the darkness, for the darkness has never overpowered it. No matter how much evil and unbelief you see in this dark world, I continue to shine brightly—a beacon of hope to those who have eyes that really see. So it's crucial to look toward the Light as much as possible. *Fix your eyes on Me*, beloved! Through thousands of good thought-choices, you can find Me—"see" Me—as you journey through this life. My Spirit can help you persevere in the delightful discipline of keeping your eyes on Me. *Whoever follows Me will never walk in darkness but will have the Light of Life.*

JOHN 8:12; EPHESIANS 1:5 NLT;
JOHN 1:5 AMP; HEBREWS 12:2

I AM KING OF KINGS *and Lord of lords, dwelling in dazzlingly bright Light!* I am also your Shepherd, Companion, and Friend—the One who never lets go of your hand. Worship Me in My holy Majesty; come close to Me, and rest in My Presence. You need Me both as God and as Man. Only My Incarnation on that first, long-ago Christmas could fulfill your neediness. Since I went to such extreme measures to save you from your sins, you can be assured that I will *graciously give you all you need.*

Nurture well your trust in Me as Savior, Lord, and Friend. I have held back nothing in My provision for you. I have even deigned to live within you! Rejoice in all that I have done for you, and My Light will shine through you into the world.

1 TIMOTHY 6:15–16; PSALM 95:6–7;
ROMANS 8:32; 2 PETER 1:19

*T*HOSE WHO WAIT UPON ME *will gain new strength.* Spending time alone with Me is so good for you, but it is increasingly countercultural. Multitasking and staying busy have become the norm. During the Advent season, there are even *more* things to be done and places to go. So I encourage you to break free from all the activity and demands for a while. *Seek My Face* and enjoy My Presence, remembering that Christmas is all about *Me.*

Waiting upon Me is an act of faith—trusting that prayer really does make a difference. *Come to Me with your weariness and burdens,* being candid and real with Me. *Rest* in My Presence, and tell Me about your concerns. Let Me lift the burdens from your aching shoulders. Trust that *I am able to do exceedingly abundantly above all you ask or think.*

As you arise from these quiet moments, hear Me whispering "I am with you" throughout the day. Rejoice in the *new strength* you have gained through spending time with Me.

ISAIAH 40:31 NASB; PSALM 27:8 NKJV;
MATTHEW 11:28; EPHESIANS 3:20 NKJV

I SPEAK TO YOU from the depths of eternity. *Before the world was formed, I AM!* You hear Me in the depths of your being, where I have taken up residence. *I am Christ in you, the hope of Glory.* I, your Lord and Savior, am alive within you. Learn to tune in to My living Presence by seeking Me in silence.

As you celebrate the wonder of My birth in Bethlehem, celebrate also your rebirth into eternal life. This everlasting gift was the sole purpose of My entering your sin-stained world. Receive My gift with awe and humility. Take time to explore the vast dimensions of My Love. Allow thankfulness to flow freely from your heart in response to My glorious gift. *Let My Peace rule in your heart, and be thankful.*

PSALM 90:2 AMP; COLOSSIANS 1:27;
JOHN 3:3; COLOSSIANS 3:15

P REPARE YOUR HEART for the celebration of My
birth. Listen to the voice of John the Baptist: *"Prepare
the way for the Lord; make straight paths for Him."*

Christmas is the time to exult in My miraculous incarnation, when *the Word became flesh and dwelt among you.*
I identified with mankind to the ultimate extent—becoming
a Man and taking up residence in your world. Don't let the
familiarity of this astonishing miracle dull its effect on you.
Recognize that I am the Gift above all gifts, and *rejoice in Me!*

Clear out clutter and open up your heart by pondering
the wonders of My entrance into human history. View these
events from the perspective of the shepherds, who were keeping watch over their flocks at night. They witnessed first one
angel and then *a multitude* of them lighting up the sky, proclaiming: *"Glory to God in the highest, and on earth Peace
among those with whom He is pleased!"* Gaze at the Glory of
my birth, just as the shepherds did, and respond with childlike wonder.

MARK 1:3; JOHN 1:14 ESV;
PHILIPPIANS 4:4 NKJV; LUKE 2:13–14 ESV

A s you wait attentively in My Presence, *the Light of the knowledge of My Glory shines upon you.* This radiant knowledge transcends all understanding. It transforms every fiber of your being: renewing your mind, cleansing your heart, invigorating your body. Open yourself fully to My Presence; be awed by My glorious Being.

Try to imagine what I gave up when I came into your world as a baby. I set aside My Glory so that I could identify with mankind. I accepted the limitations of infancy under the most appalling conditions—a filthy stable. There was nothing glorious about that setting, though angels lit up the sky proclaiming, "Glory!" to awestruck shepherds.

When you sit quietly with Me, the process I went through is reversed in your experience. As you identify with Me, heaven's vistas open up before you—granting you glimpses of My Glory. *I became poor so that you might become rich.* Sing hallelujahs to My holy Name!

2 CORINTHIANS 4:6; PHILIPPIANS 2:6–7;
LUKE 2:13–14; 2 CORINTHIANS 8:9

I AM *THE WORD THAT BECAME FLESH*. I have always been, and I will always be. *In the beginning was the Word, and the Word was with God, and the Word was God.* As you think about Me as a baby, born in Bethlehem, do not lose sight of My divinity. This baby who grew up and became a Man-Savior is also God Almighty! It could not have been otherwise. My sacrificial life and death would have been insufficient if I were not God. So rejoice that *the Word*, who entered the world as a helpless infant, is the same One who brought the world into existence.

Though I was rich, for your sake I became poor, so that you might become rich. No Christmas present could ever compare with the treasure you have in Me! I remove your sins *as far as the east is from the west*—freeing you from all condemnation. I gift you with unimaginably glorious Life that will never end! The best response to this astonishing Gift is to embrace it joyfully and gratefully.

JOHN 1:1, 14; HEBREWS 1:1–2;
2 CORINTHIANS 8:9 NASB; PSALM 103:12 NKJV

I AM THE GIFT that continuously gives—bounteously, with no strings attached. Unconditional Love is such a radical concept that even My most devoted followers fail to grasp it fully. Absolutely nothing in heaven or on earth can cause Me to stop loving you. You may *feel* more loved when you are performing according to your expectations. But My Love for you is perfect; therefore it is not subject to variation. What *does* vary is your awareness of My loving Presence.

When you are dissatisfied with your behavior, you tend to feel unworthy of My Love. You may unconsciously punish yourself by withdrawing from Me and attributing the distance between us to My displeasure. Instead of returning to Me and receiving My Love, you attempt to earn My approval by trying harder. All the while, I am aching to hold you in *My everlasting arms*, to enfold you in My Love. When you are feeling unworthy or unloved, come to Me. Then ask for receptivity to *My unfailing Love*.

1 JOHN 4:15–16, 18; DEUTERONOMY 33:27;
PSALM 13:5

I AM THE GREATEST GIFT IMAGINABLE! When you have *Me*, you have everything you need—for this life and the next. I have promised to *meet all your needs according to My glorious riches*. Yet My loved ones sometimes fail to enjoy the riches I provide because of an ungrateful attitude. Instead of rejoicing in all that they have, they long for what they do not have. As a result, they become discontented.

I'm training you to practice *the sacrifice of thanksgiving*—thanking Me *in all circumstances*. First, give thanks for the blessings you can see in your life. Then stop and ponder the awesome gift of knowing Me. I am your living God, your loving Savior, your constant Companion. No matter how much or how little you have in this world, your relationship with Me makes you immeasurably rich. So whenever you are counting your blessings, be sure to include the infinite wealth you have in Me. Add Me into the equation, and your gratitude will grow exponentially. Whatever you have + Me = an incalculable fortune!

PHILIPPIANS 4:19; PSALM 116:17 NKJV;
1 THESSALONIANS 5:18

I AM PREPARING YOU for what is on the road ahead, just around the bend. Take time to be still in My Presence so that I can strengthen you. The busier you become, the more you need this time apart with Me. So many people think that time spent with Me is a luxury they cannot afford. As a result, they live and work in their own strength—until that becomes depleted. Then they either cry out to Me for help or turn away in bitterness.

How much better it is to walk close to Me, depending on My strength and trusting Me in every situation. If you live in this way, you will *do* less but *accomplish* far more. Your unhurried pace of living will stand out in this rush-crazed age. Some people may deem you lazy, but many more will be blessed by your peacefulness. Walk in the Light with Me, and you will reflect Me to the watching world.

ISAIAH 64:4; JOHN 15:5; PSALM 36:9

I GIVE YOU JOY that is independent of circumstances; I give you Myself! *All the treasures of wisdom and knowledge are hidden in Me.* Because I am infinitely wise and all-knowing, you will never run out of treasures to search for.

I am a wellspring of Joy—eager to overflow into your life. Open wide your heart, mind, and spirit to receive Me in full measure. My Joy is not of this world; it can coexist with the most difficult circumstances. No matter what is happening in your life, *the Light of My Presence* continues to shine upon you. Look up to Me with a trusting heart. If you persist in searching for Me, My Joy-Light can break through the darkest storm clouds. Let this heavenly Light soak into you, brightening your perspective and filling you with transcendent delight.

Remember that you have *an inheritance in heaven that can never perish, spoil, or fade.* Since *you believe in Me, inexpressible, glorious Joy* is yours—now and forever!

COLOSSIANS 2:3; PSALM 89:15–16;
1 PETER 1:3–4, 8

I AM YOUR REFUGE AND STRENGTH, *an ever-present Help in trouble. Therefore, you don't need to be afraid of anything*—not even cataclysmic circumstances. The media are increasingly devoted to fear-inducing subject matter: terrorism, serial killers, environmental catastrophes. If you focus on such dangers and forget that I am your Refuge in all circumstances, you will become increasingly fearful. Every day I manifest My grace in countless places and situations, but the media take no notice. I shower not only blessings but also outright miracles on your planet.

As you grow closer to Me, I open your eyes to see more and more of My Presence all around you. Things that most people hardly notice, like shifting shades of sunlight, fill you with heart-bursting Joy. You have eyes that see and ears that hear, so proclaim My abiding Presence in the world.

PSALM 46:1–3; PSALM 89:15–16

*H*OW PRICELESS IS MY UNFAILING LOVE! This is truly a gift of heavenly proportions. Remember the unspeakable price I paid to secure this gift for you: I endured torture, humiliation, and death. My willingness to suffer so much for you demonstrates how extravagantly I love you.

I want you to comprehend how astonishingly rich you are in Me. I have given you the priceless treasure of My eternal Love! This gift makes you far wealthier than a multibillionaire, even if you own very little of this world's goods. So stand tall as you journey through your life, knowing that this glorious inner treasure is your portion each step of the way.

Rejoice that My Love is both priceless *and* unfailing. You can always count on it because it's even more reliable than the rising of the sun. Let My unfailing Love fill you with exuberant Joy as you walk along *the path of Life* with Me.

PSALM 36:7; 2 CORINTHIANS 4:7;
PSALM 16:11 NKJV

T RUST ME with every fiber of your being! What I can accomplish in and through you is proportional to how much you depend on Me. One aspect of this is the degree to which you trust Me in a crisis or major decision. Some people fail miserably here, while others are at their best in tough times. Another aspect is even more telling: the constancy of your trust in Me. People who rely on Me in the midst of adversity may forget about Me when life is flowing smoothly. Difficult times can jolt you into awareness of your need for Me, whereas *smooth sailing* can lull you into the stupor of self-sufficiency.

I care as much about your tiny trust-steps through daily life as about your dramatic leaps of faith. You may think that no one notices, but the One who is always beside you sees everything—and rejoices. Consistently trusting in Me is vital to flourishing in My Presence.

PSALM 40:4; PSALM 56:3–4;
PSALM 62:8; ISAIAH 26:3–4

*L*ET *MY PEACE RULE IN YOUR HEART, and be thankful.* And let My Spirit help you in this challenging endeavor. The Spirit lives in you, so His fruit—*Love, Joy, Peace*—is always accessible to you. A simple way to request His help is to pray: "Holy Spirit, fill me with Your Peace." Try sitting in a quiet place until you feel relaxed and calm. When you are thoroughly relaxed, it is easier to seek My Face and enjoy My Presence.

While you rest in My Presence, take time to thank Me for the many good things I give you. As you focus on Me and My bountiful blessings, let your heart swell with gratitude and even *leap for Joy.* One of the most precious gifts imaginable is My *robe of righteousness*—to cover your sins. This glorious *garment of salvation* is a priceless blessing for all who trust Me as Savior. The gift of eternal righteousness, purchased through My blood, provides a firm foundation for both Peace and Joy.

COLOSSIANS 3:15; GALATIANS 5:22–23 NKJV;
PSALM 28:7; ISAIAH 61:10

I AM LEADING YOU along a way that is uniquely right for you. The closer to Me you grow, the more fully you become your true self—the one I designed you to be. Because you are one of a kind, the path you are traveling with Me diverges increasingly from that of other people. However, in My mysterious wisdom and ways, I enable you to follow this solitary path while staying in close contact with others. In fact, the more completely you devote yourself to Me, the more freely you can love people.

Marvel at the beauty of a life intertwined with My Presence. Rejoice as we journey together in intimate communion. Enjoy the adventure of finding yourself through losing yourself in Me.

2 CORINTHIANS 5:17; EPHESIANS 2:10;
1 JOHN 4:7–8; JOHN 15:4

I AM THE ALPHA AND THE OMEGA, *the Beginning and the End.* My perspective is unlimited by time. Because I am infinite, I am able to see and understand everything at once. This makes Me the ideal Person to be in charge of your life. I know the ending of your earth-life as well as I know its beginning—and I know everything in between. You are finite and fallen; your understanding is limited and far from perfect. So trusting in Me rather than relying *on your own understanding* is the most reasonable way to live; it is also the most joyful.

The end of your life is not to be feared. It's simply the last step of your journey to heaven. I can see that event as clearly as I see you right now. Moreover, because I am the Omega— the End—I am already there. I will be awaiting you when you reach this glorious destination. So whenever you're feeling the strain of your journey through this world, fix your eyes on *the End*—and rejoice!

REVELATION 21:6 NKJV; PROVERBS 3:5 ESV; PSALM 73:24; HEBREWS 12:2

A S THIS YEAR DRAWS TO A CLOSE, receive My Peace. This is still your deepest need, and I, your *Prince of Peace*, long to pour Myself into your neediness. My abundance and your emptiness are a perfect match. I designed you to have no sufficiency of your own. I created you as a *jar of clay*, set apart for sacred use. I want you to be filled with My very Being, permeated through and through with Peace.

Thank Me for My peaceful Presence, regardless of your feelings. Whisper My Name in loving tenderness. *My Peace*, which lives continually in your spirit, will gradually work its way through your entire being.

ISAIAH 9:6; 2 CORINTHIANS 4:7; JOHN 14:26–27

A s you come to the end of this year, take some time to look back—and also to look ahead. Ask Me to help you review the highlights of this year: hard times as well as good times. Try to see *Me* in these memories, for I have been close beside you—every step of the way.

When you were clinging to Me for help in the midst of tough times, I comforted you with My loving Presence. I was also richly present in circumstances that filled you with great Joy. I was with you on the mountain peaks, in the valleys, and everywhere in between.

Your future stretches out before you all the way into eternity. I am the Companion who will never leave you, the Guide who knows every step of the way ahead. The Joy that awaits you in paradise is *inexpressible and full of Glory*! As you prepare to step into a new year, let heaven's Light shine upon you and brighten the path just before you.

ISAIAH 41:13; PSALM 16:11 NKJV;
PSALM 48:14; 1 PETER 1:8–9 NASB

ABOUT THE AUTHOR

S ARAH YOUNG'S devotional writings are personal
reflections from her daily quiet time of Bible reading,
praying, and writing in prayer journals. With sales of more
than 16 million books worldwide, *Jesus Calling* has appeared
on all major bestseller lists. Sarah's writings include *Jesus
Calling*, *Jesus Today*, *Jesus Lives*, *Dear Jesus*, *Jesus Calling
for Little Ones*, *Jesus Calling My First Bible Storybook*, *Jesus
Calling Bible Storybook*, *Jesus Calling: 365 Devotions for Kids*,
Jesus Today: Devotions for Kids, *Jesus Always*, and *Peace in His
Presence*—each encouraging readers in their journey toward
intimacy with Christ. Sarah and her husband were missionaries in Japan and Australia for many years. They currently live
in the United States. *Jesus Calling* was written to help people
connect not only with Jesus, the living Word, but also with
the Bible—the only infallible, inerrant Word of God.

Sarah endeavors to keep her devotional writing consistent
with that unchanging standard. Many readers have shared
that Sarah's books have helped them grow to love God's
Word. As Sarah states in the introduction to *Jesus Calling*,

"The devotions . . . are meant to be read slowly, preferably in a quiet place—with your Bible open."

Sarah is biblically conservative in her faith and reformed in her doctrine. She earned a master's degree in biblical studies and counseling from Covenant Theological Seminary in St. Louis. She is a member of the Presbyterian Church in America (PCA), where her husband, Stephen, is an ordained minister. Stephen and Sarah continue to be missionaries with Mission to the World, the PCA mission board.

Sarah spends a great deal of time in prayer, reading the Bible, and memorizing Scripture. She especially enjoys praying daily for readers of all her books.

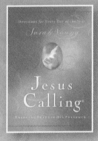
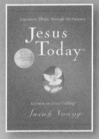
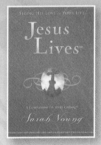

If you enjoyed this book, you may be interested in these other books from the author of *Jesus Calling*®

Jesus Calling Devotional Journal
with journaling space and prompts
ISBN 9781400322893

Peace in His Presence
quotes with inspirational images
ISBN 9780718034160

Jesus Calling 365 Devotions for Kids
adapted for children 8–12
ISBN 9781400316342

Jesus Calling Bible Storybook
Bible stories and devotions
ISBN 9781400320332

Learn more at JesusCalling.com